D1440735

THE SOCIETY FOR IRISH CHURCH MISSIONS
TO THE ROMAN CATHOLICS, 1849–1950

Manchester University Press

The Society for Irish Church Missions to the Roman Catholics, 1849–1950

Miriam Moffitt

Manchester University Press

Manchester and New York

*distributed in the United States exclusively
by Palgrave Macmillan*

BU
2880
.M63
2010

Copyright © Miriam Moffitt 2010

The right of Miriam Moffitt to be identified as the author of this work has been asserted by
her in accordance with the Copyright, Designs and Patents Act 1988.

Published by Manchester University Press
Oxford Road, Manchester M13 9NR, UK
and Room 400, 175 Fifth Avenue, New York, NY 10010, USA
www.manchesteruniversitypress.co.uk

Distributed in the United States exclusively by
Palgrave Macmillan, 175 Fifth Avenue, New York,
NY 10010, USA

Distributed in Canada exclusively by
UBC Press, University of British Columbia, 2029 West Mall,
Vancouver, BC, Canada V6T 1Z2

British Library Cataloguing-in-Publication Data
A catalogue record for this book is available from the British Library

Library of Congress Cataloging-in-Publication Data applied for

ISBN   978 0 7190 7879 8 hardback

First published 2010

The publisher has no responsibility for the persistence or accuracy of URLs for any external
or third-party internet websites referred to in this book, and does not guarantee that any
content on such websites is, or will remain, accurate or appropriate.

Typeset
by Carnegie Book Production, Lancaster
Printed in Great Britain
by the MPG Books Group

Contents

Figures

Tables

Acknowledgements

I owe a great deal of thanks to many people who helped me in the preparation of this research. I am grateful to the Irish Research Council for the Humanities and Social Sciences for their support of my research. I would like particularly to thank Professor R. V. Comerford, Dr Jacinta Prunty and the staff and fellow students at the Department of History, National University of Ireland, Maynooth whose guidance and encouragement were greatly appreciated. I am also indebted to Revd Eddie Coulter, Olive Stewart and the team of the Irish Church Missions, who not only placed their entire archive at my disposal, but organised a bottomless supply of coffee while I worked. I am grateful to the Catholic and Anglican clergy of Clifden parish, who made their records available to me, and who also supplied the essential coffee. Thanks are due also to the many people from Connemara who generously gave their time and shared their handed-down memories of the former mission and its workers.

Research for this thesis was facilitated by the staff of the following libraries and repositories, to whom I am greatly indebted: National Library of Ireland; Representative Church Body Library, Dublin; Dublin Diocesan Archives, Drumcondra; National Archives of Ireland; NUI Maynooth; NUI Cork; NUI Dublin; Irish Folklore Collection; Trinity College, Dublin; Royal Irish Academy; Valuation Office, Dublin; Allen Library, Dublin; Vincentian Archives, Dublin; Franciscan Archives, Mountbellew; Linen Hall Library, Belfast; British Library; Durham University; Birmingham University; University of Cambridge; University of Bristol; University of Leeds; New College, Edinburgh; National Library of Scotland; University of Glasgow, and the University of Aberdeen. Gratitude is also due to Martin Fagan at the Pontifical Irish College Archives in Rome for facilitating access to the draft catalogue of the Kirby Papers, New Collection. In addition, I would like to thank the facilitators of the website www.copac.ac.uk, which identified many sources in unlikely repositories. Thanks are due also to the staff of Manchester University Press, for their assistance and professionalism in the production of this book.

And finally and most sincerely, I would like to thank my family and friends for their constant help and support during the past few years.

Abbreviations

BCA	Birmingham City Archives
CMS	Church Missionary Society
CP	Copley Papers, Durham University, Special Collections
CPAS	Church Pastoral Aid Society
DDA	Dublin Diocesan Archives, Drumcondra
DED	District Electoral Divisions
DNB	*Dictionary of national biography*
DVM	Dublin Visiting Mission
EA	Evangelical Alliance
ECM	The Society for English Church Missions to the Roman Catholics
ED	Education files, National Archives of Ireland
EIM	Edinburgh Irish Mission
EPB	Early Printed Books
HCMS	Hibernian Church Missionary Society
ICM	The Society for Irish Church Missions to the Roman Catholics
IFC	Irish Folklore Commission
IRS	Irish Reformation Society
IS	Irish Society
KP, *AH*	Kirby Papers, *Archivium Hibernicum*
LAC	Ladies' Association of Charity of St Vincent de Paul
LAIS	Ladies' Auxiliary to the Irish Society
LMA	London Metropolitan Archives
NAI	National Archives of Ireland
NS	National School
NLI	National Library of Ireland
PICA	Pontifical Irish College Archives, Rome
PRO	Public Records Office

PRONI	Public Records Office of Northern Ireland
PRS	Protestant Reformation Society
RCBL	Representative Church Body Library
RIC	Royal Irish Constabulary
SBO	Saint Brigid's Orphanage, Dublin
SRS	Scottish Reformation Society
TCD	Trinity College, Dublin
TSC	Training School Committee
UCD	University College, Dublin
WCCES	West Connaught Church Endowment Society

Introduction

This study of The Society for Irish Church Missions to the Roman Catholics (ICM) will detail the efforts of the largest and most organised mission to convert the Roman Catholics of Ireland to 'biblical Protestantism'.[1] It will explore the motivations and ideologies of its supporters, its missionary methodologies, opposition encountered and the impact of the mission on Irish society. The ICM, which was founded by Revd Alexander Dallas during the Irish famine of 1845–47, emanated from the evangelical wing of the Church of England. Dallas was strongly influenced by prevailing theological issues such as the need to disseminate the scriptures and an interest in the prophecies (millenarianism). The ICM concentrated its efforts on the impoverished peasant community of Connemara in west County Galway and on the inhabitants of Dublin's slums. This work focuses on three parties: firstly, the providers of mission (principally evangelical English Protestants); secondly, its opponents (the Catholic church and latterly some sections of Protestantism), and thirdly, its convert community.

The ICM was founded to disseminate 'biblical Christianity' to the Roman Catholics of Ireland. At the very corner-stone of its foundation lay the profound evangelical conviction that Roman Catholics were destined for the fires of hell and that committed Christians were duty-bound to instruct Catholics in the knowledge of the scriptures and to sever the treacherous control of Rome over its flock.[2] Roman Catholicism was perceived to be a vast spiritual and temporal conspiracy against liberty which aimed to dominate all Christians. Its adherents were perceived as slaves of a priesthood which in turn was enslaved to the Pope.[3] The ICM's campaign to convert Irish Catholics should be seen in tandem with the horror among evangelical Protestants at the spread of the Roman religion on continental Europe, conferring a political ideology on the movement.

Since religion is one ingredient in the recipe of identity, which includes perceptions of race, language, ethnicity and ideology, the following questions must be asked: when English Protestants founded the ICM to attempt the conversion of impoverished, illiterate Irish Catholics to scriptural Protestantism, what changes did they hope would occur in the political and ethnic ideologies of the convert community? What social improvements were they seeking? To what degree did they wish to disempower the increasingly politicised Catholic clergy? To what extent were they responding to the insecurities of mid-nineteenth-century Britain? What domestic events influenced their motivations?

In Ireland the intersection of religion and politics ensures that even the most secular of episodes take on religious overtones, as religion and nationalism are not independent variables, but comprise two halves of one identity welded together by history.[4] It has been noted that 'unresolved contests' were highly visible in nineteenth-century Ireland;[5] this publication will argue that, being unresolved, these contests continued into the twentieth century. The relationship between the Catholic and Protestant communities on this island has been strongly influenced by the proselytising movement and even more so by the ensuing Catholic response. Much was written by contemporary propagandists, both for and against Protestant missions, not all of which was grounded in fact. This study aims to establish the facts surrounding the ICM's work in Ireland, to deconstruct the polemic rhetoric of both sides of the argument, to recount objectively the origins, activities, impact and legacy of the Irish Church Missions, and to address directly and support with hard evidence, claims made by both sides.

The work of the ICM is largely unexplored to date, although research has been carried out on other missionary ventures and on proselytism in general. Of the other nineteenth-century missionary ventures explored, Nangle's Achill enterprise has received most attention, while the missions of Kingscourt, Dingle, Doon and north Mayo are as yet largely unexplored.[6]

This author's recently published *Soupers and Jumpers* is the first comprehensive study of the ICM's work in Connemara. It spans the period from the beginning of mission work in the famine era to the closure of its last mission station in 1937, exploring the methodologies and influence of the ICM from the perspectives of both the missionary institution and the convert community.[7] It is, however, a case study of the Connemara missions and does not provide a comprehensive overview of the origin, development, methodologies and wider impact of the ICM.

Irene Whelan's essay 'The stigma of souperism' provides a brief overview of the ICM in Connemara while her recent publication, *The Bible war in Ireland … 1800–1840* terminates almost a decade before the ICM's inception.[8] The Canadian researcher, Desmond Bowen, explored proselytism in nineteenth-century Ireland in *Souperism, myth or reality?* and *The Protestant crusade in Ireland, 1800–1870* but does not adequately examine the work of the ICM.[9] Unfortunately, in *Souperism* Bowen confines his study to the famine years and to an area devoid of ICM influence and while his *Protestant crusade* covers the period from the Act of Union to disestablishment, it concludes before the demise of ICM activities in Connemara and when the Dublin operation was in a relatively healthy state. It provides readers with a detailed analysis of ICM operations but it neither evaluates the mission from the convert viewpoint nor questions the veracity of its advertised successes. Like Bowen's *Protestant crusade*, Paschal Majerus' study of the ICM in Connemara outlines its origin and development, and the emergence of Catholic counter-mission at macro level, but without a detailed micro-history of the convert community cannot estimate the ICM's influence or its appeal to its followers.[10]

The works of Máire Ní Shúilleabháin, John Lyons and Gerard Moran provide detailed studies of individual mission parishes,[11] while Bernard Mac Uaid and Brighid Ó Murchada have explored the impact of the ICM on the provision of education in Connemara in the nineteenth century.[12] As some of these works were written in the Irish language, while more were unpublished theses, they have been largely inaccessible to historians. Other academic appraisals of the ICM activities and Catholic counter-mission include James Murphy's exploration of the role of Vincentian parish missions in opposing the advances of proselytism,[13] Jacinta Prunty's research into the life of Margaret Aylward, the ICM's foremost opponent in Dublin,[14] and Margaret Preston's study of Dublin children's homes and schools associated with the ICM and those established to oppose its work.[15]

All the above studies give the impression that ICM missionary work in west Galway had practically ceased by 1870, while ICM publications indicate a thriving successful mission, an anomaly that will be tested in this work. The scholarly essays of Matthew Kelly and Martin Doherty on the political agenda pertaining to Protestant street preaching, while not relating specifically to the ICM, are among the few academic explorations of Protestant mission work in late-nineteenth-century Ireland.[16] The ICM's mission work in the years following disestablishment and its impact on the rapidly changing political landscape of the late nineteenth and early twentieth centuries are as yet unexamined. This work hopes to correct this deficit.

The dearth of research into the role of the Anglican church during the famine has been noted by Christine Kinealy,[17] while the 'remembering' of proselytism is addressed briefly in Niall O'Ciosáin's appraisal of the famine memories.[18] Expectional cases of proselytism in the adjoining counties of Mayo and Sligo are noted in Liam Swords' *In their own words* (Dublin, 1999), while no mention is made of the practice in his two histories of Catholicism in the north Connaught diocese of Achonry.[19] Missions to Catholics receive little consideration in histories of the Church of Ireland; in some they are omitted entirely,[20] in others they receive a passing reference.[21] Even Sedall, whose hagiographical account of Nangle's Achill mission was widely circulated, omits all mention of mission work among Catholics in his *Historical Sketch*.[22] The ICM receives at best a glancing reference in the many appraisals of the Church of Ireland published in the face of looming disestablishment, is covered in reasonable depth in Norman Emerson's essay in Phillips' *History of the Church of Ireland* over sixty years later,[23] but is sidestepped entirely in the many works which commemorate the hundredth anniversary of disestablishment.[24] Subsequent scholarship has given it little attention.[25] The most objective accounts of the ICM are found in Andrews' and Lampson's works which analyse its impact on the church.[26] Mission work among Catholics received considerable attention from the Presbyterian, Killen,[27] and is mentioned in biographies of individual bishops and clergy, with and without mission involvement, which assisted an estimation of support for the ICM within the wider church.

Evangelicalism in northern Ireland is covered in David Hempton and Myrtle Hill's *Evangelical Protestantism in Ulster society, 1870–1890* (London, 1992), which details especially the revival of 1859, but as this movement was promulgated largely through the many dissenting faiths found in the northern counties, it differed greatly from the objectives and methodologies of the centrally co-ordinated, Anglican Irish Church Missions.

The mission's monthly publications, *The Banner of the Truth* and *Erin's Hope* and its annual reports contain a wealth of information, mainly based on manuscript minutes and workers' journals. Histories of the ICM written by founders and supporters, which provide detailed but subjective accounts of the mission and its philanthropic organisations, were quoted in *The Banner* and paraphrased in the many hagiographical accounts of mission tours published in the 1850s. Details of the ICM's relief programmes are found also in publications of associated organisations. The earliest annual reports and proceedings of annual meetings outlined progress in a less guarded fashion, growing more circumspect from the mid 1850s. The above sources cast light not only on the objectives of ICM supporters, but also on its methodologies, its mission staff and its convert communities.

The most useful segment of the ICM archive was undoubtedly its annual agency books, 1856–1956, which list employees by mission and station, detailing occupation (scripture-reader, teacher, monitor, bill distributor, etc.) and wages, allowing the movements of personnel to be tracked and containing comments such as 'married, now Mrs William King', 'to America', etc. Constructing a database of this material made it possible to identify the duration of missions, years of employment, genealogical connections, rates of pay and level of training. Minute books, in contrast, yielded little insight, and in the absence of contemporary letter books, their entries were surprisingly uninformative.

Since the ICM targeted its activities at the very poor, this research concentrates on missionary operations and converts in west Galway. Research into the lives of the rural poor is more feasible than studies of urban slum-dwellers as city poor leave fewer traces. The very mobility and anonymity which the ICM sought after precludes the retention of folk memory while rapidly changing townscapes have retained little material evidence.

Some early parish registers of Connemara parishes were destroyed in the Public Record Office fire in 1922, rendering it impossible to accurately recreate or estimate the entire convert community.[28] The creation of a database from extant registers of west Galway cross-linked to the database of the ICM agency books enabled a genealogical study of converts, and of convert mission employees in particular. The ability to identify the location, duration and occupation of employees and inter-relationships of their extended families was invaluable in assessing the impact of mission involvement on the lives of converts. The Catholic registers of Clifden, Claddaghduff and Ballyconneely provided excellent information on reversions of converts, with baptisms of entire families frequently recorded, although it must be noted that Clifden Catholic records are considered to be the most illegible and fragmented in the entire country.

West Galway mission stations were located using Ordnance Survey six-inch and *Discovery Series* 1:50,000 maps, Valuation Office cancelled books, field research and local knowledge.[29] The occupants of one ICM colony (Daly Hill colony, Errismore) were identified in the Valuation Office cancelled books, which enabled an assessment of the social standing of converts with respect to their Catholic neighbours and with trained mission agents. Some idea of the Catholic perception of the ICM was gained through the schools' applications to the Department of Education (National Archives of Ireland (NAI), Education files), contemporary street-ballads (Trinity College Dublin, Early Printed Books) the Irish Folklore Commission (Schools' Collection and its own collectors' material) and recently collected local lore. Interviewees of the Folklore Commission (IFC) (1937) provided valuable insight into local perception of the mission, much of which was highly critical of the ICM: 'droch dhaoine a bhí iontú' [they were bad people].[30] It must be considered that sources such as street-ballads should not be accepted uncritically and that folklore evidence may reflect attitudes of 1930s Ireland rather than memories of the nineteenth century, as will be discussed in chapter 7.

The 1901 census, fifty years after the establishment of mission work, provided the first definitive listing of Connemara's Protestants. Efforts were made to extract the identities of children in mission homes in 1901, based on their surname. Although not a quantitative approach, it may be assumed to estimate children of 'native Catholics' with a good degree of accuracy.[31]

The underlying motivations which compelled English evangelicals to establish the ICM were assessed principally through a detailed study of its founders and supporters, which estimated their ideologies and backgrounds as revealed in their speeches and writings. William Marrable's early history of the organisation outlined not only the origin and development of the ICM, but also the mentality of mid-nineteenth-century evangelicalism.[32] A prosobiographical study of ICM office-holders and committee members was completed using standard reference texts; annual reports of other Protestant societies were examined to identify concurrent patronage and to assess trends of support, although patronage of a missionary society need not indicate ardent support for its objectives. The Edinburgh Irish Mission (EIM) was examined to compare its pan-Protestant ethos and methodology with those of the purely Anglican ICM while Sheridan Gilley's study of the Society for English Church Missions facilitated a review of an Anglican mission to Roman Catholics on English soil.[33]

Fluctuations in support for the ICM were reflected in its annual income. Since the activities of the ICM from the mid 1850s were severely curtailed by declining revenue, annual reports of other Protestant missionary societies were examined to establish whether they had experienced the same trend; the Church Pastoral Aid Society (CPAS) and the Church Missionary Society (CMS) were chosen because they represented missionary activity at home and abroad. The benevolence of English supporters was crucial to the ICM's continuance; an examination of the papers of Elizabeth Copley, one such supporter, reveals the interaction between the mission and its benefactor. The impact of the West Connaught Church Endowment Society (WCCES) on mission finances was studied, while the *Reports of the Tuam Diocesan Synod* enabled a study of the impact of disestablishment in 1869 and of the later departure of the landed classes on financial viabilities of west Galway mission-parishes, while reports of other diocesan organisations also proved useful.[34]

Attitudes and anxieties of nineteenth-century Catholicism in the face of aggressive Protestant missionary work were assessed by examining the papers of Tobias Kirby, Daniel Murray and Paul Cullen, and the writings of Frs James Maher, John O'Rourke and the tireless Daniel Cahill. These were supplemented by records of Catholic counter-missionary organisations such as the Dublin-based Saint Brigid's Orphanage and the Ladies' Association of Charity of Saint Vincent de Paul. The aims and observations of Catholic missioners were studied through published memoirs, while retrospective Catholic accounts of proselytism contribute to our understanding of attitudes of late nineteenth- and early twentieth-century Catholicism. The highly selective biographies of John MacHale published soon after his death reveal little either of the state of Catholicism in Connemara or of his reaction to the ICM,[35] while a recent biography devotes little space to proselytism, suggesting that it may have been of little relevance to the inhabitants of Tuam diocese.[36]

Irish religious periodicals were reviewed to estimate support for the ICM within Irish Protestantism. The moderate *Irish Ecclesiastical Gazette* (*Church of Ireland Gazette* from 1900) gave little space to missionary activity, while two short-lived evangelical publications gave substantial support to the ICM: *Irish Missionary Record and Chronicle of the Reformation* (Dublin, 1853–54) and *Christian Examiner and Church of Ireland Magazine* (Dublin, 1848–68).

During the ICM's period of rapid growth in the 1850s, numerous accounts of its achievements were published with balancing criticisms produced by its opponents. Disappointing results in the 1861 census, when the predicted surge in persons identifying themselves as Protestant failed to materialise, generated a considerable volume of press, as did a newspaper dialogue which claimed the mission 'stage-managed' large congregations to impress visitors.[37] As the ICM retreated to Dublin and larger provincial towns from the mid 1860s, and subsequently to Dublin alone, missionary efforts were increasingly focused on mission schools, for which little source material exists apart from agency books, *The Banner*, annual reports and the mission's many twentieth-century promotional publications.

The extent and ethos of later mission work and its location within the global reformation movement were revealed by an examination of its 1932 correspondence, which also cast light on its location within Irish Protestantism and on its relationship with its converts.[38] Biographies and correspondence of Catholic bishops reveal their perception of the ICM in the late nineteenth and early twentieth centuries, along with retrospective Catholic accounts of Protestant missions, including Fr Quigley's series of eleven journal articles 'Grace abounding' in the *Irish Ecclesiastical Record*, xx–xxii (1922–23) and Fr. Creedon's *Proselytism: its operations in Ireland* (Dublin, 1926). Fr. Padráig Ua Duinnín's fictional portrayal of a famine mission, *Creideamh agus gorta* [Faith and famine] (Dublin, 1901) is as much a revelation of Catholic opinion of the day, as of proselytism half a century earlier.

Connemara's landscape itself revealed much regarding the work of the ICM. The juxtaposition of light and shade, expanses of mountains, woods, lakes, sea and stony barren land evocatively recall the romantic literature of nineteenth-century Britain, so astutely used by the ICM in image and text in eliciting support for its cause. The prominent locations of mission churches, accessible by sea and visible even from adjacent peninsulas, underscore the influence of the ICM in the lives of Connemara's poor in the mid nineteenth century. Equally revealing is the present-day obliteration of almost all material evidence of the ICM, as when Ballinakill Select Vestry ordered the total removal of the stones of Sellerna church in 1926. The flat, dull, chalky landscape of Dallas' Hampshire parish of Wonston was equally informative, providing an understanding of his obsession with the wildness of Connemara, while the contrast between his intensely shepherded Wonston flock and the vast, largely unsupervised Irish population reveals how English supporters might have misconstrued missionary intelligence by superimposing reports of success in Ireland on their English conception of parish size and structure.

This work begins with an exploration of anti-Catholicism in the early nineteenth century, detailing its underlying political and religious agendas and outlining previous efforts to convert the Catholics of Ireland. The establishment of Castlekerke mission in famine-ravaged Connemara and the development of the Special Fund for the Spiritual Exigencies of Ireland are examined in chapter two; the expansion of the mission in Connemara and Dublin is traced in chapter three. Chapter four details the experiences of the mission from the high-point of activity in the mid 1850s to the disestablishment of the Church of Ireland in 1869, outlining the support and opposition it encountered. A case study of the Connemara missions of Errismore and Errislannan is contained in chapter five, while the later years of mission are described in chapter six. The final chapter estimates the legacy of the mission.

Although this publication includes a description of the experiences of the mission's converts and the social advantages or disadvantages of conversion, these are outlined in much greater detail in *Soupers and Jumpers*, which provides a detailed social and genealogical study of Connemara's convert community, and on the efforts of the Catholic church to frustrate the success of the mission.

Notes

1 Throughout this work, the term Catholic will be used to refer to members of the Roman Catholic church.

2 For an account of the history of the evangelical movement in general, see David Bebbington, *Evangelicalism in modern Britain: a history from the 1730s to the 1980s* (London, 2002); John Wolffe (ed.), *Evangelical faith and public zeal: evangelicals and society in Britain, 1780–1980* (London, 1995). For an account of Anglican evangelicalism see Kenneth Hylson-Smith, *Evangelicals in the Church of England, 1734–1984* (Edinburgh, 1989).

3 *Evangelical Magazine*, xxxi (1851), pp. 589–90; *Bulwark*, ii (1852–53), pp. 206–8.

4 Michael MacDonald, *Children of wrath: political violence in Northern Ireland* (Cambridge, 1986), p. 10; Tadhg Foley and Seán Ryder (eds), *Ideology and Ireland in the nineteenth century* (Dublin, 1998), p. 7.

5 Joseph Liechty and Cecelia Clegg, *Moving beyond sectarianism: religion, conflict and reconciliation in Northern Ireland* (Dublin, 2001), p. 49.

6 Meala Ní Ghiobúin, *Dugort, Achill Island, 1831–1861: the rise and fall of a missionary community* (Dublin, 2001); Irene Whelan, 'Edward Nangle and the Achill Mission, 1834–1852' in Raymond Gillespie and Gerard Moran (eds), *Mayo, a various county: essays in Mayo history* (Westport, 1987), pp. 91–112; Patrick Comerford, 'Edward Nangle (1799–1883): the Achill missionary in a new light', part i in *Cathair na Mart*, xviii (1998), 21–9, part ii in *Cathair na Mart*, xix (1999), 8–22; Thomas J. Kelley, 'Trapped between two worlds: Edward Nangle, Achill Island and sectarian competition in Ireland, 1800– 1862' (Ph.D. dissertation, Trinity College Dublin, 2004).

7 Miriam Moffitt, *Soupers and Jumpers: the Protestant missions in Connemara, 1848–1937* (Dublin, 2008).

8 Irene Whelan, 'The stigma of souperism' in Cathal Póirtéir (ed.), *The great Irish famine* (Dublin, 1995); Irene Whelan, *The bible war in Ireland: the 'second reformation' and the polarisation of Protestant Catholic relations, 1800–1840* (Dublin, 2005).

9 Desmond Bowen, *Souperism: myth or reality?* (Cork, 1970); Desmond Bowen, *The Protestant crusade in Ireland, 1800–70* (Dublin, 1978).

10 Paschal Majerus, 'The second reformation in west Galway: Alexander R. Dallas and the Society for Irish Church Missions to the Roman Catholics, 1849–1859' (MA dissertation, University College Dublin, 1991).

11 Máire Ní Shúilleabháin, *An t-Athair Caomhánach agus an cogadh creidimh i gConamara* [*Fr Kavanagh and the battle of the faith in Connemara*] (Dublin, 1984); John Lyons, *Louisburg: a history* (Louisburg, 1995), pp. 77–85; Gerard P. Moran, *A radical priest in Mayo: Fr. Patrick Lavelle, the rise and fall of an Irish nationalist 1825–86* (Dublin, 1994); Gerard P. Moran, *The Mayo evictions of 1860* (Westport, 1986).

12 Brighid Ó Murchada, *Oideachas in Íar Chonnacht sa naoú céad déag* [*Education in Íar Chonnacht in the nineteenth century*] (Dublin, 1954); Bearnárd Mac Uaid, 'Stair oideachas Bráthar Triomhadh Úird Riaghalta Sain Proinsias san naomhadh céad déag' [The history of education of the Third Order of Saint Francis in the nineteenth century] (MA thesis in history, University College Galway, 1956).

13 James H. Murphy, 'The role of Vincentian parish missions in the "Irish counter-reformation" of the mid nineteenth-century', *Irish Historical Studies*, xxii (1984), 152–71.

14 Jacinta Prunty, *Margaret Aylward, lady of charity, sister of faith: Margaret Aylward, 1810–1889* (Dublin, 1999).

15 Margaret Preston, *Charitable words: women, philanthropy and the language of charity in nineteenth-century Dublin* (London, 2004).

16 Matthew Kelly, 'The politics of Protestant street-preaching in the 1890s', *Historical Journal*, xxxxviii (2005), 101–25; Martin Doherty, 'Religion

community relations and constructive unionism. The Arklow street-preaching disturbances 1890–92' in James H. Murphy (ed.), *Evangelicals and Catholics in nineteenth-century Ireland* (Dublin, 2005), pp. 223–34.

17   C. Kinealy, *The great Irish famine: impact, ideology and rebellion* (Basingstoke, 2001), p. 149.

18   Niall Ó Ciosáin, 'Dia, bia agus Sasana: an Mistéalach agus íomha an ghorta' in Cathal Póirtéir (ed.), *Gnéithe an ghorta* (Dublin, 1995), pp. 151–63; Niall Ó Ciosáin, 'Famine memory and the popular representation of scarcity' in Ian MacBride (ed.), *History and memory in modern Ireland* (Cambridge, 2001), pp. 95–117; Niall Ó Ciosáin, 'Approaching a folklore archive: the Irish Folklore Commission and the memory of the great famine', *Folklore* (Aug. 2004), 222–32.

19   Liam Swords, *A hidden church: the diocese of Achonry, 1689–1818* (Dublin, 1997); Liam Swords, *A dominant church: the diocese of Achonry 1818–1960* (Dublin, 2004).

20   Thomas Olden, *The national churches: the Church of Ireland* (London, 1892); James Godkin, *Ireland and her churches* (London, 1867).

21   Thomas Johnston, John L. Robinson and Robert Wyse Jackson, *A history of the Church of Ireland* (Dublin, 1953), p. 259 (4 lines); John MacBeth, *The story of Ireland and her church, from the earliest times to the present day* (Dublin, 1899) (half a page); James Godkin, *Religious history of Ireland* (London, 1873) (15 pages).

22   Henry Sedall, *The Church of Ireland, a historical sketch* (London, 1886).

23   N. D. Emerson, 'Church life in the nineteenth century' in W. A. Phillips (ed.), *History of the Church of Ireland from the earliest times to the present day* (3 vols, London, 1933), iii, pp. 325–59 (15 pages).

24   R. B. McDowell, *The Church of Ireland, 1869–1969* (London, 1975); Alan Ford, James McGuire and Kenneth Milne (eds), *As by law established* (Dublin, 1995); Michael Hurley, *Irish Anglicanism 1860–1969* (Dublin, 1970).

25   Kenneth Milne, *The Church of Ireland: a history* (Dublin, 1966) (a few lines); Alan Acheson, *A history of the Church of Ireland 1691–1996* (Dublin, 1997) (three pages); Alan Acheson, *A true and lively faith* (n.p., 1992) (no mention); D. H. Akenson, *The Church of Ireland, ecclesiastical reform and revolution, 1880–1885* (London, 1971) (less than a page).

26   Thomas Andrews, *The Church in Ireland, a second chapter of contemporary history* (London, 1869); G. Locker Lampson, *A consideration of the state of Ireland in the nineteenth century* (London, 1907).

27   W. D. Killen, *The ecclesiastical history of Ireland from the earliest period to the present times* (2 vols, London, 1875), pp. 195–205.

28   The extant parish registers of the west Galway parishes are held in the Representative Church Body Library. The mission parishes include Aasleagh, Ballinakill, Renvyle, Sellerna, Ballyconree, Omey (Clifden), Errislannan, Errismore, Roundstone, Moyrus and Castlekerke.

29   The ICM was active in the following regions of west Galway: Connemara, Íar Connaught, Lough Corrib and Mask, and The Killeries. These will collectively be called the Connemara missions or, more correctly, the west Galway

missions, since it can be argued that the following missions are not strictly within the confines of Connemara: Moyrus, Killanin, Inverin, Castlekerke, Oughterard and Lough Mask. The use of Connemara to signify the entire missionary region is justifiable on the basis of the current vernacular albeit erroneous usage of the name.

30 IFC Archive, MS No. S4:307.

31 This methodology presumes that Albert Rossborough was unlikely to have come from a Catholic background while Margaret McCormick may have done; both children were in the Elliott Home in 1901.

32 William Marrable, *Sketch of the origin and operations of the Society for Irish Church Missions to the Roman Catholics* (London, 1853).

33 Edinburgh Irish Mission, *History of the mission* (Edinburgh, 1852), p. 3; Sheridan Wayne Gilley, 'Evangelical and Roman Catholic Missions to the Irish in London, 1830–1870' (Ph.D. dissertation, University of Cambridge, 1970).

34 For example prize-winners listed in the *Reports of the Tuam Board of Education* identified families whose children attended mission schools.

35 Ulick Bourke, *The life and times of the Rev. John MacHale, archbishop of Tuam and metropolitan* (Baltimore, 1882); John MacHale, *Sermons and discourses of the late most Rev. John MacHale, D.D., archbishop of Tuam*, edited by Thomas MacHale, D.D., Ph.D. (Dublin, 1883); Bernard O'Reilly, *John MacHale, his life, times and correspondence* (2 vols, New York, 1890).

36 Hilary Andrews, *The lion of the west: a biography of John MacHale* (Dublin, 2001).

37 Moffitt, *Soupers and Jumpers*, pp. 111–12.

38 1932 was chosen for two reasons: firstly, it provided a large (over 3000) sample of easily sorted material, and secondly because the Eucharistic Congress was held in Dublin in 1932 and it was mistakenly expected that this would result in increased interaction between the ICM and Catholic authorities.

Chapter 1

The origins of the Irish Church Missions: evangelicalism and anti-Catholicism in Britain and Ireland in the early nineteenth century

It is clear that Protestant missions to the Catholics of Ireland, although ostensibly religious movements, encompassed unvoiced political objectives. The religious enthusiasm which engulfed Britain and Ireland in the early nineteenth century, manifest in the rise of the evangelical party within the Established Church, inspired in many committed Christians a God-sent obligation to disseminate the scriptures to those in ignorance and error. This increased evangelical impulse coincided with, and was moulded by, the increased anti-Catholic sentiments and political ideologies of the early nineteenth century so that ultimately there was little, if any, distinction between the obligation to bring the scriptural truth to the Roman Catholic population and the desire to eradicate Romanism through the conversion of its adherents, thereby neutralising the Roman threat to Protestant Britain.

Missions to Roman Catholics: political considerations

The anti-Catholicism of eighteenth-century Britain was further fuelled by nineteenth-century concessions to Catholics such as Catholic emancipation in 1829 and the Tithe Comminution Act in 1838.[1] The sense of threat to Protestant *status quo* was amplified by the active participation of Roman clergy in these political crusades. As Irene Whelan has stated, 'the ideological and political showdown of the 1820s had consequences for denominational relations that can hardly be overstated'.[2] The momentum and success of the emancipation campaign aroused intense disquiet in among segments of the Protestant population and galvanised the connection between the promotion of evangelical religion and the defenders of Protestant rights and privilege. In the early decades of the century, the campaign to convert Roman Catholics became synonymous with the preservation of Protestant interests, while concessions to Catholics were considered the fruits of a Jesuitical plot to overthrow the Protestant presence, not only in Ireland but throughout the empire. Parliamentary reforms imposed on the Church of Ireland in 1833 were viewed as a further weakening of the Protestant status and the increase in the government grant to Maynooth (1845) was perceived as an unpardonable indulgence of a false and seditious religion.

Efforts to eradicate or contain popery encompassed not only doctrinal, but also social and economic objectives as political ideologies developed which blamed Ireland's backwardness and lawlessness on its adherence to Catholicism.[3] This resulted in a concerted effort to eradicate Irish popery and led to the formation of numerous societies which attempted to convert Irish Catholics, of which the Irish Society (1818) was the most far-reaching. Indeed, the conversion of Ireland became the focus of evangelicalism in England in the first half of the nineteenth century.[4] These missionary efforts among Irish Catholics became known as the Second Reformation. This may be described as occurring in two phases. Phase one encompassed the conversion impetus of the late 1820s, principally under the auspices of the Irish Society at Kingscourt (County Cavan), Ventry (County Kerry) and Doon (County Limerick), and is detailed by Irene Whelan in *The Bible War in Ireland*. Phase two, which was more ambitious, began with the establishment of the ICM during the Irish famine of 1845–48.

The actual term 'the Second Reformation' is misleading as efforts to convert Irish Catholics to the reformed faith had continued since the sixteenth century and were, in fact, a continuation of the Tudor and Stuart reformation. The elimination of Catholicism in Ireland was long seen as essential for the maintenance of Protestant power, as observed by William King, archbishop of Dublin (1650–1729): 'either they or we must be ruined'.[5] In the intervening centuries, efforts were made to eradicate, or at least contain, Romanism by parliamentary statute and by the provision of Protestant schooling so that, when numerous bible societies were established in the early nineteenth century, Ireland's Catholic clergy were alert to 'hidden dangers' masked as educational facilities.

The anti-Catholic sentiments which flourished in Britain and Ireland in the first half of the nineteenth century held traction at all levels of society. It is claimed that evangelical religion had more support among the upper classes in Ireland than in England,[6] and many of the landed elite certainly embraced the evangelical movement which was gaining popularity within the Church of Ireland. Many Irish landowners promoted scriptural education on their estates, which were maintained by the numerous mission societies established for this purpose both within and without the Established Church. These Irish evangelicals formed a closely knit community of aristocrats, often connected by marriage, and included the earls of Roden, Clancarty, Lorton, Gosford, Cavan, Bandon, Lanesborough and Mayo, all of whom would embrace the work of the ICM – in its initial years, at least.

Efforts to eradicate, or at least contain, Catholicism were equally supported by English aristocrats, some of whom owned Irish estates or were connected to Ireland. An Irish connection was not essential, however, as the perceived threat of a rising Catholic body politic, coupled with the conviction that the smile of God rested on Protestant Britain, prompted many noteworthy persons to lend their support to crusades against the Roman 'whore of Babylon'. The intensity of anti-Catholic fervour in mid Victorian Britain has been outlined by Denis Paz, Frank Wallis and John Wolffe, who demonstrate the sense of threat felt by the ultra-Protestants of Britain in the face of an increasingly public acceptance and toleration of the Roman church in terms of political concerns and of religious observance.[7]

Anti-Catholicism was fostered among lower social classes in English towns, directly and indirectly, by the many popular Protestant organisations in operation by the 1850s such as the Protestant Institute in Islington, where significant funds were raised for the ICM. As John Wolffe stated, through membership of these associations, those who began with strong but inarticulate racial, nationalist or anti-Catholic prejudices were enabled to graft a spiritual dimension to them and thus to acquire the distinction which came from engaging in a religious crusade.[8] Hymns, an effective method of influencing public opinion, fostered anti-Catholicism, such as the following which demanded: 'Let Babylon's proud altars shake/And light invade her darkest gloom/The yoke of iron bondage break/The yoke of Satan and of Rome!'[9] Popular anti-popery spectacles, such as the annual procession on 5 November at Lewes in Sussex, proliferated and frequently degenerated into violence.

The onset of the Irish famine of 1845–48, with its resulting deluge of destitute famine migrants into the cities of Britain, greatly increased the appeal of organisations wishing to contain or eradicate the extent and influence of Romanism. For those embracing millenarian beliefs, the cause held additional appeal (see below). The restoration of the English Catholic hierarchy in 1851 and the ensuing furore would further intensify anti-Roman sentiments, increasing the attraction of the ICM. This coincided with the high-water mark of Protestant activity in the 1840s and early 1850s, symbolised by the foundation of the National Club (1845) and in Reformation Societies.[10]

The establishment of the ICM, initially founded as the Special Fund for the Spiritual Exigencies of Ireland, provided an outlet through which anti-Catholic fervour could be vented and turned to a useful and productive purpose: to effect the conversion of Irish Catholics to scriptural Protestantism and thereby neutralise the political threat posed by the Roman clergy, or the 'truth-hating ministers of a persecuting bible-hating church', as they were described.[11] When a parliamentary investigation occasioned by increased agrarian violence revealed that all of Ireland, excluding Ulster, was beset by violent ribbonism, many English became convinced that the unrest was a 'conspiracy against property fomented by the Popish hierarchy'.[12]

Undeniably, England was urgently concerned about the inflow of Irish migrants to English cities, where it was unsympathetically claimed that they fled 'under the *pretence* of a pressure from death and famine'.[13] Over 300,000 Irish migrated to England between 1841 and 1851, and in 1851 the Irish Catholic population of London was estimated at 200,000, a fact which gave 'catalytic boosts' to the forces of anti-popery.[14] Britain's Protestants could not afford to stand idly by while the religion, culture and very ethos of the empire were under threat. The fact that many believed the Second Coming to be imminent lent an increased urgency to the crisis.

Scotland was a favourite destination for the Irish emigrant and the Edinburgh Irish Mission (EIM) was founded in 1842. Its work achieved an increased profile from 1847 following the arrival of large numbers of famine immigrants. Its aims were two-fold: firstly to rouse Protestants to resist Roman advances and its 'pernicious' clergy, which were considered to be attempting the conversion of Edinburgh's Protestants, and secondly to rescue Catholics from their 'fearful position'. Unlike the ICM, the EIM openly acknowledged its political aims and attempted to combat popery's three-pronged onslaught on Britain. It reported that the Romish advance in parliament, in the tractarian movement and in the influx of Irish Catholics had succeeded to the extent that numerous Catholic churches and convents had been stealthily founded in Protestant Scotland by 1852.[15]

In contrast to the ICM, the EIM employed evangelical men of all denominations. It was actively supported by notable dissenting clergymen, such as James Begg, founder of the famously anti-Catholic *Bulwark*. Begg advised that all publicly funded support of Catholicism, especially the Maynooth grant, should be withdrawn and that 'Missions to Papists' should be established throughout England and Ireland, promising that 'Babylon shall without doubt ultimately fall'.[16] The EIM, like the ICM, rejoiced in the conversion of Catholic priests such as James Forbes, who joined the Free Church of Scotland and became an active missionary. His superintendent, the Irish-speaking Revd Patrick M'Menemy, was a convert of the Presbyterian Church in Ireland.[17]

The methods employed in Edinburgh, and indeed in city missions throughout the country, were later adopted by the ICM: employing missionaries, visiting agents and Irish teachers, it held day and Sunday schools for children, along with prayer meetings, inquiry classes and Sabbath services. Although the EIM asserted that its war was 'not against papists themselves, but against popery', intense sectarian hostilities frequently resulted in violence and victimisation of Catholics.[18] Protestant–Catholic tensions in the slums were intensified by the presence of large numbers of Ulster Protestant migrants, giving rise to frequent 'Orange and Green' riots. These, however, were caused more by existing animosities and by anti-Catholic propagandists, rather than by mission activity itself.

By the end of 1851 the mission reported that between 300 and 400 persons had renounced the Church of Rome in Edinburgh. A mission was established at Glasgow to counteract the growing numbers of convents, and its work was extended to Perth, Dundee and Montrose. The EIM was soon operative outside Scotland, with agents working among the Catholic populations of London, Liverpool and other cities, as it was evident to ultra-Protestants that, rather than curbing the Romish influence, parliament would further endow Catholicism.[19] Britain's Protestants were urged to cast off their 'sinful lethargy' so that the multitudes in 'popish darkness' might be rescued and British Protestantism safeguarded. Its supporters were repeatedly reminded of the need to strengthen the EIM as the 'Antichristian apostasy was mustering all its forces … in all parts of Christendom' and could only be thwarted by an extension of the EIM to every town in the kingdom.[20]

The EIM was not alone in its crusade to safeguard the Romish souls of Scotland: the Scottish Reformation Society (1851), which also grant-aided missions in rural Ireland, supplied mission funds to Glasgow, Edinburgh and Dundee, and to other large towns where Romanists are 'multiplying year by year, and perishing for lack of knowledge within the sound of the Gospel'.[21] Speakers of Scots Gaelic were employed to deal with Celtic popery 'of both our own Highlands and of Ireland'.[22] In the 1850s, the ICM would send Irish-speaking agents to work among Irish Catholics in Glasgow (it is unclear whether they functioned independently or under the auspices of a Scottish society).[23] No precise date for the demise of the EIM has been identified; evidence suggests that it ceased to exist in the early to mid 1860s. Missions to Catholics were maintained after that date under the auspices of the Home Mission of the Free Church of Scotland but not specifically directed at Catholics from Ireland.[24]

Non-sectarian mission work had been carried out in an urban context by organisations such as the London City Mission, whose scripture readers and lay visitors had operated in the slums of the capital since 1835. It reflected the 'religious boom' of the Victorian era, primarily a middle-class phenomenon which inspired missioners to instil those in ignorance with a knowledge of the scriptures and a love of God.[25] They were also motivated by a somewhat patronising need to imbue the poor with their own virtues of cleanliness, thrift, sobriety and industry. Following the establishment of the ICM in 1849, its supporters recognised the inconsistency of attempting to convert Catholics in Ireland while neglecting those closer to home, founding The Society for English Church Missions to the Roman Catholics (ECM) in 1853 in which many ICM personnel were also active.[26] The ECM concentrated its operations in London's slums, most especially in Robert Bickersteth's parish of St Giles, where both its methodologies and those of the counter-missionary forces closely mirror the ICM's experiences. Lack of success and decreased finances forced the quiet dissolution of this movement in 1858.[27] In 1853, Revd Samuel Garrett, curate at St Giles, informed supporters of mission's 'effective progress' and prayed that it would 'aim an effectual blow at the Apostasy'; he was forced to admit, late in life, that 'though at one time there seemed fields white to the harvest, these hopes died away'.[28]

The Special Fund for the Spiritual Exigencies of Ireland, the direct fore runner of the ICM, was established in London in 1846 to attempt the conversion of the Catholic population in Ireland by capitalising on famine conditions. It was founded by Revds Alexander Dallas and Edward Bickersteth to provide funding for Dallas' newly adopted missionary venture at Castlekerke, County Galway, as discussed in the following chapter. Its committee consisted of members of the aristocracy, MPs, London businessmen and English clergymen, many of whom were ardent millenarianists.[29] Some Irish supporters, including the duke of Manchester and the earl of Roden, had long supported the much-publicised missionary movements at Achill, Doon, Ventry and Kingscourt and were unquestionably inspired by religious motivations, although many were aware that support could be attracted by more earthly considerations. As Robert Bickersteth, later bishop of Ripon, 1857–84, remarked, 'Whilst, however, our object is strictly religious and not political, it is capable of being defended on political grounds.'[30] He appealed to the vulnerability of those threatened by the Irish influx when he said, 'And what do we anticipate from this movement? Let those who can be influenced by no higher consideration, be influenced by this. We confidently anticipate a great social amelioration. (Hear, hear).'[31] Speaker after speaker at ICM annual meetings reassured listeners of the gain it would be to England when the 'Irish problem' was solved. Audiences were repeatedly told that England had tried to conquer and govern Ireland by political means, and that the bible would succeed where the imposition of law had failed; that the root of the 'Irish problem' lay in Catholicism and until this was eradicated, no other method, oppressive or conciliatory, would be effective:

> what keeps Ireland in her present condition? ... Why is it that with all the means and appliances that have been used ... Ireland shows no symptom of improvement ... The reason is obvious: it is that you have been fostering the evils of the country *pari passu* with the almost desultory effects which have been made to bring the gospel to the hearts of her people.[32]

Supporters were assured of the social and political benefit of converting Ireland's Catholics. Dallas himself stated: 'That which is beneficial to Ireland will ultimately be of advantage to England.'[33] Even John Bird Sumner, archbishop of Canterbury (1848–62) warned of the danger of 'constant immigration from Ireland of men who have imbibed superstition from the cradle'.[34] Supporters were promised that 'an enlightened people will supply their place' if the ICM was successful and that

> [England's] agricultural districts and manufacturing towns, which now teem with Irish emigrants, carrying with them popery, in all its degrading and debasing forms, will be relieved of such a burden as this; an enlightened people will supply their place; and instead of demoralising the inhabitants of England, by the vices and deceptions of Romanism, and feeding the cravings of a vulture-like priesthood, will disseminate (if they are educated in Ireland in the truths and doctrines of vital Christianity) peace and goodwill amongst men.[35]

For some English people the superiority of England's economy, social structure and political stability was unequivocally due to her Protestantism: 'See England! great industrious, peaceful and prosperous, because a free people – a Bible-reading, liberty-breathing, and free-thinking people ...'[36] The perception of the Catholic Irish as idle and wasteful was confirmed by the success of the Ulster economy compared with the Romanist provinces of Ireland, a view shared by Edward Nangle of Achill.[37] Ireland's topography and geology were misrepresented to supporters, who were told that the 'Roman Catholic population starves in the richest land in Ireland, while Protestants thrive on her inferior soils'.[38] It promised to be of enormous benefit to the economies of both countries if the Irish Catholics could be transformed into industrious Protestants as existed in Ulster. This was reinforced in Macauley's *History of England*, which outlined 'the blighting effect of popery ... wheresoever it has had the ascendancy'[39] and also by the fact that Protestant England was spared the attempted social revolutions that had occurred in Catholic Europe, beginning with the French revolution and continuing in Austria, interpreted as proof of the divine protection of the elect.[40] The potential social improvement was outlined in 1852 by John O'Callaghan, ICM missionary at Castlekerke, who painted a very rosy pen-picture of refined, restrained converts contrasting with 'savage' Romanists:

> A few years ago the people of this place were sunk in ignorance and superstition, but they are now surprisingly intelligent, peaceable, and all, more or less, acquainted with God's Word ... On Sundays, the Romanists meet together after mass to play at cards, to drink whiskey, to curse, and to fight, or may be seen at work as on the other six days; while the converts after prayers and Sunday school, remain at home with their families, or go to the houses of the Readers to receive instruction, remembering to keep holy the Sabbath day [41]

The ICM considered that the famine had broken the stranglehold of the Catholic clergy on their flock, mostly through resentment regarding the distribution of relief, thereby rendering Catholics amenable to Protestant approaches: 'The tyranny and coercion of these priests very generally disgusted the people',[42] a sentiment echoed to supporters of Presbyterian missions.[43] According to Revd Dallas, the Catholics of Ireland viewed the famine as punishment from God for the 'conduct of the priests'.[44] The insidious power of the Roman clergy was repeatedly outlined to supporters, warning of the danger 'to have men calling themselves "Priests of God" exercising this power ... against law, against institutions, against the connexion between Ireland and England, against all that makes us safe ...'[45]

It appears that there was some truth in the ICM's assertion that Connemara peasants had disassociated somewhat from their church, as their trust in religion was shattered by the famine experience.[46] It was considered essential that a suitable alternative to Catholicism be offered, since anarchy might ensue if the Catholic clergy lost their grip on the people and Protestantism did not step into the void.[47] It was darkly hinted that if a Catholic was 'roused to enquire' but did not become 'a Protestant and a true Christian, the chances are that he becomes an infidel'.[48]

Another contributing factor to the ICM's support in the initial years was the restoration of the Catholic hierarchy in England in 1851 and the ensuing close relationship between Rome and English Catholicism.[49] The injudicious comments of Cardinal Wiseman that 'Catholic England ... [was] restored to its orbit in the ecclesiastical firmament' sparked the furore of the Papal Aggression which occupied many minds and newspaper columns in England, both Catholic and Protestant, in the early 1850s.[50] The introduction of continental religious orders into Britain amplified the Protestant conviction that Catholicism, both Irish and continental, was encroaching on Britain. It was considered essential that this consolidation of Catholicism on English soil be resisted, as Rome was the root of all evil and Britain God's chosen Israel.[51] The English public was reminded of the political nature of the struggle against Rome and also informed that continental Protestants were exposed to intense persecution as popery gained in strength throughout Europe.[52] The resulting nationwide, pan-Protestant lunge against Catholicism gave additional impetus to the ICM's cause as the British public grew more hysterical about an impending Romish onslaught. Supporters at the ICM's 1852 annual meeting were urged

> if you would keep that [English life] and would not have that life tainted by the pestilential breath which would wither all, if you would not have these flowers of English virtue blackened by that poison blast, which would blow over them and leave them hateful to the eye and odious to every sense, then guard against the principles of Jesuitry – resist the power of Popery. (Loud and protracted applause)[53]

Thus the ICM answered the needs of an element of British society which felt threatened and besieged by the encroachment of Catholicism both from Ireland and continental Europe. In supporting the ICM, which promised to overthrow Catholicism, even the lowliest Englishman could play his part in holding back the looming attack on Britain and on the Established Church of England and Ireland.

Support for missions to Roman Catholics:
religious considerations

From the viewpoint of a mid-nineteenth-century evangelical, popery or Romanism was not based on the scriptures but was grounded on a collection of orders, rites and traditions, while evangelicalism, in contrast, was firmly based on the Word of God. Bebbington has defined four fundamental tenets of evangelicalism as conversionism, activism, biblicism and crucicentrism,[54] to which, arguably, a fifth may be added: individualism.[55] Evangelicals, through an understanding of the scriptures (biblicism), cognisant of their own sinfulness and aware that they have been saved by Christ's death (crucicentrism), are reborn in the truth (conversionism) and resolve to bring others to learn the Word of God (activism), with whom a personal relationship can be formed (individualism). Therefore, the very essence of evangelical Christianity compels the believer to introduce the Gospel to others and to save those in ignorance and error from the certain prospect of eternal damnation. This compulsion to spread the Gospel, which underpinned the foundation of the Irish Church Missions, took its lead from the scriptures.[56] In Ireland, the consequences of disseminating a scripturally based religion differed from experiences in other English-speaking countries, as most of its population was Roman Catholic, which overlaid the religious crusade with sectarian and political agendas.

Although only a small section of the Church of England was evangelical in the early nineteenth century, the evangelical influence among parish clergy had grown significantly by 1835 and it had achieved some notable positions of authority within the Established Church.[57] By 1850 about one-third of Anglican clergymen were evangelical, including many of the brightest and best. It was from this section of the Church of England that the ICM drew its support.[58] The focus of mid-nineteenth-century English evangelicalism was the conversion of Irish Catholics,[59] perceived as a threatening extension of the despotic power of Spain and Rome.[60]

The growth of English evangelicalism resulted in the formation of parish organisations, many of which were missionary in character, such as the Church Missionary Society (1799) and the Church Pastoral Aid Society (1836). This paved the way for the formation of ICM auxiliary or parish associations, founded to ensure a continuing income derived from a lower social order than its aristocratic patrons. The ties of pan-Protestant evangelicalism were frequently stronger than connections within Anglicanism itself[61] and in its early years, at the height of the anti-Catholic hysteria of the 1850s, much support was given to the ICM from regions where dissent was numerically strong.

Evangelicalism and evangelical societies flourished in Ireland in the early nineteenth century, promoted by graduates of Trinity College, Dublin, especially through the influence of men such as Henry Monck Mason, James Digges La Touche and Thomas Lefroy.[62] Many of these men were of pivotal importance in existing missions to Roman Catholics and would initially lend support to the newly formed Irish Church Missions.

Evangelical hostility to Catholicism, which it considered the 'deadly and implacable foe of revealed truth',[63] originated primarily from the fact that most Catholics did not personally read the bible, but relied instead on the interpretation of others and on non-scriptural doctrines and devotional practices. Irish Catholics in the mid nineteenth century were not forbidden to read the scriptures, although many Catholic clergymen did not encourage the practice.[64] Some Catholic clergy argued that illiterate peasants were not capable of personally interrogating the scriptures as 'The bible is not a book easily understood, even by well educated persons ... an illiterate convert, therefore, accepts the new religion on the worst kind of authority, that of ignorant bible readers', arguing that it should be interpreted by Catholic clergy.[65] Protestant mission supporters capitalised on this discouragement to read the bible, as in this 'supposed discussion' (written by a deputation secretary of the Hibernian Bible Society) said to be 'a fair representation of the controversies ... between the people and the priests':

> Priest: Did I not tell you, Barney, that the Bible is a dangerous book, and
> not fit for the common, ignorant sort of people to read. It has turned your

head; you are a proof that it is much better in every respect that the priests should study it, and take the right meaning out of it, and explain it to the people.[66]

The indefatigable Catholic polemicist Dr Daniel Cahill (1796–1864), who published over 100 counter-missionary pamphlets, repeatedly insisted that Catholics were permitted to read the scriptures, arguing in 1856 that over a quarter of a million bibles had been sold in Ireland in the previous twenty years.[67] In 1846, even before Dallas' arrival in Connemara, John MacHale, archbishop of Tuam (1834–81), published an Irish translation of the New Testament, followed by translations of other parts of the scriptures. That these works each ran to at least two editions proves that there was a demand for bibles among Irish Catholics.[68] It was the deference of Irish Catholics to their clergy in matters of scriptural interpretation that most enraged evangelical Protestants, who made no distinction between an outright ban on Catholics reading the scriptures (which was never in force) and the requirement to rely on their clergy for direction in their interpretation (which certainly was). This reliance of Irish Catholics on their clergy was fundamental to evangelical opposition to Catholicism and frequently denounced: 'how can a Roman Catholic be free? His reason is in fetters, his conscience is in the priest's hands and his Bible is closed.'[69] Catholicism was seen as a 'really blasphemous counterfeit of God's own truth'[70] and Connaught described as the most superstitious province in Ireland, where the 'sordid disposition of the priests ... [confirmed the] marked antipathy of their priests towards Biblical instruction'.[71]

Catholics' reliance on clerical interpretation of the scriptures had political overtones, an influence which was increasingly feared through the era of Catholic emancipation and anti-tithe agitation. Although the ICM was non-political in nature, members were told of the 'absolute despotism' exercised by priests over a people 'hoodwinked, nay, blindfolded by superstition', astutely reminding supporters of the 'spirit of persecution, that wants only the power to rival the malice of the days of Mary'.[72] ICM supporters applauded Dallas' assertion that the ICM provided the best safeguard to Romish encroachment on England since 'when you are thinking of the best method of repelling that aggression on our shores which has awakened so deep an interest in every Protestant breast and English heart ... the best method is to carry the war into the enemy's country'.[73] This sentiment was echoed by persons advocating Presbyterian missions to Roman Catholics. Stuart Moody, a member of the Free Church of Scotland, urged that

We are bound to employ every means at home to check the growing strength of this fiery serpent, that is nestling within our bosom; but the most effectual of all methods of prevention is for us to send forthwith a band of devoted missionaries to Ireland to convert the Roman Catholics in their own homes ...[74]

Many differences existed between mid-nineteenth-century evangelical Christianity and Roman Catholicism.[75] Anglican doctrine as laid down in the Thirty-Nine Articles (1571) considered Catholic doctrines, such as purgatory and transubstantiation, to be false and without biblical foundation.[76] Evangelicals condemned non-scriptural Catholic doctrines such as transubstantiation[77] and Dallas insisted that 'Roman Catholic religion is not Christianity' since the Council of Trent had been 'wholly opposed to the Scriptures', giving detailed doctrinal argument against its doctrines and practices such as justification by faith, purgatory, invocation of saints, the veneration of Mary, transubstantiation and Apostolic Succession.[78] Traditional Catholic practices such as the veneration of images were criticised, and in particular the veneration of Mary was denounced, as in the following conversation reported in *Erin's Hope*, which told of an Irish child who prayed daily to Mary but reportedly knew nothing of God or Christ:

> 'Who made her?' She did not know. 'Have you ever heard of God?', 'No, never.' 'Have you ever heard of Jesus Christ?', 'No, never'. 'Have you ever heard of the Virgin Mary?' 'Oh, yes;' she knew all about the Virgin Mary. 'And what do you know about her?' 'Oh, I pray to her every day to save me'.[79]

Catholicism was considered immensely inferior to Protestantism since 'the more debased the idolatry by which man is enslaved, the farther is man removed from the knowledge of that true God', and was viewed as 'an apostasy of St. Paul'.[80] It was believed that 'should a [Catholic] soul try to approach Almighty God in prayer, *Rome has entirely cut it off* by raising within it the monstrous idol of the Virgin'.[81] Mission supporters were reminded that the Pope had proclaimed himself 'under the warranty of false credentials, Christ's vicar on earth' and was 'pointedly contrasted with ... true Christianity'.[82]

The increasing tendency towards millenarian beliefs, and especially the prevalence of pre-millennial beliefs, was an important influence in fostering missions to Catholics. It has been shown that ideologies of British nationalism, anti-Catholic sentiments and millenarianism, although prevalent since the 1820s, were 'at their most influential at a popular level from the 1840s onwards', while Dallas acknowledged in 1847 that discussion of the prophecies had been 'scarcely mooted in religious society' twenty years earlier.[83]

Millenarianism, which predicted Christ's second coming as foretold in scripture, identified Rome as the Antichrist, the Whore of Babylon, the beast of Revelation and other biblical images representing forces of evil, and considered that the 'Christian who put his hope in her help, and not in Christ' was 'outside the Evangelical scheme of salvation and could not be saved'.[84] Pre-millennial convictions were increasingly held by the upper classes, promoted especially by John Nelson Darby, an Irish clergyman who argued that the Second Coming of Christ would occur before the millennium (the thousand year reign of the saints), thereby conferring an increased sense of urgency on the cause of converting Romanists.

ICM supporters interpreted crises such as 'cholera, famine after famine, fever, dysentery and the extensive system of emigration' as signs of the impending Second Coming of Christ (providence)[85] and believers were urged to effect the fall of the Romish Antichrist so that they might be able to announce 'Babylon, the great, is fallen, is fallen'.[86] The conversion of Jews to scriptural Protestantism was also considered essential for the fulfilment of the prophecies.

Evangelicalism and Roman Catholicism shared a number of doctrines. Both claimed a monopoly on the truth (one true church), as evidenced by contemporary signs (providence) and were convinced that all means to convert unbelievers to the perceived truth were justifiable (error has no right).[87] England's nineteenth-century evangelicals were certain that theirs was the one true church: 'Blessed be God for our English Protestantism, because it *is* Bible Christianity',[88] and that they were responsible for the salvation of Ireland's 'utterly apostate' Catholics, who were unquestionably bound for eternal damnation.[89] The righteousness of their cause was without question since Protestantism had 'as many aspects of GOOD as Popery itself has of EVIL'.[90] Catholicism was equally confident in its own divine merits, claiming its own monopoly on salvation and striving to rescue converts to Protestantism whom it believed to be unquestionably destined for the fires of hell.[91]

Both Roman Catholicism and evangelical Protestantism shared an urgent sense of responsibility to bring the Gospel to those in ignorance. A resolution passed at the foundation of the Church Missionary Society stated that it was the 'duty of every Christian to endeavour to propagate the Gospel among the heathen', while the Catholic Mill Hill Fathers were founded in London in the 1860s 'for evangelising the heathen'.[92] Even as Irish Catholics were combating proselytism at home, they were sending missionaries abroad to save foreign souls. All Hallows Seminary, Dublin opened to train missionaries in 1842 and the seminary of the Society of Missionaries for Africa was opened in Cork in 1879. There are significant similarities between the way the Protestant and Catholic missions portrayed both the 'native' or 'target' populations and the ideology of converting those in ignorance. Fiona Bateman aptly summarises the assumptions of missionary discourse which, she argues, can be applied to both Catholic and Protestant missions with equal validity:

> Missionary efforts to spread civilisation and Christianity (always inextricably linked in the discourse) were based largely on a notion that the benighted target populations had no religion which was deserving of the name and that their poor living conditions, laziness, and immoral behaviour were bound up in their state of religious ignorance ...[93]

Evangelical Protestants considered that missionary work among Irish Catholics had long been neglected by Protestant churches in Ireland,[94] but now hoped that 'God's time for breaking up this darkness has come'[95] and that the conversion of Ireland's Catholics would be undertaken since 'millions of our countrymen ... are in the depths of the darkness which results from this imposition left to work in all the unchecked evil of hereditary corruption'.[96] Contemporary Catholic missioners were equally concerned to gather souls for the Lord, writing in 1853 that it was 'a lamentable truth that 500 millions of our fellow creatures throughout the world are ... buried in the darkness of idolatry, and given up to the evils of heathen superstition'.[97] Charles Bernard, later Protestant bishop of Tuam, outlined the Protestant duty to rescue Catholics from eternal damnation:

> Did you ever consider – my friends – that there is an awful responsibility in the possession of a Bible – an awful guilt in keeping back from others its saving truths ... Shall we see them involved in vital error, falling almost to the zero of vital infidelity, know that their path leads them not to God, and yet raise no warning voice?[98]

Faced with such perceived deviation from scriptural truth, evangelicals considered that heretical opposition to the bible should not only be suppressed but should be overcome, and that all methods which might result in the eradication of the enemy Church of Rome were justifiable (error has no right).[99] This explains the ICM's adoption of methods considered questionable, even at the time, by other segments of Protestantism, such as the conditional distribution of relief in mission schools.

Both Catholic and Protestant powers utilised Christian mission as a powerful weapon of cultural expansion. Catholic 'White Fathers' who laboured in Africa were reminded that '*Nous travaillons aussi pour la France*' [We also work for France],[100] while John Phillip, superintendent of the London Missionary Society, reported that its missionaries were 'extending British interests, British influence and the British empire'.[101]

The choice of Ireland as a location for missionary enterprise was governed by its proximity to England, the adventitious arrival of famine conditions and the mass emigration of poor Irish to England. The formation of the ICM coincided with the nineteenth-century explosion of world mission, which was greatly facilitated by improved navigation techniques.[102] Popular accounts of missions to foreign lands, which combined exploration and evangelisation, as typified by David Livingstone (1813–73), fostered an interest both in the fascinating savagery of foreign 'natives' and in their 'depraved' religious rites. Ireland and its native population were romantically portrayed in mission literature, with wind-swept Connemara depicted as having palm trees and its population described as being 'as savage as the South Sea islanders'.[103]

While English opinion of the 'barbarous Irish' was constant, English estimates of the degree to which the Irish might be 'improved' varied. As Europeans came into contact with cultures of the new world, some leading English thinkers proposed the idea that the Irish were so barbaric and pagan that they could not be reformed and should be subdued.[104] The ICM was advised against attempting to 'improve' the Irish, suggesting instead that the Irish should be encouraged to emigrate so that the 'Anglo-Saxon could take his place',[105] as 'these unfortunate persons have small, ill-shaped skulls with foreheads villainous low'.[106] Other opponents reminded the ICM that the historian, Macauley, had stated that it was a remarkable fact that 'no Christian nation, which did not adopt the principles of the Reformation before the end of the sixteenth century, should ever have adopted them. Catholic communities have, since that time, become infidel and become Catholic again; but none has become Protestant.'[107]

In spite of such reservations, evangelical theology was underpinned by the conviction that people were equal in their capacities to hear and understand the scriptures, evidenced by the work of the CMS in Africa and Asia, and English efforts to spread the Gospel at home and abroad continued apace. In 1851, nearly 500,000 guineas were raised for this purpose.[108] Despite opposition to missionary work among Irish Catholics on ethnicity grounds and of the lack of support from existing proselytising societies such as the Irish Society, as discussed in the following chapter, the evangelical obligation to rescue Ireland's Roman Catholics from certain eternal damnation resulted in the formation of the ICM. Alexander Dallas was pivotal in the establishment of the Special Fund for the Spiritual Exigencies of Ireland in 1846, remodelled as the Society for Irish Church Missions to the Roman Catholics in 1849, driven by his evangelical compulsion to bring Irish Catholics to the scriptural truth. Without his efforts, the ICM would never have come into being.

Previous efforts to convert Irish Catholics

Although the Tudor reformation was of pivotal importance in the history of Ireland, few Irishmen embraced the Protestant faith. Efforts towards widespread conversion were only undertaken in the nineteenth century, but never on so large a scale as the ICM.[109] Recent assessments of proselytising activities in eighteenth-century Ireland show that conversion efforts concentrated on the provision of education and that little direct missionary work was undertaken until the early nineteenth century.[110] Irish Catholicism had long been blamed for its disloyalty and backwardness in marked contrast to the social and political advances wrought in Protestant England. The barbarous/civilised dichotomy influenced many aspects of Protestant thought from the twelfth to the seventeenth and eighteenth centuries. As Liechty has attested, 'the Irish Reformation became another English method – along with colonisation, warfare, and anglicisation – for subjugating and civilising Ireland'.[111] Some clerical propagandists contrasted '[Protestant] civility in language, dress, diet and housing with [Catholic] barbarism'[112] while others, in contrast, disagreed with the assumption that 'the Irish nation before the English came among them were a rude, uncivilised people and governed by barbarous laws and customs'.[113]

Irishmen, of all creeds and classes, appreciated the merits of educating the children of the poor. In the wake of the 1798 rebellion, organisations such as the Association for Discountenancing Vice reminded landlords of their duty to provide scriptural education on their estates, informing them that the native population of Wales and Scotland had been transformed by exposure to the scriptures.[114] Numerous societies such as the Hibernian Bible Society (1806), the Society for Promoting the Education of the Poor (1811) and the Irish Society (1818) were formed to deliver a scriptural education on a nationwide scale and, in their initial decades, were attended by equal numbers of Protestants and Catholics. The origin and operation of organisations founded to disseminate the scriptures have been traced in detail by Irene Whelan, who has shown that they attracted considerable numbers of Catholics until the Roman clergy voiced their disapproval in the mid 1820s, prompted more by a desire to restrict access to the scriptures rather than by an actual fear of proselytism.[115]

As the campaign for Catholic emancipation escalated in the second and third decades of the nineteenth century, a political and ideological doctrine developed which held that Ireland's problems could ultimately be attributed to its Catholicism.[116] Protestants were galvanised to resist the growth of a Catholic body politic and the positions of scriptural societies and the Catholic church became polarised. Protestants feared that Catholic emancipation was sought, not as an end in itself, but as the beginning of a process to establish the political and educational supremacy of Irish Catholics, and to obliterate the Protestant presence in Ireland.[117] Numerous evangelising societies were formed, many of which utilised the Irish language and the inducement of education, as Protestants – principally but not exclusively of an evangelical disposition – sought to effect change in the ethnicity and ideologies of Irish Catholics and thereby safeguard Ireland and, by extension, Britain, from the subversive influence of the Roman religion.

Efforts to convert the Catholic peasantry were not confined to Anglicanism. The (Congregationalist) London Hibernian Society for the Diffusion of Religious Knowledge in Ireland (1804) and the Baptist Society for Promoting the Gospel in Ireland (1814) commanded a considerable presence, especially in counties Mayo, Sligo and Roscommon in the province of Connaught. Supporters of proselytising missions, both within and without the Established Church, believed their efforts were directed by the divine hand of God, as proven by the success of similar missionary endeavours in foreign lands and by the defeat of Napoleon. They were horrified at the passing of Catholic emancipation in 1829, described as 'the evil tree [which] bringeth forth fruit',[118] and bemoaned the creation of the national school system in 1831 which deprived mission societies of their principal *modus operandi* in all but a handful of locations.

Doctrinal objections to Roman Catholicism instilled English evangelicals with a God-sent obligation to rescue those trapped in the errors of Rome. The duty to disseminate the scriptural truth throughout Ireland was further accentuated by the knowledge that England had 'forced papal despotism on Ireland' in the twelfth century and ICM supporters were reminded that they could not ignore their responsibility to Ireland 'without bringing on ourselves retributive, national punishment'.[119] Missionary zeal had established missions among England's urban poor and sent countless agents to foreign lands, but the neighbouring island had been left in error and darkness.[120] ICM supporters were reminded in 1850 that 'You send it [the Gospel] to the cannibals of New Zealand ... why not send it to Ireland: Surely you are more interested in Ireland than in those distant countries (Hear.) You are married as it were to Ireland, and be the union for better or for worse, you cannot break it.'[121]

Efforts to convert the Catholics in the west of Ireland were undertaken by numerous organisations from the early nineteenth century, especially but not exclusively by the Established Church. Since its inception in 1818, the Irish Society (IS) was active in north Mayo/south Sligo and in districts of east Galway and south Roscommon. The introduction of proselytising missions to a district was dependent on committed landowners and clergymen, such as the mission near Boyle, County Roscommon introduced by Lord Lorton of Rockingham, and those near Ballinasloe facilitated by Lord Clancarty. Similarly, in the decades immediately preceding the famine, scriptural schools were established in Connemara, at Ballinahinch on the Martin estate, at Renvyle on the Blake estate, and in the town of Clifden, facilitated by funds from the Island and Coast Society and the Kildare Place Society. In spite of scriptural schools of this nature, educational provision was sparse in the impoverished west of Ireland. This was remedied by the introduction of the national school system in 1831, which diminished the appeal of scriptural schools in most districts. However, John MacHale's exclusion of national schools from his Tuam diocese created an educational void which facilitated the uptake of the ICM's services.

Evangelical clergymen of the Church of Ireland were deployed in Connemara from 1820, in the episcopate of archbishop Trench (1819–39), including Revds Charles Seymour at Clifden, Brabazon Ellis at Moyrus (Carna), Anthony Thomas at Ballinakill and Mark Anthony Foster at Tully.[122] Revds Foster and Ellis, along with Hyacinth D'Arcy of Clifden, were instrumental in establishing the Connemara Christian Committee in 1836, dedicated to evangelising among the Catholic population.

Among the many societies of the Established Church which had attempted the conversion of Ireland's Catholics prior to the foundation of the ICM, the most prominent were the Irish Society (IS) and the Achill Mission (AM).[123] The Achill Mission and the ICM were similar in terms of methodology, unequivocally denouncing Catholicism and offering education and relief only to those needy who chose to convert, which differed markedly from the tactics of the more moderate IS.

The IS was founded in 1818 'for promoting the education of the native Irish through the medium of their own language' and intended to 'afford the same advantages for education to all classes of professing Christians'. It attracted substantial support from landlords such as Lord Farnham at Kingscourt in Cavan and Lord Ventry in Kerry, who attempted to foster Protestantism on their estates in the 1820s and 1830s, and it commanded ongoing support from the Irish clergy. John MacHale, Catholic archbishop of Tuam, 1834–81, had considerable contact with the IS when bishop of Killala (1825–34), as the society was very active in north Mayo. In fact, the missions of the Presbyterian church and the Anglican Irish Society were greatly facilitated by MacHale's exclusion of national schools from the Killala diocese.

The IS taught the Irish-speaking peasantry to read, using the Irish bible as a textbook: 'the people began with no other desire than to hear the Irish, but by-and-by the work of God rubbed off the scales and they saw the light, at first dimly, then more clearly'.[124] The daughter of John Alcock, a life-long IS activist, described the

> remarkable movement in the direction of Protestantism ... more wonderful because it was not the result of controversy, not the work of zealous missionaries, but mainly of the quiet private study of the Scriptures, through which hundreds of intelligent, though uneducated persons in

different parts of the country, and without communication with each other, were led by the Divine Spirit, at the same time, to the knowledge of the same truths.[125]

The IS was confined to educational methods but its offshoot, the Ladies' Auxiliary of the Irish Society (LAIS) employed scripture readers. In 1848, the LAIS employed fifty-one scripture readers while the IS employed 738 teachers, most of whom were untrained Irish teachers, but the Society was not active in west Galway.[126] In stark contrast to ICM methods, it was IS policy to employ Catholics as teachers, insisting that

> the teachers be as far as practicable respectable Irish speaking Roman Catholics, Protestants may sometimes be appointed, but only when no competent Romanist can be obtained, and in every case the teacher must be able to speak and understand as well as read the language and must be located amongst the Roman Catholic population ... the pupils [must] be, with very few exceptions, Roman Catholics. Converts may be admitted into the classes but <u>original</u> Protestants <u>very rarely</u> and only when the superintendent thinks it would not be prudent to exclude them. In every case the pupil must be able to speak and understand Irish.[127]

Revd Alexander Dallas, founder of the Irish Church Missions, was frustrated by the Irish Society's slow rate of progress and at its employment of Catholics. The ICM would later copy the IS practice of employing untrained Irish teachers, who worked unobserved among their neighbours, less conspicuous without a formal schoolhouse: 'A teacher's schoolroom was his own close, dark cabin, where after the day's work was done, his neighbours gathered round the hearth'.[128] However, in marked contrast to the IS, the ICM only employed those who had openly converted. Although the IS provided mission schools in a small number of locations, its work mostly consisted of informal Irish teaching. It operated two training schools in County Limerick, for schoolmasters at Ballingarry and for scripture readers at Doon.[129] These schools, with the one at Achill (see below), provided trained agents in the initial days of the ICM, while the IS Collegiate school at Ventry and the Irish Missionary College at Ballinasloe ensured a supply of Irish-speaking students for the ministry.[130]

The IS was unworried by its slow progress and allowed its scholars to remain Catholic, saying that few 'as far as we can learn, leave Romanism; but who can tell the blessed effects of the study of that Word to multitudes of such persons'.[131] In 1850, an unidentified western district of the IS had 1,299 Catholic pupils out of a total of 1,477. This lack of urgency for conversion should not be interpreted as a tolerance of Catholicism as many IS supporters were ardent millenarians and the Society congratulated itself that hundreds had 'been brought to renounce Papal error and join themselves to our Scriptural church'.[132] Revd John Alcock preached that the 'Sovereign Pontiff in Rome is the Anti-Christ ... by this conclusion you put all Roman Catholics outside the pale of salvation'.[133] The IS reported that Catholic clergy initially approved of its provision of education, but many were forced to oppose it as their hierarchy came to appreciate the danger it posed to Catholicism.[134] In spite of Catholic opposition, the IS did not engage in controversial denunciations of Catholicism, consistently maintaining a steady, almost understated, attack on popery, exclusively through the provision of education.

In contrast to the moderate IS, the AM engaged in direct argument with the Catholic church. In 1834 Revd Edward Nangle founded his colony on the impoverished island off County Mayo in the diocese of Tuam, which, like Connemara, had a pressing need for temporal relief and education. Considerable similarities existed between the Achill and west Galway missions: both occupied a similar landscape; both were founded by persons external to the area; both founders were initially drawn to the region by famine conditions and were warned of the folly of their endeavours by persons with more experience of mission work; both separated the collection of funds for missionary work from monies used for orphan homes and temporal relief; both solicited support from sympathetic Protestants by outlining the persecution of converts and mission staff; both encountered the formidable opposition of John MacHale, Catholic archbishop of Tuam; Catholic clergy ordered a boycotting of all persons connected with both missions; opposition national schools with Roman Catholic patronage were swiftly opened in both regions, and in both missions the reliability of the convert numbers is open to question.[135]

When Dallas first turned his attention to the west of Ireland in 1845, the Achill mission was at its peak, busily advertising its thriving mission colony, schools, church, dispensary, orphan houses, hotel and training school.[136] The appeal of Achill for tourists retained the cause in the public eye, even if publicity was not always favourable. Mr and Mrs Hall severely criticised the AM, asserting that it was administered by a committee 'the greater number of whom probably have never visited the settlement',[137] and Asenath Nicholson scathingly observed in 1844–45 how the trifling payment to convert-workers would 'never give them the palatable well-earned board round which their masters sit, and which they have earned for them by their scantily-paid toil'.[138] She was even more critical on her second visit to Achill in 1847, denouncing the mission for overworking its converts whom it paid with meagre rations of Indian meal.[139]

The similarities between the AM and the ICM may be explained by shared personnel. Three out of four trustees of the AM were founding members of the ICM.[140] Financial problems in the AM forced a merger with the well-resourced ICM in 1852, which continued until 1856, when discord between the two societies,[141] coupled with a declining ICM income, forced a dissolution.

The early nineteenth century saw the establishment of numerous missions to Catholics promulgated through the dissenting churches. The Home Mission of the Synod of Ulster operated missions to Roman Catholics from the early 1830s. By 1840, when the 'Synod of Ulster' and the 'Presbyterian Synod of Ireland distinguished by the name Seceders' were amalgamated to form the General Assembly of the Presbyterian Church in Ireland, the annual income of the Home Mission was £3,088.[142] It initially focused its operations on three locations: Kerry, north Mayo/south Sligo (termed the Connaught mission) and a midland mission centred on the town of Parsonstown (Birr). The Home Mission soon appreciated the need for Irish-speaking missionaries for its Kerry and Connaught missions, reporting in 1842 that there were only six men capable of preaching in Irish across all Protestant denominations.[143] Both the Anglican Irish Society and the General Assembly of the Presbyterian Church in Ireland attempted to correct this deficit by instituting bursaries for theological students with a knowledge of Irish in Trinity College, Dublin (Irish Society) and in the Theological College, Belfast (General Assembly) and, from 1840, it became mandatory that candidates for the Presbyterian School of Divinity in Belfast should study the Irish language for at least six months.[144]

By the mid 1840s, and prior to the onset of the famine, a concerted Presbyterian effort was underway to convert the Catholic population. It promised that 'no field is as promising as the Irish speaking population of our own land',[145] since 'the net of the gospel could as easily be thrown over this country just now, as a net over a shoal of herrings'.[146] In 1843 a Bi-centenary Fund was established to 'aid in the erection of houses of worship for Presbyterians in the south and west; to afford protection to converts from popery; and to such other objects as are included in an extraordinary effort for the benefit of the Roman Catholics of Ireland'. Within a year the Fund stood at £16,000, a portion was withdrawn to supply churches in the south and west and the remainder allocated for 'the instruction of the Irish-speaking population'.[147]

The annual income of the Home Mission averaged £4,000 in the early 1840s, a large portion originating in Scotland. Groups of ladies in Scottish towns and cities established auxiliary associations to gather funds for mission work among Irish Catholics, often 'adopting' mission workers, as when they funded Revd Michael Brannigan, a convert from Rome, to work in the north Mayo station of Ballinglen.[148] In 1842, the Home Mission announced the formation of a Ladies' Association in Glasgow, which 'like its sister in Edinburgh ... takes a special interest in the instruction of the native Irish, through the medium of their own language'.[149] As might be expected, Scottish supporters of missions to Catholics aligned themselves with the evangelical Free Church at the Disruption of 1843. Members of the Free Church were informed in 1847 that 'with the exception of Birr, in King's County ... the great sphere of Presbyterian missionary effort is in Connaught' and a report presented to the Free Church urged: 'Let us go quickly to our knees and pray for Ireland – let us go to our coffers and give for Ireland – let the people go to their ministers and lend them to Ireland – and let her ministers go to Ireland, and plead with her in the name of our God, who giveth us the victory in Jesus Christ our Lord'.[150]

Presbyterian missions were operated in a manner similar to those of the Irish Church Missions. Children were taught in day schools; adults were instructed in a more informal manner. A controversial approach was adopted in both instances and the 'errors of Rome' clearly outlined. The missions operated on a more modest scale than the extensive Irish Church Missions; an orphanage was established in the town of Ballina and an agricultural/industrial school at the mission's farm in Ballinglen, near Ballycastle in north Mayo, and a small number of Presbyterian schools were founded in the region between Dromore West (south Sligo) and Ballycastle (north Mayo).

Although the ICM, which was officially founded in 1849, shared the objectives of the mission societies established in the early decades of the century, it was born into a markedly different atmosphere and encountered a more robust and resistant response from both the clergy and laity of the Roman Catholic church. The social, economic and political aspirations of the Roman Catholic majority advanced significantly in the first half of the nineteenth century. Several factors have been identified behind this trend: the growth of a substantial Catholic middle class, the influence of Maynooth-trained clergy, the increased provision of education for the masses, the passing of Catholic emancipation in 1829, and the development of a Catholic body politic.[151]

The boom in agricultural commodities which marked the years of the Napoleonic Wars, followed by the contraction of the market from 1816, impacted greatly on the development of Irish Catholicism. The merchant classes, in which many Catholics were prominent, prospered during the long war against France. Traders and farmers benefited most from the increased cost of commodities. Their social superiors, the landlords, struggled to meet increased prices without a parallel increase in income, as much of their land was let on long leases at fixed rents. Traders or merchants were well positioned to offer mortgages on lands held by Protestants. Enabled to purchase land in fee since 1793, many enterprising Catholics bought farms outright or foreclosed on indentures; this occurred throughout the early nineteenth century, but especially in the wake of the famine. Although the impact on the tenantry was minimal, the gradual advancement of middle-class Catholics into the landowning classes added to a heightened sense of Catholic confidence. The growth in wealth of merchant classes facilitated the construction, or reconstruction, of Catholic churches, initially in cities and towns but later throughout the more prosperous rural areas. Connemara, a very deprived district devoid of a resident Catholic middle class, benefited little from this expansion in Catholic infrastructure prior to the famine, although many Catholics purchased sections of famine-bankrupted estates in Connemara in the Encumbered Estates Court from 1850. In the Dublin diocese the emergence of a confident Catholic middle class is best exemplified by the ambitious church-building programme that marked the episcopate of Daniel Murray (1823–52).

The campaign to force through Catholic emancipation politicised the Catholic population. This had been promised at the Act of Union in 1800 but was granted only when Daniel O'Connell mounted a formidable agitation, assisted in great measure by Catholic clergy. The laity was now enabled to take its place, not only at local level, but in parliament. Municipal reform enabled Catholics to play a full role in urban politics and to assume posts of responsibility and status, as in 1841, when Daniel O'Connell became Lord Mayor of Dublin. The Catholic 'body politic' had arrived.

From 1795, clergy were trained in Maynooth seminary, as continental seminaries were closed in the aftermath of the French revolution. The 'Maynooth priest' has often been contrasted unfavourably with former 'gentlemanly' continental clergy, being less cultured and more politically inclined. This observation may reflect the changing nature of Irish Catholicism in general as a Catholic political awareness developed from the 1820s. By 1853 half the priests in Ireland were Maynooth ordained. Although these men came from 'better off' families, they came from less wealthy families than had continental seminarians. This reflects the dissemination of literacy and prosperity downwards through the social orders of Catholicism as money, influence and education came within the grasp of many, but remained far outside the aspirations of the very poor. The tenor of Irish Catholicism was altered as the nineteenth century progressed, and especially as the threat of proselytism mounted under famine conditions with the 'liberal Catholicism of Troy, Murray, and O'Connell' giving way to a defensive alliance between the Catholic clergy and laity.[152]

The creation of the national school system in 1831 brought literacy within the reach of many, though the requirement of joint local funding placed a heavy burden on the poorest communities. It was established to correct the perceived iniquities of the state-sponsored Kildare Place Society, which Catholic authorities had long viewed as a proselytising agency. The transfer of government grants from the Protestant Kildare Place Society to the non-denominational National Board of Education was considered by many Protestants as an erosion of their advantages and as an indulgence of the 'heretical' Catholic religion. From the outset the Church of Ireland and the Presbyterian Church remained independent of the National Board, although the Church of Ireland placed its schools under the National Board in 1860. Many Catholic bishops also had serious reservations about the system, most notably John MacHale of Tuam. Several lay-supported national schools had been introduced into the Tuam diocese during the tenure of his predecessor but were forced to close following MacHale's appointment. His exclusion of national schools from the Tuam diocese, where the impoverished laity were unable to fund alternatives, provided the Irish Church Missions with a vast geographical area practically devoid of educational facilities. It was through the medium of education, and especially through the education of children, that the ICM would concentrate its efforts and experience its greatest successes.

The demographic shifts occasioned by the 1840s famine – impacting most tragically on the vast 'underclass' of landless cottiers and rural poor – also helped to create a Catholic middle class, both secular and clerical, which was more confident, assertive and politicised. Opportunities opened up for Catholics reared in the decades after Catholic emancipation and educated in the admirable state-funded schools; this generation was more confident about its social status and its right to participate in public life. Power was indeed gradually passing from the Protestant minority to the Catholic majority. As the century progressed, further reform of franchise and land ownership would tip the balance further to the detriment of Protestant interests as previously held confessional advantages were distributed according to class rather than creed. Sectarianism was at a low ebb at the start of the nineteenth century; it increased steadily as Protestants reacted to the agitation for Catholic emancipation and to the forced removal of confessional privileges, and as Catholics responded to the first phase of the 'Second Reformation' at Farnham, Dingle, Doon and Achill. Interdenominational tensions and distrust were cultivated in both communities.

The climate into which the ICM stepped in 1849 was very different from that which greeted the arrival of the IS in 1818. The IS met a largely impoverished and uneducated Catholic population, devoid of educational facilities, dissociated from the political process, and harbouring little resentment towards the Protestant churches. Over the next forty years the ground shifted continually. From a Protestant viewpoint, concessions were repeatedly made to Catholic pressures, eroding long-held privileges. From a Catholic viewpoint, 'fair play' was eventually extended to all, regardless of creed. The ICM encountered a population which in most areas of the country had considerable wealth and access to education, and where its middle class could aspire to political success. Understandably, it chose to locate its efforts in Connemara and the Dublin slums, areas where the advances of the previous half century had made the least headway.

Notes

1 See, for example, James Dixon, *Letters on the duties of Protestants with regard to popery* (London, 1840), p. 5.

2 Irene Whelan, *The bible war in Ireland: the 'second reformation' and the polarization of Protestant-Catholic relations, 1800–1840* (Dublin, 2005), p. 232.

3 Irene Whelan, 'The stigma of souperism' in Cathal Póirtéir (ed.), *The great Irish famine* (Dublin, 1995), p. 136; Whelan, *Bible war, passim*; Christine Kinealy, 'Potatoes, providence and philanthropy: the role of private charity during the Irish potato famine' in Patrick O'Sullivan (ed.), *The meaning of the famine* (London, 1997), p. 144.

4 John Wolffe, *The Protestant crusade in Great Britain, 1829–1860* (Oxford, 1991). This entire book is concerned with the evangelical struggle to defeat or at the very least to contain Catholicism, principally in Ireland.

5 Quoted in Dáire Keogh, *Edmund Rice and the first Christian Brothers* (Dublin, 2008), p. 17.

6 Whelan, *Bible war*, p. 14.

7 D. G. Paz, *Popular anti-Catholicism in mid Victorian England* (Stanford, 1992); Frank Wallis, *Popular anti-Catholicism in mid-Victorian Britain* (Lampeter, 1993); Wolffe, *Protestant crusade*.

8 John Wolffe, 'Evangelicalism in mid-nineteenth-century England' in R. Samuel (ed.), *Patriotism: the making and unmaking of British national identity* (London, 1989), pp. 194–5.

9 *Missionary hymns (composed and selected for the public service at the annual meetings of the London Missionary Society and for the prayer meetings of auxiliary societies in town and country)* (London, 1830), p. 12.

10 Many ICM office-holders were members of the National Club (including the duke of Manchester, earl of Cavan, earl of Roden, Viscount Bernard, marquis of Blandford, Charles Frewen, G. A. Hamilton, C. A. Moody, J. Napier, J. Plumptre, W. Verner, John Colquhoun, Dibgy Mackworth, Edward Bickersteth, Robert Bickersteth, and Lord Ashley, later earl of Shaftesbury). National Club members in 1848 in Wolffe, *Protestant crusade*, pp. 212–14; ICM, *Annual Reports*, 1850–60.

11 *The Warder*, 4 Oct. 1856.

12 *Report of speeches at the National Club meeting* (London, 1852); *The religious state of Ireland* (London, n.d.), p. 221; 'Man of Sin', *Evangelical Magazine and Missionary Chronicle* (1851), p. 209; *John Bull*, No. 2, 1852, p. 696. For an exploration of the English perception of the influence of Irish Catholic clergy, see Robert James Klaus, *The Pope, the Protestants and the Irish: papal aggression*

and anti-Catholicism in nineteenth-century England (New York, London, 1987), pp. 173–99 and Wolffe, *Protestant crusade*, pp. 198–246.

13 Letter from 'Alpha', *Christian Guardian*, June 1851.

14 John Garwood, *The million peopled city: or one half of the people of London made known to the other half* (London, 1853), p. 245; Theodore Hoppen, *The mid-Victorian generation, 1846–1886* (Oxford, 1998), pp. 440, 443.

15 Edinburgh Irish Mission, *History of the mission* (Edinburgh, 1852), p. 3.

16 James Begg, *A handbook of popery; or, text-book of missions for the conversion of Romanists: being papal Rome tested by scripture, history and its recent workings ... with an appendix of documents* (Edinburgh, 1852), pp. 319–26.

17 Edinburgh Irish Mission, *Conversion of the Rev. James Forbes, Roman Catholic priest in Glasgow* (Edinburgh, 1852); James Edmund Handley, *The Irish in modern Scotland* (Cork, 1947), p. 102.

18 See for example, Handley, *The Irish in modern Scotland*, pp. 95–6. Following a deputation from the 'great Protestant meeting at Greenock', the Catholic Constable Bradley, of Edinburgh, was dismissed for arresting Protestant youths who had smeared filth on a priest's door.

19 *Bulwark*, 1851–52, pp. 9, 59–60, 76, 200, 217–18; Edinburgh Irish Mission, *Missions for the conversion of Irish Romanists in the large towns of England and Scotland explained and recommended, being the Report of the Edinburgh Irish Mission for the year 1851, with the list of subscriptions* (Edinburgh, 1852), pp. 2–3.

20 *Free Church Magazine*, July 1851, pp. 216–18.

21 *The position of popery in Great Britain and the means of resisting it in Scotland, being an account of the operations of the Scottish Reformation Society for the year 1860* (Edinburgh, 1861), pp. 12–13.

22 Edinburgh Irish Mission, *Appeal in reference to the extension of the Edinburgh Irish Mission and Protestant Institute, addressed to the friends of Protestantism* (Edinburgh, n.d.), p. 4.

23 See, for example, obituary of Revd Tim Clesham, *Banner of the Truth*, July 1894, p. 13.

24 See, for example, Free Church of Scotland, *Home Mission and Church Extension Committee, financial report of the Home Mission and Church Extension Fund Committee. May 1864* (Edinburgh, 1864).

25 E. R. Wickham, *Church and people in an industrial city*, quoted in Hugh McLeod, *Religion and society in England, 1850–1914* (London, 1996), p. 3.

26 Robert Bickersteth, *The designed end of affliction; a sermon preached at St. John's Church, Clapham ... March 24, 1847* (London, 1847), pp. 72–3. Persons involved in both the ICM and the ECM included Robert Bickersteth, Daniel Wilson, Captain Francis Maude, Captain Henry Trotter, Sir Peregrine Maitland, Sir Thomas Blomefield, William Cadman, John Plumptre, Arthur Kinnaird and Captain Francis Vernon Harcourt.

27 Sheridan Wayne Gilley, 'Evangelical and Roman Catholic missions to the Irish in London, 1830–1870' (Ph.D. dissertation, University of Cambridge, 1970), p. 95.

28 English Church Missions, *Annual report, 1853* (London, 1853), p. 15; Samuel

Garrett, *Recollections,* quoted in Gilley, 'Evangelical and Roman Catholic missions to the Irish', p. 236.

29 Duke of Manchester, Lord Henry Cholmondely, Lord Ashley (later Lord Shaftesbury), Sir W. R. Farquhar, Bart., Sir Thomas Blomefield, Bart., Sir George Otway, Bart., Hon. Capt. Francis Maude, Hon. Arthur Kinnaird, John Plumptre, MP, John Colquhoun, MP, Rear Admiral Hope, Capt. Henry Trotter, John Bridges, Esq, J. E. Gordon, Esq., Alexander Gordon, Esq., John Paul Dean, Esq., Robert B. Seely, Esq., John Bridges, Esq., Revd Alexander Dallas, Edward Bickersteth, Revd F. Ford, Revd Daniel Wilson, Revd Edmond Holland and Revd T. R. Birks, listed in *Further report and appeal of the committee of the special fund for the spiritual exigencies of Ireland* (n.p., n.d.).

30 J. E. Gordon, *A letter to the Rev. Edward Bickersteth* (n.p., 1847), pp. 9–11; ICM, *Report of the proceedings of first annual general meeting,* p. 13.

31 ICM, *Report of the proceedings at the third annual meeting,* p. 9 (spoken by Revd Robert Bickersteth).

32 ICM, *Report of the proceedings of the first annual general meeting,* p. 6, (spoken by Revd T. Nolan).

33 A. R. C. Dallas, 'The present position of popery and Protestantism in Ireland. A lecture, etc.' in Church of England Young Men's Society, *Six lectures on Protestantism Delivered before the north of London auxiliary to the Church of England Young Men's Society in October, November and December 1851* (London, 1852), p. 159.

34 *Charge to the archdeacons and clergy of the diocese of Canterbury* (Lambeth, 1850), reproduced in Gilley, 'Evangelical and Roman Catholic missions to the Irish', p. 72.

35 William Marrable, *Sketch of the origin and operations of the Society for Irish Church Missions to the Roman Catholics* (London, 1853), p. 451.

36 Irish Reformation Fund, *Report of the General Irish Reformation Fund for the restoration in Ireland of her primitive religion, and the necessary protection of converts for the years 1847 and 1848* (Dublin, 1847), p. 2.

37 Edward Nangle, *Protestantism in Ireland, the essence of a sermon, preached in the octagon chapel, Bath, on Sunday, July 5th, 1835, on behalf of the Protestant missionary settlement, in the island of Achill* (Bath, 1835), p. 23.

38 'Reformation in the West', *The Times,* reprinted in *Connaught Watchman,* 15 Oct. 1851.

39 ICM, *Report of the proceedings of first annual general meeting,* p. 13.

40 Eugene Stock, *History of the Church Missionary Society* (4 vols, London, 1899–1916), i, p. 88; Klaus, *The Pope, the Protestants and the Irish,* p. 126.

41 *Statement of the Society of the Irish Church Missions to the Roman Catholics* (n.p., 1852), p. 3.

42 William Marrable, *Sketch of the origin and operations of the Society for Irish Church Missions to the Roman Catholics* (London, 1853), p.10. For an exploration of the perception of the famine as a special 'mercy', calling sinners to the 'Evangelical Truth', see Peter Gray, 'Ideology and the famine' in Cathal Póirtéir (ed.), *The great Irish famine* (Dublin, 1995), pp. 86–103.

43 Stuart A. Moody, *Ireland open to the Gospel* (Edinburgh, 1847), p. 35.

44 Alexander Dallas to Irish Society, 21 October 1846, in Irish Society, *Quarterly Extract No. 83* (Dublin, 1847).

45 ICM, *Report of the proceedings at the third annual meeting, 30 April 1852* (n.p., n.d.), p.11 (spoken by J. C. Colquhoun).

46 Testimony of Fr Éamonn Ó Conghaile in Raymonde Standún and Bill Long, *Singing stone, whispering wind: voices of Connemara* (Dublin, 2001), p. 168.

47 Public consciousness was very aware of the threat of anarchy which had abounded on the continent. The popularity of Lord John Russell in the aftermath of the failed Chartist riots attests to the terror of radicalism intrinsic in the English population of the time.

48 ICM, *Report of the proceedings at the third annual meeting*, p. 10 (spoken by Revd Robert Bickersteth).

49 For the background to the restoration of the Catholic hierarchy in Britain see Klaus, *The Pope, the Protestants and the Irish*, pp. 68–101.

50 Quoted in Gerald Parsons, *Religion in Victorian Britain*, i, *Traditions* (Manchester, 1988), p. 148.

51 Wolffe, 'Evangelicalism in mid-nineteenth-century England', p. 189.

52 National Club, *Address to the Protestants of the United Kingdom by the committee of the National Club. The progress of foreign popery as affecting English safety. Fourth series, No. VIII* (London, 1852); Anonymous, *Results of an investigation into the cases of Protestant persecution on the continent* (London, 1854); Pierce Connelly, *The coming struggle with Rome, not religious but political; or, words of warning to the English people* (London, 1852); Anonymous, *Cardinal Wiseman and the canon law of Rome, 'The Oscott Provincial Synod' or can the cardinal be a loyal subject of Queen Victoria?* (Edinburgh, 1852); John Napier, *England or Rome, who shall govern Ireland? a reply to the letter of Lord Mounteagle* (Dublin, 1851).

53 ICM, *Report of the proceedings at the third annual meeting*, p. 11 (spoken by J. C. Colquhoun).

54 D. W. Bebbington, *Evangelicalism in modern Britain: a history from the 1730s to the 1980s* (London, 2002), pp. 2–17.

55 John Wolffe, *Evangelicals, women and community: study guide* (Milton Keynes, 2000), p. 20.

56 Luke 4:43 [I must preach the kingdom of God in other cities also for therefore I am sent], quoted in Sarah Davies, *Other cities also; the story of mission work in Dublin* (Dublin, 1881), p. 1. (Sarah Davies was editor of *Erin's Hope*.)

57 Kenneth Hylson-Smith, *Evangelicals in the Church of England, 1734–1984* (Edinburgh, 1989), pp. 67–8. (C. B. Sumner, bishop of Winchester; J. B. Sumner, bishop of Chester; Henry Ryder, bishop of Lichfield and Coventry; Henry Raikes, chancellor of the diocese of Chester; Henry Law, archdeacon and canon of Wells Cathedral; William Dealth, chancellor of the diocese of Winchester; C. J. Hoare, archdeacon and canon of Winchester Cathedral.)

58 Boyd Hilton, *The age of atonement: the influence of atonement on the social and economic thought, 1795–1865* (Oxford, 1988), p. 26; Klaus, *The Pope, the Protestants and the Irish*, p. 138.

59 Wolffe, *The Protestant crusade in Great Britain*. This entire book is concerned with the evangelical struggle to defeat, or at the very least to contain, Catholicism.

60 David Hempton and Myrtle Hill, *Evangelical Protestantism in Ulster Society, 1870–1890* (London, 1992), p. 81.

61 For example the Anglican ICM supporter, Elizabeth Copley, was even more personally involved with the Scottish Presbyterian mission at Ballinglen, County Mayo than with the ICM.

62 Whelan, *Bible war*, pp. 62–6.

63 Charles Stuart Stanford, *A handbook to the Romish controversy: being a refutation in detail of the creed of Pope Pius the Fourth on the grounds of scripture and reason: and an appendix and notes* (Dublin, 1868), p. iii.

64 James Maher, *Letters of Rev. James Maher, D.D., late P.P. late of Carlow-Graigue, on religious subjects, with a memoir*, ed. by the Right Rev. Patrick Francis Moran (Dublin, 1877), p. 493.

65 John O'Rourke, *The battle of the faith in Ireland* (Dublin, 1887), p. 530.

66 William Smyth Burnside, *The Connemara peasant; or, Barney Brannigan's reasons, in a discussion with the priest of his parish, for reading the scriptures without asking the priest's leave* (Dublin, 1854), pp. 2, 7. This work should not be confused with the work of William Carleton, a convert to Protestantism but an opponent of aggressive proselytism, who wrote *The clarionet, the dead boxer and Barney Branagan* (London, 1850).

67 D. W. Cahill, *Sixth letter from the Rev. Dr. Cahill to his Excellency, the earl of Carlisle* (Dublin, 1856), p. 7.

68 John MacHale, *The new testament of our Lord and Saviour Jesus Christ; translated from the Latin vulgate; diligently compared with the original Greek; and first published by the English College at Rheims, A.D. 1582 with annotations, a chronological index, table of references, etc. With the approbation of his Grace the Most Rev. Dr. Mac Hale, Archbishop of Tuam* (Tuam, 1846 and 1863); John MacHale, *An Irish translation of the book of Genesis, from the Latin vulgate with a corresponding English version, chiefly from the Douay ...* (Tuam, 1859 and 1868); John MacHale, *An Irish translation of the holy bible: from the Latin vulgate; with a corresponding English version, chiefly from the Douay; accompanied with notes from the most distinguished commentators* (Tuam, 1861 and 1868); John MacHale, *Craobh urnaighe cráibhthighe, tioinssuighthe ar an Sgriobhain Dhiadha, agus rannta toghtha na h-Eaglaise .... Second edition. Irish and English* (Dublin, 1866). See also Anonymous, *Protestantism essentially a persecuting religion, by another convert from Anglicanism* (York, 1853), p. 87.

69 John Gregg, quoted in Anonymous, *Two months in Clifden, Co. Galway, during the summer of 1855* (Dublin, 1856), pp. 3–4.

70 William Fitzpatrick, quoted in Charles Bullock, *What Ireland needs, the gospel in the native tongue* (London, c.1880) p. 18.

71 L. J. Nolan, *A third pamphlet* (Dublin, 1838), p. 5.

72 Alexander Robert Charles Dallas, *Popery in Ireland, a warning to Protestants in England, etc. being a lecture delivered before the Islington Protestant Institute on Monday, January 18th, 1847* (London, 1847), pp. 24–6.

73 ICM, *Report of the proceedings at the second annual meeting, held on the 2nd of May 1851* (n.p., 1851), (spoken by Alexander Dallas).

74 Moody, *Ireland open to the Gospel*, pp. 84–5.

75 These differences still exist, although more tolerant and pluralist attitudes generally prevail.

76 Article XII, the Catholic doctrine of purgatory, is 'repugnant to God'; Article XXVIII, transubstantiation, is 'repugnant to the plain words of Scripture'. The more extensive Presbyterian Westminster Confession (1649) outlines in detail its objections to Roman Catholicism, stating that 'religious worship is to be given to God ... and to him alone: not to angels, saints ... nor in the mediation of any other' (Chapter XXI). It plainly states in Chapter XXV that the 'Pope of Rome [is] that man of sin and son of perdition'.

77 James Hatherell, *A City wholly given to idolatry. A sermon [on Acts xvii. 16] preached in aid of the Irish Church Missions to the Roman Catholics* (London, 1860), p. 13.

78 A. R. C. Dallas, 'The Christ of Romanism, not the Christ of Scripture, a lecture delivered before the Church of England's Young Men's Society, 28 February 1851' in *Lectures delivered before the Church of England's Young Men's Society for aiding missions at home and abroad* (London, 1851), pp. 15–37. For further treatment of the doctrinal errors of Catholicism see also A. R. C. Dallas, *Real Romanism, as stated in the creed of Pope Pius the Fourth* (London, 1845); Dallas, *Popery in Ireland, a warning to Protestants in England, etc.*; A. R. C. Dallas, *The point of hope in Ireland's present crisis* (London, 1849); A. R. C. Dallas, *Lecture delivered at the Town Hall, Brighton ... on the sacramental delusions of Romanism* (Brighton, 1851); A. R. C. Dallas, *A sermon preached by the Rev. Alexander R. C. Dallas ... in the church of St. Dunstan's-in-the-west, Fleet Street on Wednesday evening, May 14th, 1857, in behalf of the Society for Irish Church Missions* (London, 1851); A. R. C. Dallas, *The present position of popery and Protestantism in Ireland. A lecture, etc.* (1852); A. R. C. Dallas, *A popish political catechism. The reprint of an old tract preserved in a volume of 'Pamphlets mostly relating to Dissenters,' in Oriel College Library. To which is added some extracts from authorized and approved Romish writings* (London, 1867).

79 *Erin's Hope*, 1853, p. 4.

80 Hatherell, *A City wholly given to idolatry*, pp. 5–6, 13.

81 John Garrett, quoted in Henry Stewart Cunningham, *Is 'Good news from Ireland' true? Remarks on the position and propect of the Irish Church Establishment* (London, 1865) pp. 34–5 (his italics).

82 Dallas, 'The present position of popery and Protestantism in Ireland', p. 5.

83 Wolffe, 'Evangelicalism in mid-nineteenth-century England', p. 195; Alexander R. C. Dallas, 'The Promised Land' in *Good things to come: being lectures during Lent, 1847, at St. George's, Bloomsbury* (London, 1847), p. 4.

84 Wolffe, 'Evangelicalism in mid-nineteenth-century England', p. 189; William Conybeare, *Church parties, an essay* (London, 1854), pp. 5–6.

85 Marrable, *Sketch of the origin*, p. 8; Hempton and Hill, *Evangelical Protestantism*, p. 94.

86 John Cumming, *The church: a sermon preached in St. George's Church, Edinburgh,*

June 4, 1856 on behalf of the Society for Irish Church Missions to the Roman Catholics (London, 1856), p. 19.

87 The relevance of these doctrines both in a historical setting and in the light of present-day inter-denominational relations in Northern Ireland is discussed in Joseph Liechty and Cecelia Clegg, *Moving beyond sectarianism: religion, conflict and reconciliation in Northern Ireland* (Dublin, 2001), pp. 67–71.

88 Dallas, 'The present position of popery and Protestantism in Ireland', p. iv of preface written by W. W. Champneys.

89 Society for Irish Church Missions, *Early fruits of Irish missions* (6th edn, London, 1852), p. 20.

90 *The Irish Missionary Record and Chronicle of the Reformation*, Nov. 1852.

91 Gilley, 'Evangelical and Roman Catholic missions to the Irish', p. 109; Donal Kerr, *'A nation of beggars'? Priests, people and politics in famine Ireland, 1845–52* (Oxford, 1994), p. 207.

92 Lawrence Nemer, 'Anglican and Roman Catholic attitudes on missions: a comparison of the Church Missionary Society with the Society of St. Joseph of the Sacred Heart for Foreign Missions in their home structures and life between 1865 and 1885' (Ph.D. dissertation, University of Cambridge, 1978), pp. 5, 29.

93 Fiona Bateman, 'Defining the heathen in Ireland and Africa: two similar discourses a century apart', *Social Sciences and Missions*, xxi (2008), 78.

94 Dixon, *Letters on the duties of Protestants*, p. 51.

95 Anonymous, *What are the Irish Church Missions?* (London, 1855), p. 5.

96 *Banner of the Truth*, Feb. 1851, p. 24.

97 *All Hallows' Annual* (Dublin, 1852–53), p. 22.

98 Charles Bernard, *What is truth? A sermon preached on behalf of the Society for Irish Church Missions* (Cork, 1854), pp. 7–8.

99 This doctrine was developed in the fourth and fifth centuries by St Augustine to justify the use of state coercion to suppress heretical opponents who were viewed as radically in error, having no right to hold their beliefs. Joseph Liechty and Cecelia Clegg, *Moving beyond sectarianism: a resource for young adults, youths and schools* (Dublin, 2001), p. 35.

100 Stephen Neil, *Colonialism and Christian missions* (London, 1966), p. 349.

101 John Philip, *Researches in South Africa* (2 vols, London, 1828), i, p. ix.

102 Jean Comby, *How to understand the history of Christian mission* (London, 1996), pp. 115–34.

103 *Second report of the West Connaught Church Endowment Society 1863* (Dublin, 1863), pp. 44–6. (J. C. Colquhoun quoted therein; this comment referred to Inisturk Island off the Connemara coast.) The October 1854 issue of *Erin's Hope* included a drawing of Connemara which included palm trees. See also Anonymous, *Stories about the mission work in Ireland*, No. 1 (Dublin, 1854), p. 8.

104 Liechty and Clegg, *Moving beyond sectarianism: religion, conflict and reconciliation in Northern Ireland*, p. 67.

105 William Conyngham Plunket, *A short visit to the Connemara missions …* (London, Dublin, 1863), pp. 25–6.

106 W. L. Clay, *The prison chaplain, a memoir of the Rev. John Clay* (London, 1861), p. 569, quoted in Gilley, 'Evangelical and Roman Catholic missions to the Irish', p. 103.

107 Quoted in Cunningham, *Is 'Good news from Ireland' true?*, pp. 35–56.

108 *Classified guide to London*, 1851, quoted in Jacinta Prunty, 'The geography of poverty: Dublin 1850–1900: the second mission of the church with particular reference to Margaret Aylward and co-workers' (Ph.D. dissertation, National University of Ireland, 1992), p. 122.

109 For an explanation of the failure of the reformation in Ireland, see Aidan Clarke, 'Bishop William Beddell, 1571–1642' in Ciarán Brady, *Worsted in the game: losers in Irish history* (Dublin, 1989); Crawford Gribben, 'The forgotten origins of the Irish evangelicals' in Robert Dunlop (ed.), *Evangelicals in Ireland: an introduction* (Dublin, 2004).

110 Miller argues that each denomination ministered to its own flock while Hayton shows how aggressive missionary work was promoted through charity schools. David Miller, '"Presbyterianism and Modernisation" in Ulster', *Past and Present*, lxxx (Aug. 1978), 73; David Hayton, 'Did Protestantism fail in early eighteenth-century Ireland? Charity schools and the enterprise of religious and social reformation' in James McGuire, Alan Ford and Kenneth Milne (eds), *As by law established* (Dublin, 1995), pp. 175–9. See also J. C. Beckett, *The making of modern Ireland, 1603–1923* (2nd edn, London, 1981), p. 183.

111 Joseph Liechty and Cecelia Clegg, *Moving beyond sectarianism, religion, conflict and reconciliation in Northern Ireland*, p. 81.

112 Giraldus Cambrensis, *The history and topography of Ireland*, trans. by John J. O'Meara (rev. edn, Portlaoise, 1982), pp. 102–3, 118; Nicholas Canny, *From reformation to restoration: Ireland 1534–1660* (Dublin, 1987), p. 10; Toby Barnard, 'Improving clergymen' in McGuire, Ford and Milne (eds), *As by law established*, p. 137.

113 Written by Anthony Raymond (1675–1726), quoted in R. V. Comerford, *Ireland* (London, 2003), p. 63.

114 Whelan, *Bible war*, pp. 77–8.

115 Ibid., pp. 105–7.

116 Ibid., *passim*; Kinealy, 'Potatoes, providence and philanthropy', p. 144; Hempton and Hill, *Evangelical Protestantism in Ulster society*, pp. 81–102.

117 Whelan, *Bible war*, p. 129.

118 Dixon, *Letters on the duties of Protestants*, p. 5.

119 ICM, *Report of the proceedings at the first annual meeting, held on the 26th April 1850* (n.p., 1850), p. 22 (spoken by Revd Dr Mortimer O'Sullivan); Alexander Dallas, *The story of the Irish Church Missions, part 1* (London, 1867), p. 2; Edward Bickersteth, *Special Fund for the Spiritual Exigencies of Ireland* (n.p., 1848), p. 1.

120 The Anglican CMS was formed in 1799, the pan-Protestant London Missionary Society in 1795, and the British and Foreign Bible Society in 1804.

121 ICM, *Report of the proceedings of first annual general meeting*, p. 9 (spoken by Revd T. Nolan).

122 Whelan, *Bible war*, pp. 248–50.

123 The Established Church was involved in the following societies: Irish Society, Ladies' Auxiliary Irish Society; Incorporated Society for Promoting English Protestant Schools in Ireland; The Additional Curates Fund Society for Ireland; Ragged School Society; Sunday School Society for Ireland; Hibernian Bible Society; Society for the Education of the Poor (Kildare Place); Island and Coast Society; Church Education Society; The Scripture Readers' Society; Ladies Hibernian Female School Society; The Priests' Protection Society; The Parochial Visitors' Society; The Board of Erasmus Smith Schools; Irish Reformation Society; The Association for Promoting the Knowledge and Practice of Christian Religion. In addition to these a number of societies specific to dissenting religions were operative: Presbyterian, Methodist, Wesleyan Methodist and Baptist.

124 Quoted in Desmond Bowen, *Souperism: myth or reality?* (Cork, 1970), p. 84.

125 Deborah Alcock, *Walking with God, a memoir of the Ven. John Alcock by his daughter* (London, 1887), pp. 127–8.

126 ICM Archive, Irish Society, quarterly extract no. 84, p. 590.

127 ICM Archive, IS minutes, 7 Apr. 1857.

128 Alcock, *Walking with God*, p. 126.

129 *The Irish Society Record, containing a general statement of the society's progress as shewn in extracts from the reports and correspondence of its superintendents and other friends* (Dublin, 1852), p. 3.

130 *The Irish Society Record* ... (Dublin, 1854); *The seventh report of the Irish Missionary School, Ballinasloe for the year ending 21ˢᵗ December 1853* (n.p., n.d.).

131 *The Irish Society Record* ... (Dublin, 1850), p. 8.

132 Ibid., p. 7.

133 John Alcock, *Antichrist, who is he, two sermons preached on Wednesday evenings, 22 and 29 March, 1848 in Christ Church, Cork* (Cork, 1848), p. 55.

134 *The Irish Society Record* ... (Dublin, 1850), pp. 5–6.

135 Nangle first visited Achill during the 1831 famine. When he attempted to establish the mission he was told that he was going on a 'wild goose chase to Achill'. Meala Ní Ghiobúin, *Dugort, Achill Island, 1831–1861: the rise and fall of a missionary community* (Dublin, 2001), pp. 8, 10, 15, 17–18, 22–3, 38, 40.

136 The Achill training school establishment, situated at its Mweelin settlement, was originally established to receive and train convert priests but later was used to train scripture readers. Nangle had been instrumental in founding the Priests' Protection Society, which aided convert priests. Thomas J. Kelley, 'Trapped between two worlds: Edward Nangle, Achill Island and sectarian competition in Ireland, 1800–1862' (Ph.D. dissertation, Trinity College Dublin, 2004), p. 209.

137 Mr and Mrs Hall, *Ireland north and west, its character and scenery in one volume* (Boston, n.d.), pp. 395–6.

138 Asenath Nicholson, *The bible in Ireland ('Ireland's welcome to the stranger; or, excursions through Ireland in 1844 and 1845 for the purpose of personally investigating the condition of the poor')*, edited with an introduction by Alfred Tresidder Sheppard (London, 1926), pp. 262–3.

139 Asenath Nicholson, *Annals of the famine in Ireland*, edited by Maureen Murphy (Dublin, 1998, first published 1851), p. 105.

140 Hon. Somerset Maxwell, Right Hon. Joseph Napier, MP and George Hamilton MP. The fourth Achill trustee was Revd Edward Nangle.

141 The ICM quarrelled over the administration of the Achill mission and was annoyed that Nangle solicited funds in England specifically for Achill. Kelley, 'Trapped between two worlds', p. 264.

142 *Report of the Home Mission of the Synod of Ulster* (Belfast, 1840).

143 *Second annual report of the Home and Foreign Mission of the General Assembly of the Presbyterian Church in Ireland: July 1842* (Belfast, 1842), p. 19.

144 *Minutes of the General Assembly of the Presbyterian Church in Ireland, consisting of the General Synod of Ulster and the Presbyterian Synod of Ulster, distinguished by the name Seceders, held in Belfast, July 1840* (Belfast, 1840), p. 17.

145 *Fourth annual report of the Home and Foreign Mission of the General Assembly of the Presbyterian Church in Ireland: July 1844* (Belfast, 1844), p. 7.

146 Moody, *Ireland open to the Gospel*, p. 28.

147 *Third annual report of the Home and Foreign Mission of the General Assembly of the Presbyterian Church in Ireland: July 1843* (Belfast, 1843), p. 17.

148 *Third annual report ... Home and Foreign Mission of the General Assembly*, p. 45.

149 *Second annual report ... Home and Foreign Mission of the General Assembly*, p. 21.

150 Moody, *Ireland open to the Gospel*, p. 88.

151 Patrick Corish, *The Irish Catholic experience: a historical survey* (Dublin, 1985), pp. 151–91; S. J. Connolly, *Priests and people in pre-famine Ireland* (Dublin, 1982), *passim*.

152 Dáire Keogh, 'The Christian Brothers and the Second Reformation in Ireland', *Éire-Ireland*, xl (spring/summer 2005), p. 58.

Chapter 2

Getting started: Alexander Dallas' mission at Castlekerke, 1846

The ICM, informally founded in 1846, functioned over the following decades to convert Irish Catholics to scriptural Protestantism. The ICM functioned to answer a number of needs, both of the providers of mission and of the recipient community. In examining both the foundation of the movement and its *modus operandi*, the principal question to be asked is, whose needs did the Society serve? Was it formed to supply the need of the Roman Catholics of Ireland for a scriptural religion? Or was it established to meet their more earthly needs such as education, food, clothing and shelter? Or was it founded to meet the needs of the English ultra-Protestants who wished to curb the influence of Catholicism, which they perceived to be flooding over both England and Ireland? Or was there also another, less obvious need, that of the recently settled Protestant population of Connemara for a Church of Ireland infrastructure in their newly adopted neighbourhood?

The life and influences of Revd Alexander R. C. Dallas (1791–1869)

The ICM was founded as a direct result of the labours of the Hampshire clergyman, Alexander Dallas, whose life and opinions can be evaluated through his many writings, including his autobiography, *My Life*.[1] Desmond Bowen's biographical account shows how Dallas' mid-life disillusionment with the spiritual state of his English parish left him in search of an alternative crusade.[2] Dallas, who served as a commissariat officer in the Napoleonic war and subsequently lived a 'high life', was ordained in 1821 and experienced an evangelical conversion in 1824. He came to the attention of the reforming evangelical bishop Charles Bird Sumner who, in 1829, appointed him rector of Wonston, the most valuable parish in Winchester diocese with a net annual income of £900 in 1851, where he was to remain until his death.[3] In spite of this, Dallas' life was beset with financial worries.

Wonston parish was developed greatly by Dallas, who founded a school

46

2.1 Revd Alexander Dallas.
Source: *The Banner of Truth*, Oct. 1895.

at Sutton Scotney, built a new school at Wonston and instituted a meticulous system of 'parent encouragement tickets' to ensure attendance at day and Sunday schools; this 'benevolent despot' arrogantly ran his parish with military efficiency[4] and was obsessed with numbers, minutely documenting attendances at service and communion.[5] Dallas' fascination with head-counts and presumption that attendance equalled devout conviction would form a crucial part of the ICM's methodology. He appears to have been genuinely but patronisingly concerned for his labouring parishioners.[6] From the late 1830s it is clear that Dallas was disappointed with the devotion of his Wonston flock.[7]

Dallas' writings reveal that he had not always held anti-Catholic views; he did not consider Ireland's 1822 famine a divine punishment[8] and lack of finances alone prevented his marrying a Catholic in his youth.[9] His increasing anti-Catholicism was in line with local contemporary attitudes[10] and appears to have sprung out of his increased interest in prophecies from the 1830s, which brought him into contact with leading millenarianists, such as Revd Edward Bickersteth, who were strongly to support the conversion of Irish Catholics.[11]

The attention of Revd Dallas was drawn to Ireland in 1839 when Anthony Thomas, formerly missionary curate in Connemara and then secretary of the Jews' Society, invited him to the Dublin annual meeting of the Irish Society for the Conversion of the Jews.[12] From 1840 Dallas attended annual meetings of religious societies in Dublin and came into contact with the Irish Society. Dallas hinted at missionary work in Ireland in 1843 in his millennial work, *The Prophecy upon the Mount*, writing that 'the Gospel is to be preached in the different languages of the world'.[13] He was more direct by 1846, arguing in military terms: 'Not more surely did the British army fight the battle of all Europe on the plains of Waterloo, than do the spiritual clergy and laity of the Church of Ireland fight at this moment against the apostasy of Rome, for the Christians of England as well as for themselves.'[14]

By 1848 Dallas was disillusioned with his Wonston parish, where he acknowledged that he was unpopular and that he encountered a 'distressing case of ignorance or resistance to the truth'.[15] An unhappy home-life (Dallas and his first wife lived apart for a number of years before her death in 1847), coupled with parochial dissatisfaction, left his crusading personality unfulfilled. By then he was 57 years old and might have been expected to live out his life as rector of his rural parish. As Bowen states, 'unfortunately or otherwise for Ireland's religious history, this was not to be'.[16]

Connemara in 1846

The immense material needs of the poor in nineteenth-century Ireland, and especially in Connemara, are widely acknowledged, where destitution was reported even before the onset of the famine in 1845.[17] The population of Ballinahinch barony in County Galway, wherein the ICM concentrated most of its missionary efforts, increased by 82 per cent between 1821 and 1841 but was reduced by 12,000 persons or over one-third between 1841 and 1851.[18] In 1846, 1,800 families in Ballinakill parish were 'in a state of destitution' and in 1847 over 86 per cent of the population of Clifden Poor Law Union were dependent on government rations.[19] The famine in Connemara continued into 1848, to be closely followed by epidemics of fever and cholera. A letter-writer to *The Tablet* urged readers to give assistance to 'their starving fellow-creatures' via Franciscan Brothers from Clifden and Roundstone monasteries who toured England raising relief funds.[20] The material needs of the Catholic poor of Dublin during and after the famine years are also without question.[21] As those evicted throughout rural Ireland gravitated to the capital, the already crowded slums of Dublin swelled with the impoverished and the dispossessed.

By 1847, the formal provision of religion in Connemara was only recovering from the restrictions of the penal laws, although archaeological evidence proves that Christianity was long established in Connemara.[22] Mass attendance in west Galway in 1834 was among the very lowest in the country.[23] In the large diocese of Tuam, there were only 130 churches, ten slated, the remainder thatched with mud walls;[24] Clifden parish had one place of worship for every 170 Protestants and for every 3,492 Catholics.[25] Three Catholic clergymen served the vast parish of Clifden in 1835, containing the half-parishes of Claddaghduff and Ballindoon (total population of 13,568 in 1841). Mass was held twice on Sundays in Clifden, attended by 1,000 to 1,200 persons, while about 600 attended mass in each of the two outlying chapels. Dallas was aware that the religious needs of Connemara's Catholics were inadequately supplied,[26] a fact acknowledged by the Catholic church: 'I hear several parishes are vacant, and no priest can be found to fill them, being unwilling to face the hardships'.[27] Contemporary observers attributed much of the ICM's advances in Connemara to the poor infrastructure of Catholicism, as in Leenane where the local community was a great distance from either church or priest.[28] In 1847, Paul Cullen (archbishop of Armagh 1850–52, Primate and archbishop of Dublin, 1852–78) told Tobias Kirby of rumours that priests in the Tuam diocese were reluctant to serve in the most stricken regions for fear of starvation and fever;[29] five years later a Vincentian missionary commented that in Glan, a fruitful region of Castlekerke mission, 'at the best of times, the people seldom heard Mass or saw a priest'.[30] Even Fr Quigley, who described Catholic clergy of the famine era as 'great and glorious men and priestly soldiers', admitted serious deficiencies in the pre-famine Catholic infrastructure.[31]

The Achilles heel of the Catholic church in the Tuam diocese was its failure to provide accessible education for the poor.[32] The fact that only 200 out of Connemara's vast school-age population were enrolled at school in 1835 proves the educational want in Connemara,[33] which was further exacerbated by John MacHale's exclusion of national schools.[34] Without doubt, this enticed the ICM to the region as 'education was put under a ban and anathema in these parts'.[35] In 1850 there were almost no convents northwest of a line from Galway to Drogheda, while they were relatively commonplace in the wealthier southeast of the country.[36] A similar disparity existed within the diocese, with most schools concentrated in its more prosperous eastern section; four schools operated in the Cathedral town of Tuam[37] while few schools existed in the impoverished region of Connemara. This lack of educational facilities created a ready market for the ICM's missionary advances.

Through his acquaintance with Anthony Thomas, former curate at Ballinakill, Dallas would have been aware of the dearth of schools in the diocese and also of the previous missionary endeavours in Connemara in the days of (Protestant) Archbishop Trench (1819–39). Trench had personally funded two curates in Ballinakill and Roundstone to preach the 'Word of Life to the Poor Roman Catholic multitude'.[38] He founded the Connaught Home Missionary Society in 1836 which sent Revd Thomas Coneys, later first Professor of Irish at Trinity College, Dublin and subsequently an ICM missionary, to 'go everywhere throughout Connemara and neighbouring islands ... preaching in Irish from village to village'.[39] The Franciscan monasteries at Clifden and Roundstone were founded in the 1830s to counteract this influence.[40] Connemara had clearly more to recommend it to Dallas as a missionary location than its lack of education, but it must be acknowledged that the provision of schooling was the approach most likely to appeal to the mission's ultimate recipients, i.e. the poor of Connemara. MacHale admitted that the poor were unable to pay for schooling but denied that his exclusion of national schools created an educational void which the ICM eagerly filled.[41]

Although uninterested in secular education, MacHale was determined that his people would be thoroughly instructed in their faith. In 1840 he compiled a catechism which was translated into Irish and adopted for use by Irish bishops. He purchased 100 copies, to promote a 'more effective diffusion of the genuine scriptures in the Irish language with approved notes and comments'.[42]

At the onset of the ICM's activities, Dublin's Catholic infrastructure was in an equally embryonic state. Although Daniel Murray, archbishop of Dublin 1828–52, had 'reformed the people of Dublin, quadrupled his clergy',[43] the needs of the capital's poorest Catholics were largely unserved, despite the erection of ninety-seven churches during his tenure, and the provision of at least one poor school per parish, along with orphanages, hospitals, sodalities, confraternities and charitable institutions.

Although their religion was not scriptural in nature, Irish Catholics did not see themselves as lacking in spirituality. They did, however, have considerable temporal needs which were fulfilled by the mission, such as the distribution of relief during the famine. Even MacHale admitted that most converts came from the very poor, often the 'victims of eviction'.[44] In fact Dallas was twice mistaken for the relieving officer, at Derrygimla and at Streamstown.[45] By identifying and responding to the material needs of the poor, the ICM forged contact with the neediest segment of Irish society, who pragmatically accepted the aid proffered. The peasantry of Connemara and the slum dwellers of Dublin, desperately in need of education and relief, were swift to avail of the ICM's benevolence.

Getting started: mission work among the Irish Catholics

Although The Society for Irish Church Missions to the Roman Catholics
was not officially formed until 1849, Alexander Dallas has been associated
with efforts to convert the Catholics of Ireland prior to the onset of the
Irish famine in 1845. Through his friendship with Anthony Thomas, he
became acquainted with members of the Society at Easter meetings in
Dublin from 1840 but grew frustrated at the slow progress made by the IS,
complaining that many of its long-term pupils 'were as constant at Mass as
ever'.[46] By its founding ethos, the IS was precluded from direct missionary
work and was confined to educational methods. However, the LAIS funded
scripture readers to work directly among the Catholic population. The
LAIS was prohibited from publicly collecting funds, but raised funds by
corresponding with like-minded friends. It was Dallas' introduction to
Fanny Bellingham, an active member of the LAIS, that 'opened an entire
change in the course of the story'.[47]

Dallas considered that a direct controversial approach was needed
to convince Irish Catholics of the errors of Romanism, 'to disabuse
their minds of the false notions of Christian truth which they possess'.[48]
Dismayed that the Irish Society met this advice with 'disapprobation
and rejection',[49] he confined his communications to Fanny Bellingham,
with whom he devised a plan to circulate his pamphlet, *A voice from
heaven to Ireland, or a look out of Ireland into Germany*, among literate
Irish Catholics. Aware of a current government survey of crops, Fanny
Bellingham arranged that chosen agents would survey the countryside,
identifying educated Catholics to whom copies of the pamphlet in English
and Irish were dispatched with military precision from Bristol, Manchester,
Birmingham, Liverpool, Edinburgh and London. Twenty thousand texts
were simultaneously delivered throughout Ireland on 16 January 1846,
arriving 'like flakes of snow from Heaven'.[50] Dallas later told how 'Paddy
was fairly perplexed' by their arrival and how Catholic clergymen attempted
to intercept and destroy the tracts.[51] This venture was funded by Enoch
Durant, a member of the London Irish Society.

According to Dallas' own account, his colleagues in the Irish Society
did not expect these publications to 'stir the minds of a large number
of Roman Catholics'; they considered the enterprise an 'absurdity' and
withheld their support.[52] Bellingham, who knew 'Christian persons' who
employed scripture readers on their estates, introduced Dallas to Captain
and Mrs Blake who lived in the Irish-speaking region of Doon on the
north shore of Lough Corrib in impoverished west County Galway, just
east of Connemara.[53] With the strong support of her clergyman, Revd
Edwin Moore of Cong, Mrs Blake had started a scriptural school for girls.

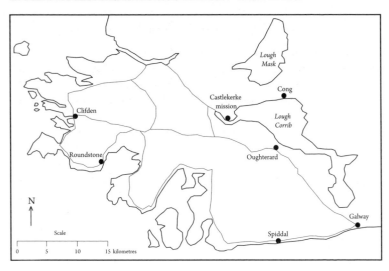

2.2 Castlekerke mission

After visiting the region, Dallas agreed to adopt the work and undertook to finish the schoolhouse, provided she allowed him to 'instruct them in the truth of the gospel in contrast with the falsehoods of Rome'.[54] This was to be Dallas' first mission in Ireland, romantically named 'Castlekerke', although the actual townland was called Drumsnauv.[55] It should be noted that, even at this early juncture, Dallas' missionary efforts were focused on children.

Dallas found himself without a sponsor when his wealthy benefactor, Enoch Durant, refused to fund the venture. His problem was solved by the onset of the famine when the thought was suggested of procuring funds to afford relief to the children at Castlekerke school; 'a channel was thus opened, through which the streams of charity flowed, to maintain many souls within the reach of the gospel salvation, who would otherwise have passed out of the body into their spiritual darkness'.[56]

Clearly Dallas not only utilised the famine to entice the starving to interact with mission agents, but also used the destitution of the Irish to raise mission funds: 'the awful famine of 1847, with its attendant horrors in 1848 worked wonderfully for its [mission's] development'.[57] An account of a starving family describes the destitution:

> the humble and distressed state of Margaret Martin, and ten in family, who are in a starved state. She did not get a morsel of the relief this fortnight; and six days after depriving her of the relief, a boy twelve years old dropped down dead with starvation; and three days after another boy died ...[58]

Dallas considered that the famine and consequent disease had prepared the people to receive 'those consolations which the glorious Gospel of God can alone impart'.[59] He continued to inform both the English public and Irish Catholics about Ireland's religious state; his letter on 'The Real State of Ireland' was published in the *Morning Herald* of 11 October 1846, and when the famine of 1845–47 began to exert its toll on the country, he circularised Irish Catholics with *The Food of Man*, saying 'as the priests had cursed the food which God had provided for his soul, God had withdrawn his blessing from that which he usually provided for his body'.[60] He concentrated his missionary efforts on Castlekerke, where the LAIS funded a scripture reader and Dallas' own parish of Wonston provided funds for a teacher.[61]

The conviction of the 'errors of Romanism' among evangelical Protestants was reinforced by the onset and extent of the Irish famine of 1845–47, interpreted by many as God's vengeance on sinful Ireland for having stubbornly clung to its Catholicism, its justifiable punishment foretold in the Scriptures:

> Son of man, when the land sinneth against me, by trespassing grievously, then I will stretch out mine hand upon it, and break the staff of the bread thereof, and will send famine upon it, and will cut off man and beast from it. (Ezekiel, xiv, 13)

Nangle, founder of the Achill mission, observed how 'Surely God is angry with this land. The potatoes would not have rotted unless He sent the rot to them.'[62] Economists and politicians also promoted this attitude. The evangelical Trevelyan described the famine as 'a direct stroke of an all-wise and all-merciful Providence',[63] while the Benthamite, non-interventionist policies of the Peel government attested to the widely held opinion that Ireland was responsible for its calamities and that punishment had been sent to it by God. Sir James Graham, home secretary, wrote to Sir Robert Peel that 'The Sword, the Pestilence and the Famine are the instruments of his displeasure: the canker worm and the locust are his armies ... doubtless there is a God who judgeth the Earth!'[64]

Under the exigencies of the famine of 1845–47, Irish Catholics were perceived as providentially open to mission overtures: 'Ireland is on the very point of a crisis, which, by the blessing of God, will rise her sons to the happy condition of a Protestant people.'[65] Edward Nangle, of the Anglican Achill mission considered it 'a great seed time'.[66] Members of other Protestant denominations also saw the famine as a proselytising opportunity; the Presbyterian, Thomas Armstrong, was bitterly disappointed when the English failed to capitalise on Ireland's famine conditions for ethnic and religious change[67] and the Dublin *Protestant Watchman* advised Lord John Russell that he 'must endeavour to bring the knowledge of God to every cabin in Ireland'.[68] In contrast, the Society of Friends refused the request of Emily and Rebecca Irwin for funds to establish a scriptural school at Boyle, County Roscommon. Although these ladies considered that Catholics had 'greatly lost their faith in their church and their clergy and are now ready to receive sounder instruction', the Quaker committee could not countenance 'anything of a party or sectarian character' and considered 'the present particularly unsuitable for proselytising'.[69] While some ICM supporters merely saw the famine as a heaven-sent opportunity, many truly sympathised with the plight of the starving. Hugh M'Neile reminded his congregation that 'Plagues, pestilences, famines ... [were] national punishments for Sin', but urged them to 'send food, or money, or both'.[70]

Dallas' adoption of Castlekerke marked the transfer of his attentions from Ireland's literate Catholics to its impoverished peasant community. From then his missionary activities were focused on Ireland's poorest, where their very poverty provided a compelling means of inviting their interest. In Castlekerke in April 1847 ten shillings was shared daily among the sick and twenty pounds worth of seed, and 'shoes and coarse clothing' were issued at the day and night-schools, where enrolments were 116 and 143 respectively, enabling Castlekerke to 'smile with oats and potatoes in hopeful greenness'.[71] The distribution of food, and especially soup, at mission schools and services gave rise to the term 'souper', which signified a mission agent. Converts were known by the derogatory term 'jumper', probably a corruption of the Irish verb 'd'iompaigh' which means to have turned.

Dallas insisted that starving Irish peasants were doctrinally motivated to avail of mission services; the improbability of this is clearly shown in extracts from a singular scripture reader's journal, where the avid interest of Irish Catholics for the Gospel is juxtaposed with the misery of starvation: 'I have now upwards of forty in the Sunday Scripture class; there the father and children sit side by side, the little one assisting the parent to read, and all eagerly answering the questions ... no one refuses to listen to the truth ... the "relief-fund" has kept many from starving, and restored many sick to health'.[72]

Castlekerke's mission agents laboured very successfully among the Catholic population, aided by copious supplies of mission relief. Paul Cullen informed Rome that 140 of 150 families in the Glan district had 'perverted', which clearly was a cause of great concern to the *Propaganda Fide*.[73] When progress in Castlekerke necessitated an Irish-speaking clergyman, Dallas insisted on employing an Anglican, although Irish-speaking Methodist and Presbyterian clergy were more readily available. In 1848, he persuaded Bishop Thomas Plunket of Tuam to ordain Castlekerke scripture reader, John O'Callaghan, an erstwhile Maynooth seminarian.[74] It has been argued that Plunket strongly supported the ICM to atone for his previous absenteeism from the diocese, which had evoked reprimands from Primate Beresford and Lord Eliot, the chief secretary.[75] Three generations of Plunket bishops were to provide staunch support for the ICM.[76]

The location of Castlekerke on the shores of Lough Corrib ensured easy access to lakeside communities in Cong parish on the north shore (Tuam Catholic diocese) and in Oughterard parish on the south shore (Galway Catholic diocese). Soon Castlekerke mission had schools at Farnaught, Cornamona, Glan, Lyons, Kilmilkin and Cappaunalaurabaun. Castlekerke's location was suitable for publicising its successes as it was easily reached from Galway city. Lough Corrib was navigable eastwards as far as Menlo, only three miles west of Galway. From there it was possible to travel by boat to the post-town of Oughterard (where the ICM established a hostel) and on to the lakeside mission stations of Castlekerke and Glan, enabling committed evangelicals to view the significant advances on popery.

The success of Castlekerke confirmed Dallas' opinion of the advantages of direct controversial mission but he could not persuade the IS to adopt this approach.[77] The IS wished the venture well but did not expect success.[78] Failing to inspire the Irish clergy to launch an aggressive campaign against Roman principles or to enlarge the operations of the IS, Dallas established the 'Special Fund for the Spiritual Exigencies of Ireland' to work aggressively among Ireland's Catholics, as there were 'fields white to the harvest at Glan, and at Kilmilkin'.[79] The Fund set about establishing direct missionary work in Ireland, but first had to choose a suitable location and settled on the region of west Galway. According to Dallas, this was decided when Enoch Durant, viewing a map of literacy in Ireland as found in the 1841 census, pointed to west Galway and said

> To make the experiment effective, the Mission should be carried on where ignorance is greatest and the advantages are fewest. The difficulties will, of course, be greater; but the success will be more telling, and more likely to convince the Irish clergy.[80]

It is extremely doubtful whether this was the case. It appears improbable that the arch-strategist Dallas would randomly choose a mission location and coincidentally find it an extremely impoverished area, devoid of education, where Catholicism was badly organised, where evangelical missionary curates had laboured for decades, and where sympathetic landowners had already started the work.

The London epicentre of anti-Catholicism was Exeter Hall, which housed meetings of Protestant societies of an evangelical, missionary and anti-Romish flavour, including the ICM. Many persons closely involved in the ICM, as committee members or as vice-patrons, had previous involvement in attempts to disseminate the Gospel to those in ignorance, either among the Catholics of Ireland, the irreligious of England or the heathens of foreign countries. Other ICM supporters were involved in avowedly anti-popery political pressure groups such as the National Club, Evangelical Alliance and Scottish Reformation Society. Association with these societies might suggest a desire to contain or eradicate popery.[81] As R. B. McDowell has stated, 'if one wishes to study any community, it is vital to discover on what grounds its leaders were selected, and what types of men were placed in posts of high responsibility'.[82]

From the outset, the ICM attracted considerable support from London businessmen and peers of the realm, many of whom were already associated with other religious causes. For example, Lord Henry Cholmondeley (later marquis of Cholmondely), Francis Maude and John Labouchere were trustees and actively involved in the running of the recently built St Paul's church (1847), a CPAS-funded mission for seamen in London, which they ensured was free from any Romish tendencies.[83] John Labouchere was also a trustee of the Church of the Holy Trinity in Westminster whose rector, William Cadman, was a leading evangelical and an ICM committee member.[84] The foundation of a seaman's church is proof of their desire to extend the scriptures to persons frequently outside their range. In the case of such evangelically minded persons, the extension of this effort to Irish Catholics is entirely understandable. The marquis of Blandford, author of The Blandford Act, 1856, which enabled the division of extensive parishes, was a vice-president of the ICM. It can be assumed that he was motivated to support the ICM because of a desire to provide religious facilities for non-attenders. Many persons who promoted the work of the ICM had built churches throughout Britain, sometimes in the capacity of landowner.[85]

A close network existed among evangelical activists, evident from an investigation of those associated with the ICM. Christ Church, Barnet, was principally funded by Captain Henry Trotter (also active in the English Church Missions), who built a school, a minister's house and a church in 1852, and gave the living to Revd William Pennefather, then ministering at Trinity Church, Walton, where Revd Edmond Holland was trustee.[86] All three gentlemen were ICM committee members. While Captain Trotter was personally extending facilities for Anglican worship in London, he was simultaneously doing likewise in Ireland under the auspices of the ICM, and throughout England through the ECM.

Some ICM supporters had previously engaged in attempts to convert Irish Catholics, mostly through the auspices of the Irish Society. Lord Farnham, father of Somerset Maxwell, had established a mission colony on his Kingscourt estate; Francis Maude was treasurer of the Irish Society; and Revd William Pennefather, whose sister was married to Somerset

Maxwell, had been struck by the spiritual destitution of Connemara and established a parish church at Roundstone in 1843.[87] Another sister of William Pennefather was married to James O'Brien, bishop of Ossory, who strongly promoted the ICM's Kilkenny mission (see chapter 4).[88]

Just as the great number of ICM committee members and vice-presidents were involved with the CPAS, indicating their desire to impart the Gospel to others, involvement with the CMS can be assumed to indicate a similar inclination. Research shows that fifty-one persons active in the ICM were also associated with the CPAS, and ninety-five were associated with the CMS while thirty persons were associated with both the CPAS and CMS.[89]

Protestant missions to Catholics can be viewed as either the dissemination of the scriptures among Catholics or as the eradication of Catholicism as an objective *per se*, although the boundaries between these ideologies remain indistinct. The fact that Francis Maude and Lord Henry Cholmondeley (also associated with the CPAS) were vice-presidents of the Irish Reformation Society (IRS) could suggest as great an interest in eliminating Popery as in converting Irish Roman Catholics. Cholmondely, a very moderate politician, did not 'refuse attention to claims for necessary reforms'.[90] As with the earl of Roden (see below) this moderation may not have extended to the toleration of Roman Catholics. However, the fact that he fostered the development of churches among the non-churchgoing English population suggests that the elimination of popery may not have been his sole motivation. Similarly, Sir Arthur Cotton, president of the CMS and Protestant Reformation Society (PRS),[91] provides another example of ambiguous motivations among ICM supporters.

The speeches and writings of ICM supporters invariably championed the anti-popery of the mid nineteenth century and fuelled the sense of anxiety experienced by evangelicals.[92] Typical was the output of Sir Christopher Lighton, Bart., who purchased land at Sellerna, near Clifden, County Galway 'for the purpose of advancing the reformation'.[93] Of the thirty-eight committee members of the General Irish Reformation Society in 1850, ten were associated with the ICM[94] and many signed a memorial to the queen following the imprisonment of the Madiai in Tuscany for their practice of Protestantism (1851).[95] Admiral Vernon Harcourt chaired a lecture delivered by the famously anti-papist dissenting Scottish clergyman, Revd John Cumming, D.D. entitled 'The Pope, the Man of Sin', the text of which was published by the British Society for Promoting the Religious Principles of the Reformation.[96] However, as Vernon Harcourt was a founding member of the CPAS and was active in establishing churches throughout England, it is not possible to ascribe purely anti-papist views to his involvement with the ICM.[97]

Table 2.1 shows that most ICM supporters who were MPs were conservative in politics.[98] As evangelicals saw it: 'Popish superstition advanced while Whig infidelity paved the way.'[99] There were some notable exceptions to this; the earl of Aberdeen, Lord Calthorpe, Arthur Kinnaird (11th Baron), earl of Shaftesbury and Earl Cairns were all liberals. There was, however, great variation among the politicians, with some conservative politicians holding moderate religious views and some liberals appearing extreme in their defence of Protestantism. Dudley Ryder, second earl of Harrowby (conservative), voted for the repeal of the Test Acts and in favour of the grant to Maynooth.[100] In contrast, the liberal MP, Arthur Kinnaird (10th Baron, ICM vice-president 1852–87) was president of the Scottish Reformation Society.[101] He and his wife were involved in many Protestant educational and philanthropic causes and were strong supporters of exclusively scriptural education.[102] He was a partner in the banking house Ransom & Co., ICM bankers, as was his son, Arthur Kinnaird (11th Baron).

Table 2.1 Political inclinations and place of education of ICM committee members who were MPs

Name	Politics	University	College
Aberdeen, Lord	L	Oxford	
Calthorpe, Lord	L		
Cowper, William	L		
Gordon, Alexander	L	Cambridge	Trinity
Harrowby, 3rd earl of	L	Oxford	Ch. Ch.
Kinnaird, Arthur (10th Baron)	L		
Shaftesbury, 7th earl of	L		
Harrowby, 2nd earl of	MC	Oxford	Ch. Ch.
Dynevor, Lord	MC	Oxford	Ch. Ch.
Hoare, Joseph	MC		
Arbuthnot, George	C	Cambridge	Trinity
Blanford, 6th marquis of	C	Oxford	Oriel
Bandon, 2nd earl of	C	Oxford	
Bandon, 3rd earl of	C	Oxford	Oriel
Bandon, 4th earl of	C		
Broderick, William	C	Oxford	Baliol
Brooke Bridges, Sir William	C	Oxford	Oriel
Cairns, 1st earl	C	Dublin	
Cholmondeley, 4th marquis of	C		
Cholmondeley, 5th marquis of	C	Oxford	
Clancarty, 3rd earl of	C	Cambridge	St. John's

Name	Politics	University	College
Colquhoun, John	C	Oxford	Oriel
Farquhar, Sir W.	C		
Fitzwalter, Lord	C	Oxford	Oriel
Frewen, Charles	C	Cambridge	Trinity
Hamilton, George	C	Oxford	Trinity
Kennaway, Sir John	C	Oxford	Baliol
Kinnaird, Arthur (11th Baron)	C	Cambridge	Trinity
Jermyn, 1st earl	C	Cambridge	Trinity
Lanesborough, 5th earl of	C		
Lefroy, Anthony	C	Dublin	
Lifford, 3rd Viscount	C	Oxford	Ch. Ch.
Maxwell, Somerset	C	Oxford	Baliol
Mayo, 5th earl of			
Moody, Charles A.	C	Oxford	
Napier, Sir Joseph	C	Dublin	
Roden, Viscount –1854	C		
Roden, 3rd earl of	C		
Roden, 4th earl of	C		
Roden, 5th earl of	C		
Plumptre, J. P.	C	Nat. & Un. Univ	
Ryder, Granville	C		
Stewart, William	C	Cambridge	St John's
Verner, Sir William	C		

Note: L = liberal, MC = moderate conservative, C = conservative, Ch. Ch. = Christ Church, Nat. & Un. Univ. = National and United University
Source: *Crockford's clerical directory* (London 1865, 1883, 1910, 1921); M. Stenton, (ed.), *The who's who of British members of parliament* (Hassocks, 1976); M. Stenton and S. Lees (eds), *The who's who of British members of parliament* (Hassocks, 1978).

Very often the fiercest denunciations of the Irish in Britain were penned by Scotsmen.[103] The strongly anti-Catholic James Edward Gordon, Conservative MP for Dundalk, was a founder of the British Society for Promoting the Religious Principles of the Reformation (later Protestant Reformation Society). When his extreme views cost him his seat in 1832, he turned his attention to orchestrating the No-Popery crusade of 1834–36 and organised the Protestant Association as a focus for the anti-Catholic campaign.[104] His fellow Scotsman, John Colquhoun held extreme views on the Irish question, the Irish educational system[105] and the influx of Irish Catholics, complaining that 'in the very streets of London, and in the streets of every city and town of England, and Scotland ... the same mighty Rome stands up and defies our government, tramples on our laws, dethrones our Sovereign, laughs at our Parliament, calls together its own synods, passes its own laws'.[106]

The parliamentary speeches of Lord Ashley, MP for Dorset (later earl of Shaftesbury) and Sir R. H. Inglis, MP for Oxford University, highlight the ultra-Protestant stereotyping of Catholics common in the 1850s and reveal the underlying beliefs which underpinned their hostility to Catholics. R. H. Inglis (1786–1855), a founder of Exeter Hall, had opposed Catholic emancipation, Jewish relief bills, the Maynooth Act and the repeal of the Corn Laws. He is claimed to have accurately represented the views of country squires, being 'an old fashioned Tory, a strong churchman with many prejudices'.[107]

The viewpoints of most ICM supporters lay within the extremes of the moderate views of the earl of Harrowby on the one hand and R. H. Inglis on the other. Some, like the earl of Harrowby, supported concessions to non-Anglicans. (His support for the ICM may have been influenced by the conversion of his grandson, Revd George Dudley Ryder, to Catholicism in 1845.) Others, like the earl of Roden, Grand Master of the Orange Order, although described as 'a firm friend to religious toleration', most 'steadily maintained the Protestant principles on which the institutions of the country are based'.[108]

Most ICM committee members who were MPs opposed any attempt to interfere with the Church of England, such as Charles Frewen, who was 'opposed to concessions to the Roman Catholic church'.[109] Earl Cairns and Sir Joseph Napier were typical of this class of politician. Napier actively opposed the movement for Roman Catholic emancipation, Jewish emancipation, opening diplomatic relations with Rome, removal of tithes, and he was rightly described after his death as representing an 'indubitable type of the Protestantism of the North of Ireland in its best form'.[110] When Mr Monsell introduced the Roman Catholic Oaths Bill, Cairns moved an amendment to secure Protestant government and worship in the United Kingdom. He presided at the ICM's annual meeting for the four years before his death in 1885, not thinking it 'beneath the duty of the Lord Chancellor of England openly to advocate the cause of the missions in Ireland'.[111]

When the education of ICM committee members is examined, no clear pattern emerges. Of those whose place of education is identifiable, the majority appear to have been Oxford educated, especially among lay supporters. This is surprising, given that Cambridge is accepted as the nucleus of English evangelicalism. This may tentatively be taken to indicate that clergy were influenced by evangelicalism and were doctrinally motivated, whereas secular supporters experienced more complex motivations.

It is widely acknowledged that Alexander Dallas held millenarian views, as did Revd William Marrable, co-founder of the ICM. Other ICM supporters who were known millenarianists include Revd Edward Bickersteth, earl of Shaftesbury, Revd Hugh M'Neile and James Hatley Frere. The writings of many clerical members of ICM committees demonstrate millenarian convictions.[112] Supporters with Irish connections who held strong millenarian beliefs, and who had championed previous missionary work among Irish Catholics, included the earl of Roden and duke of Manchester.[113] Sir John Kennaway (ICM vice-president 1863–1916) was president of the CMS and also of the London Society for Promoting Christianity among the Jews. Robert Bickersteth, a frequent speaker at the ICM's annual meetings, demonstrated strong millenarian opinions, and Isaac Brock, ordained as a Connemara missionary, transferred to the Jews' Chapel, Bethnal Green, London.[114] Millenarianism was not confined to the earlier years of the ICM: Revd J. B. Barraclough (committee member 1919–27) was association secretary of the Jews' Society, 1875–81, head of the Jew's Society Mission, 1881–84 and chaplain to the London Jew's Society, 1881–91.[115]

It is difficult to objectively assess the motivations of the founders and early supporters of the ICM. Sir Henry Cholmondely provides a good example. His involvement with the CPAS and as a trustee in city churches indicates a desire to bring the Gospel to the poor, while his association with the Irish Reformation Society suggests that he was interested in the elimination of popery. His example proves that these aims were not mutually exclusive. However, to date no evidence has been found to ascribe to him social, political or economic motivations. He may have been influenced by family connections: his sister was married to a cousin of Fanny D'Arcy (neé Bellingham), who played a pivotal role in the foundation and development of the ICM.

Accepting the evangelical fears that the Church of England was under attack: from within in the shape of Tractarianism and ritualism (from 1833); from Ireland in the shape of an incursion of Roman Catholics (from 1845); from Rome in the shape of the re-established Roman hierarchy (1851); from dissent and Rome, in the state in the admission of Catholics and Dissenters to parliament (1829), and admission of dissenters to grammar schools (1860) and to Oxford and Cambridge (1854 and 1856); from non-Christians, in the emancipation of Jews (1858); it is easy to understand the attraction of the possible conversion of Roman Catholics. Involvement with the ICM provided a sphere of activity where supporters could play some part in holding back the boulder of religious pluralism which was rolling over their country.

The timing of the foundation of the ICM was opportune. When Alexander

Dallas initiated mission work at Castlekerke in 1846, or when he founded the ICM in 1849, he had no inkling of the future uproar of Papal Aggression and the intensity of anti-Catholic feeling that would be generated. To a large extent, the ICM was in the right place, at the right time, to take advantage of the rising sectarian temperature of the early 1850s. In the early decades of the nineteenth century, evangelical objections to Catholicism were primarily underpinned by doctrinal issues. By the mid century, and especially after the influx of famine migrants, this had acquired social, political and economic elements. These component factors were interwoven and subject to individual variation, rendering an absolute analysis of the motives of ICM founders and supporters impossible, except to state that each one was convinced of the 'errors of Romanism', the need for its eradication, the threat it posed to Protestant England, the doctrinal supremacy of Protestantism, the industrious and lawful nature of Protestants, and the certainty of a transformation in the character of converts, as evangelical contempt for Catholicism emanated 'not only from its doctrinal "heresies" but also from its social and political consequences'.[116]

At the local level, a small but significant group of persons also influenced the progress of the ICM in Connemara, which had become increasingly 'settled' in the early nineteenth century by families such as the Blakes at Renvyle, the D'Arcys at Clifden and the Martins at Ballinahinch, where their residences formed 'English settlements like "oases in the waste"'.[117] The establishment of scriptural schools by these families and the posting of evangelical missionary curates by Archbishop Trench paved the way for the ICM, which promised a Protestant infrastructure by way of churches and schools. Revd Wall, landowner at Errislannan, circulated his friends with the following letter, which he also published in the December 1852 issue of the *Irish Missionary Record and Chronicle of the Reformation*. Although a clergyman, his motivations were clearly more social and political than religious, urging support from 'all ye who would wish to see the blessings of CIVILISATION, INDUSTRY, CONTENTMENT, LOYALTY AND PEACE grow up in this remote and unvisited peninsula, instead of BARBARISM, SLOTH, DISCONTENT, DISAFFECTION AND TURBULENCE ...' (his capitals). In common with many other Connemara landlords, Revd Wall succeeded in having a church erected on his estate, sited almost opposite his main gate. Over a hundred years later, his great-granddaughter exclaimed, 'what incredible conceit. And what a vivid picture those few lines give of the attitude of the Protestant landowner fired with missionary zeal'.[118] Although many Connemara landowners believed that the conversion of Catholics was desirable, their support for the ICM may have been weaker had the Church of Ireland infrastructure in the region been better established.

Notes

1 Alexander R. C. Dallas, *My life, &c* (n.p., n.d. [1869]).

2 Desmond Bowen, 'Alexander R. C. Dallas, warrior-saint of Wonston, Hampshire' in Paul T. Phillips (ed.), *View from the pulpit: Victorian ministers and society* (Toronto, Cambridge, 1977).

3 *Religious census of Hampshire, 1851* (Winchester, 1993), p. 123.

4 Alexander Robert Charles Dallas, 'A word from the pastor to his flock', *Wonston Weekly Calendar*, 1837, No. 18; Alexander R. C. Dallas, *The pastor's assistant. Intended to facilitate the discharge of the pastoral office in the Church of England* (3 vols, London, Wonston, 1842), p. 211; Peter Clarke, *Dever and Down: a history of the parish of Wonston* (Winchester, 2002), p. 74.

5 For example, see Alexander R. C. Dallas, *Pastoral superintendence: its motive, its detail and its support* (London, 1841), p. 360, where he states that, 'There are 73 houses where no inhabitant is a communicant, 23 where every adult is, 22 where heads of house are, 17 where wives are, 6 where some member is, making 78 houses where some person is.'

6 Alexander R. C. Dallas, *The pleasure-fair* (London, 1843); Alexander R. C. Dallas, *Harvest hints for Christian labourers* (London, 1843).

7 For instance he admitted in 1836 that in forty-nine out of 143 households 'no persons make a reasonable and consistent profession'. In 1840 he observed that sixty-four former communicants no longer attended church, twenty of whom had declined during the previous year and that over half of parish households did not attend church. Dallas, *Pastoral superintendence*, pp. 154–5, 360.

8 Alexander R. C. Dallas, *A sermon upon the present distress in Ireland, preached at Highclere, in the county of Hants, etc.* (London, 1822) p. 27.

9 Dallas, *My life*, pp. 181–3.

10 Shirley Matthews argues that anti-Catholicism in Hampshire increased markedly between the 1820s and the 1850s in '"Second string" and "precious prejudice": Catholicism and anti-Catholicism in Hampshire in the era of emancipation' in James H. Murphy, *Evangelicals and Catholics in nineteenth-century Ireland* (Dublin, 2005), pp. 85–96.

11 His first published work on millenarianism appeared in 1841; eleven works on millenarianism published between 1841 and 1851 have been located (see bibliography).

12 Alexander R. C. Dallas, *The story of the Irish Church Missions, part 1* (London, 1867), pp. 12–15; J. D. Sirr, *A memoir of Power Le Poer Trench, last archbishop of Tuam* (Dublin, 1845), pp. 630–3.

13 Alexander R. C. Dallas, *The prophecy upon the Mount; a practical consideration of Our Lord's statement respecting the distinction of Jerusalem, His own appearing and the end of the age* (London, 1843), p. 120.

14 Alexander R. C. Dallas, *What shall we do for Ireland?* (Wonston, 1846), p. 2.

15 Alexander R. C. Dallas, *My church-yard. Its tokens, and its remembrances* (2nd edn, London, 1848), pp. 3, 17–18, 100–1.

16 Desmond Bowen, *The Protestant crusade in Ireland, 1800–70* (Dublin, 1978), p. 212.

17 Henry McManus, *Sketches of the Irish highlands: descriptive social, and religious. With special reference to Irish Missions in west Connaught since 1840* (London, Dublin, 1863), p. 9. (The author remarked in 1840 that due to the herring decline: 'Roundstone ... is the very picture of desolation'.)

18 Maeve Mulryan Moloney, *Nineteenth-century elementary education in the archdiocese of Tuam* (Dublin, 2001), p. 13. In 1841 the population was 33,456, in 1851 it was 21,349; a decrease of 12,116 persons or 36 per cent.

19 NAI, Relief Commission Papers, Incoming Correspondence, Ballinahinch Barony, MS No. 5111, Hyacinth D'Arcy to Relief Commission, 5 Aug. 1846; Christine Kinealy, *This great calamity: the Irish famine 1845–1852* (Dublin, 1994), p. 151; Kathleen Villiers-Tuthill, *Patient endurance: the great famine in Connemara* (Dublin, 1997), *passim*.

20 Letter from 'An Englishman', *The Tablet*, 1 July 1848.

21 For an exploration of the impact of the famine, and especially of fever and cholera in Dublin, see William P. MacArthur, 'Medical history of the famine' in R. D. Edwards and T. D. Williams (eds), *The great famine* (Dublin, 1994, first published 1956), pp. 273–4, 286.

22 265 sites of religious significance have been identified in west Galway (120 ecclesiastical remains, eight crosses, 137 holy wells); see Office of Public Works, *Archaeological inventory of county Galway, west Galway including Connemara and the Aran Islands* (Dublin, 1993), p. 23.

23 See map in Emmet Larkin, 'Before the devotional revolution' in James H. Murphy (ed.), *Evangelicals and Catholics in nineteenth-century Ireland* (Dublin, 2005), p. 23.

24 E. J. Quigley, 'Grace abounding', *Irish Ecclesiastical Record*, xx (1922), 570.

25 *First report of the Commissioners of Public Instruction, Ireland, with Appendix*, HC 1835 (45), xxxiii, pp. 34d–35d.

26 Dallas, *The story of the Irish Church Missions, part 1*, p. 105.

27 Paul Cullen to Tobias Kirby, Liverpool, 2 Sept. 1847 in Patrick J. Corish (ed.) 'Irish College, Rome: Kirby Papers', edited by Patrick J. Corish, *Archivium Hibernicum*, xxxi (1973), p. 30. Many clergy of all denominations died of famine fever during the famine years.

28 Anonymous [Angelo Maria Rinolfi], *Missions in Ireland: especially with reference to the proseltizing [sic] movement; showing the marvellous devotedness of the Irish to the faith of their fathers, by one of the missioners* (Dublin, 1855), p. 260.

29 Pontifical Irish College Archives, Rome (PICA), MS No. KIR/NC/1/1847/8, Paul Cullen, Liverpool, to Tobias Kirby, 2 Sept. 1847.

30 Vincentian Archives, 'Life of Fathers Dowley and Lydon', p. 106.

31 *Irish Ecclesiastical Record*, xxi (1923), 28.

32 Gerard Moran, *The Mayo evictions of 1860* (Westport, 1986), p. 22.

33 *Second report of the Commissioners of Public Instruction in Ireland, 1835*, xxxiv (47), pp. 52–4d.

34 For an explanation of MacHale's reasons for excluding national schools, see Mulryan Moloney, *Nineteenth-century elementary education*; Bernard O'Reilly, *John MacHale, his life, times and correspondence* (2 vols, New York, 1890), ii, p. 450; Ulick Bourke, *The life and times of the Rev. John MacHale, archbishop of*

Tuam and Metropolitan (Baltimore, 1882), pp. 107–8; John MacHale, *Sermons and discourses of the late most Rev. John MacHale, D.D., archbishop of Tuam*, edited by Thomas MacHale, D.D., Ph.D. (Dublin, 1883), p. 280.

35 *Dublin Evening Mail*, 11 Nov. 1851.

36 See map in Caitríona Clear, *Nuns in nineteenth century Ireland* (Dublin, 1987), p. 38.

37 St Jarlath's College (1800), Presentation Convent (1835), Franciscan Brothers (1839), Convent of Mercy (1846).

38 Sirr, *A memoir of Power Le Poer Trench*, pp. 611–17.

39 Ibid., pp. 611–17; Irene Whelan, 'The stigma of souperism' in Cathal Póirtéir (ed.), *The great Irish famine* (Dublin, 1995), pp. 141–6.

40 Bearnárd Mac Uaid, 'Stair oideachas Bráthar Triomhadh Úird Riaghalta Sain Proinsias san naomhadh céad déag'[The history of education of the Third Order of Saint Francis in the nineteenth century] (MA dissertation, University College, Galway, 1956), p. 108.

41 Letter from John MacHale to Cardinal Fransoni, Tuam, 17 Aug. 1852 in O'Reilly, *John MacHale*, ii, p. 432; *Freeman's Journal*, 21 Sept. 1852.

42 *Catholic Directory*, 1841, p. 307; Dublin Diocesan Archives, Drumcondra (DDA), Minutes of bishop's meeting, 11 Nov. 1841.

43 Catholic Truth Society, *A roll of honour, Irish prelates and priests of the last century, with preface by Most Rev. John Healy, D.D., archbishop of Tuam* (Dublin, 1905), p. 103.

44 Oliver J. Burke, *The history of the Catholic archbishops of Tuam, from the foundation of the see to the death of the most Rev. John McHale of Tuam* (Dublin, 1882), p. 343.

45 Alexander R. C. Dallas, *The story of the Irish Church Missions. Continued to the year 1869, etc.* (London, 1875), p. 49; A[nne] Dallas, *Incidents in the life and ministry of the Rev. Alexander R.C. Dallas A.M.* (London, 1871), p. 391.

46 Dallas, *The story of the Irish Church Missions, part 1*, p. 42.

47 Ibid., pp. 12–34.

48 Ibid., p. 30.

49 Ibid., p. 24.

50 Dallas, *The story of the Irish Church Missions, part 1*, p. 60.

51 Ibid., pp. 47–64; *Banner of the Truth*, 1 Apr. 1863, p. 55.

52 Dallas, *The story of the Irish Church Missions, part 1*, pp. 47, 50.

53 Ibid., p. 62.

54 Ibid., pp. 89–90.

55 Alexander Dallas, *Castelkerke* (London, 1849), pp. 1–15.

56 Dallas, *The story of the Irish Church Missions, part 1*, p. 93.

57 Ibid., p. 61.

58 Dallas, *Castelkerke*, pp. 42–3.

59 Dallas, *Incidents in the life*, p. 390.

60 Dallas, *The story of the Irish Church Missions, part 1*, p. 84.

61 Ibid., p. 93.

62 *Achill Missionary Herald*, Feb. 1847.

63 Charles Trevelyan, *The Irish crisis* (London, 1848), p. 147.

64 Quoted in A. N. Wilson, *The Victorians* (London, 2002), p. 76.

65 ICM, *Annual report*, 1852, p. 23.

66 *Achill Missionary Herald*, 26 May 1849.

67 Thomas Armstrong, *My life in Connaught, with sketches of mission work in the west* (London, 1906), pp. 58, 95–6.

68 'Letter to the Right Hon Lord John Russell', *Protestant Watchman*, 12 May 1848.

69 Emily and Rebecca Irwin to Society of Friends, 7 Oct. 1847 and draft reply, 15 Dec. 1847, quoted in Liam Swords, *In their own words: the famine in north Connaught* (Dublin, 1999), pp. 231, 258–9.

70 Hugh M'Neile, *The famine, a rod of God, its provoking cause – its merciful design: a sermon preached in St. Jude's Church, Liverpool on Sunday, February 2, 1847* (London, 1847), pp. 8, 41.

71 Dallas, *Castelkerke*, pp. 20–2.

72 Ibid., pp. 41–3.

73 Peadar MacSuibhne, *Paul Cullen and his contemporaries, with their letters, 1820–1902* (5 vols, Naas, 1965), iii, p. 91.

74 Dallas, *The story of the Irish Church Missions, part 1*, pp. 131–6; Dallas, *Castelkerke*, pp. 87, 92.

75 Bowen, *Protestant crusade*, p. 217; Desmond Bowen, *Souperism: myth or reality?* (Cork, 1970), pp. 157–79.

76 Thomas Plunket, bishop of Tuam 1839–67; William Conyngham Plunket, bishop of Meath 1876–85, archbishop of Dublin 1885–97 (nephew of Thomas Plunket), and Benjamin John Plunket, bishop of Tuam 1913–19, bishop of Meath 1919–26 (son of William Conyngham Plunket).

77 Dallas, *The story of the Irish Church Missions, part 1*, p. 103.

78 *Proceedings of the Irish Society*, Sept. 1847, p. 30.

79 Dallas, *The story of the Irish Church Missions, part 1*, pp. 102–3; Dallas, *Castelkerke*, p. 119.

80 *Banner of the Truth*, Apr. 1867, p. 22.

81 For the purposes of this study, the following societies were examined: Irish Society; The Island and Coast Society; London Hibernian Society; The Church Pastoral Aid Society; The (Hibernian) Church Missionary Society; Evangelical Alliance; Reformation Societies, Irish, British, Scottish and Protestant.

82 R. B. McDowell, *Historical essays, 1938–2000* (Dublin, 2003), p. 144.

83 Lord Henry Cholmondeley and Hon. Francis Maude to Revd Dan Greatorex, concerning works to Church spire etc., London Metropolitan Archives (hereafter LMA), MS Nos P93/PAU2/68 and P93/PAU2/90/1–4, Sep.–Nov. 1864; MS No. P93/PAU2/31, 12 June 1863, Thomas Richardson, Vicar of St Matthew, Pell Street to John Labouchere, explains that Mr Louder, of 'the very high party' is trying to gain an ecclesiastical district which would 'subvert' the work of the sailors' church, and must be stopped.

84 LMA, MS No. P89_TRI/137, Records of Holy Trinity Church, Westminster (1857); MS No. P89_TRI/89, John Labouchere 16 Portland Place, Middlesex, Esq. is listed among the trustees of the Trinity District National Schools; *Crockford's clerical dictionary* (London, 1883), p. 183.

85 For example, Lord Calthorpe (ICM vice-president 1862–66) built St George's church (1838) and St James' church, both in Edgebaston, Birmingham (1852). Unlike the London churches previously described, these churches were not invested in trustees. The livings of both were perpetual curacies until 1885 when they became vicarages, both in the gift of Lord Calthorpe. Birmingham City Archives (BCA), MS Nos EP58 and EP54.n, Records of the Ecclesiastical Parish of St James, Edgbaston.

86 LMA, MS Nos DRO/107/K/02/001 and DRO/107/F/04/012, Records of Christ Church, Barnet: Saint Alban's Road, Barnet; Robert Braithwate, *The life and letters of Rev. William Pennefather* (London, n.d.), pp. 221, 267.

87 Braithwate, *William Pennefather*, pp. 65, 77–99.

88 Thomas J. Kelley, 'Trapped between two worlds: Edward Nangle, Achill Island and sectarian competition in Ireland, 1800–1862' (Ph.D. dissertation, Trinity College Dublin, 2004), p. 32.

89 See Miriam Moffitt, 'The Society for Irish Church Missions to the Roman Catholics, 1850–1950' (Ph.D. dissertation, National University of Ireland, Maynooth, 2006), Appendix III.

90 M. Stenton (ed.), *The who's who of British members of parliament* (Hassocks, 1976), p. 76.

91 *Annual report of the Protestant Reformation Society*, 1894.

92 For example, Daniel Wilson, *The Church of England in danger. A letter to the Vicar of Islington upon his recent pamphlet 'Our Protestant faith in danger'. By one of his parishioners* (London, 1850); Samuel Minton, *Romish tactics and Romish morals* (London, 1851).

93 Christopher Lighton, *Does Rome teach salvation by faith alone? If not is her teaching Christian?* (n.p., n.d.); Scottish Association for the relief of Irish children attending scriptural schools, *Report for 1851, with notes of two months' residence among the Irish Church Missions in west Galway and Mayo* (Edinburgh, 1851), p. 20.

94 *Fourth Report of the General Irish Reformation Society for the restoration in Ireland of her primitive religion, and the necessary protection of converts* (Castle-Douglas, 1850), earl of Roden (president), earl of Lanesborough (vice-president), earl of Gainsborough (vice-president), Lord Ashley, MP, later Lord Shaftesbury (vice-president), Lord Henry Cholmondeley (vice-president), The Hon. Somerset Maxwell (vice-president), Sir William Verner, Bart. (vice-president), J. P. Plumptre, esq., MP (vice-president), J. C. Colquhoun, MP (vice-president) and Sir T. Blomefield Bart. (committee member). Francis Maude was a vice-president in the years 1847–48.

95 Frank Wallis, *Popular anti-Catholicism in mid-Victorian Britain* (Lampeter, 1993), pp. 103–7. ICM members included the marquis of Cholmondely, and the earls of Cavan, Shaftesbury, Roden and Clancarty.

96 John Cumming, *The Pope, the Man of Sin, a lecture … third thousand* (London, n.d. [1851]).

97 *Report of the Church Pastoral Aid Society* (London, 1893).

98 In table 2.1 Alexander Gordon is listed as conservative, which was his inclination during the 1850s when he was involved with the ICM. Later in life

he became a liberal. Stenton, *The who's who of British members of parliament*, i,
p. 159.

99 'The semi–infidel or liberal, the Papist and the Tractarian', *The Record*, 14 Sept.
1846. See also J. C. Colquhoun, *On the object and uses of Protestant Associations*
(London, 1839), p. 11.

100 *Dictionary of national biography (DNB)* (London, 1886), L, p. 45.

101 *Report of the Scottish Reformation Society*, 1860.

102 *DNB*, xxxi, p. 189; Wallis, *Popular anti-Catholicism*, p. 100 (Church Missionary
Society, the Malta Protestant College, the Lock Hospital, Dr Barnardo's
Homes, the London City Mission, Aged Christians' Society, British Ladies'
Female Emigration Society, Foreign Evangelisation Society, Calvin Memorial
Hall at Geneva, Union for Prayer, Zenica Bible and Medical Mission, and the
Young Women's Christian Association).

103 James Edmund Handley, *The Irish in modern Scotland* (Cork, 1947), pp. 93–131;
Revd J. A. Wylie, Professor of the Protestant Institute in Scotland, 'Rome's
Grand Missionary Institute, or her use of the Irish for swamping England', in
Rome and civil liberty (London, 1864), pp. 164–70.

104 John Wolffe, *The Protestant crusade in Great Britain, 1829–1860* (Oxford,
1991), p. 75.

105 J. C. Colquhoun, *The system of national education in Ireland, its principle and
practice* (Cheltenham, 1838).

106 ICM, *Report of the proceedings at the third annual meeting*, p. 11 (spoken by
J. C. Colquhoun).

107 Wallis, *Popular anti-Catholicism*, p. 68; *DNB*, xxix, pp. 6–7.

108 Stenton, *The who's who of British members of parliament*, i, p. 212.

109 Ibid., i, p. 151; ibid., i, p. 34 (J. P. Plumptre voted against emancipation of
the Jews); ibid., i, p. 49 (William Broderick was 'a firm supporter of our
constitution and staunch adherer to the Protestant church'); ibid., i, p. 314
(Sir W. Farquhar would not vote for the abolition of church rate unless some
provision was made for the fabric of churches); M. Stenton and S. Lees (eds),
The who's who of British members of parliament (Hassocks, 1978), ii, p. 81 (Sir
William Henry Houldworth 'supported Sunday closing bill and every attempt
to destroy church establishments').

110 *DNB*, xl, p. 65.

111 ICM, *Annual report*, 1884, pp. 13–14.

112 Stenton and Lees, *The who's who of British members of parliament*, ii, p. 119;
Irish Ecclesiastical Gazette, 9 Nov. 1906; James Hatley Frere, *Preface to the
second edition of the great continental revolution containing remarks on the
progress of prophetic events during the year 1848–49* (London, 1849). For
further examples of millenarian writings of ICM supporters see T. R. Birks,
On the principles of prophetic interpretation (London, 1841); T. R. Birks, *The
two later visions of Daniel* (London, 1846); H. H. Beamish, *What, where and
who is Anti-Christ?* (London, 1854). For an exploration of the impact of
millenarian thought see D. W. Bebbington, *Evangelicalism in modern Britain:
a history from the 1730s to the 1980s* (London, 2002), p. 82; Wallis, *Popular
anti-Catholicism*, pp. 29, 95.

113 Myrtle Hill, *The time of the end: millenarian beliefs in Ulster* (Belfast, 2001), p. 34.
114 *Banner of the Truth*, July 1871, p. 41, Robert Bickersteth, *A sermon preached at the Episcopal Jews' Chapel, Plastine Place, Bethnal Green, on Thursday, May 5, 1853, before the London Society for Promoting Christianity amongst the Jews* (London, 1853); Robert Bickersteth, *The state of Jews before the Lord's second coming* (London, 1854); *Crockford's clerical directory* (London, 1865), p. 81.
115 *Crockford's clerical directory* (London, 1921), p. 81.
116 David Hempton and Myrtle Hill, *Evangelical Protestantism in Ulster society, 1870–1890* (London, 1992), p. 81.
117 Digby Neave, *Four days in Connemara* (London, 1852), p. 21; Villiers-Tuthill, *Patient endurance*, p. vii; Whelan, 'The stigma of souperism', p. 136.
118 Alannah Heather, *Errislannan: scenes from a painter's life* (Dublin, 1993), p. 5.

Chapter 3

The expansion of missionary work, 1846–52

Small-scale work among Connemara's Catholic population had been undertaken for two decades prior to the foundation of the ICM. Archbishop Trench of Tuam (1819–39) had personally funded two missionary curates at Roundstone and Ballinakill.[1] Societies such as the Island and Coast Society undertook localised missionary work, and Hyacinth and James D'Arcy, sons of John D'Arcy founder of Clifden, twenty miles west of Castlekerke, had also contemplated missionary work among the Catholic population.[2] By 1839, along with Colonel Thompson of Salruck near the Killaries, they had planned a mission settlement along the lines of Nangle's colony at Achill which was postponed only by the onset of the famine.[3] Fanny Bellingham met Hyacinth D'Arcy when visiting Clifden in 1845, and after the establishment of the successful Castlekerke mission, she had introduced him to Dallas. D'Arcy's settlement plan was shelved in favour of Dallas' more ambitious scheme for the total conversion of Connemara's Catholic population where 40,000 persons 'stood so greatly in need of the light carried by a Christian mission'.[4] Hyacinth D'Arcy played a pivotal role in the ICM's progress in Connemara. Following the sale of his father's estate in the Encumbered Estates Court, Hyacinth was ordained by Thomas Plunket in 1851 and served as parish clergyman and ICM superintendent in Clifden until his death in 1874.[5] He married Fanny Bellingham in 1850. ICM activity in Connemara was managed at a local level by Hyacinth and Fanny D'Arcy, by Hyacinth's brother, James (mission accountant) and James's wife, Mary.

Few detailed accounts exist of the very beginnings of mission work in Connemara but it is known that work began in January 1848. Schools were soon established at Clifden, Fakeragh, Ballyconree, Errislannan and Sellerna, where John MacHale's exclusion of national schools created an educational void eagerly filled by the ICM.[6] Although adults were invited to services and discussion classes, missionary work was particularly aimed at children, who swiftly availed of the education delivered in the ICM's scriptural schools. Funds for individual schools were raised by interested supporters, such as Jane Deborah Moore of Lisburn, who raised funds for the Moyrus mission. She had long been involved in scriptural education in County Down and offered her services to Revd Dallas after hearing him preach on behalf of the ICM in Lisburn in 1851. She communicated by letter with like-minded friends and attracted 6,000 subscribers from the 30,000 invitations issued, enabling the erection of a church, school and parsonage on three acres of land granted by local landlord, Colonel Thompson. Moyrus church, which was 'free from all tractarian taint or form of doctrine', was consecrated in July 1853 when fifty-one converts were confirmed.[7] Clifden and Barnahalia schools were built with monies raised by Miss Dickson; Renvyle, Duholla and Aillebrack were funded by Mrs Marrable; Cleggan by Mr Twining and Miss Beddome, and Lettermore was funded by an anonymous donor.

By March 1851 west Galway had twenty-one congregations with 3,892 regular attendants, and its twenty-nine mission schools were attended by 2,858 children.[8] *The Banner* reported that ICM schools were attended by 'sick and hungry scholars', who were 'fainting from hunger' when relief did not arrive and who preferred to attend mission schools rather than go to the poor house where 'they would have treble the quantity of food for their bodies, but lost that for their souls'.[9] This contradicts Catholic evidence that association with the ICM was facilitated by mission agents going 'from cabin to cabin, and when they find the inmates naked and starved to death, they proffer food and raiment, on the express condition of becoming members of their conventicle'.[10] Contemporary Presbyterian missions in north Mayo, which also distributed relief, were equally certain that Romanism had been overcome, but appreciated the importance of relief. A Presbyterian catechist proclaimed:

> How many children, do you think, we have attending this school? It is scarcely credible, if I had not seen it with my own eyes – no less than two hundred and fifty boys and girls; this is truly amazing, considering this is one of the darkest places in Ireland, where Popery has long reigned undisturbed; I am told there is not one Protestant in all the parish. The meal I have got will not give half of the scholars their breakfast for a week. I visited the school on Friday, and attempted to distribute a very small portion of meal to the most starving, in a house; but the scholars got word round, and in one minute the house was crowded, all crying for a little meal.[11]

Between 1848 and 1877, sixty-four stations were established in west Galway (see figures 3.1 and 3.2), some of which were relatively short-lived while others persisted for decades. In 1851, Thomas Plunket, bishop of Tuam, Killala and Achonry, diverted the income of the vacant deanery of Tuam to west Galway, where he divided the union of Ballinakill into the mission parishes of Ballinakill, Renvyle, Sellerna, Ballyconree, Clifden,

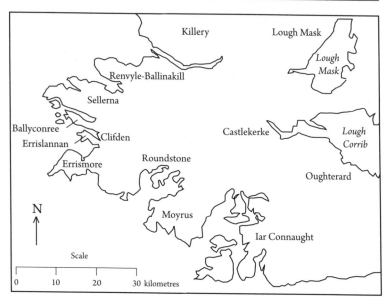

3.1 Missions in Connemara.
Drawn by Miriam Moffitt, 2009.

Errislannan and Errismore.[12] Observing the progress of Protestant mission in his Tuam diocese, Lord Plunket unsuccessfully attempted to extend its influence to his adjoining dioceses of Killala and Achonry and transferred Edward Nangle from Achill to Skreen in April 1852 to consolidate the work of the Second Reformation in the northern section of his territory.

The number of converts confirmed in 1851 provides proof of the ICM's early success, which enabled supporters to optimistically proclaim that 'the district which was so characteristically Romanist, is now characteristically Protestant'.[13] Mission success was measured by convert numbers, of which candidates for confirmation were considered the most reliable (table 3.1). This tactic was standard practice among all missionary organisations; the IS told its supporters that 700 former Catholics were confirmed at Doon and 800 in North Mayo in 1848–49.[14] In 1849 Thomas Plunket confirmed 401 Connemara converts, in 1851 another 727 were 'brought to the knowledge of the truth through the instrumentality of the Society for Irish Church Missions' and in 1852 a further 535 were confirmed.[15] Readers of *The Banner* learned that the bishop of Tuam confirmed 247 converts and 12 original Protestants on his 1853 confirmation tour, consecrating churches at Arran, Aasleagh, Sellerna, Clifden (replacement church), Errislannan, Knappagh, Ballycroy, Bunlahinch and Ballyovie.[16] (Arran and Ballycory churches were founded by the Irish Society.) By then the ICM was confidently

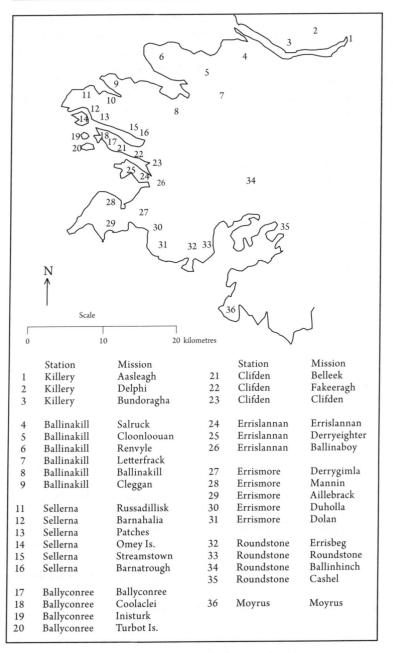

	Station	Mission		Station	Mission
1	Killery	Aasleagh	21	Clifden	Belleek
2	Killery	Delphi	22	Clifden	Fakeeragh
3	Killery	Bundoragha	23	Clifden	Clifden
4	Ballinakill	Salruck	24	Errislannan	Errislannan
5	Ballinakill	Cloonloouan	25	Errislannan	Derryeighter
6	Ballinakill	Renvyle	26	Errislannan	Ballinaboy
7	Ballinakill	Letterfrack			
8	Ballinakill	Ballinakill	27	Errismore	Derrygimla
9	Ballinakill	Cleggan	28	Errismore	Mannin
			29	Errismore	Aillebrack
11	Sellerna	Russadillisk	30	Errismore	Duholla
12	Sellerna	Barnahalia	31	Errismore	Dolan
13	Sellerna	Patches			
14	Sellerna	Omey Is.	32	Roundstone	Errisbeg
15	Sellerna	Streamstown	33	Roundstone	Roundstone
16	Sellerna	Barnatrough	34	Roundstone	Ballinhinch
			35	Roundstone	Cashel
17	Ballyconree	Ballyconree			
18	Ballyconree	Coolaclei	36	Moyrus	Moyrus
19	Ballyconree	Inisturk			
20	Ballyconree	Turbot Is.			

3.2 Mission stations in west Galway, 1848–1937.
Drawn by Miriam Moffitt 2009.

reporting that Connaught had upwards of 10,000 converts with 'hundreds of thousands' of additional enquirers.[17] The earl of Roden promised that the ICM would soon be active throughout the entire country[18] and in 1851 Dallas had even informed London audiences that Ireland was by then 50 per cent Protestant.[19] Many mission opponents disputed the ICM's claimed successes; a Catholic critic later observed how 'in the early souper campaigns, arithmetic was a very weak point with the holy and upright purveyors of Protestantism'.[20]

Table 3.1 Convert confirmations in Connemara, 1851

Mission station	No. confirmed	Mission station	No. confirmed
Castlekerke	34	Salruck	30
Kilmilkin	15	Clifden	66
Cornamona	24	Barnatrough	55
South Corrib	23	Errislannan	11
Glan	9	Ballinaboy	11
Oughterard	49	Derrygimla	76
Inverin	20	Aillebrack	20
Spiddal	6	Duholla	23
Roundstone	21	Moyrus	35
Sellerna, incl. Cleggan, Claddaghduff & Omey	84	Ballyconree	78
		Connemara Orphan's Nursery	37

Source: Thomas Plunket, *Convert confirmations* ... (London, 1851), pp. 11–13.

Mission school pupils were directly and controversially instructed in the scriptures and in the errors of Rome. Bishop Plunket told converts that they had been baptised in a 'corrupt and apostate Church' but had been 'emancipated from the slavery of the Anti-Christ ... into the glorious light of Protestant purity and truth'.[21] Adult meetings were attended by large numbers of 'inquirers', such as the 500 persons observed by John Gregg at Sellerna in 1850,[22] but schoolchildren were seen as crucially important in bringing the message into their homes. They were taught to recite verses of scripture in the Irish language, so that 'by means of the dear little missionaries, the seed was sown broadcast'.[23] In 1853, Revd Ryder of Errismore told of 2,000 mission pupils 'reading the Word of God for their parents and their relatives'.[24] Anti-Catholicism was fostered by ensuring that pupils daily learned one of the 'twenty-four Reasons for leaving the Church of Rome',[25] creating 'little three or four year old converts in the nurseries intensely hating Popery'.[26]

Many of the ICM's early schoolchildren were quickly trained as scripture readers; one traveller observed a class of forty-five trainee readers in Hyacinth D'Arcy's house; in October 1852 the training school was transferred to Dublin.[27] Following the practice of the Irish Society, long-term pupils were employed as 'text teachers' or 'Irish teachers' to work among neighbours; payment was conditional on their attracting eight pupils.[28] In contrast to the Irish Society, these teachers had officially and openly converted to Protestantism.

The immense efforts to alleviate the dreadful destitution of the district are clear from the numerous publications detailing the early years of mission work as poverty compelled many of Connemara's poor to avail of the mission's feeding programme.[29] In January 1851, 9,872 persons were fed in mission schools and an additional sick 433 tended.[30] Clifden's glebe house at Ballyconree was acquired as an orphanage where seventy-eight children were housed in 1851, and in addition several orphans slept in schoolhouses while more were dispersed among converts; Glenowen was soon acquired for a girls' orphanage and a separate infants' nursery was founded.[31] Hyacinth D'Arcy described how he found

> three miserable little children crouched up in the corner ... they begged
> so hard not to be sent away ... we resolved that they should have their ¾d.
> worth of meal a-day and the knowledge of Jesus ... we now have 125 orphans,
> 493 fatherless and 115 motherless; total 733.[32]

The ICM insisted that conversions were won on the basis of doctrinal convictions, a claim contested from the outset by Catholic authorities. Even after famine conditions had abated, considerable long-term benefits attached to conversion, such as housing in mission cottages and employment as Irish teachers, as discussed in chapters 4 and 5.[33] Supporters were reassured that converts, realising the 'errors of Romanism', were drawn to the scriptural truth, such as the young Connemara boy who said 'the priest tells you that you err if you know the scriptures, but Christ tells you that you err not knowing the scriptures', and how another refused to fix his roof during a storm lest he break the Sabbath.[34]

Between 1849 and 1856, additional schools were opened throughout Connemara, so that thirty-six ICM schools or stations were operative by 1856. Churches were built in prominent locations at Ballinakill, Sellerna, Errislannan and Moyrus in the 1850s, strategically placed to ensure easy access by sea, followed in the 1860s by churches at Renvyle, Errismore and Castlekerke and in 1871 by Ballyconree and Omey Island. Stations were arranged in missions, each under the control of a missionary; each station consisted of a school with one or two teachers. Most had at least one scripture reader and others were significantly larger; for example in 1856

Sellerna had a staff of eight: a clergyman, five scripture readers and two teachers.[35] Nangle's Achill mission had published useful textbooks such as the *Irish and English Spelling Book* which taught Irish vocabulary and sample sentences to complete beginners and contained translations of short scriptural extracts and useful sentences: 'Ná bhíodh eagla ort' [Don't be afraid], 'Ba mhaith liom a bheith a caint leat' [I would like to speak to you], 'Is maith an obair Dia a mholadh' [Praising God is good work], 'Labhar leis an duine uasal' [Speak to the gentleman], 'Is cathair alnn [álainn] Lonndon [London is a lovely city].[36]

Following its success in west Galway, the Special Fund for the Spiritual Exigencies of Ireland was officially reconstituted as the Society for Irish Church Missions to the Roman Catholics on 29 March 1849, to 'communicate the Gospel to the Roman Catholics and converts of Ireland by any and every means which may be in accordance with the United Church of England and Ireland'.[37]

Prior to the commencement of a formal ICM presence in Dublin, Fanny Bellingham had organised missionary work among the Catholic population with Revd Charles Fleury via the Dublin Visiting Mission (DVM). By 1850 the DVM was associated with the ICM, with Revd Fleury supervising and training agents at the ICM's Townsend Street premises.[38] In preparation for mission work, Fanny Bellingham had divided the poor parts of Dublin city into 'districts for the labourers' and the richer parts into districts where ladies might gather the necessary funds.[39] Direct mission work began with controversial classes at Bow Street in St Michan's parish in the north inner city; scripture readers invited Catholics to attend schools, classes and services, functioning as a link between the 'teachers and the taught', which was considered essential since 'ignorant Roman Catholics will not go to the well of life for themselves'.[40]

The evangelical movement gained in strength in the early nineteenth century and by the arrival of the ICM in 1849 a large body of influential evangelical clergy existed in Dublin. The dean and chapter of Christ Church Cathedral favoured clergy with a strong evangelical leaning and appointed to parishes in their giving, clergy with a firm commitment to the work of the ICM, of which the most significant were Charles Stanford and William Marrable.[41] By the mid 1850s, the Dublin mission provided an impressive range of services (see table 3.2). After the establishment of a headquarters at Townsend Street in 1849, many of Dublin's leading evangelical clergy became involved with the ICM: Charles Stanford, rector of St Michan's, later of St Thomas'; his curate Charles Fennell McCarthy, ICM Dublin superintendent 1852–77; John Gregg, Trinity church. As editor of the *Christian Examiner*, Charles Stanford was influential in championing the ICM and also wrote its textbook on controversy, which became a nineteenth-century best-seller, indicating the degree of inter-confessional distrust in nineteenth-century Dublin.[42] The book, described as 'the perfect sword, sharp-edged and cutting asunder many a theological knot', sold 13,000 copies between 1854 and 1869, when another 3,000 were printed.[43]

In Dublin as in west Galway, the ICM targeted the very poor and initiated mission work in areas well documented in housing and sanitary reports as being among the most destitute in nineteenth-century Dublin.[44] Its headquarters was located adjacent to the Lock Hospital in Townsend Street, 'one of the strongholds of Satan ... [where] Sin of all kinds abounded'.[45] Agents reported visiting the dying in dark cellars and described the difficulty of discussing religious matters with the poor while 'their poor bodies are in want of the common necessities of life'.[46]

Slum-dwellers were visited in their homes by male scripture readers, who read tracts from the bible and invited the poor to attend at mission lectures and services. The empathy of mission workers for the poor has to be questioned as most came from middle-class families or from farming backgrounds in Connemara, as discussed in the following chapter. A group of wealthy ladies including Mrs Whately (wife of Richard Whately, Protestant archbishop of Dublin, 1832–63) and Mrs Ellen Smyly became closely involved with the ICM's work in Dublin, undertaking the temporal wants of pupils and converts.[47] In 1850 Mrs Smyly established her first Ragged School at Harmony Row, off Grand Canal Street, and later opened others throughout Dublin, followed by residential children's homes.[48]

The role of women as fundraisers, organisers and mission agents deserves some comment. When donor-gender of ICM support was studied, it emerged that funds from male and female donors were equal in value, more females with small donations contrasting with fewer males contributing sizeable amounts. Legacies also divided roughly equally between male and female benefactors. Women were important in terms of raising the profile of the mission. It is evident from the correspondence of Fanny and Mary D'Arcy with mission benefactor, Elizabeth Copley, that long periods of time were expended in writing letters which outlined the necessity of the work and the progress made. As editor of *Erin's Hope*, Sarah Davies devoted her life to publicising the work of the ICM and its children's homes, producing, in later years, four detailed accounts of the mission's child-focused work in Dublin.[49]

The ICM offered females a well-paid career in teaching but at a lower wage than male teachers. Many of its schools were staffed entirely by females at a time when openings for women were limited. While it can be argued that the ICM did not facilitate females to engage in crusading missionary work in the way that Amy Carmichael laboured in the Presbyterian missions

Table 3.2 ICM homes and schools, Dublin, 1850–1900

Begin	End	Location	Description	Comment
1850	1855	St Michan's Schoolroom, Bow St.	Inquiring class & Sunday School	
1852		27 Townsend St.	Sunday Ragged Schools	
1852	pre 1856	Mount Brown	Sunday Ragged Schools	to Luke St
1852	1853	rear of 27 Townsend St.	Girls' and infants' Ragged Schools	
1852		27, later 53, later 167 Townsend St.	Ragged Day School for Boys	
1852		Mission House, Townsend St.	Ragged Boys' School	
1852		Grand Canal St. (corner Grattan St.)	Ragged Boys' School	
1852		Grand Canal St. (corner Grattan St.)	Night School for Boys	
1852		Grand Canal St. (corner Grattan St.)	Sewing class for women	
1853		Mission House, Townsend St.	Licensed for public service	
1853	1857	Weavers Hall, later Skinners Alley	Ragged Boys' School	to Coombe
1853		Lurgan St.	Ragged Schools	
1853	1862	Weavers Hall, later Skinners Alley	Girls' and infants' Ragged Schools	to Coombe
1853	1890	19 Luke St.	Girls' and infants' Ragged Schools	to Rath Row
1853		18 Luke St.	Female Training School	
1856	1856	Oriel St., St Thomas' parish	Sunday School	
1856	1857	Irishtown	Ragged Boys' School	forced to withdraw
1857		Coombe Schools	Ragged Boys' School	
1857		Fishambe St.	Ragged Sunday School	
1858		52 Townsend St.	Boys' Dormitory	
1859		Birds' Nest, 12 York Road, Kingstown	Children's Home	

Begin	End	Location	Description	Comment
1861		Grand Canal St.	Boys' Dormitory	
1861		Luke St.	Girls' Home	
1862		Coombe	Girls' and infants' Ragged Schools	
1868		Coombe	Boys' Home	closed 1922
1870		Luke St.	Girls' Home (a second home)	
1872		167/168/169 Townsend St., later to Bray, later to Charlemont St.	Elliott Home for Waifs and Strays	
1883		168 Townsend St.	Home for Big Lads	
1888		18 Hawkins St.	Helping Hand Home	
1890		Rath Row	Girls' and infants' Ragged Schools	

Compiled in 2005 by Miriam Moffitt from annual published reports of the ICM, Dublin Visiting Mission and Smyly schools and homes, ICM minute books and agency books, modelled on table by J. Prunty in *Margaret Aylward, lady of charity, sister of faith: Margaret Aylward, 1810–1889* (Dublin, 1999), p. 43.

in India, neither did it enable male workers to develop individual spheres of work.[50] By rotating its agents every few years, individual workers were unable to forge permanent links with their target communities. This may have facilitated a conception of an institutional mission but probably curbed the popularity and potential of individual workers. Lay agents, although an integral part of mission work, were totally controlled by their ordained missionary, who in turn received his directions from London. The opportunities offered to individuals in foreign missions were not available within the tightly regulated confines of the ICM.

As an organisation, the ICM was dominated by males and all positions of power relating to mission work belonged to men. Female involvement was confined to the nurturing or child-focused aspect of the work; its orphanages were mostly administered by middle- and upper-middle-class women. Women's influence, which was considerable, was nurtured through the monthly publication, *Erin's Hope*, which romantically described the lives of children saved from the dual affliction of popery and destitution. By giving names and personal information of individual children, *Erin's Hope* promoted an intimate connection between supporters and the work of the mission, in contrast to the *Banner of the Truth* whose content was more didactic in nature. Although separate committees ran individual schools, the same persons sat on many committees. Mrs Whately raised funds for the Mission Church in 1853 while her daughter sourced the funds for Townsend Street Ragged School.[51] These homes and schools undoubtedly rescued children from the most terrible poverty. They functioned as a unit with children transferred between homes; some catered for younger children while the 'Helping Hand' home in the Coombe catered exclusively for older boys, where they grew 'accustomed to the habits of civilised life'.[52] There is no evidence to suggest that any distinction was made between spiritual, educational and relief programmes of the homes and schools. Margaret Preston has observed how 'Smyly's proselytising was made clear throughout her records and overshadowed her benevolence' and argues that the blatant agenda of the homes inflamed sectarian tensions.[53] This frequently resulted in violence, as when a mob of 3,000 persons attacked the Coombe mission schools.[54]

The ICM employed a variety of methods to disseminate its message to Roman Catholics: handbills and placards; house-to-house visiting; wayside conversations; controversial classes; discussion lectures; day, evening and Sunday schools; homes for destitute children, and church services. In 1852, mission agents made 33,980 home visits.[55] Controversial classes and sermons caused particular offence to Catholics as by nature they criticised long-held traditions and beliefs, such as Revd Ryder's sermon on the invocation of saints.[56] The ICM circulated a list of topics for discussion in advance of meetings.[57] In 1850 approximately 10,000 handbills advertising sermons and controversial classes were distributed weekly in Dublin, and were also printed in the daily newspapers and on placards displayed throughout the city.[58] The subject matter of the ICM's sermons, as identified in a collection of over 400 handbills, demonstrates its confrontational approach or 'active missionary efforts of an aggressive character'.[59] Catholic opposition was quickly aroused and organised and the animosity experienced by the mission is clear from the two entrances to the Mission Church in Townsend Street, one through the Mission House and another less visible entrance through Rath Row, 'for the Nicodemuses who came in secret … shivering poor ones who clustered round the stove … hearing the good news of a home prepared in heaven even for them'.[60] The mission quickly grew to the stage where Dublin's nine municipal wards were systematically covered by agents. As in west Galway, success was estimated by attendance at mission schools and services and great progress was reported in the ICM's annual reports and in the separate reports of the DVM. Table 3.3 shows that the ICM employed over 500 agents within five years after its inception.

Table 3.3 ICM agents, schools, scholars and income, 1849–54

Year	Missions	Clergy	Agents	Total	Schools	Scholars	Income (£)
1849	11	14	97	111	29	2110	4674
1850	18	13	141	154	39	2532	6285
1851	23	30	257	287	69	2941	12689
1852	33	44	359	403	81	3572	28962
1853	44	59	487	546	98	4962	37183
1854	41	56	462	518	112	6982	40039

Source: Anonymous, *What are the Irish Church Missions?* (London, 1855), p. 8; ICM, *Annual reports*, 1850–1854

As well as managing its west Galway and Dublin missions directly, the ICM funded 'Local Committees for Missions' where the support of ten clergymen in adjacent parishes was ensured. In these missions, two clergymen toured the district while the remaining eight took care of parish work. The increase in local committees from eleven in 1850 to forty-four in 1853 confirms the substantial support given to the movement by Irish clergy, especially for the duration of the merger with the Irish Society (1853–56), as by 1853 the ICM was active in twenty-seven out of thirty-two counties.[61]

The marketing of mission

The poisoned charm that long had cast
Its deadly spell around
Now link by link is yielding fast
To the Gospel's magic sound.[62]

The Irish Church Mission marketed its missionary operation to the Protestants of England on three key premises: firstly, that Ireland was in dire need of scriptural religion and that its Catholic population eagerly sought access to the bible; secondly, that the errors of Rome were likely to further encroach on England, and, thirdly, that social, political and cultural benefits would accrue to Ireland, and more importantly to England, if the conversion of Ireland were effected. By consciously and subconsciously answering combinations of the above needs, the ICM was able to enlist a considerable degree of support, especially in its first decade of operation. The mission made use of the contemporary movements of the mid nineteenth century to influence its target audience: anti-Catholicism, romanticism, millenarianism and the evangelical philanthropic impulse.

The production of serial and occasional publications was a cheap and effective means of communicating directly with its supporters. The publication of its own annual reports (from 1850) and its monthly magazines *The Banner of the Truth* (1850) and *Erin's Hope* (1853) ensured a regular outflow of positive publicity. In addition, in the early 1850s, approximately every three months, the mission produced 'Occasional Papers', detailing its operations and appealing for funds. Very soon after its inception, the origins and objectives of the society were outlined in full in Alexander Dallas' *Castelkerke* and William Marrable's *Sketch of the origin and operations of the Society for Irish Church Missions to the Roman Catholics*.[63] The latter work included a description of the entire missionary operation of the early 1850s, an itinerary for visiting the missions and a section on 'the duty of Englishmen towards Ireland', concluding with a strongly worded appeal for funds.

The ICM also publicised its work by directly encouraging supporters to visit the missions and to report publicly its advances on Romanism since 'Every traveller, convinced of the reality of the work, becomes an important witness'.[64] One such mission tourist was Robert Backhouse Peacocke who, 'finding them to exceed all he had been led to anticipate ... [decided] carefully to record what he heard and saw'.[65] The invariable content of these tour accounts demonstrated that Ireland was wild, demoralised and outside the realms of civilisation, with a population hungering and thirsting for a free Gospel, having lost all respect for the priests and popish practices, coming in their tens of thousands out of the darkness of enslaving Romanism into the liberation and light of the pure Protestant truth.

Six editions of the mission's own publication *Early fruits of Irish missions* were printed between 1850 and 1852, and in 1860 the ICM published *A mission tour book in Ireland* (London, 1860), which proposed itineraries and cautioned against speaking to local Roman Catholics. One such visitor, John Garrett, outlined in detail the answers given to him by his Connemara car-man, who told of 'relief given in the time of the famine' and that the poor were 'ready to listen so long as money was being spent' and that 'the whole movement is a very doubtful one'.[66] In retrospect, the car-man seems to have accurately analysed the situation. Garrett, however, stressed to his readers that opinions from such sources were not to be trusted.

Sales of *The Banner* and *Erin's Hope* ensured increased publicity of a positive nature while their profits further buttressed fund-raising efforts. Numerous individual accounts of mission tours were privately published, generally as pamphlets. An analysis of these shows the decreasing interest of the mainstream public in the ICM's work from the mid 1850s, with little publicity emanating from outside the mission.[67] The launch of the West Connaught Church Endowment Society resulted in a temporary increase in the output of mission literature in 1860–64. It can be argued that, in the light of declining publicity, *The story of the Irish Church Missions, parts 1 and 2* were published in 1867 and 1875 to keep the cause in the public eye.

In the 1850s, the ICM ensured that its operations were reported in contemporary newspapers such as the *Dublin Christian Examiner, The Times* (London), *The Standard, The Warder, The Record* and *The Rock*.[68] The content of provincial papers clearly shows considerable mission support among the Protestants of the west of Ireland.[69] The tone of the newly founded *Galway Express* (1853), which was 'devoted to the maintenance of Protestantism and to the advancement of the commercial, agricultural and trading interests of Ireland', is noteworthy.[70] In its first two years, it was vehemently anti-Catholic, devoting large sections of the paper to doctrinal argument which repeatedly outlined the 'errors of Romanism', as in the reputed conversation between an Anglican minister and a Catholic priest published on 3 September 1853. By 1855, while remaining decidedly Protestant, unionist and conservative, content was dominated by secular news such as the Crimean war, parliamentary debates and agricultural advice. It continued to mention ICM events such as meetings and controversial lectures, but with less enthusiasm than formerly.

Just as local newspapers copied articles from national newspapers, as when the *Connaught Watchman* reprinted 'Reformation in the West' from the London *Times*,[71] national newspapers relied on local reporting of persecutions endured by converts. Reproductions of lengthy extracts of annual reports in the national media ensured that the general public heard of successes, such as when readers of *The Times* (London) read in 1863 that 30,000 Irish Catholics had converted during the previous two years.[72] Irish supporters were sometimes informed of mission activities via a circuitous route. The *Ballina Chronicle* of 12 December 1849 reported an ICM meeting in Exeter Hall, London, where it was announced that the bishop of Tuam had confirmed over 400 Connemara converts.

It was vital for the success of the ICM that the English public be convinced of the need in Ireland for scriptural religion. To that end, the mission maintained that the errors of Rome needed to be clearly and frequently outlined. Supporters were assured that theirs was the only truth since 'We stamp as error ... we know no path of life but the strait [sic] and narrow way'.[73] Catholicism was described as 'a nominal church, utterly apostate ... willing to keep her children without the True Christ and without hope',[74] and elsewhere supporters learned that Romanism in Ireland was a 'strange mixture of the *horrible* and the *ludicrous*'.[75] Dublin clergyman, William Marrable, described Catholicism as using 'Holy wafers, ashes, oil, candles, spittle, beads, crucifixes and pictures'; to this list he added charms, scapulars and holy wells. Devotions of this type were blamed for the prevalence of 'murder, drunkenness, idleness, Sabbath-breaking and excesses of every kind'.[76] English children learned how ignorant Irish children described the bible as 'the jumper's book ... the devil's book'[77] and the idolatrous veneration of saints and images was outlined to supporters as in figure 3.3 where a monk was shown forcing a pupil to worship a holy picture.

The ICM cause benefited greatly from the publicity of the mid-nineteenth-century pan-Protestant missions to Catholics which also reinforced the Irish need of the scriptures in the mind of the mainstream British public.[78] James Taylor's account of Presbyterian missions warned that 'Popery would perpetuate its dark reign' and the publications of the Scottish Reformation Society remonstrated Protestants who were blind to the danger.[79] Missions to Irish Catholics in London and Scotland similarly generated a large volume of material to interest English Protestants in the conversion of Romanists, urging them to use 'all scriptural means to expose and arrest the progress of this gigantic evil'.[80]

ICM supporters were told that the English were 'responsible for having forced papal despotism on Ireland' in the twelfth century and therefore had a duty to bring Irish Catholics to the scriptural truth.[81] The responsibility of converting Irish Catholics was placed on the shoulders of the English public, since 'millions of our countrymen, within a day's journey of most of our homes, are in the depths of the darkness ... in all the unchecked evil of hereditary corruption'.[82] The famine, perceived as a punishment from God, afforded the English an unprecedented opportunity to evangelise

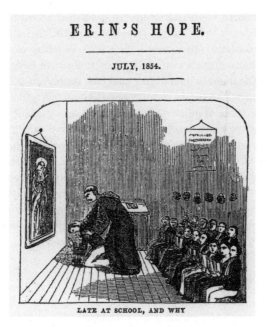

3.3 'Late at school, and why';
Catholicism as portrayed in *Erin's Hope*, July 1854.

the Irish as 'the scourge of God had done its work ... and those who have
been for so long fast bound by priestly tyranny, and whose spirits have been
crushed under the yoke of ignorance and superstition, are beginning to be
set free'.[83]

The impression given in *The Banner* and in other ICM publications
is that the ideology of conversion, the justification of the cause and the
perpetuation of anti-Catholic feeling were more important than actual
mission work and especially more important than the experiences of the
convert community. The following is typical of the pronouncements of the
ICM: 'The fact that the officers of the Society are being brought into close
contact with such a masterpiece of Satan as Popery, seems to induce in them
the zeal and faithfulness of men in earnest.'[84]

By repeatedly outlining to an English audience the need to rescue Irish
Catholics from the errors of Rome, the ICM successfully mobilised a large
body of supporters, most of whom merely donated money or organised
collections. Those more dedicated visited Dublin and Connemara and
recorded their observations. Writers of mission tours told and retold the
same story of the origin of the ICM, taken from Dallas' or Marrable's works.
Since success was measured in terms of convert numbers, attendances at

school and church featured strongly in published accounts of mission tours, with tales of the 'steady increase of converts',[85] invariably backed up with actual numbers present at various stations, telling of schools filled with eager children, such as those seen by the earl of Roden in 1852.[86] Continuing the trend of quantifying converts, supporters learned that by 1855 the mission had grown to forty-one stations and 6,982 pupils.[87]

A frequent tactic of mission writers was the reproduction of 'supposed conversations' in which former Irish Catholics were shown as fervently attached to personal reading of the scriptures: 'no reports ... can convey an adequate idea of the eager manner in which the Irish Romanists *drink in* and feed upon Scripture truth ...'[88] A typical example, reported to have taken place between a Clifden priest and a mission pupil, demonstrates how the hold of the Catholic clergy on their flock was supposedly weakened by the arrival of the ICM. It was reported that this interaction concluded with 'Little Mickey' being physically attacked by the curate.

Father Ned	You are a jumper.
Little Mickey	Yes, I am, Sir.
Father Ned	You are going to hell, then.
Little Mickey	No, I am not, Sir, for the blood of Jesus Christ, his Son, cleanseth us from all sin.
Father Ned	You learned that in that wicked book of yours, the Bible.
Little Mickey	It is not wicked, it is God's own book.
Father Ned	It is wicked, and anyone who reads it will be lost.
Little Mickey	Well then, I am not ashamed of the Gospel of Christ, for it is the power of God unto salvation to everyone who believeth.[89]

Catholic responses to the mission's continuous imaginary dialogues of persons who 'seemed seriously impressed' and 'earnestly seeking' were unsurprisingly sceptical. Patrick Murray, Professor of Theology at Maynooth 1838–82, accurately described the literary skills of 'these clumsy fabricators' who put into the mouths of uneducated Catholics 'words and phrases, with which the aforesaid Catholics are just as familiar with as they are with the technical terms of scholastic theology ...'[90] Catholic opponents of the ICM also used unlikely language and reported supposed conversations where Protestants were defeated in theological argument, such as in *David and Goliath* where a Catholic hedge-school pupil engaged four determined Protestants in sophisticated doctrinal argument and eventually claimed success to the incredible extent that the pamphlet ended with all four praying to the 'Illustrious Queen of Grace and Majesty' and reciting the Hail Mary.[91]

In the mission's reproductions of supposed conversations, converts and pupils at mission schools were generally shown to be intelligent and capable of successful argument with mission opponents, especially with Catholic clergy.[92] In contrast, Irish adults were frequently shown as being of lower intellect; their western accents and use of English were scoffingly related; one adult explained the word mortal as 'Asy kilt' [easily killed].[93] Converts and Catholics alike were quoted verbatim, the use of phonetic spelling conveying authenticity and simplicity to mission reports. Mrs Dallas told of a respectable convert-farmer near Lough Corrib in the 1860s who told her, 'sure and didn't I learn the Gospel from ye when ye preached at the Glan Schoolhouse some twenty years back; and my cabin was over the mountain yonder'[94] and a convert's perception of the arrival of nuns in Clifden was described: 'didn't I see one of them goin' up to the Convint [sic] with the priest, and she had a white piece across her forehead ... there was big min [sic] and women, as well as girls and gossoons, thryin to see what ailed her face'.[95] The sophisticated language placed in the mouths of Connemara Irish-speaking peasants prompts questions about the veracity of mission reports, such as the account of the death of the illiterate Irish-speaking Errismore convert detailed in chapter 5.

The social improvement wrought by the mission was greatly emphasised and much use was made of the appeal of 'cleanly and nice looking children ... rescued from the depths of Roman superstition and darkness, singing so sweetly the praises of their great Deliverer'.[96] This image was bolstered by the publication of hymns and addresses, reputedly sung by children or converts in which their love of the bible was contrasted to their previous existence in darkness and error, as in the following two stanzas from 'Welcome to Mr Dallas' which told how 'dark popery ruled ... in slavery's chains'. Accounts of performance of such addresses were relayed to supporters; in this instance a copy was sent to the English benefactor, Elizabeth Copley, telling her it 'drew tears from the eyes of many present', reinforcing the idea of a mission district filled with loyal British subjects.[97]

II

As the pillar of cloud guided Israel by day
So God in His mercy directed your way;
To the land where oppression and slavery reigned
As the name of the Saviour was loudly profaned.

III

Dark popery ruled and our souls did remain
The victims of woe bound in slavery's chains;
And Ireland lay passive while her birthright was gone
None caring for souls though Christ died to atone.

Omey islanders were similarly portrayed as having broken free from the control of the priests, singing 'their favourite' hymn, which stated that 'And never more shall priest of Rome / Beguile us with a lie / For every Omey Islander / Can know the reason why!'[98] Another address to Revd Dallas told of how the Irish had formerly been taught to hate and fear the English, but now welcomed them to Ireland: 'Welcome to the Saxons here / Whom once we learned to hate and fear / But now a free and happy band / We love and bless their noble land'.[99] This publication included four lengthy addresses to Mr Dallas and concluded that 'The feelings expressed in these verses are not beyond those which fill the hearts, and bind them, not to Mr Dallas alone, but to the Saxon and the Protestant, of whom he is the only representative known and loved by them.' By placing verse of this unlikely nature in the mouths of Irish-speaking Connemara children, and by portraying them as now welcoming the Saxon whom 'once we learned to hate and fear', the ICM promised to its English audience an ability to effect ideological and political change.

Increased love of England was frequently related as a by-product of religious conversion, for example supporters were assured that 'Converts from Rome look on them as their dearest friends ... though once they were taught to hate them by the priests of Rome.'[100] Loyalty to the crown was fostered among children in ICM homes; the queen's birthday was celebrated with tea and cake in Ballyconree orphanage.[101] The civilising impact of mission work and the dissemination of English were emphasised,[102] while tour-books told how the Castlekerke clergyman called upon the children for their usual 'Three cheers for the Queen!'[103] Folklore evidence confirms the colonising aspect of mission work, telling how ICM teachers gave instruction on manners and customs: 'Bhíodh múinteoir acu ansin a'léigheamh na mBíobla dóibh agus a'thabhairt teagaisc dóibh ina mbéarraí is ina nósanna féin' [There was a teacher there reading the bible to them and giving advice on his own type of manners and habits.][104]

'Basking in the sunshine of divine favour', England attributed its commercial prosperity to its adoption of the Protestant faith and considered that all Ireland's problems could be solved if the ICM were successful.[105] Mission publications placed great emphasis on the social improvement expected, contrasting industrious Protestants with drinking, gambling Romanists: 'Wherever you find a band of converts, you find a band of well ordered, industrious and peaceable subjects.'[106] Readers were constantly told of the civilising effect of the ICM; one tourist told how his party 'met a group of lads, generally attended by a Scripture Reader ... all clean and intelligent looking. "Jumpers of course?' we asked the driver. "They are, yer Annur [your honour] – going to the Monthly Meeting in Clifden"'.[107] Elsewhere readers learned that 'the change in character evinced in the peaceable demeanour of the converts is in striking contrast to their former conduct'[108] and that Castlekerke and Kilmilkin converts were 'young men, clean, respectable, and Protestantised, with an upright manly bearing, quite different from their appearance in 1845 and from the Roman Catholics around'.[109]

In addition to social improvement, it was reported that political gain would follow the conversion of Ireland. The mission played on the fear that Protestants might suffer at the hands of the numerically superior Catholics. Dallas repeated stories of the 1798 rebellion heard in his childhood, telling London audiences of the 'massacre of the Protestants of Ireland, ... planned and plotted for two years at least ... when the Papists rose up and slew the Protestants wherever they found them ...'[110] The Catholic practice of confession and absolution was condemned since 'the easy rate at which absolution may be procured, either before or after commission of the said act, accounts for its operation upon the ignorant and superstitious'.[111] Speaking at the annual meeting in 1852, John Colquhoun outlined the political danger posed by Irish Catholic priests:

> I bid you to remember what it is to have men calling themselves 'Priests of God' exercising this power ... against law, against institutions, against the connexion between Ireland and England, against all that makes us safe.[112]

There is much evidence that the language of the ICM was heavily influenced by the romantic movement. Dallas was a cousin of Lord Byron; Dallas' father had written extensively on the poet and Dallas himself edited the three-volume work, *Correspondence of Lord Byron, with a friend*, which was, in fact, the correspondence between Lord Byron and Dallas' father.[113] Queen Victoria's acquisition of Balmoral in the Scottish highlands in 1847 reinforced the romantic appeal of dramatic rural landscapes. The integrity of 'mountain-men' was praised by Prince Albert, who admired the 'honesty and sympathy which distinguished the inhabitants of mountainous countries'.[114] The essence of romanticism, the valuing of feeling above calculation, is to be found in the emotive deathbed scenes of converts who remain true to the Protestant faith, as in the dying Connemara orphan who said, 'I am not crying for I know Jesus; and if you knew him you would not cry ... I long to be with Jesus.'[115]

Compilers of mission-tour accounts employed emotive language to capture the drama of Connemara's landscape, where the light of the Gospel was repeatedly contrasted with the darkness both of the district and of Romanism. Dallas told a Clifden audience how converts were 'turned from darkness to light and from the power of Satan to God',[116] and comments such as 'especially does the lonely grandeur of the hills powerfully affect the meditative mind'[117] were frequently encountered.

The Banner told its readers how mission tourists were astounded by the 'wild beauty' of west Galway and, on witnessing the packed schoolrooms and large convert congregations in a district which had until recently been 'sunk in the grossest darkness', were inspired to exclaim 'What hath God wrought!'[118] Supporters learned that Castlekerke was 'almost a Killarney in miniature'[119] and Wordsworth's 'Daffodils' springs to mind when reading the following:

> There, as in solitude and shade, I wander
> Through the green isles, or rest upon the sod,
> Awed by the silence, I reverently ponder
> THE WAYS OF GOD.[120]

Lithographs in published accounts of mission tours portrayed idyllic rural scenes, such as the 'Examination at Castlekerke School' (see figure 3.4), which depicts an orderly group of children, girls in clean white pinafores, hands joined in fervent prayer, standing at a lakeside, against a backdrop of a nearby wooded hill and faraway forbidding mountains. Urban missions were depicted in equally romantic terms, the Coombe Ragged School was described as 'a candle set up on a candlestick; its light shines around, and penetrates into very dark places'.[121]

Millenarianism was another contemporary movement which greatly influenced the ICM's principal founders and early supporters. It was Dallas' interest in the conversion of Jews which had originally brought him to Ireland and most clerical members in the early years had associations with societies such as the Mission to the Jews. Supporters, many of whom held premillenial convictions, held that the Second Coming was imminent, as regularly outlined in Dallas' lectures and writings, which told that 'The time is perhaps close at hand, when the blast of the ram's horn, divinely placed at the lips of the Lord's people shall be heard, and then ... by the power of God, this wall of Jericho, this high wall of Romanism, shall fall flat down; and great will be the fall thereof!'[122]

The ICM used its publications to promote a sense of urgency around the Second Coming. Revd James Mecredy, missionary at Inverin, reported in 1860: 'Therefore when I look abroad or at home, I see evident signs that a movement is going on, whose tendency is the destruction of the Anti-Christ.'[123] A sense of urgency and a need to immediately eradicate Catholicism are evident from ICM publications. For instance, when seeking funds to open a school at Barnahalia in Connemara, *The Banner* reported that there was a danger of Jesuits opening a school there.[124] Supporters were repeatedly told that were it not for lack of resources, Catholicism could be eliminated in Ireland. In 1851 Dallas told supporters that Ireland had 'a majority of Protestants in Ireland at this time: – include the half

3.4 Examination at Castlekerke School.
Source: Earl of Roden, *Progress of the Reformation in Ireland*
(2nd edn, London, 1852), p. 68.

million [in workhouses] and the majority would barely be on the side of the Romanists'.[125] The mission persistently claimed that one final drive would tip the balance and from then the conversion of Ireland would be unstoppable and, over the following decades, supporters were assured that a large portion of the Catholic population of Ireland was on the brink of conversion.[126]

The mission appealed to the philanthropic impulse of Victorian England, correctly telling how thousands were kept alive by mission relief in Dublin and Connemara in the famine years and early 1850s. A series of *Stories about the mission work in Ireland* outlined in emotive language the plight of orphans and the mission's efforts to provide each child with 'two meals of stirabout a day'.[127] On the back covers of these pamphlets was written 'Subscriptions in aid of the Food for the Schools will be gratefully received by Mrs [Fanny] D'Arcy, Clifden, Connemara or Miss [Sarah] Davies, 13 Merrion-Square North, Dublin.'[128] Publicity was given to the ICM's work by other Protestant societies, such as the Scottish Association who wrote

> Besides these 78 orphans [in the orphanage] there are, connected with the Connemara schools, 120 more. These poor things are supported on ½ lb. of stirabout given in school, with an additional ½ lb. In nearly all the schoolhouses, three or four of these forlorn ones sleep on the floor, others are dispersed among the converts, to whom a trifle is paid for sheltering

them; and, in many instances, the unbought compassion of their neighbours provides them a home.[129]

Even after the extreme destitution of the famine years had passed, the mission appealed to the charitable nature of the English to provide essential relief. A letter from Revd Ryder of Errismore in *Erin's Hope* told of a little girl who couldn't attend school until she had been given clothes.[130] In later years, the tone of *Erin's Hope* became almost totally philanthropic, appealing to charitable rather than religious motivations.

Recruitment and deployment of mission agents

In its early days, the ICM depended on personnel trained in the existing missions of Achill and Dingle[131] or recruited from the wider Protestant community.[132] In the 1850s many of its clergymen were converts: William Kilbride of Derrygimla (trained in Achill), John Conerney of Moyrus (1855–74) and Sellerna (1874–85), Roderick Ryder of Ballyconree (1851–52) and Errismore (1852–85), and William Kennedy of Castlekerke, Bunlahinch and Dublin were all converts from Rome, as was the convert-priest, William Burke, who had previously 'paralysed a proselytising effort in County Clare'.[133] Many non-convert clergymen had spent time in missionary districts: both Joseph Duncan of Ballinakill and Charles Seymour of Tuam had formerly worked in Achill.[134]

Many clergy had been educated in the Irish Missionary College at Ballinasloe,[135] founded by Revd James Lancaster, secretary of the Connaught Auxiliary of the Irish Society, to train clergymen in the Irish language.[136] When John Gregg visited in 1850, he found seventeen pupils learning Irish to enable them to preach in Irish-speaking districts.[137] According to Patrick Egan, it closed long before the end of the nineteenth century.[138] Biographical details of original Protestant mission agents are elusive as few memoirs have been identified.[139] Those located indicate ultra-Protestant tendencies, such as the Ulsterman, Clarke, schoolteacher at Oughterard, who treasured a picture of King William crossing the Boyne which had been in his family for generations, and R. Steele, an Ulster Baptist, who observed that 'As Christians we saw enough of Popery in Ireland to make us detest it, and pity its victims'.[140] Although a dissenter, Steele was invited to work for the ICM in Connemara but soon left the Society to teach in England. Richard Hobson from Hacketstown, County Carlow became interested in the ICM after reading in the *Carlow Sentinel* of beatings suffered by readers and spent eleven years working as scripture reader in Louth and North-Eastern mission. Hobson's sister, Caroline entered the ICM Female Training School in 1862, and taught in Galway from 1864 to 1867.[141]

Soon after Castlekerke and Connemara missions became established, converts were trained as mission agents, their fluency in Irish being an important asset. For example Dallas described the conversion of Walter Griffin of Glan soon after the opening of Castlekerke; by 1850 Walter's occupation was 'scripture reader'.[142] In 1852 a bilingual convert had replaced the Ulsterman Clarke at Oughterard and mission teacher, Daniel Gibbons has been identified as Spiddal's first convert.[143] Many mission tourists commented on the youthfulness of agents, mostly 'young people belonging to the schools, – their ages varied from 10 years to 20'.[144]

Little direct evidence exists to detail the role of female agents. In fact, interaction with individual agents of either sex is limited as our knowledge is obscured by the layering of religious and cultural ideologies on the descriptions of actual missionary experience. Figure 4.1 demonstrates that mission workers formed a self-contained community, as outlined in the following chapter. While most foreign missions preferred to dispatch married couples to faraway lands, the majority of ICM agents were young and single when recruited and subsequently married fellow workers. These mission-couples formed the backbone of the ICM's work, especially in Connemara; some had adopted the Protestant faith prior to the establishment of the ICM, others were converted through its efforts. They clearly were concerned for the welfare of their pupils, temporal as well as spiritual, and were obviously moved by the poverty of the district.

The married couple Pat Cafferkey and Honor MacHale, converts of Nangle's Achill mission, provide an example of agents from a previous missionary community. These transfered from Achill to Connemara in 1858, taught at Moyrus 1858–67, Streamstown 1867, Barnatrough 1868–74, Ballinahinch 1874–77 and Moyrus until Honor's death in 1894 and Pat's in 1901.[145] This practice of rotating married couples throughout the mission network was common, especially in west Galway. Until the 1890s, women were only employed as teachers, whereas men could alternate between teaching and scripture reading according to need; after 1890 women could serve as bible women. On the death of a spouse, it was common for the remaining person to continue in ICM employment, irrespective of whether husband or wife died first, as in the case of the above Cafferkeys and of Mrs Hawkshaw, whose husband Charles died in 1868, after which Mrs Hawkshaw taught in Ballinaboy, Letterfrack, Fakeragh, Cleggan and Renvyle until she died in 1878 at the age of eighty-three. This involved moving residence about every two years, which must have been quite distressing for an elderly woman.[146]

From an early date many converts were trained as scripture readers and teachers; many, like Tom Nee and Tim Cleshan, were subsequently ordained as missionary clergymen. Tom Nee entered the Training School in 1856 and, with his teacher-wife Maria, rotated round the Connemara

3.5 Ballyconree mission school,
where Thomas and Maria Nee taught from 1868 to 1870.
Source: ICM Archive, Magic Lantern Slide.

missions from 1858 to 1870, after which he was appointed Instructor at the Male Training School in Dublin, and Inspector of Schools in 1875. From his ordination in 1886 until his death in 1919 he served as the missionary at Errismore in Connemara. Alannah Heather unkindly referred to the elderly Thomas Nee as the 'senile old rector of eighty-six ... [who] sometimes brought with him his much younger wife, who had been a school-teacher'.[147] Revd Ryder's account of Errismore mission in *The Banner* described a 'most active and zealous' Dublin agent, whose father had died during the famine and who had attended Derrygimla school. This person has been identified as Tim Clesham from Mannin in Errismore mission. He moved to Glasgow with another ICM agent to work among the Irish, was later ordained and ministered at Aasleagh from 1874 until his death in 1894. A Catholic clergyman reportedly observed that 'no one knows the great extent of the harm he has done to the faith'.[148]

Opposition to the activities of the Irish Church Missions

From its inception, the Irish Church Missions provoked opposition from the Catholic church as its aggressive stance was deliberately confrontational. Its public denouncement of the errors of Rome and its exposures of Catholic superstition not surprisingly led to equally public counter-attacks.

This struggle for the souls of the poor was fought out on the battleground of tenement-streets and in the media at local, national and international levels. Catholic forces attempted to influence their more educated co-religionists with a propaganda war of sermons and countless polemic productions in both the public and private media, while simultaneously targeting the underprivileged with increased parochial visiting and alternative sources of education and relief. The ICM's indisputable early successes understandably caused great anxiety in the Roman Catholic church, which mounted a disjointed defence.

The nineteenth-century Irish Catholic church was legally hampered from providing for its poor so that organised Catholic philanthropy was in its infancy in Ireland when the ICM was founded. Penal laws forbade the endowment of Catholic charities (9 Geo.2.c.3), which was partially relieved by Catholic emancipation in 1829. In 1832 Catholics were permitted to grant lands for the building of churches and schools (2&3 Will.4.c.115) but it was only in 1860 that Catholic charities were freed from legal restrictions.[149] Consequently Irish Catholicism was hindered by acts of parliament from providing for its poor or from organising philanthropic and educational alternatives to the ICM for more than ten years after the foundation of the mission.[150]

The explosion of Protestant mission in foreign countries in the early nineteenth century was condemned by the Roman congregation responsible for Catholic missions, *Propaganda Fide*: 'The biblical societies are sewing [sic] error all over the globe … We have come to understand everywhere the need to oppose the gigantic efforts of the Protestant Bible society …'[151] The establishment of similar missions in Catholic Ireland triggered a vigorous response as the attention of the Catholic hierarchy was drawn to the movement's undeniable advances. In 1848 Peter FitzMaurice, parish priest of Clifden, wrote to Daniel Murray, archbishop of Dublin (1823–52) that

> Proselytism was never so rampant as now. There is a staff of nineteen peripatetic Bible readers (or jumpers) under the command of a bankrupt landlord of Clifden doing all the mischief in their power. The funds of the British Association are perverted to their unholy purpose, viz. the changing of bad Catholics, and of course worse Christians, into good hypocrites.[152]

One ICM supporter observed how its success had 'already filled the hearts of the priests of the Church of Rome with fear and anxiety'.[153] Correspondence between Daniel Murray and the renowned English convert, Henry Wilberforce, proves that the Irish hierarchy was intensely concerned about proselytism in Connaught. An editorial in *The Nation* entitled 'Proselytism – the Church by "soup" established' told how the west of Ireland was 'deserting the ancient fold' and that a class of Protestants 'more bigoted and anti-Irish ... [was] growing up from the recreant peasantry'.[154] It soon became evident that an especial threat was posed to Catholicism in Dublin, where the work of proselytising societies, of which the ICM was the most aggressive, was well established during the bishopric of Daniel Murray. In 1851, even before his elevation to the see of Dublin, Paul Cullen (archbishop of Armagh 1850–52, archbishop of Dublin and Primate 1852–74) was aware of the extent of the problem, writing that in Dublin 'The number of proselytising schools is prodigious ... seventy or eighty in Dr Murray's own parish, and in St Michan's',[155] and a Dublin priest recorded that '"I understand there are no fewer than three thousand of our poor children already in their schools", says one priest to another. "Three thousand indeed!" responded his friend, "double the number and you will be nearer the truth"'.[156] Nationalist and Catholic newspapers detailed the growth and potential danger of the ICM, reporting that

> agents of that foul and abominable traffic are every day opening new schools of perversion, and are founding new churches for the accommodation of their purchased congregations ... Shall the soupers and tract-distributors accomplish the work which all the force of England, for three hundred years has been unable to effect? [157]

> Its agents and emissaries, from the great organiser Parson Dallas, and the wealthy fanatics of Exeter Hall, down to the meanest Bible-reader in Connaught, are continually at work; and God only knows all the evil they have wrought. But it is full time at least to cease ignoring such a malady. It is full time – and God knows there is good cause – to preach a crusade against it ... We repeat, that it is not Tuam, nor Cashel, nor Armagh that are the chief seats of successful proselytism, but this very city in which we live [Dublin].[158]

The *Freeman's Journal* denounced the duality of proselytism and relief, asserting that there was 'something particularly revolting to a manly mind in seeing men hired to go into the hovels of famine and misery, and with a Bible in one hand and a soup-ticket in the other, holding out the alternative of death'.[159]

The Catholic church had considerable experience in refuting exaggerated claims of mission success elsewhere in Ireland[160] and, although aware that the ICM laboured aggressively among its very poor, Catholic authorities quickly contradicted the mission's claims of vast attendances at mission schools. In one Dublin parish of 50,000 persons where the ICM claimed attendances of up to 6,000, Catholic clergy insisted that only 150 children were *in situ*, whose parents 'in the extremities of their distress, permitted their famishing offspring to enter such schools for a time' and Catholic curates in the very poorest localities reported their 'utter ignorance of those multitudes said to be in attendance at schools dangerous to religion'.[161]

Connemara's Catholic clergy fought an incessant war against the activities of the ICM.[162] From the beginning, they refuted the enormous successes claimed by the mission, as in a letter from Archbishop John MacHale in the *Freeman's Journal* of 8 December 1849. Although the ICM could accurately claim enormous success in its early years, converts began to revert once the extreme famine conditions had passed; from the early 1850s priests reported the return of 'many of these deluded creatures during the past two years ... especially when they entertain fears of their last end drawing near'.[163]

In spite of such scepticism at the ICM's claimed successes, the Catholic church waged an aggressive multi-pronged counter-missionary campaign against proselytism. The Catholic hierarchy presented a united front against proselytism although it was divided on issues such as national education and tenant rights; in 1847 it sent a memorial to the Lord Lieutenant regarding proselytism.[164] In their eyes, this onslaught was not a 'Second Reformation' but rather an extension of the three-century war between truth and error; and Paul Cullen, recently arrived from Rome, was the very personification of Tridentine militism.

Tobias Kirby, rector of the Irish College in Rome, acted as a conduit for information from the Irish bishops and clergy to the Vatican. Bernard Burke, parish priest of Westport, wrote to him in 1853 regarding proselytism in Connemara and Achill.[165] Correspondence from Ireland to *Propaganda Fide* also outlined the scale of the problem, especially in the Tuam diocese, where it was partly ignored by John MacHale.[166] Paul Cullen wrote a detailed report in 1851, telling that Oughterard (Catholic diocese of Galway) was 'a parish of Jumpers and Bible Readers' where the Protestant bishop of Tuam had recently confirmed hundreds of 'perverts'.[167] Although Rome decreed that visiting Catholic missioners should be dispatched into areas subject to proselytising, MacHale refused access to external missions, undertaking the work personally: 'Dr. MacHale denies perversions in his diocese ... He believes it would be a slur to let in strangers.'[168]

Although MacHale had supported Michael Slattery of Cashel in proposing Paul Cullen as archbishop of Armagh, tensions between the Gallican MacHale and ultramontane Cullen increased once Cullen appeared on the Irish scene.[169] Over the decades animosity between the archbishop and Primate, which was greatly exacerbated by the appointment of Cullen's ally, John MacEvilly, as bishop of Galway in 1857, dominated the politics of the Irish Catholic church and created a schism in Irish Catholicism which facilitated the work of the ICM.

The first aggressive action to combat proselytism in west Galway took place in Oughterard, where a successful Vincentian mission was held in June 1852. As Lawrence O'Donnell, bishop of Galway, was unavailable,

Archbishop MacHale confirmed over 3,000 persons in Oughterard.[170] Continuing on to Glan, the most successful station of Castlekerke mission, where 'the ravages of proselytism were most fearful',[171] he laid the foundation stone for a church and received many converts back to Catholicism, including ten scripture readers.[172] Many claimed they were bribed to become Protestant. Patrick Sullivan testified in August 1852 that

> 1, Patrick Sullivan, son of the late Michael Sullivan of Oughterard, so solemnly declare that I abandoned the Roman Catholic faith from no conscious motive, but was induced thereto by motives of self-interest – being paid five shillings a month as a Bible reader. I do also declare, in the presence of witnesses, that I am sorry for this apostasy, and I voluntarily make this reparation for the scandal given to the Roman Catholic Church – the only reparation I can make, on the eve of my departure for America. I also declare that I am not moved to make this declaration by any motive of interest – I make it freely from my heart.
>
> Patrick Sullivan, Bible-reader, aged nineteen years
>
> (Witnesses)   Michael Joyce, Patrick Fitzpatrick (householders).[173]

Dr MacHale's efforts to retain total and sole control of his diocese were undermined by the direct intervention of the Vatican. He resisted a summons to Rome in 1851 to explain the state of his diocese, explaining that he could not leave his flock when the wolf was literally on them. In spite of successful counter-missionary efforts in Oughterard, aggressive counter-missionary work was not readily undertaken in the Tuam diocese until the following year, possibly prompted by Cullen's accurate observation to Kirby in November 1852 that the 'proselytisers still working, and no one working against them in the west'.[174] The following year, MacHale was forced to admit two Rosminian missionaries, Frs Rinolfi and Lockhart, to undertake parish missions.

The following chapter will show how, from reluctant beginnings, the Catholic church developed parish-based organisations which zealously policed the poor and distributed relief; established free or 'ragged' Catholic schools; provided parish missions to foster greater involvement of the poor in church activities; and organised the social ostracism of convert and mission communities, which was especially effective in west Galway, while its polemicists published lengthy tracts decrying the ideology and methodology of proselytism in general and of the ICM in particular. The improvement of the Catholic infrastructure was underway before the arrival of the ICM and a number of Catholic charitable organisations were in place, especially in Dublin.[175] The arrival of aggressive proselytising missions galvanised Catholic authorities and focused services in locations targeted by proselytism.

Notes

1 J. D. Sirr, *A memoir of Power Le Poer Trench, last archbishop of Tuam* (Dublin, 1845) pp. 639–42.

2 Bearnárd Mac Uaid, 'Stair oideachas Bráthar Triomhadh Úird Riaghalta Sain Proinsias san naomhadh céad déag' [The history of education of the Third Order of Saint Francis in the nineteenth century] (MA, University College, Galway, 1956), p. 163.

3 Irene Whelan, 'The stigma of souperism' in Cathal Póirtéir (ed.), *The great Irish famine* (Dublin, 1995), p. 143.

4 Alexander R. C. Dallas, *The story of the Irish Church Missions, part 1* (London, 1867), pp. 105, 124–9.

5 ICM Archive, ICM minutes, No. 576, minute book 2, 25 July 1851.

6 Anonymous, *Stories about the mission work in Ireland*, No. 7 (Dublin, 1854), p. 6.

7 J. P. Garrett, *A brief memoir of Miss Moore* ... (3rd edn, Belfast, 1867), pp. 5–22.

8 *Banner of the Truth*, 1851, pp. 102–3.

9 Ibid., 1851, p. 124.

10 DDA, Murray Papers, William Flannelly, parish priest of Ballinakill to Daniel Murray, 6 Apr. 1848.

11 Stuart A. Moody, *Ireland open to the Gospel* (Edinburgh, 1847), pp. 58–9.

12 ICM Archive, ICM minutes, book 2, No. 7, 7 June 1851.

13 Robert Bickersteth, *Irish Church Missions, a sermon etc.* (London, n.d.), p. 5.

14 J. D. Sirr, *The children of the light and their obligations* ... (London, 1851), p. 364.

15 *Statement of the Society for Irish Church Missions to the Roman Catholics*, London, Jan. 1852; *Report of the Society for Irish Church Missions*, 1853, p. 13.

16 *Banner of the Truth*, 1853, pp. 136–7,156–60.

17 William Marrable, *Sketch of the origin and operations of the Society for Irish Church Missions to the Roman Catholics* (London, 1853), p. 44; Earl of Roden, *Progress of the reformation in Ireland: extracts from a series of letters written from the west of Ireland to a friend in England in September 1851* (2nd edn, London, 1852), p. 33.

18 Roden, *Progress of the reformation*, p. 81.

19 Alexander R. C. Dallas, 'The present position of popery and Protestantism in Ireland. A lecture etc.' in Church of England Young Men's Society, *Six lectures on Protestantism Delivered before the north of London auxiliary to the Church of England Young Men's Society in October, November and December 1851* (London, 1852), pp.193–4.

20 E. J. Quigley, 'Grace abounding, a chapter of Ireland's history', *Irish Ecclesiastical Record*, xxi (1923), p. 131.

21 Thomas Plunket, *Convert confirmations* ... (London, 1851), pp. 11–13.

22 John Gregg, *A missionary visit to Connemara and other parts of the county of Galway* (Dublin, C. 1850), pp. 25, 34.

23 Anonymous, *Stories about the mission work in Ireland*, No. 7, p. 7.

24 Joseph Denham Smith, *Connemara, past and present* (Dublin, 1853), p. 106.

25 *Second annual report of the Connemara Orphans' Nursery* (Wonston, 1852), p. 16.

26 James Maher, *The letters of Rev. James Maher, D.D., late P.P. of Carlow-Graigue, on religious subjects, with a memoir*, ed. by the Right Rev. Patrick Francis Moran (Dublin, 1877), p. 393.

27 ICM Archive, ICM minutes, book 5, No. 930, June 1852 and No. 1030, 5 Oct. 1852; Robert Backhouse Peacock, *The reformation in Ireland. Notes of a tour amongst the missions in Dublin and West Galway in ... September 1852* (2nd edn, London, 1853), p. 46.

28 Vincentian Archive, 'Life of Fathers Dowley and Lydon', p. 97.

29 Gregg, *A missionary visit to Connemara*, p. 34.

30 Fanny Bellingham, *Fourth account of the fund entrusted to Miss Fanny Bellingham ... for the relief of the converts and children of Connemara* (Wonston, 1851).

31 Scottish Association for the relief of Irish children attending scriptural schools, *Report for 1851, with notes of a two months' residence among the Irish Church Missions in west Galway and Mayo* (Edinburgh, 1851) pp. 12–14.

32 Hyacinth D'Arcy to Fanny Bellingham, 12 Feb. 1850, in Bellingham, *Fourth account ... Fund for the Relief of the Converts*, p. 10.

33 Miriam Moffitt, *Soupers and Jumpers: the Protestant missions in Connemara, 1848–1937* (Dublin, 2008), pp. 25, 115–16.

34 ICM, *Report of the proceedings at the second annual meeting, 2nd May 1851*, pp. 6, 20.

35 The ICM employed the following at Sellerna in 1856: George Shea (clergyman), John Tobin, William Mannion, Pat Gallagher, Thomas King, Thomas Longstone (scripture readers), and Joseph and Maria Palmer (teachers). ICM Archive, ICM agency books, 1856, Sellerna.

36 *An Irish and English spelling-book for the use of schools, and persons in the Irish parts of the country* (Achill, 1849).

37 ICM Archive, ICM minutes, No. 223, 1 Mar. 1850.

38 *Dublin Visiting Mission in Connexion with Society for Irish Church Missions, Report for 1869* (n.p., 1870) p. 1, quoted in Jacinta Prunty, 'The geography of poverty: Dublin 1850–1900: the social mission of the church with particular reference to Margaret Aylward and co-workers (Ph.D. dissertation, National University of Ireland, 1992), p. 132; A Fellow Worker, *Patient continuance: a sketch of the life and labours of the late Rev. Doctor MacCarthy of Dublin* (Dublin, 1878), p. 4.

39 Anonymous, *'Them also', the story of the Dublin mission* (2nd edn, London, 1866), p. 4.

40 Ibid., pp. 75, 271.

41 John Crawford, *The church of Ireland in Victorian Dublin* (Dublin, 2005), p. 114.

42 Charles Stuart Stanford, *A handbook to the Romish controversy: being a refutation in detail of the creed of Pope Pius the Fourth on the grounds of scripture and reason: and an appendix and notes* (Dublin, 1868); Desmond Bowen, *The Protestant crusade in Ireland, 1800–70* (Dublin, 1978), p. 242.

43 Quoted in Crawford, *The church of Ireland in Victorian Dublin*, p. 56.

44 Prunty, 'The geography of poverty', p. 132.

45 'Them also', p. 15.

46 *Thirteenth report of the Dublin Mission Visiting Branch of the Society for Irish Church Missions to the Roman Catholics for the year ending December 31st, 1861* (Dublin, 1862), p. 5.

47 Margaret Preston, *Charitable words: women, philanthropy and the language of charity in nineteenth-century Dublin* (London, 2004), pp. 74–82.

48 *The early history of Mrs Smyly's homes and schools*, speech by Miss Vivienne Smyly (grand-daughter) given 29 May 1976 (n.p., n.d.).

49 Sarah Davies, *Holly and Ivy, the story of a winter Birds' Nest* (Dublin, 1871); Sarah Davies, *Wanderers brought home* (Dublin, 1871); Sarah Davies, *St. Patrick's armour: the story of the Coombe Ragged School* (Dublin, 1880); Sarah Davies, *Other cities also; the story of mission work in Dublin* (Dublin, 1881); Sarah Davies, *Helping hand, the story of the Coombe Boy's Home* (Dublin, 1881).

50 See, for example, Myrtle Hill, '"Women's work for women": the Irish Presbyterian Zenana Mission, 1874–1914', in Rosemary Raughter, *Religious women and their history: breaking the silence* (Dublin, 2005), 82–97.

51 'Them also', pp. 16–17, 20; *Banner of the Truth*, 1852, pp. 63–4.

52 Davies, *Helping hand*, p. 15.

53 Preston, *Charitable words*, pp. 74–82.

54 Davies, *St. Patrick's armour*, pp. 26–7.

55 Marrable, *Sketch of the origin*, pp. 26–7.

56 Copley Papers, Durham University, Special Collections (CP), MS No. GRE/G18/1/157.

57 These included Rule of Faith, Penance, Extreme Unction, Justification by Faith Only, Transubstantiation, Sacrifice of the Mass, Purgatory, Worship of the Virgin Mary and Saints, Indulgences, Image Worship, Doctrine of Intention, Supremacy of the Pope, Idolatry of the Church of Rome, Fallibility of the Church of Rome and Apostasy of the Church of Rome. *Report of the Society for Irish Church Missions to Roman Catholics*, 1850, p. 41.

58 'Them also', p. 13.

59 ICM Archive, ICM minutes, No. 4473, 28 Nov. 1867.

60 'Them Also', pp. 14, 21.

61 In 1850 'Local Committees for Missions' operated at Ballinasloe with Loughrea, Longford, Lisnaskea, Annadaff, Sligo, Askeaton, Tralee, Enniscorthy, Portarlington, West Meath and Meath; *Report of the Society for Irish Church Missions to the Roman Catholics*, 1850, p. 33; In 1853, 'Local Committees for Missions' operated at: Dublin South, Dublin North, Monkstown, Wicklow, Wexford North, Wexford South, New Ross, Ossory or Kilkenny, Callan, Leighlin or Carlow, Killishandra, Mohill, Strokestown, Athlone, Nenagh, Parsonstown, Portarlington, Edenderry, Ferbane, Ballinasloe, Westmeath, Longford, Edgeworthstown, Meath, Balbriggan, Drogheda, Boyle, Carrick-on-Shannon, Elphin, Sligo, Lisnaskea, Clones, Newry, Belfast, Roscrea, Celbridge, Belturbet, Lisburn, Athy, Booterstown and Iniskeen; *Report of the Society for Irish Church Missions to the Roman Catholics*, 1853, p. 19.

62 Scottish Association, *Report for 1851*, p. 19.

63 A. R. C. Dallas, *Castelkerke* (London, 1849); Marrable, *Sketch of the origin*.

64 *Banner of the Truth*, May 1852.

65 Peacock, *The reformation in Ireland*, preface.

66 John Garrett, *Good news from Ireland. An address to the archbishops and bishops of the Church of England* (London, 1863), p. 60.

67 This includes all publications identified in the major repositories of the British Isles or to which any reference was made in mission literature. While this listing aims to be as comprehensive as possible, it omits those for which dates of publication are not stated or cannot be estimated with a substantial degree of certainty.

68 ICM Archive, ICM minutes, No. 2919, 23 Sept. 1858.

69 *Ballina Chronicle*, *Connaught Watchman*, *Mayo Constitution* and *Galway Express*.

70 *Galway Express*, 5 Feb. 1853.

71 *Connaught Watchman*, 15 Oct. 1851.

72 *The Times*, 27 June 1863, copied from ICM *Annual report*, 1863, p. 40.

73 Charles Bernard, *What is truth? A sermon preached on behalf of the Society for Irish Church Missions to Roman Catholics in the parish of St. Multose, Kinsale on Sunday, November 12th, 1854* (Cork, 1854), p. 7.

74 Society for Irish Church Missions, *Early fruits of Irish missions* (6th edn, London, 1852), p. 20.

75 John Elliott Howard, *The island of saints, or Ireland in 1855* (London, 1855), p. 157.

76 Marrable, *Sketch of the origin*, p. 7.

77 *Erin's Hope*, 1860, pp. 171–2.

78 Michael Brannigan, *Connaught Mission, its past and present* (n.p., n.d. [c.1848]); James Carlile, *Fruit gathered from among Roman Catholics in Ireland* (London, 1848); James Carlile, *Birr mission, obituary of Mary Kehoe* (n.p., 1851); William Crotty, *The mission in Connemara* (Belfast, n.d.); Andrew Ross, *Ballinglen, Killala, County Mayo, Ireland* (n.p., 1851).

79 J. W. Taylor, *A month's visit to Connaught and its mission stations* (Edinburgh, London, 1849), p. 64.

80 Edinburgh Irish Mission, *The true way of dealing successfully with popery, being the report of the Edinburgh Irish Mission for the year 1850, with the list of subscriptions* (Edinburgh, 1851); Edinburgh Irish Mission, *Appeal in reference to the extension of the Edinburgh Irish Mission and Protestant Institute, addressed to the friends of Protestantism* (Edinburgh, n.d.), p. 2.

81 ICM, *Report of the proceedings at the first annual meeting, held on the 26th April 1850* (n.p., 1850), p. 22. (Spoken by Revd Dr Mortimer O'Sullivan.)

82 *Banner of the Truth*, Feb. 1851, p. 24.

83 Society for Irish Church Missions, *Early fruits of Irish missions*, p. 4.

84 Mr Andrews of Wimbledon, member of London Committee, speaking at 1862 annual meeting, *Banner of the Truth*, 2 June 1862, p. 84.

85 Thomas Plunket, *The West Galway Church Building Fund, an appeal from the bishop of Tuam* (Dublin, c.1860), p. 2.

86 Ballinaboy (108), Ballyconree (170), Fakeragh (80), Derrygimla (156), Streamstown (151), Sellerna (250 incl. adults), Salruck (80 converts), Bundoragha (35), Aasleagh (85), Kilmilken (60 converts), Gertacurragh (56 converts); Roden, *Progress of the reformation*, pp. 10–34.

87 Anonymous, *What are the Irish Church Missions?* (London, 1855), p. 8.

88 Peacock, *The reformation in Ireland*, p. 1 of preface.

89 *Erin's Hope*, 1854, p. 64.

90 Patrick Murray, *The mendacity of souperism in Ireland, a letter to Edward G.K. Browne, Esq.,* ...(London, 1861), p. 7.

91 Hugh Joseph O'Donnell, *David and Goliath, or the complete victory of a Mayo hedge-school pupil* ... (Dublin, 1853), p. 160.

92 For example see interaction between William Dooley, Irish teacher at Barnatrough and an unnamed priest in *Banner of the Truth*, Jan. 1852, pp. 12–13.

93 Anonymous, *A day at Clifden* (London, 1853), p. 16.

94 Mrs A[nne] Dallas, *Incidents in the life and ministry of the Rev. Alexander R.C. Dallas A.M.* (London, 1871), pp. 520–1.

95 Anonymous, *Two months in Clifden, Co. Galway, during the summer of 1855* (Dublin, 1856), p. 28.

96 Catherine Hartland Inglis, *Notes of a tour through the south and west of Ireland; with some account of the operations of the General Irish Reformation Society* (Castle Douglas, 1850), p. 15.

97 CP, MS No. GRE/5/48, Mary D'Arcy to Miss Copley, 1 Mar. 1858.

98 Anonymous, *Two months in Clifden*, p. 18. This portrayal of Omey contrasts with later violence towards mission staff when a 'valued Lay agent was ... severely kicked ... feared he has received an injury for life', 'Explanation of a set of six diagrams' in Society for Irish Church Missions, *A mission tour book in Ireland, showing how to visit the missions in Dublin, Connemara, etc.* (London, 1860), p. 42.

99 Scottish Association, *Report for 1851*, p. 20.

100 Marian Freyer, *Connemara, its social and religious aspects* (Galway, 1861), p. 76.

101 *Galway Express and General Advertiser for the counties of Galway, Mayo, Roscommon, Clare and Limerick*, 20 June 1866.

102 Freyer, *Connemara*, p. 77.

103 Garrett, *Good news from Ireland*, p. 55.

104 IFC Archive, A77:238, spoken by Micheál O'Maoláin, Baile Nua, Cleggan, Ballinakill.

105 John Wolffe, 'Evangelicalism in mid-nineteenth-century England' in R. Samuel (ed.), *Patriotism: the making and unmaking of British national identity* (London, 1989), i, p. 189.

106 From a sermon by Revd Edward Bickersteth, reproduced in the ICM, *Annual report*, 1852, p. 11.

107 Anonymous, *A day at Clifden*, p. 6.

108 Quoted in Peacock, *The reformation in Ireland*, p. 72.

109 Bellingham, *Fourth account* ... *Fund for the Relief of the Converts*, p. 2.

110 Dallas, *The story of the Irish Church Missions*, part 1, p. 8; Dallas, *Protestantism in Ireland*, p. 33.

111 David Alfred Doudney, *A run through Connemara. By the editor of the 'Gospel Magazine,' and 'Protestant Beacon'* (London, Dublin, 1856), p. 4

112 *Report of the proceedings at the third annual meeting, 30 April 1852* (London, 1852), p. 11.

113 Alexander R. C. Dallas, *Correspondence of Lord Byron, with a friend* … (3 vols, Paris, 1825).

114 Christopher Hibbert, *Queen Victoria: a personal history* (London, 2000), p. 177.

115 M., *Connemara. Journal of a tour, undertaken to inquire into the progress of the reformation in the west of Ireland. By M.* (Dublin, 1852), p. 12.

116 *Galway Express*, 23 Apr. 1859.

117 Denham Smith, *Connemara, past and present*, p. 40.

118 *Banner of the Truth*, Sept. 1860, p. 137.

119 Llewelyn Wynne Jones, *The new reformation in Ireland: or striking facts and anecdotes illustrating the extent and reality of the movement* (London, 1852), p. 32.

120 Quoted in frontispiece to Denham Smith, *Connemara, past and present.* Denham Smith was a congregational minister at Kingstown who accompanied Dallas on a visit to Connemara.

121 Davies, *Other cities also*, p. 37.

122 Dallas, *Protestantism in Ireland*, p. 196.

123 ICM, *Annual report*, 1869, p. 50.

124 *Banner of the Truth*, Feb. 1852, p. 31.

125 Dallas, *Protestantism in Ireland*, pp. 193–4.

126 ICM, *Annual report*, 1890, p. 9.

127 Anonymous, *Stories about the mission work in Ireland*, No. 5 (Dublin, 1854), p. 14.

128 Anonymous, *Stories about the mission work in Ireland*, Nos 1, 2, 4, 5, 7 (Dublin, 1854).

129 Scottish Association, *Report for 1851*, p. 20.

130 *Erin's Hope*, 1866, p. 14.

131 For example, the parents of Callaghan McCarthy, ICM agent at Tourmakeady, were Dingle converts. P. M'Closkey, *Trial and conviction of a Franciscan monk at Mayo spring assizes, 1852* … (Dublin, 1852), p. 15.

132 For example, see entry in 1858 ICM agency book stating that 'Joseph and Maria Palmer (neé Winder) have returned to England'. ICM Archive, ICM agency books, 1858, Sellerna.

133 J. G. MacWalter, *The Irish reformation movement in its religious, social and political aspects* (Dublin, 1852), p. 242; the author of this very polemical book was also a convert; Roden, *Progress of the reformation*; John Gregg, *A missionary visit to Achill and Erris, and other parts of the county of Mayo* (Dublin, 1850), pp. 31, 34.

134 Meala Ní Ghiobúin, *Dugort, Achill Island 1831–1861: the rise and fall of a missionary community* (Dublin, 2001), pp. 18, 31.

135 Among the ICM clergymen educated in Ballinasloe Missionary College were John Crampton, Henry Fleming, Benjamin Irwin, Robert and Edward Murphy, and Brent Neville. *Irish Ecclesiastical Gazette*, Nov., Dec. 1858; ICM Archive, ICM agency books, 1856–99.

136 Patrick Egan, *The parish of Ballinasloe: its history from the earliest times to the present day* (Dublin, 1960), p. 254.

137 Gregg, *A missionary Visit to Connemara*, p. 5.

138 Egan, *The parish of Ballinasloe*, p. 255.

139 R. Steele, *Footprints in the hands of time* (London, 1882); Richard Hobson, *What hath God wrought, an autobiography. Richard Hobson. With an introduction by the Right Rev. F. J. Chavasse* (London, 1913).

140 Peacock, *The reformation in Ireland*, p. 27; Steele, *Footprints*, p. 7.

141 Hobson, *What hath God wrought*; ICM Archive, ICM agency books, 1862–67.

142 Dallas, *Castelkerke*, pp. 99–105; Representative Church Body Library (RCBL), Marriage register, Oughterard, MS No. P. 169/3/1, entry No. 16.

143 James Mecredy, *A brief narrative of the reformation in Iar Connaught* (Dublin, 1854), p. 5.

144 Scottish Association, *Report for 1851*, pp. 12–14; see also M., *Connemara. Journal of a tour*, p. 16.

145 ICM Archive, ICM agency books, 1856–1903.

146 Moffitt, *Soupers and Jumpers*, pp. 145–6.

147 Alannah Heather, *Errislannan: scenes from a painter's life* (Dublin, 1993), p. 75. Frances Stewart, later Mrs Nee, was a probationer 1892–93 and a qualified teacher 1893–95, when she left to marry Revd Thomas Nee. His first wife, Maria, died in December 1893, *Banner of the Truth*, Jan. 1894, p. 8.

148 *Banner of the Truth*, April 1868; *Banner of the Truth*, July 1894.

149 DDA, MS No. Cullen, 328/4 file 1, laity, Jan.–June 1871, *Report from the select committee on conventual and monastic Institutions*, 23 June 1871; Prunty, 'The geography of poverty', p. 108.

150 Desmond Keenan, *The Catholic Church in nineteenth-century Ireland: a sociological study* (Totawa, New Jersey, 1983), pp. 115–37.

151 *Annals of the propagation of the faith*, 1823, quoted in Jean Comby, *How to understand the history of Christian mission* (London, 1996), p. 119.

152 DDA, MS No. 2002, Peter FitzMaurice to Daniel Murray, 25 June 1848.

153 Bickersteth, *Irish Church Missions, a sermon etc.*, p. 6.

154 *The Nation*, 20 Nov. 1852.

155 Paul Cullen to William Walsh, 8 Nov. 1851, quoted in Desmond Bowen, *Paul Cardinal Cullen and the shaping of modern Irish Catholicism* (Dublin, 1983), p. 135.

156 Quoted in William Meagher, *Notices of the life and character of his grace, Most Rev. Daniel Murray, later archbishop of Dublin* (Dublin, 1853), p. 122.

157 *The Nation*, 20 Nov. 1852.

158 *The Tablet*, 8 Nov. 1851.

159 *Freeman's Journal*, 23 Aug. 1850.

160 Luke Walsh, *The Home Mission unmasked ...* (Belfast, 1844), *passim*.

161 Meagher, *Notices ... Rev. Daniel Murray*, p. 125.
162 Moffitt, *Soupers and Jumpers*, pp. 69–84.
163 For example, see letter from Fr Mylotte, curate of Ross (Clonbur), near Castlekerke, *Galway Mercury*, 20 Dec. 1851.
164 PICA, MS No. KIR/NC/1/1847/10, Paul Cullen to Tobias Kirby, 29 Oct. 1847.
165 Bernard Burke to Tobias Kirby, Westport, 15 Oct. 1853 in 'Irish College, Rome: Kirby Papers', edited by Patrick J. Corish, *Archivium Hibernicum*, xxxi (1973), p. 14, hereafter referred to as Kirby, *AH*.
166 Paul Cullen to Tobias Kirby, 28 Oct. 1852, Paul Cullen to Bernard Smith, Dublin, 13 July 1852, and Paul Cullen to Bernard Smith, 7 Nov. 1852 in Kirby, *AH*, xxxi (1973), pp. 43–4.
167 Quoted in Bowen, *Paul Cardinal Cullen*, p. 170.
168 Paul Cullen to Tobias Kirby, Dublin, 13 July 1852 in Kirby, *AH*, xxxi (1973), p. 43.
169 Bowen, *Paul Cardinal Cullen*, pp. 88–99.
170 Vincentian Archive, 'A memoir of the Congregation of the Mission in Ireland, England and Scotland' by Thomas McNamara in 1867, with important appendices added shortly before his death in 1892 and 'Life of Fathers Dowley and Lydon'.
171 Vincentian Archive, 'Life of Fathers Dowley and Lydon', p. 106.
172 Máire Ní Shúilleabháin, *An t-Athar Caomhánach agus an cogadh creidimh i gConamara* [*Fr Kavanagh and the battle of the faith in Connemara*] (Dublin, 1984), p. 51.
173 D. W. Cahill, *Eighth letter of the Rev. Dr. Cahill to his Excellency, the earl of Carlisle* (Dublin, 1856), pp. 10–11.
174 PICA, MS No. KIR/NC/1/1852/53, Paul Cullen to Tobias Kirby, Dublin, 4 Nov. 1852.
175 Keenan, *The Catholic Church in nineteenth-century Ireland*, pp. 115–40.

Chapter 4

The mission loses momentum, 1853–69

By the end of 1852 the operations of the Irish Church Missions had grown to an impressive extent with an extensive infrastructure and promising convert communities in both Dublin and Connemara, supplemented by smaller 'local' missions scattered throughout the country. Archdeacon Stopford's unofficial census of the western missions confirmed the existence of thriving congregations in 1851.[1] In the early 1850s funds teemed into the Society's coffers, its appeal greatly increased by the onset in England of the Papal Aggression of 1851. To most supporters the ICM's objective of the total conversion of Ireland seemed imminently achievable; many considered the movement unstoppable and hoped that 'ere long Ireland will become a Protestant country',[2] an aspiration that ultimately went unfulfilled. Factors which impeded the development of the Irish Church Missions included the aggressive Catholic response to its proselytising efforts, the diminishing appeal of anti-popery causes in Britain from the mid 1850s and a decline in Irish support for the mission. This should not suggest an end to the efforts and successes of the ICM, which persisted in its efforts to rescue souls from Rome, albeit reduced in size and efficacy. Over the following decades, and well into the twentieth century, the mission continued to exert an influence, especially in the slums of Dublin and in Connemara.

The operations of the ICM, 1853–69

The impressive growth of the Irish Church Missions in its early years resulted in the establishment of numerous schools, churches and children's homes in Connemara and Dublin. Although the rate of conversions slowed after the Catholic church mounted an aggressive campaign to frustrate the ICM's efforts, the mission continued to expand, but more slowly than before. In its literature, the mission stressed the ethnological and political change in converts and by 1854 Protestant fears of Catholic clerical influence had been mollified by the ICM's assertion that 'the power of priestly influence is wonderfully broken'.[3] Although ICM income declined from 1854 (see figure 4.3, p. 00), the mission continued to function effectively, especially through the agency of child-focused proselytism. New mission schools were opened throughout Connemara, parish churches were enlarged and, by 1865, eleven new mission churches had been established.[4] The existing orphanages in Dublin and Connemara were supplemented by new homes at Nead na Farraige at Spiddal and a Boy's Home in Galway, and by Aasleagh Orphanage which was later opened in Leenane. On a countrywide basis, however, there was a severe contraction of mission stations (see Appendix).

The ICM continued to work as before with trained agents engaging in house visiting, teaching, controversial classes and discussion lectures, supplemented by the work of Irish teachers who interacted with their neighbours at local level. The mission never regained the momentum of its early years and small-scale conversions replaced the communal surge towards Protestantism. The ICM continued to benefit from the publicity afforded to other missionary endeavours, as when the Presbyterian, Dill, reported in 1852 that the 'dense clouds of Popery' were rising from the land,[5] although the missionary operations of other Protestant societies also declined markedly from the mid 1850s.

Scripture readers of the ICM visited the homes of the poor in both Connemara and Dublin, reading portions of the bible and distributing tracts. They tried to establish a relationship with their clients, visiting and revisiting the same families in an effort to persuade the poor to attend mission services and to send their children to the mission schools. This coincided with extensive attempts in mid-nineteenth-century Britain to 'improve' the poor through exposure to the scriptures, and the ICM's efforts to save 'non-scriptural Romanists' should be seen in tandem with the expansion of mission to the 'irreligious poor' taking place in Britain. There were, however, a number of distinct differences between Protestant missions to the poor in Ireland and in Britain.

The London organisation, the Metropolitan Visiting and Relief Association (1843) depended on middle-class females who visited London's poor on a voluntary basis. The ICM, in contrast, utilised male scripture readers who had undergone a period of training and who received a wage (£4 a month if trained, £2 a month for probationers). It did not imitate the practice of employing trained, working-class females as bible-women although the Ranyard mission (1857) had considerable success with this approach in London. It is likely that the ICM benefited by the employment of trained agents and would have probably achieved a greater degree of success if women visitors had been engaged in domestic visiting, as its agents would have encountered significant numbers of women when visiting tenements. Females who had passed through the ICM Training School were only employed as bible-women from 1898.

Another crucial difference between the missions to the poor in Ireland and in Britain was that most of the British poor were nominally Protestant whereas most of the poor in Ireland were at least nominally Catholic. This resulted in a confrontation between the Catholic church, which claimed the ownership of the souls of the Irish poor, and the Protestant missions, which sought to equip them with a knowledge of the scriptures. The fact that the Irish poor identified themselves with the Roman religion hindered the ICM's success as, unlike their British counterparts, those who availed of ICM services and relief offered were forced to discard long-established loyalties. The majority of the poor 'knew' they were Catholic although their knowledge of Roman doctrine or teachings and their attendance at mass were probably minimal, and their belief systems may have been closer to folk religion than to a clearly defined appreciation of Catholic tenets. This contrasted with the situation in Britain where Protestant missions did not challenge deep-seated, multi-generational loyalties when they attempted to sweep the 'irreligious poor' into church and church-based schools and societies.

The ICM depended on the benevolence of English Protestants and maintaining a steady correspondence with supporters was part of the work of mission personnel. The regular correspondence between Fanny and Mary D'Arcy of Clifden and the wealthy benefactress, Elizabeth Copley of Hampton Court, confirms the degree of support for ultra-Protestant causes among a segment of society. It would be easy to dismiss ICM workers as religious zealots, but the letters of Fanny and Mary show they were genuinely concerned for the well-being of their converts. In contrast to the faceless fund-raising ladies of England, such as Elizabeth Copley, these women worked at the coal-face of mission, entering the most miserable of cabins and labouring in very unpleasant and at times unsafe circumstances. Both Fanny and Mary were 'born to better things'. Fanny was daughter of John Bellingham, Castlebellingham, County Louth; Mary's father was a naval man, the inspecting commander of Clifden coastguard district.[6] Fanny and Mary's correspondence reveals that their efforts to feed and care for the converts and children ranged from obtaining clothes to providing dry beds, which contradicts the mission's insistence that it never provided assistance.

> 1100 to be daily fed, nearly 200 of whom are total orphans ... the mission's funds seem to be coming in & we are kept in weekly in anxious waiting upon God for the daily bread for these schools ... it is this wh[ich] occupies all my spare moments as I have to keep incessantly writing to collect £34 <u>each</u> <u>week</u> without a society committee or any extra help except friends ...[7]

> The continued wet weather renders the present dormitory unfit for habitation,
> it is almost impossible to place the beds so as to keep them dry.[8]

The mission capitalised on Miss Copley's ultra-Protestant sentiments, reassuring her of the mission's success 'notwithstanding the opposition that the devil and his agents bring to bear against it'[9] and urging that she purchase land near its mission at Sellerna which would benefit from 'the countenance and support of a Protestant landlord'.[10] Mary D'Arcy empathised with Miss Copley's sense of threat, reminding her that it was important 'to expose the errors of Romanism and to raise the Standard Protestant Scriptural truth against its deadly although often (as is the case in England) insidious advances'.[11] Every effort was made to inform Miss Copley of the social and political changes wrought in mission pupils, reproducing addresses which gave thanks for the truth 'Which we found in that Book she so wisely has sent / Instead of the Pope, or the Catholic Rent ...'[12] and reassuring her of the children's avid interest in the marriage of the Princess Royal.[13]

Within a few years of its inception, a large portion of the mission's trained staff came from its convert community. It is evident that the children of labourers benefited much less from ICM involvement than did children of farmers. This may account for the very early falling away of labourer involvement in the missions. Analysis of the 108 mission agents who married in the west Galway mission churches between 1847 and 1928 shows that they were eight times more likely to be drawn from the farmer families than from labouring backgrounds. Henry Wilberforce had commented on this facet of mission when he claimed that in addition to receiving food and clothes and housing, converts of a 'somewhat higher class' were employed as scripture readers and teachers.[14] Schoolmasters and scripture readers were paid an average of £60 per annum in 1856, with school-mistresses being paid £42 yearly.[15] In 1861, the national school-teacher at Cleggan was granted £15 per annum, which was on a par with payment rates for national school teachers at the time.[16] The possibility of social advancement was observed by Clifden's parish priest, who remarked, 'Just look at the readers with their tail-coats, their Bibles ... sitting at their smoking tea tables. Little wonder they'd be fond of the stirabout.'[17] Social improvement through association with the mission was derided in contemporary street-ballads, as in the following:

> O ye Biblemen, Soupers and Jumpers, no wonder ye work for your pay,
> For ye knock out an illegant [sic] living by leading poor souls the wrong
>   way.
> But its little ye care for the murder of any unfortunate souls,
> While you have, instead of wet lumpers, your beef, and your bacon and
>   rowls.

With canting, blaspheming and lying, ye hypocrites! ain't ye afraid?
Och, give up your lies and your souping, and take to some honester trade.[18]

Figure 4.1 shows the frequent intermarriage of families with ICM involvement and the tendency of children of ICM workers to enter the employment of the ICM. This section of research draws on an inter-linking of two databases, that of ICM agency books and of extant registers of west Galway Church of Ireland parishes in the RCBL. Despite the incomplete nature of the parish registers for west Galway, a high degree of intermarriage among families with mission associations is revealed, showing that mission agents formed a self-contained pool within the wider community of west Galway.

Armed with literacy and a knowledge of English, a considerable number of ICM staff emigrated, for example Dominic Cafferkey, who on leaving the ICM Male Training School in 1857 was stationed at Clonluan, Bunlahinch, Spiddal and Inverin until his emigration to Canada in 1864.[19] Some trained agents resigned to work for other missionary societies, such as Michael O'Sullivan of Salruck, who left Connemara to work in Edinburgh under the direction of John Hope. O'Sullivan regretted leaving the ICM, which brought 'me, my wife and whole family, parents, brothers, &tc., out from the darkness and delusions of a false religion, under which we were once bound slaves'.[20] Some agents are listed as having gone to England, America and Australia; others are simply listed as having 'emigrated'. The majority who left the Society 'resigned' or 'discontinued' or simply vanish from the records. Although the lists of persons who emigrated to England, America and Australia are by no means complete, they represent people who had been trained by the Society and in whom a considerable investment had been made. It must be stated that the ICM often lost the services of experienced agents, for example mission-teacher Tim O'Connell, who emigrated to America in 1870, had given fourteen years' service. In view of the decreasing finances of the ICM, it is probable that many were dismissed rather than resigned, but it is impossible to quantify how many staff were forcibly removed.

In 1860, William Conyngham Plunket, later archbishop of Dublin, with the support of his uncle, Thomas Plunket, bishop of Tuam, proposed the formation of the West Connaught Church Endowment Society to provide a fund to endow the recently formed western parishes.[21] With the exception of Ballycroy, near Erris in north Mayo, all WCCES parishes were under the auspices of the ICM.[22] The ICM missions which received funding were Moyrus, Errismore, Errislannan, Ballyconree, Sellerna, Renvyle, Aasleagh and Castlekerke; i.e. those missions which were not original parishes of the Church of Ireland.[23]

In his biography of W. C. Plunket, Frederick How stated that the WCCES

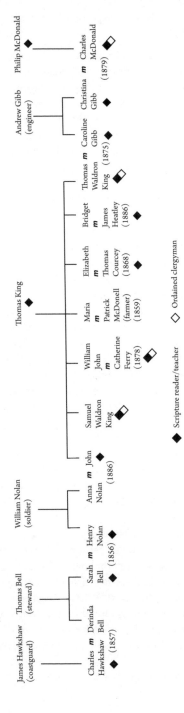

4.1 Intermarriage in a sample of families employed by the ICM in Connemara

was founded, not only to provide funds for the west Galway parishes, but so that 'English readers may have some little notion of another aspect of the Roman Church, other than the more or less attractive one which is carefully exhibited in England'.[24] The need for this organisation was outlined in the *Irish Ecclesiastical Gazette*, which explained a new society was needed to provide a permanent source of funding for mission parishes, thereby freeing ICM funds for expenditure on new conquests.[25] It should be noted that the establishment of the WCCES by Lord Plunket and his nephew, W. C. Plunket, coincided with the negative publicity regarding the very public 'War in Partry' when Lord Plunket evicted large numbers of tenants who refused to send their children to mission schools (discussed later).[26]

A large fundraising operation was set in motion in the early 1860s with much publicity awarded to the work of the ICM, such as Revd W. C. Plunket's *A book for tourists in Ireland* and *A short visit to the Connemara missions* and John Garrett's *Good news from Ireland*.[27] Annual reports of the WCCES detailed its progress and fundraising meetings were held at which supporters heard how Connemara's peasant converts eagerly sought endowments for their districts.[28]

The WCCES was well supported; Richard Whately of Dublin gave £700 to the fund. By 1862, £6,200 had been received, enabling the permanent endowment of the newly formed parishes of Moyrus and Sellerna.[29] Subsequently eight ICM parishes (plus Ballycroy) were to receive endowments amounting to the interest of £25,000; each parish usually received £75 per annum. In 1865, fifteen more churches awaited endowment but there is no evidence that the WCCES widened its sphere of activity.[30] However, the endowment of the WCCES had an extremely important impact in maintaining the viability of individual mission parishes.

The ICM was aware by the mid 1860s that the halcyon days of the early 1850s had passed and that its crusade was losing momentum. In Connemara, the work had become parochial rather than missionary as forthright mission work among the Catholic population had declined.[31] In 1867, after twenty years of missionary effort, Dallas spoke of ICM agents and missionaries, not as aggressive rescuers of those trapped in the errors of Rome, but as 'defensive agents in parishes invaded by Roman Catholic missionaries'.[32] By then, the cause of converting Irish Catholics no longer appealed to the majority of Protestants and the mission's claimed successes had been tarnished with allegations of bribery and ineffectiveness. Many of its founders were ageing or already deceased, its original cohort of converts and mission agents were growing old; Revd Dallas himself was approaching eighty years of age. In spite of irrefutable evidence to the contrary, the mission continually insisted that advances on Romanism were being effected and 'the war, which has lasted for more than twelve centuries

4.2 Moyrus church.
Source: *The Banner of Truth*, Jan. 1881.

between the Church of Christ and the Antichristian confederacy of Rome, seems to be drawing to its final issue'.[33]

In 1868, Revds Auriol, Cory, Edward Bickersteth and Charles F. McCarthy toured the missions and published recommendations on the future direction of the ICM.[34] Although some agents were still practising 'aggressive' missionary work, these clergymen noticed a 'turning in' on the part of some workers. Many agents were second generation converts who had endured a lot of violent opposition; many others had been forced to emigrate.[35] These clergymen made the crucial recommendation that, because of extreme pressure brought to bear on rural converts, future work should be concentrated in towns and cities where people were less conservative. This paved the way for the withdrawal from west Galway to Dublin and larger towns, although by 1870 the end of the Connemara missions was still decades away. This should not be seen as a weakening of the crusade against Catholicism; the ICM's objective was reiterated in April 1869 as to rescue 'fellow-subjects in Ireland from the deadly and soul-destroying thraldom of the Romish apostasy', but rather a realisation of the strength of social and family bonds in rural Ireland.[36]

Catholic opposition to the Irish Church Missions

The Catholic church mounted a multi-faceted campaign against the ICM, developing parish-based organisations, providing parish missions, alternative sources of education and relief, and, especially in the rural district of Connemara, inciting the total ostracism of the mission and its convert community.

Development of parish-based organisations

Catholic activists realised that the most effective answer to Protestant missionary activity was the distribution of food and clothing, the provision of free schooling and the establishment of alternative Catholic facilities for destitute children in areas of extreme poverty. It formed societies of 'St Vincent de Paul ... [and] multitudinous assemblies of Christian Doctrine Societies ... to watch over the poor lost little ones'.[37] In Dublin, this was principally undertaken by the ICM's most formidable opponent, Margaret Aylward (1810–89), who devoted the last forty years of her life to combating proselytism by exposing the extent of Protestant missionary efforts and by providing Catholic alternatives to mission relief.[38] St Brigid's Orphanage (1856) and St Brigid's Schools (1861) were established in Dublin by Margaret Aylward and her co-workers to answer the needs of those most likely to succumb to the 'conditional' relief of the ICM.

In 1851 Aylward introduced the Ladies' Association of Charity of St Vincent de Paul (LAC) into the central Dublin parishes of St Mary and St Michan where the ICM was especially active.[39] The lady-members visited the poor in their homes, distributing relief, encouraging or even harassing the poor to attend to their Catholic duties. Paul Cullen greatly supported the LAC, addressing its annual meetings in 1856 and 1861, granting it a place on the annual charity sermon list and providing it with funds to distribute food and clothing to the poor.[40]

The LAC's tactics were remarkably similar to those of the ICM, their zealous perseverance bringing many to mass and confession. They patrolled the 'wretched lanes and courts', mirroring counter-missionary tactics undertaken in London where the unintended result of militant Protestantism was the policing of slum areas by 'the Catholic priest and his lay allies'.[41] They controlled the poor through promises of clothes and food for good attendance at Catholic schools.[42] The ICM acknowledged that competing system of Catholic relief in the Coombe district of Dublin, where the LAC rewarded those who distanced themselves from the ICM's 'Weavers' Hall' school.[43] In 1852, the LAC made 3,591 visits to 200 families, attempting to instruct the poor in Catholic doctrine and also in parenting and household management.[44] They perceived their mission as two-fold: firstly to win back those who had converted to Protestantism or were in perilous contact with the ICM, and secondly, to 'encourage' nominal and lapsed Catholics to come in closer communion with their church, as in the case of a man they 'visited over and over again' until he attended confession.[45] Like the ICM, they were ever watchful at death-beds, providing beads and crucifixes, ensuring that the dying would receive the last rites and, above all, would die as Catholics.[46]

Although the reports of the LAC and the ICM concurred on the poverty of nineteenth-century Dublin, they differed on its causes. The ICM asserted that poverty stemmed from Catholicism and sinfulness,[47] reinforcing the accepted stereotyping of the poor and the Catholic. Aylward, in contrast, protested that sinfulness was caused by poverty, which ran counter to the accepted Victorian paradigm that an individual was responsible for their personal circumstances.[48] However, in spite of her empathy with the poor, Aylward was unsympathetic to the 'excuses, equivocations and lies' of those who sent their children to mission schools, insisting that 'poverty was no excuse for treason'.[49]

St Brigid's Orphanage (SBO), a boarding-out institution which was an offshoot of the LAC, was established in 1856 to protect children suffering the 'double calamity of spiritual and physical destitution'.[50] The SBO admitted children considered at risk of being placed in Protestant homes, especially those associated with the ICM. The SBO was based on an 'outdoor system' where children were reared in foster homes, usually farms in counties Dublin and Wicklow. Great emphasis was placed on religious instruction and foster parents received premiums when the child achieved milestones such as knowing a determined amount of catechism by heart.[51]

It was claimed that persons associated with the ICM frequently offered childcare, schooling, training and employment to the poor on condition that they convert, for example the children of prostitute Matilda Geraghty to whom Mrs Smyly had reportedly offered '£5 for the two children, and 8s. a week to turn Protestant'.[52] Entries in the registers of the SBO, which contain testimonies, accompanied by verifiable details such as names and addresses, asserted that reversion to Catholicism was difficult as Mrs Smyly sought repayment of costs incurred. For example, in 1864 the Birds' Nest released three Rooney children on payment of £33 15s.[53] It appears the poor fully understood the criteria for admission to all available charities and astutely exploited inter-confessional competition to obtain relief, as when Mary and Michael Tyrrell were admitted to St Brigid's after their mother threatened to bring them to ICM superintendent, Revd Charles McCarthy.[54]

Catholic educational and philanthropic facilities were introduced to the Connemara parishes targeted by the ICM but at a slower pace than in the capital, partly due to the intransigence of John MacHale, archbishop of Tuam, and partly due to the scarcity of middle-class Catholics, as discussed below.

Provision of free schooling for the poor

The provision of free schooling for the poor was an especially potent weapon in the battle for souls as both Catholic and Protestant authorities were conscious of the importance of instructing young children at an impressionable age; as explained by one Catholic polemicist: 'a dew-drop on the baby plant may warp the giant oak for ever'.[55] Paul Cullen was alert to the ICM's threat to Catholic children, believing a 'war, most insidious and malignant' was being fought 'with the hope of perverting the children of the poor'.[56] The case study of Errislannan and Errismore missions in chapter 5 will show that their concern was justified, as the school-going cohort of 1848–55 proved the most fertile in terms of lasting converts, an assertion that is defended even more clearly in *Soupers and Jumpers*.[57]

Catholic authorities considered it essential to prevent attendance at mission schools, placing the onus of passing on the Catholic faith on the shoulders of Irish parents who were repeatedly warned that children would be better off dead than at mission schools.[58] Contempt for those who placed their children in Protestant homes and schools was also disseminated among the illiterate via street-ballads: 'Her child she sold for paltry gold / To Kingstown he did go, ma'am / From mother's breast to vulture's nest / The robin'll be a crow, ma'am.'[59]

The ICM's Ragged School, first located at Weavers' Hall, then New Row and later at the Coombe, was founded to 'enter the stronghold of Popery' where children and adults lived in the most abject poverty in a district severely lacking in education provision.[60] Through organisations like the LAC, Catholic authorities successfully aroused the laity to oppose this and other schools of the ICM. Catholic hostility soon turned to violence with mission schools in Weavers' Hall and Luke Street attacked by a mob of 3,000 persons and children forcibly removed so that, by 1857, Paul Cullen could boast that 'Souperism is dead in Dublin ... the people are very excited against them'.[61] St Brigid's schools were established in the 1860s 'to withdraw the children of the neighbourhood from Protestant and proselytising schools', and in 1863 they took over the former Ragged Schools at West Park Street, directly opposite the ICM's Coombe Schools.[62] The Catholic Ragged School, St Brigid's and Francis Street Catholic schools were enlarged to provide additional places.[63] As with the Franciscan schools in John MacHale's Tuam diocese, these remained independent of state control. A description of St Brigid's pupils provides an assessment of mission-school pupils since both drew from the same community:

Their parents are in and out of jail ... through the temptation of drink totally neglect their children ... they are squalid and naked ... usually grow up without the knowledge or practice of religion ... it is from this class of children that the proselytisers fill their orphanages, houses and asylums, robbing them of their faith.[64]

By harnessing the Catholic middle class to fund alternative schooling for the poor and to conduct a vigilant campaign towards the ICM, the threat of slum proselytism was brought under control. By 1865, extreme hostility towards the mission had abated to the extent that the ICM reported that the mission was 'to be let alone'.[65] The battle for the souls of Dublin's poor was not over however. It would continue for decades, albeit on a reduced scale.

The Irish Church Missions was aware of the lack of a middle class in the west of Ireland, where the onus of counter-mission fell squarely on the shoulders of Catholic parish clergy, who regularly appealed for funds to establish Catholic schools in Connemara. Fr Kavanagh sought funds in the *Catholic Directory* to establish a convent in Oughterard and Michael Mulkerrin, parish priest of Killanin (Spiddal), informed readers of *The Telegraph* that his parishioners were exposed to 'incessant and most trying temptations to lure them from the holy faith of their sainted forefathers'.[66] When the Synod of Thurles (1850) decreed that Catholic children could attend national schools in districts where no Catholic alternative was available,[67] Rome ordered Archbishop MacHale to provide schools which would educate the young 'without any peril to their faith'.[68] Parish schools were established in Oughterard parish at Leam and Glan (Galway diocese) which remained independent of the national board for a decade.[69] In his own diocese of Tuam, MacHale tolerated but did not champion the foundation of national schools, which Connemara's Catholic clergy founded from the mid 1850s, causing a large decrease in mission-school attendance.[70] For instance three schools were opened between 1853 and 1861 to oppose the efforts of the ICM's Sellerna mission.[71] Numbers at the ICM's Connemara schools fell from 1,500 during the famine to 700 in 1853, when it was claimed that pupils were drafted in 'from different and distant parts, in order to form a stranglehold there'.[72] This decline in mission involvement following the establishment of rival national schools was also observed in other areas of missionary activity such as north Mayo, where attendances at Presbyterian mission schools declined from 2,000 to 870 between 1852 and 1854.[73] On a national scale, attendances at ICM schools continued to decline, from 18,873 to 13,195 between 1856 and 1858.[74]

In spite of the success of national schools in halting the progress of proselytising missions, John MacHale continued to prefer schools under his direct control, such as the Franciscan schools at Clifden, Roundstone and Tourmakeady, telling readers of *The Tablet* of 22 January 1853 that proselytism vanished when faced with the Franciscans' 'self-sacrificing zeal'. Education was withheld from most of the Tuam diocese until national schools were introduced on a comprehensive scale after MacHale's death in 1881.

The provision of Catholic parish missions

Cullen knew that it was inconceivable that MacHale would admit the degree of his difficulties, as MacHale continued to condemn national schools and denied that there was any proselytism in his diocese.[75] Following a report in the Protestant *Dublin Evening Mail* of 18 February 1852 that over 10,000 persons had renounced popery in Connemara, Cullen informed Tobias Kirby, his successor at the Irish College in Rome, that MacHale still denied the 'awful … falling away' around Clifden and refused to admit any form of counter-missionary force. Cullen suggested that a trip to Rome might change MacHale's mind.[76]

Cullen's assertion that MacHale denied the presence and danger of the ICM is not wholly true. The failure of the ICM at Castlekerke and Oughterard may be partly attributed to their location in the Catholic diocese of Galway to which John MacEvilly was appointed in 1857 and where he quickly adopted an aggressive system of counter-mission. MacEvilly, a friend and ally of Margaret Aylward, was aware of the multi-pronged counter-missionary tactics adopted in Dublin. He quickly sent a Vincentian mission to Oughterard and reported later that year that not even a 'vestige of the accursed system of souperism' existed after their visit,[77] an assertion he retracted the following year.[78] Oughterard mission school continued for decades after MacEvilly's triumphant claim, although the existence of a school should not suggest healthy attendances, as local sources suggest that it attracted few pupils.[79] Michael Kavanagh, parish priest of Oughterard, asked as early as 1853 'How long will the English people remain in darkness … [There are villages] from two to nine miles from Oughterard, of whose inhabitants, not one, even in those days when famine stalked the land, ever became a Jumper'.[80]

Catholic authorities were correct about the ICM's lack of progress at Oughterard and Castlekerke, as by then proselytism was on the wane in that region.[81] Further west, however, Connemara lay open to the ICM's advances where MacHale's obstinacy deprived thousands of Ireland's poorest of even the minimum educational provision as parish clergy could only establish a limited number of national schools without the official and financial support of their archbishop.

Dr MacHale's efforts to retain total and sole control of his diocese were undermined by the direct intervention of the Vatican. He ignored a summons to Rome in 1851, explaining that he could not leave his flock when the wolf was on them. Aggressive work was not undertaken in the Tuam diocese until early 1853, possibly in response to Cullen's accurate observation to Kirby in November 1852 that MacHale was giving a free hand to the ICM.[82] The following year, MacHale reluctantly admitted the Rosminian priests, Frs Rinolfi and Lockhart, to undertake parish missions.

Catholic parish missions usually lasted one or two weeks and involved up to three sermons daily, covering subjects such as commandments and sacraments, and giving catechetical instruction, sometimes interpreted by Irish-speaking Christian Brothers.[83] A memoir from the Vincentian order, which was already effective in the heavily proselytised area of Dingle, describes how the formation of lay organisations was an essential element and was crucial for the perpetuation of their influence.[84] A Christian Doctrine Confraternity would be first established to provide catechetical instruction; then a Living Rosary Confraternity, which was concerned with the furnishing and maintenance of the church building; then a Temperance Society; then conferences of the Society of St Vincent de Paul and the Ladies' Association of Charity. In this regard, Catholic authorities were heavily reliant on literate middle-class members to reinforce their message. Following a successful five week parish mission in Oughterard in 1852, male and female Sodalities of the Christian Doctrine, a Sodality of the Sacred Heart, a Sodality of the Living Rosary, and a branch of the Society of the Saint Vincent de Paul were established.[85] Irish-speaking Vincentian missionaries, who promised to report directly to Paul Cullen, were employed in the Galway diocese, while Rosminians, who spoke no Irish, were engaged in the Tuam diocese by MacHale.[86]

A triumphant account of the successful parish missions in the Tuam diocese in 1853–54 told of the defeat of the 'proselytising charlatans' who had formerly posed such a threat. It reported that Clifden Catholic church could not accommodate the vast congregations and that 150 persons reverted in Roundstone.[87] Even Paul Cullen was forced to acknowledge their success.[88]

Considerable evidence exists that Catholic missions pressurised converts to revert to their former faith, as when 300 converts reverted in Oughterard in 1852 with 'wonderful and edifying sorrow for their crime'.[89] These missions instilled a vigilance among the Catholic clergy, who were ever watchful for 'defections', patrolling their flock to ward off 'the devouring wolves in sheep's clothing'.[90] In the days when mission relief provided the surest or even the sole means of survival, many considered it best to live a Protestant and die a Catholic; one Connemara landowner even asserted that Catholics pretended to convert with the collusion of the priests.[91] Such ambiguity was unacceptable after the onset of aggressive counter-mission; converts could no longer be 'Soupers on week-days and Catholics on Sundays'.[92] The tendency and obligation to return to Catholicism at death were reinforced by street-ballads which told of converts pleading for forgiveness.[93] This caused great tension at death-bed scenes with ICM missionaries and priests battling over the dying, as when Revd George Shea of Sellerna and Fr Patrick Roynayne fought at the bedside of Michael Kinnealy.[94]

To appease Rome, John MacHale called two provincial synods at Tuam in 1854 and 1858, ostensibly to improve church discipline, administration of the sacraments and religious instruction. The 1858 synod stipulated priests could not denounce any person from the altar, which some clergy ignored with impunity.[95]

While the successful Catholic missions of the 1850s caused most converts to return to their former faith, some converts remained steadfastly Protestant. For most of these persons, the benefits of mission involvement, such as employment and housing, outweighed the consequences of social exclusion, although most converts eventually reverted. Frs Downey and Lydon observed a difference between these more committed converts and those who quickly reverted under the pressure of parish missions. Those who remained Protestant for a considerable time became 'reluctant Catholics' who 'if they did not become good practical Catholics, seemed at least to have abandoned the camp of the enemy'.[96] In contrast, Harriet Martineau was critical of Catholic and Protestant missions alike, remarking that 'The Catholic and Protestant zealots seem to be trying, as for a wager, which can fastest drive the people into an ignorant contempt of all faiths whatever'.[97]

Ostracism and persecution of ICM converts and mission staff
Lay Catholic opposition to the ICM mainly took the form of social ostracism and direct violence against the convert community, an effective tactic in the closely knit communities of west Galway. James Murphy has shown that, in Dingle in the early 1840s, ostracism was a spontaneous reaction in which Catholic missioners played no part.[98] In contrast, the Catholic laity of Connemara seemed to excuse their 'pervert' neighbours, especially those driven by destitution to send their children to mission schools. Consequently, ostracism was ordered from on high by Archbishop MacHale, parish clergy and visiting missionaries, who ordered that Catholics should

> separate themselves completely from intercourse with the Jumper ... not to
> speak to them, not to lend or borrow from them; not to allow them into their

homes nor upon their land ... they were directed to sign themselves with the cross everytime they met one in public or in private.[99]

This tactic proved very successful and ICM supporters claimed that many were prevented from openly converting 'knowing the many things they have to give up if they come out'.[100] Opposition extended to violence against converts and mission agents, with frequent destruction of personal and mission property, such as the burning of Widow O'Donnell's house in Errismore (see chapter 5). Hyacinth D'Arcy considered that this episode was motivated by 'religious animosity' fuelled by persistent priestly denunciations of 'readers and all who listened to them, and especially those who harboured them'.[101]

ICM supporters were informed of violence endured by mission personnel via annual reports and the *Banner of the Truth*, which gave monthly accounts of the 'provocation and insult' endured at the instigation of the Catholic priests.[102] It reported that persecuted and socially isolated converts were boycotted in business and therefore depended on the ICM for employment. Many were physically assaulted, such as those in Ballyhane, where

> Pat Jordan was whipped on the road by a priest. Ann O'Mally, a little school-girl was hit with a stone. Biddy Houghty and Mary Jordan were hunted and struck with stones ... Pat. Archibold was publicly denounced for selling meal to the 'jumpers' and was obliged to refuse them, lest his house would be burned ... Mrs Staunton with three in family, earned her living by spinning wool, she can get no employment now. Mrs Burke, with four in family, supported herself similarly, and is similarly situated. Mrs Marks, two in family, had to leave her service ...[103]

Protestant newspapers, in both Ireland and England, such as *The Irish Missionary Record and Chronicle of the Reformation* (Dublin, 1852–54), published detailed reports of violence endured by mission agents. Catholic clergy were inevitably depicted as instigators,[104] as at Roundstone where priests, monks and boatmen 'lately entered the mission house, beat the boys, and drove them out'.[105] It should be noted that the geography of violent outrages in 1853 coincided with the western mission tour of Frs Rinolfi and Lockhart.[106] The concurrence of street violence and Catholic missions can also be established in Dublin, where serious rioting in the Coombe coincided with a Vincentian mission at the parish of St Nicholas of Myra, Francis Street.[107]

Catholic clergy insisted that those who died as Protestants could not be buried in Catholic graves. Such was the case of Connemara convert, John Halloran, who withstood his family's efforts to fetch Fr Roynayne. The previous Sunday, the priest had preached that Halloran's soul was in hell, that his neighbours should not pray for him and that he should not be allowed burial in his family plot. George Shea, ICM missionary at Sellerna assured supporters that Halloran had 'died in peace with God ... trusting in him alone for salvation'.[108]

There is ample evidence of social ostracism and exclusive dealing, consistent tactics of Catholic opposition throughout west Galway. In Spiddal and Inverin for instance, Revd Mecredy reported that he could obtain neither school premises nor lodgings for his schoolteacher, that nobody would deal with mission personnel and that he knew many converts who were beaten for attending service.[109] Undoubtedly converts 'suffered daily insults and nightly outrage' for their association with the ICM[110] and countless examples were reported by mission tourists.[111] For example, it was claimed that a Catholic landlord near Clifden evicted eight convert families without notice and knocked down their houses, refusing to accept their rent.[112]

Most of all, Catholic clergy feared the influence of Irish or text teachers, whose payment in early years depended on their attracting the interest of their neighbours. Catholics were warned to 'Bless yourselves when you meet them. Don't have anything to do with them'[113] and John MacHale exhorted Tuam Catholics to 'avoid the deadly enemy ... [who] would rob you of your soul, by gaining wages for apostatising'.[114]

Those who availed of mission relief were ridiculed in street-ballads. 'The Spriggers' lists some of Oughterard's converts and 'Soup House Mhuigh-iorrais' names James Lyden, a convert scripture reader who worked in Connemara from the early 1850s until his death in 1918.[115] Some ballads were considered highly inflammatory, for example Martin Power was arrested in Back-Lane during rioting in the Coombe for singing ballads of a 'seditious nature', especially the song entitled *The Devil among the Soupers*.[116] These songs were often long-lived, remembered for longer than the events or persons they sought to immortalise; the following Dublin ballad was sung for Lucy McDiurmid when she collected material for her 2006 publication:

> Now Maisie Brown was terrible poor
> The neighbours said she was on the flure
> Now she rides to hell in a coach and four
> Since she prayed with Mrs Smyly.[117]

Social exclusion of persons with mission associations extended to mothers of mission pupils, who were not churched following the birth of children, and in the fishing communities along the Connemara sea-board converts were excluded from the vital fishing trade.[118] Ostracism continued for decades after the intense violence had abated. By present-day standards, the tactics of the Catholic church appear harsh but it must be remembered that Catholics were convinced that certain and eternal damnation awaited those who meddled with Protestantism. Just like the committed Protestants of the day, Catholics 'knew' they belonged to the one and only true church.

Once a Catholic individual or a family were 'identified with the ICM, intense local resentment forced most to emigrate',[119] but probably not as many as the mission claimed after its low convert numbers were exposed by the 1861 census. As will be discussed later, some explanation was necessary as great advances against Catholicism had been claimed which did not materialise. Revd Archdall (later bishop of Killaloe) promised a Dublin audience in 1857 that 'The time is coming. The light is becoming too strong ... This will be a Protestant land – may I live to see it.'[120] The ICM's reliance on the 'emigration excuse' was scathingly mocked by Catholic polemicists, who enquired the whereabouts of the vast number of converts long before the 1861 census: 'Where then are the millions who have been emancipated from Popish errors, and who have openly left the Church of Rome?', scoffingly inquiring the whereabouts of the convert community: 'there is a fatality about it – it never appears. The converts are carried off by emigration ... The country remains as Popish as ever. The schools, too have, in great part, like the ghosts of inquirers and converts, become invisible.'[121] Low convert numbers were, in fact, due to landslide reversions to Catholicism once the severity of the famine and its aftermath had abated, and after the Catholic church had mounted a concerted campaign against proselytism.

Catholic polemical opposition

The forum for public debate on the merits or otherwise of Protestant mission was the pulpit and the public press. Among the most prolific clerical letter-writers were Archbishop Paul Cullen, Fr James Maher of Graigue, County Carlow (uncle of Paul Cullen), Daniel Cahill of Dublin and Patrick Lavelle of Partry. These men eloquently informed the Irish and English public that the ICM utilised famine conditions to undermine the Catholic faith of the Irish peasant, which 'he and his fathers had ever held to God',[122] writing open letters to persons in authority which were published in the English and Irish media and sold in pamphlet form.[123] Catholic clergy rejected invitations to engage in direct controversial debate, aware that a previous dialogue had provided abundant publicity for the Protestant cause,[124] while Cullen's pastoral of 1857 forbade the laity from taking part in controversial discussions.[125]

Catholic polemical writings reveal a number of approaches which were subtly combined to increase their appeal and influence. An effective tactic was identifying allegiance to Catholicism with loyalty to the Irish nation. Other tactics included accusing the ICM of capitalising on destitution or offering bribes for conversion, questioning its claimed successes, denouncing the Protestant faith and condemning the ICM's use of controversialism.

Professor Comerford has outlined how the foundations of the inter-relationship between Irishness and Catholicism were laid down in the seventeenth century and disseminated through writings such as Geoffrey Keating's *Foras feasa ar Éirinn [Compendium of knowledge about Ireland]* (1634), the prologue of which comprises a rebuttal of Giraldus Cambrensis and other writers such as Spenser whom Keating considered to have denigrated the Irish.[126] It is clear that the Catholic church saw nineteenth-century proselytism as an extension of the religious struggle that had persisted for centuries. Drawing from an armoury of Jacobite sectarian rhetoric, counter-missionary tactics emphasised the 'deep rooted attachment of the Irish people to the faith'.[127] Fr Cahill told how the Irishman 'received his faith more than two thousand years ago and has never for a moment swerved from it since',[128] while Fr Maher asked whether the Irish were to reject 'the faith of our forefathers, for which we have bled for centuries ...'.[129]

Harnessing the already extant religious and political tensions of nineteenth-century Ireland, the Catholic authorities combined the ideologies of Irishness and Catholicism to synergistic effect, as when Clifden's parish priest urged his congregation: 'Let them never think, boys, that the evergreen flourishing three [sic] shall be routed out of Catholic Clifden and the pale yally [sic], orange, faded flower planted in its stead',[130] while another chronicler told of 'the power of persuasion which Protestantism possesses when enforced at the point of a bayonet or administered through the medium of stirabout'.[131] Street-ballads were also astutely employed to reinforce the connection of Britishness and Protestantism and equally between Irishness and Catholicism, even among the illiterate. Connections of this nature had long been forged and many of these ballads were penned prior to the establishment of the ICM, but the onset of this campaign of aggressive proselytism provided a renewed opportunity to give voice to nationalist resentments and to nurture this connection. These ballads and anthems rejoiced in the triumph of the Roman church over Protestant missionaries by cleverly linking the former oppression of Catholicism under penal laws with contemporary missionary onslaught:

> Years have passed of sad succession,
> Under many a tyrants reign,
> Slaves we were to their oppression,
> And wore their poisoned fettered chains,

By Harry, Bess, Calvin and Luther,
Our blessed clergy suffered sore,
But to their legal legislation,
Romans won't submit no more.[132]

Folklore evidence reveals the success of such rhetoric in fostering a connection between the ICM and the British establishment. For instance, eighty years later, an elderly Franciscan Brother in Clifden incorrectly asserted that ICM schools were government backed, an allegation entirely without foundation, while an Oughterard resident (also incorrectly) recalled that 'government soup-houses' had been established at Oughterard, Glan, Glen Gabhla and Castle-Kirk [sic], 'to entice the starving to change their religion'.[133] The dual involvement of some Protestant landlords of Connemara in both government-relief schemes and proselytism may explain mistaken 'memories' that government relief was only distributed to those who converted.[134]

The writings of Daniel Cahill (1796–1864) in particular did much to facilitate this perception. In an extensive letter-writing campaign which ran to at least thirteen published letters, the lord lieutenant, the earl of Carlisle, was accused of taking part in the 'Irish Souper affair' on the basis of a £5 donation to the Coombe Ragged Schools where, according to Dr Cahill, Dublin's poor were asked 'to foreswear their creed, to perjure their conscience, to learn hypocrisy and to foster malignity'.[135] Although there is no evidence to support Cahill's claim that the ICM was government backed, its activities must be viewed in the context of proselytism in general as several Protestant orphanages which accepted Catholic children were in receipt of government grants.[136] It must also be remembered that, from the outset, ICM supporters hoped that the mission would effect change, not only in the religious beliefs of Irish Catholics, but also in their political and ideological allegiances.

The popular appeal of Dr Cahill's letter-writing campaign to English notables may be estimated from the many songs composed in his honour, which contain copious derogatory references to Protestantism as the creed of Cromwell, Bess, Neddy, Harry, Luther and Calvin and which clearly identify the English conquest of Ireland with efforts to eradicate Catholicism.[137] Rhetoric of this type which reinforced existing beliefs that conversion represented, not merely the loss of one's faith and birthright but also a treacherous coupling with the English enemy, ultimately contributed to the presumption that to be wholly Irish, one had to be Catholic, as discussed in chapter 7. Fr Maher's output was more moderate and measured, posing the most pertinent question of all, 'Could men change their convictions or be converted from one faith to another, when the intellect is deranged, and no thought rests on the mind but to get food?'[138]

Catholic writers appealed to the English press to expose how Ireland was under siege from the proselytisers, charging that it was cruel and cowardly to 'torture starving creatures to change the religion and that success was only achieved because the country was starving'. Fr Cahill confidently promised that Irish Catholics would maintain a steadfast allegiance to Catholicism in spite of the mission's 'soup and bacon theology', and asserted that, were conditions in Ireland to improve, 'the soup-kitchens of these hypocrites [would be] without one Irish beggar'.[139] Paul Cullen repeatedly outlined the fact that the ICM targeted the most vulnerable section of society using 'a system of pecuniary proselytism ... to make converts by bribes and gold ... by the many bigoted and fanatical haters of Catholicity'.[140] In an obvious attack on Mrs Whately and Mrs Smyly, he appealed to Dublin's liberal Protestants to distance themselves from the 'fanatical agents of proselytising societies ... the wives and daughters of dignitaries of the Establishment, and of doctors and other professional men ...'.[141]

From the outset the ICM was forced to refute allegations of bribery as 'utterly groundless', as will be discussed later.[142] The mission's provision of children's homes was condemned as 'opprobrious bribery and kidnapping of the children of the starving, naked poor'[143] and while Catholic polemicists admitted it was charitable to feed the hungry and clothe the naked, they considered it the work of Satan to induce 'the recipients to renounce the religion of their fathers'.[144]

Catholic writers attacked the distribution of 'infamous tracts' which 'slander our creed'[145] and denounced scripture readers as a 'vulgar, illiterate horde of agents' who produced 'fabulous accounts of thousands and tens of thousands of conversions, where none exist'.[146] Mission agents were particularly reviled as 'ignorant, uneducated and characterless' persons who worked where 'poverty and distress press most heavily on the people'. It was claimed that their efforts 'irritate[d] the people beyond endurance', often resulting in violence which invariably resulted in court verdicts which were 'gratifying to the Bible-readers'.[147] The threat of reprisals against mission staff was frequently voiced; *The Telegraph* insisted that Irish Catholics would no longer ignore 'the open and outrageous attacks made upon their faith and their clergy'.[148] Similarly, Fr Cahill warned of the social discord caused by the 'treacherous Protestant Church' in trying to 'rob' Ireland of her faith while she lay 'in her bed of sickness'.[149]

The writings of some Catholic polemicists reveal an outright contempt for the 'lying practice of infidel Protestantism',[150] described as 'the grossest imposture ever practiced on the credulity of mankind, substituting falsehood and lies, and immorality, and vengeance, and exile, and death, for the merciful laws of Christ, and the eternal charities of God'.[151]

By the mid 1850s Catholic writers were claiming a certain degree of success, telling that 'the vile Soupers are gone', their system 'entirely failed', with converts returning 'with tears and supplications, begging pardon of God and the Church for the scandal they committed'.[152] They were encouraged by the reduction in support for the ICM and in 1857 Fr Maher reassured his readers that 'The good sense of [Irish] Protestants has at length become disgusted with it – they will have no more of it'[153] and in 1866 told that the English were beginning to 'view the subject aright'.[154] However, the following year he admitted the English public were unaware that the movement was an 'enormous fraud on the public' and a 'sham reformation', pleading that

> Oh if the press would but let England see things as they really are, the vile system of lying, of collecting money, the cunning and hypocrisy of the proselytisers, and the sufferings and tears of the poor, the harassing of conscience, and insults for adherence to the faith of their fathers, to which they are subjected, we would soon see an end to this nefarious proselytising traffic.[155]

The intensity of religious hostility in the mid nineteenth century between Roman Catholicism and evangelical Protestantism cannot be overstated, as both sides vehemently protested their own viewpoint. We cannot appreciate the depth of feeling that prompted Henry and Robert Wilberforce, converts to Catholicism and sons of the renowned evangelical William Wilberforce, to purchase land and actually move from England to Connemara to counteract the progress of the ICM.[156] Even Dallas acknowledged that criticism from a Wilberforce would carry more weight among the English public 'than MacHale or Cullen'.[157]

Henry Wilberforce waged public campaign to draw the attention of the English public to the ICM's methodologies. As secretary of the Catholic Defence Association, he publicly criticised the ICM, contrasting the 'fundamental rule of the society' that funds could not be used for temporal relief with the mission's feeding programme, dismissing the ICM's claims that 'a few benevolent individuals … collect small subscriptions'.[158] Wilberforce questioned the sincerity of the ICM's converts, asserting that many 'pretended converts' declared on their death-beds that they had always been 'Catholics at heart'. Astutely reading the situation, Wilberforce stated that it was quite possible that 'one agent be employed in teaching and another in bribing … [and] that the bribery fund may be kept separate from the school fund'.[159] This was to be the basis of George Webster's charges, as discussed later.

The decline in English support for the ICM

The appeal of converting Irish Catholics resonated with the ultra-Protestants of Britain in whom anti-Catholic sentiments had been nurtured during the first half of the nineteenth century, and most especially during the protests against the granting of Catholic emancipation (1829), the increase in the grants to Maynooth (1845) and the restoration of the Roman Catholic hierarchy in Britain (1851). The fortuitous timing of the establishment of the ICM placed it in an advantageous position to capitalise on these movements.

The 1840s and 1850s campaigns against the Maynooth grant, and against the Papal Aggression of 1851–52, drew support from Protestants of all denominations.[160] However, by the mid 1850s the decline in anti-Catholic sentiment in Britain was obvious. The demise of the movement has been dated to 1860 by John Wolffe and to 1862 by Theodore Hoppen, after which time few attempts were made to regulate Catholicism by parliamentary means.[161] The fall-off in subscriptions to the ICM from 1854 reflected a shift in evangelical preoccupation from Irish to continental Catholicism and increased anti-nunnery activity.

From an ultra-Protestant viewpoint, ongoing parliamentary discussion regarding Catholicism was necessary to keep the cause in public view. The division in the anti-Catholic vote in 1851, which led to the defeat of Disraeli's motion to censure the prime minister, Lord John Russell, over his handling of the Papal Aggression, marked the demise of united Protestant parliamentary agitation.[162] Shaftesbury noted in 1851 that parliamentary anti-Catholicism was political rather than religious and that many Anglicans viewed evangelical agitation suspiciously because of its association with Dissent.[163] In the absence of a united cause to rally against, internal schisms along denominational lines surfaced in formerly well-supported interdenominational societies, resulting in infighting and duplication of efforts.[164] The second phase of anti-Maynooth agitation in 1851–52 was clearly concentrated in Scotland, with less backing in England and scarcely any support in Ireland. The dominance of Dissent over Anglicanism in Scotland ensured that opposition to Maynooth did not automatically translate into support for the Anglican Irish Church Missions.[165]

In the face of divisions in parliament along party lines, and internal tensions in evangelical societies along denominational lines, cohesive Protestant agitation began to crumble, albeit slowly. The advancement of constitutional Protestantism was further weakened by the replacement of the Derby government with the Aberdeen coalition. The disintegration of parliamentary Protestantism must be viewed in tandem with an increasingly militant Catholic parliamentary presence. The temporary hiatus in the Maynooth debate coincided with a switching of Protestant preoccupations from the conversion of Ireland to religious liberty abroad, triggered by the Madiai episode. The anti-convent movement also gained prominence at this time, with claims that women were involuntarily detained, coupled with demands for inspection and regulation of convents. By the mid 1850s, as the threat of Catholicism was superseded by the Crimean War and ensuing economic difficulties at home, disintegrating Protestant organisations were unable to rouse public interest in the defeat of Catholicism and the cause of converting Ireland waned. At the collapse of the Aberdeen government in 1855, Derby wrote that the time was 'singularly inopportune for the agitation of any question connected with such a subject' i.e. inopportune to resurrect ultra-Protestant causes.[166]

The third revival of the anti-Maynooth campaign in 1855–56 showed that although English support had increased considerably from a fairly small baseline, the cause no longer attracted the interest of the mainstream public. By then the momentum and support base of the anti-popery movement had suffered an 'unmistakable decline' and a number of anti-Maynooth candidates lost their seats in the general election of 1857.[167] Although publications such as *The Record* and *The Bulwark* attempted to keep it in the public eye, in the absence of a successful campaign against Catholicism, the protection of Protestantism slipped from view, accelerated by the death of many who had led the cause since the 1830s.[168] This decline in anti-Catholicism was to some extent reversed during the 1860s and 1870s but took the shape of fervent campaigns against ritualism and convents as by then the public had lost interest in political Protestantism and aggressive attempts to convert Roman Catholics.

The importance and appeal of the ICM within nineteenth-century anti-Catholicism may be gauged by comparing its income at the height of the anti-popery movement with that of the better-known pan-Protestant Evangelical Alliance. Table 4.1 clearly demonstrates that the ICM commanded vastly more support than did the Evangelical Alliance. Decreasing anti-Catholic fervour was mirrored in the ICM's declining income (see figure 4.3). This was exacerbated by the lack of success evident from the 1861 census when the great results promised by the ICM did not materialise, as discussed later. Mission income was severely affected by the dual problems of decreasing English interest in ultra-Protestant concerns and an obvious lack of success. Ongoing accusations of improper conduct, charges of bribery and distaste at the mission's use of controversy exacerbated its precarious financial position. In future decades, the ICM would be further side-lined within the power structures of the empire when the Conservative party, in response to the growing secularisation of the

Table 4.1 Annual incomes (£) of the Irish Church Missions and Evangelical Alliance, 1850–59

	1850	1851	1852	1853	1854	1855	1856	1857	1858	1859
Irish Church Missions	6,285	12,689	28,962	37,183	40,039	39,030	31,217	29,093	26,530	N/A
Evangelical Alliance	1,508	1,421	1,222	1,408	N/A	N/A	2,415	2,340	N/A	1,716

Source: ICM and Evangelical Alliance annual reports, 1850–59

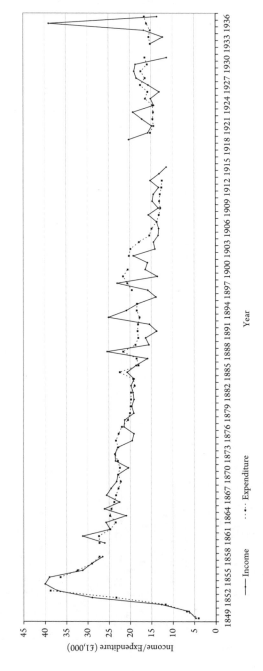

4.3 ICM income and expenditure, 1849–1937. Source: ICM, *Annual reports*, 1850–1937

United Kingdom, toned down its association with the Anglican church following Gladstone's convincing defeat of Disraeli in 1880.

The decline in income between 1855 and 1900 was not uniform across Britain. Monies remitted directly to the ICM headquarters in London did not decline to the same degree as auxiliary subscriptions. In the decade 1860–69, direct subscriptions declined by 9.17 per cent compared with a decrease in auxiliary subscriptions of 20.64 per cent.[169] From this may be inferred that, while the more 'dedicated' ultra-Protestants continued to support the cause, remitting their subscriptions directly to the London office, some rural clergy discontinued parish collections. The ICM's declining income might be ascribed to the decline in the prominence of evangelicalism within Anglicanism from the mid century, but since both the ICM and CPAS were centred in the evangelical party of the Church of England, given the increasing income of the CPAS, this argument is not valid.[170] The aims of both societies were similar: the dissemination of the Gospel to persons in ignorance, either the irreligious of England or the Catholics of Ireland. For a brief period, in the early 1850s, the incomes of the societies were approximately equal, but while that of the CPAS continued to increase, the ICM's income experienced a steady decline from the late 1850s.

It would be tempting to ascribe to the differing fortunes of the CPAS and ICM a disinclination among English people to convert other nationalities to Protestantism. This hypothesis, however, does not stand up to scrutiny. When the income of the CMS is examined, it is evident that the English contributed generously and consistently to the conversion of persons in foreign lands.[171] Since the English supported the dissemination of the Gospel at home (the CPAS) and abroad (the CMS), lack of missionary zeal cannot explain the decline in support for the ICM. In this light, the decreasing interest of the British public in the conversion of Irish Catholics reflects the changing direction of evangelicalism in the mid nineteenth century and confirms a political dimension to British anti-Catholicism.

Decline in Irish support for the ICM

Although most Protestants were in favour of winning Catholics to the scriptural truth, many came to criticise the ICM because of its alleged bribery of converts, its use of controversialism and its exaggerated claims of success. Kilkenny Protestants alerted the public to the ICM's use of controversy in 1856, prompting a letter-writer to *The Times* to ask 'why will Exeter Hall not leave Ireland alone?'[172] ICM methodologies in Kilkenny drew stinging criticism from leading Protestants, although the mission had the strong support of the evangelical bishop of Ossory, James O'Brien, who insisted that where parish clergy were unsuited 'for the rougher work of controversy', they should thankfully accept the assistance offered.[173] In 1855, James Tidmarsh, mayor of Kilkenny, rebuked ICM scripture readers for going

> about in the streets of the city and into the abode of wretchedness and misery, and to provoke controversies and thereby collect crowds and thereby cause disgraceful scenes, by using provoking language in scoffing at the mysteries of their religion.[174]

Ongoing violence towards mission agents, which was regularly reported in the Protestant media, resulted in the ICM frequently charging some of Kilkenny's Catholics with assault.[175] Protestant magistrates were unsympathetic to the plight of mission agents and Kilkenny's mayor argued that ICM scripture readers should be 'considered as provoking a breach of the peace'.[176] Over the following years, Kilkenny's Protestant community were to regularly protest at the Society's presence and the conduct of its scripture readers, causing the matter to be raised in the House of Lords, where a local magistrate was quoted as saying that he would not accept evidence of scripture readers, unless corroborated by an alternative source.[177] Bishop O'Brien's refusal to withdraw the ICM, although requested by leading Protestants, resulted in additional negative publicity from the Protestant community, whose letters to the Protestant *Kilkenny Moderator* were reproduced in the *Catholic Telegraph*.[178] Although not successful in closing the Kilkenny mission (which functioned until 1892), the publicised concerns of Kilkenny's Protestants damaged the ICM by drawing attention to unrest caused by its methodologies and by exposing that it did not command the unanimous support of Irish Protestantism.

The ICM was an English organisation, founded and driven by English evangelicals, with all important decisions made by its London committee; the lack of influence of persons with experience of Ireland seriously undermined the feasibility of the enterprise. In 1853 an unsuccesful merger took place between the ICM and the Irish Society, which comprised the Dublin Irish Society, the Irish Society of London and the Ladies' Auxiliary of the Irish Society. The union was eagerly sought by the London Irish Society but unsuccessfully resisted by the Irish Society of Dublin (which was mainly peopled by Irish clergy).[179] The rationale for the merger was the futility of four societies collecting funds in England for the same purpose, but while all societies may have shared the objective of converting Ireland's Catholics, there was little similarity between the methodologies of the IS and ICM; the controversialism of the ICM contrasting with the softly-softly approach of the IS. The ICM arrogantly remarked that 'the

Irish Society may be chiefly employed in preparing the ground, the Society for Irish Church Missions may be better adapted for bringing the crop to perfection'.[180] The IS greatly resented the ICM's insistence that it withdraw from all areas outside of Cashel, Limerick and Cork dioceses, as it was compelled to relinquish a large number of long-established stations, such as those of north Mayo which were soon closed by the ICM. The merger, planned at the zenith of the ICM's popularity, became a great financial burden as ICM income started to decline sharply.

Above all, the ICM's controversial approach greatly unsettled IS supporters. Dallas' arrogance and single-mindedness rendered him insensitive to the feelings and opinions of others. There was no place in the newly formed union for the traditionally mild approach of the IS as the ICM had no interest in providing education to those unwilling to openly convert. On 31 March 1856, after a trial three year period, the merger was dissolved, reflected in the ICM withdrawal from former IS stations in 1856. The differing methodologies were explained by Revd John Alcock at the IS annual meeting following the dissolution of the merger: 'The Irish Society was pushed out of its original, quiet, easy, simple progressive way of circulating the Scriptures among the peasantry in their own tongue, their mode of action was altered, and experience has now taught them that the alteration was not an improvement.'[181]

The IS complained that it had suffered financially from the episode and from 1856 its teachers were trained, not by the ICM, but by the Church Education Society.[182] The Dublin Irish Society reconvened, but not the Irish Society of London or the Ladies' Auxiliary of the Irish Society, although until 1902 the ICM's annual reports were entitled 'Report of the Committee of the Society for Irish Church Missions to the Roman Catholics with which is incorporated the late Irish Society of London'.

The popularity of the IS among Irish clerics may be attributed to its non-confrontational approach. It was more interested in bringing Catholics into contact with the scriptural truth than with their outward conversions. Its reports told of 'Roman Catholics coming out of the bondage of Rome, and ranging themselves on the side of the Church of the Reformation ... Roman Catholic teachers, Roman Catholic pupils, Roman Catholics attending meetings to be examined in the teaching of the Book of Life'.[183] In a thinly veiled rebuke of the ICM in 1862, the IS told of how it was welcomed back into Bandon, from where the ICM had recently withdrawn. 'The old Irish Society is still alive in the memory of numbers of people. Everywhere we hear it spoken of as part of the good old times, and often welcomed amongst us again.'[184]

The support of Irish Protestants was initially extended to the ICM but partially withdrawn after the dissolution of the merger between the IS and the ICM (1853–56). The Irish Society had long attracted substantial support among Irish Protestants, who well understood the need for a non-aggressive approach. Without the insight and wisdom of these Irish Protestants, policies were formed and decisions made by London committees so socially, culturally and geographically removed both from mission providers and recipients that the likelihood of permanent successful conversions was negligible. By antagonising this important segment of the Irish church, the ICM alienated many who might otherwise have backed its work, reflected in a diminution in Irish support from the mid 1850s. However, by placing all power in a central committee in London, the ICM prevented a splintering of its mission, as happened when Scottish supporters of the Presbyterian missions to north Mayo seized ownership of its flagship mission at Ballinglen, as discussed later.

Protestant objection to the ICM's use of controversy

Even among those who favoured the conversion of Irish Catholics, a large number disapproved of the combative approach of the Irish Church Missions, lamenting the 'hindrances to missionary work arising from … offensive controversy'.[185] Many considered this to be more likely to 'raise opposition and hatred' than to 'win men from error to the truth'.[186] Examples of ICM teachings and handbills include:[187] 'The popish mass is an invention of the Priests for personal homage; and a diabolical doctrine of grovelling idolatry'.[188] Controversial classes were less prevalent in Dublin's affluent parishes where middle-class Protestants were unhappy with the ICM's divisive methods and had no desire to attract the wrath of Paul Cullen.[189] Its methods were sharply criticised in 1869 by Thomas Andrews, an Irish Protestant who remembered how the mission's duty to spread the Gospel was deemed sufficient to justify 'the most objectionable means'. He recalled the 'constant irritation' to the Catholic population and 'thoroughly doubted' the ICM's claimed successes.[190]

Some Protestants objected to the offensive description of Catholicism which the ICM considered as merely elucidating 'the errors of Rome'; others objected because they feared Catholic reprisals. The Englishwoman, Matilda Houstoun was well acquainted with the ICM's work near her Connemara estate and was wholly in favour of converting Catholics to the scriptural truth. She was, however, highly critical of the ICM's missionaries, who had, she considered, 'but a little "knowledge", and a still smaller amount of tact … [but were not] deficient in *zeal* … [having] more than enough of that often dangerous quality'. She considered the local missionary a 'graceless zealot', whose practices such as referring to the virgin as 'a sinful, unrighteous woman' were counter-productive and insulting to Catholics, and who strove to provoke his 'priestly opponents to the bitterest wrath'.[191] She recorded that the entire enterprise was 'wholly unsuccessful' and that 'the pseudo-converts ... owed their salvation to the large Charity of Exeter Hall'.[192] Other Protestants, like Sir Digby Neave, recorded the progress made by the mission and thoroughly approved of its controversialism, which he felt was necessary to separate the Roman Catholics from their superstitious faith.[193] It may be assumed that Matilda Houstoun's twenty years' sojourn in Connemara generated a more informed opinion of the ICM and its methods than did Digby Neave's visit of four days.

Many Irish Protestants, mindful of their numerical inferiority, feared the consequences of the mission with good reason. James Godkin commented that children attending a parish school in Dublin were 'hooted ... though previously they had not been molested'.[194] This quote refers to the parish of St Michan, Dublin, where Revd Stanford's weekly controversial classes were attended by some 700 persons in 1850, resulting in much tension and outright conflict.[195] During the tenure of his two successors, when no controversial work had been undertaken, there was little trouble; but 1866 saw the resurgence of interdenominational tension following the appointment of Revd William Marrable to the parish and the recommencement of controversial classes. The conduct of some mission agents was a cause of concern for parish clergymen. Godkin described instances when clergy, regretting the arrival of controversial missionaries, were forced to 'shut up the schools and lecture-rooms, on account of the alleged misconduct of the lay missionaries'.[196]

Writing from the safety of England, Revd George Venables criticised Protestants who withheld the scriptural truth from Catholics 'for fear of a little opposition' and explained that 'outrageous opposition always ceases after three or four years'.[197] He complained that tolerant Protestants must have 'but a very insignificant idea of the errors of Romanism or they would not be deterred by opposition', but acknowledged that some agents might 'be possessed with a spirit of controversy in which love may be lacking'.[198] Former staunch supporter, Revd William McIlwaine of Belfast, severed his connection with the ICM in 1860 because of the Society's 'utter mismanagement' of its operations, explaining that since the ICM was administered from England, its agents were inadequately supervised and its funds wasted. He argued that the ICM had ignored advice to *Festina Lente*, seeking that all Ireland's Catholics were to be 'instantaneously converted' which justified the use of any methods. He criticised the means employed and described the ICM's ordained missionaries as 'raw, untrained, and often ill-qualified young men' and its lay agents as 'all of an inferior class ... incapable of writing English grammatically'.[199]

Evidence of Protestant disquiet at the ICM's controversial methods may be gleaned from Clifden Protestant Marian Freyer's 1861 publication which sought 'to contradict the many false statements made by enemies of the Irish Church Missions'. She acknowledged indifference among her coreligionists and regretted that many 'wish[ed] to live in peace with all men'.[200] *The Banner* admitted that many Protestants withheld support because of 'that objection they entertain to controversy'.[201] Others withheld support through apathy[202] or because they considered the cause unnecessary 'because those whom we seek to convert are already called by the sacred name of Christians'.[203] The *Christian Examiner* condemned this complacent attitude, unable to comprehend why foreign missions were supported 'while there is utter indifference to and entire neglect of those who are in equally absolute darkness at home'.[204] Recent scholarship confirms that an increasing appreciation of the 'communal strife' occasioned by proselytism caused even militant Protestants to be 'more circumspect and cautious about their missionary activities'.[205]

Protestant opposition of grounds of bribery

In 1847 there had been intense, outspoken criticism of a group of Belfast clergymen who formed the 'Fund for the Temporal Relief of the Suffering Poor of Ireland through the Instrumentality of the Clergy of the Established Church'. The object of this movement was to provide relief and spiritual succour to the distressed so that 'advantage may be taken of these providential circumstances'.[206] This movement quickly encountered intense opposition as many Protestants disapproved of offering assistance on condition of conversion.[207] Thus, at the formal establishment of the ICM in 1849, which resembled a re-embodiment of the 1847 movement, the ICM committee for missions was quick to defray suggestions of bribery or of capitalising on want. Nevertheless, many Protestants remained sceptical.[208]

Archbishop Whately denounced the 1847 movement, asserting that 'all the grace of charitable action is destroyed if we present ourselves as seeking to take an ungenerous advantage of misery and convert our benefactions into a bribe to induce men to do violence to their consciences'.[209] Opposition was even raised in parliament, where Lord Brougham said in 1847 that to raise monies to convert destitute Catholics was 'one of the most diabolical devices for sowing dissention where only charity should prevail'.[210] Newspapers were equally vehement in their opposition, the *Banner of Ulster* criticised it, stating,

> at a time when such frightful destitution is prevalent, it is surely most unwise to put forth denominational peculiarities in such an offensive form and this to give the impression that proselytism is to be the basis of charity. We regret

this movement all the more as it is likely to interfere with the other efforts made in the cause and to add to the existing calamity, the element of religious animosity.[211]

The committee of the ICM were very much awake to potential allegations of bribery and, from the outset, insisted that it did not, and would not, distribute relief of any sort.[212] Not all Protestants were convinced by its pledges. Several newspapers were outspoken against ICM methods, especially in relation to the temporal rewards offered, for example the *Northern Whig* suggested that persons of integrity should not support the ICM as

> There is a difference between *inducing* a child or man to do what he believes to be wrong, and *striving to convince* him that what he believes to be wrong is really not so. The former process 'addresses arguments to his hunger'; it endeavours to feed him into Protestantism. Happily, there are within the Irish establishment men who, loving their Church much, love honour and fair dealing more.[213]

Other denominations faced the dilemma of providing food while attempting to disseminate the scriptures. The Home Mission of the Presbyterian Church openly acknowledged the necessity to feed the starving:

> there will still be such opportunity of extending the hand of mercy to the poor and the needy, as will make room for the message of the gospel. Irrespectively of this, indeed, it is our duty to feed the hungry and clothe the naked ... but along with the bread that perisheth, giving freely the bread of life to every one that will receive it.[214]

Objections on the grounds of bribery surfaced from within Protestantism from the mid 1850s when George Webster, curate of Archbishop Whately's chaplain Dr West, raised concerns about the ICM's tactics in the impoverished Dublin parish of Irishtown.[215] Both West and Webster, who had ready access to the archbishop, were staunch opponents of ultra-Protestantism and especially of the ICM.

In 1855 Webster alleged that ICM agents distributed bread to needy Catholics at the end of proselytising services and that it paid a man to impersonate a Catholic and be defeated in argument at a controversial meeting in Irishtown. The ensuing controversy triggered a sworn inquiry in 1857, presided over by Archbishop Whately. The conduct of the inquiry was somewhat strained when Alexander Dallas cautioned a respectable parishioner of the possibility of libel and only proceeded when Whately forced him to concede immunity from prosecution. The ICM neither admitted nor denied the allegations, merely saying it had no knowledge of what had happened two years earlier. When Dallas promised that his proselytising movement would have 'glorious fruit', Whately asked for evidence of the blossoms.[216]

The verdict of the inquiry was puzzling. Whately accepted Dallas' explanation for why money was handed to an attendant at the above discussion but said that it was an unwise action and totally ignored the issue of distributing food to the poor on condition that they attend service. He pointed to the 'absence of proof of any positive good results' and banned the ICM from Irishtown, writing that 'for the present, there was an uncompensated evil of much acrimonious feeling ... [in place of] those quieter approaches of good which had formerly attested'.[217]

The episode was revived six years later when George Webster, then chancellor of Cork Cathedral, preached a sermon in which he stated that the ICM had 'bribed their supposed converts and that he could prove they had done so'.[218] In the interim, the public had grown aware that other missionary societies had bribed converts to provide weak Catholic opposition at controversial discussions, as when it was proven that James Mathison was paid by John Hope to participate and be defeated by advocates of scriptural Protestantism at public meetings in Glasgow.[219] Much of the ensuing debate between Webster and the ICM hinged on the definition of bribery, which the ICM defined as 'giving money or anything else to Roman Catholics to declare themselves Protestants', while Webster insisted that it was the granting of temporal relief to anyone 'for the purpose of tempting him to do what his conscience condemns'.[220] He insisted that this was what the ICM did when they gave food and clothes to Catholics to induce them to listen to instruction in the Protestant faith. This was the complaint of the LAC, which said that the poor were 'lured by the offer of a small cut of bread, and then obliged in return to listen to blasphemous language and a sermon from the minister'.[221] The controversy, which was conducted in the public press in both England and Ireland, was subsequently reproduced in three pamphlets: a careful selection of correspondence published by the ICM,[222] the *Only Complete Copy* containing the entire correspondence edited by 'Four Rectors'[223] and a third written by John C. Colquhoun, ICM chairman, to answer the publication of the 'Four Rectors'.[224] Regrettably, these 'Four Rectors' did not identify themselves even during the ensuing controversy, which renders this exposé less authoritative.

The central focus of the debate was whether it was right or wrong to offer a reward to anyone to go against strongly held personal or religious convictions. Some mission supporters disapproved of offering inducements. ICM clerical secretary Henry Eade wrote that, 'To offer a bribe would be unworthy of a Christian, not to say of an honest man', but explained the difficulty of inviting Catholic interest, since 'the fetters which enslave the

Roman-catholics [sic] are all the more dangerous because they are bound upon the conscience'.[225] Some supporters approved of enticing Catholics by means of relief as this 'lies in the line of a people's true progress' [226] (doctrine of error has no right), saying that if this approach facilitated their hearing the Gospel, 'we should deem the deed not only lawful, but obligatory'.[227] Others believed that it was morally wrong to offer inducements, arguing that bribery of any sort was unacceptable.[228]

The ICM countered such criticism by insisting that it never distributed temporal aid, but interestingly also stated that even if it *had* enticed people to go against their conscience, neither the ICM nor the people concerned would have done wrong since 'it is not sinful to induce a man to go against a *defiled* conscience'.[229] The ICM constantly refuted all allegations of bribery, asserting that although it could not check the 'private liberality of individuals', it would not 'be the channel of this relief, however needy the supplicant', insisting that its entire income was spent in seeking to win converts from Rome 'by the faithful exhibition of the doctrines of Christianity, and by an exposure of the delusions of Romanism'.[230] Critics of the ICM's methods, such as Arthur Dann, protested that it was 'mere quibbling' to shift the responsibility upon the 'kind and charitable ladies' who organised the mission's temporal relief schemes.[231]

Local memories assert that the ICM distributed a meat-based soup on Fridays and vegetable soup on other days to force Catholics to go against their beliefs.[232] The reluctance with which Connemara's poor availed of mission relief is substantiated by poetry evidence:

> Is doilbh liom ceangail le Cailbhin is Liútar claon,
> Ach golfairt mo leanbh 's a gcreacadh gan trioc gan tréad
> Thug sruthanna ó' m' dhearcaibh s'na gcaisibh is tuirlingt déar.[233]

[It makes me sad to have anything to do with Calvin or perverse Luther/But the lamenting of my children and their ruination without belongings or livestock/Brought tears streaming from my eyes.]

The ICM's argument that its distribution of relief and mission work were distinct was patently false. It may have been possible to disguise the connection in Dublin, as the food and shelter were provided by persons who, strictly speaking, were not employed by the mission. In the case of the western missions, aid was distributed via schoolteachers to pupils in avowedly ICM schools. Irrefutable evidence of the distribution of aid to converts exists in the fact that Hyacinth D'Arcy signed the accounts of the Fund for the Relief of the Converts and Children of Connemara which blatantly contradicts the ICM's above assertion that 'they will not be the channel of this relief, however needy the supplicant'.[234] The very existence of printed receipts for the Fund for the Relief of the Converts and Children of Connemara, signed by Fanny D'Arcy, demonstrates that mission relief was a structured and sanctioned practice.[235] These receipts state that the fund 'relieves the sick, the widows, the fatherless, and others in their distress; and God has given it His blessing in its bringing many to hear of Jesus'. Similar funds operated for the relief of poverty in Dublin. Revd Webster's public criticism made the Protestant population increasingly aware that allegations of bribery hovered over the ICM. By 1866, even former supporters, such as Revd Arthur Edwards, were criticising the dual role of the ICM as provider of relief and disseminator of scriptural religion.[236]

Protestations at the ICM's lack of success

The ICM appears to have experienced a considerable degree of success and popularity in the early 1850s but fairly soon even Protestants began to question its advertised advances. Objective outsiders, such as John Forbes, Mr and Mrs Hall and Lord Osborne (all English Protestants) used the press to expose the ICM's exaggerated claims.[237] Forbes found little evidence of Protestantism in Clifden unless he specifically sought it out and maintained that the Society's assertion that the region was characteristically Protestant must be viewed as 'the expression of an amiable and sanguine enthusiasm'. He believed that most converts would return to their former religion if the country became prosperous and found that many who had converted during the extreme years of the famine had reverted by late 1852, although a Catholic national-school teacher correctly expected that some children would remain Protestant, which was also the opinion of Lord Osborne's informant, who thought that child converts were genuine but was unsure about adults.[238] Forbes stated that material relief not doctrinal conviction was at the root of these conversions, writing that Catholicism had been temporarily overcome 'by carnal, not spiritual weapons'.[239] The Halls agreed that the movement was *bona fide* but thought that the ICM's claim of 30,000 converts was 'probably an exaggeration', acknowledging that destitution had encouraged conversions and that mission relief alleviated the material wants of the poor.[240] They praised the social improvement wrought by the ICM, writing that children had been 'instructed in better habits' and taught 'to praise God and be thankful'.[241]

The results of the 1861 census, which were placed before the public in May 1863, tolled the death knell for any hope of ongoing widespread support within the Protestant communities of either country. In common with many British Protestants, ICM supporters had believed in the mission's claimed successes. Readers of the Scottish *Free Church Magazine* were told that Catholics outnumbered Protestants by only 500,000 as a direct result of missionary work, Dallas had asserted in 1851 that Ireland was already 50 per cent Protestant, and the earl of Roden reported in 1852 that over 10,000 Roman Catholics had left the Church of Rome in the Tuam diocese alone.[242] Archdeacon Stopford published an unofficial census of the 1851 Protestant populations in the Galway mission parishes which indicated vast congregations.[243] This showed that in eight parishes in the Tuam diocese, the Protestant population increased from 779 in 1834 to 2,482 in 1851, at a time when the overall population of these parishes decreased from 64,455 to 47,220 (see table 4.2).[244] One supporter estimated the Irish Protestant population as two million in 1857,[245] and in 1859 former ICM missionary, Revd Dalton, accurately estimated the total population of Ireland as approximately six million but was seriously off-target in his estimate of the Protestant-to-Catholic ratio, suggesting 2.5 million Protestants and 3.5 million Catholics.[246] Supporters, confident that the work of the ICM was 'progressing towards its completion', eagerly awaited the results of the 1861 census to prove the mission's successes.[247] But whereas the ICM promised a considerable increase in Protestant numbers, the actual population of the Established Church fell by over 100,000 between 1834 and 1861, from 800,730 to 693,357 (see table 4.3).

Far from Revd Dalton's prediction of 2.5 million, in 1861 the population of the Established Church did not even reach 700,000. In spite of this irrefutable evidence, ICM supporters persisted in manipulating figures to prove the success of their crusade. W. C. Plunket wrote that the *'Church population had not only been relatively increased but actually increased'* (his italics), arguing that Methodists were included in Established Church figures in 1834 and excluded in 1861 and that the Established Church percentage had grown by almost 2 per cent.[248] George Venables, previously 'in great distress' on account of the census results, was reassured by Plunket's explanation; other Protestants were not so easily mollified. Even Venables acknowledged some degree of exaggeration by some 'well-meaning but injudicious friends' who had romantically described missionary progress 'in terms too glowing'.[249]

Unsurprisingly, the disappointing census results attracted the attention of the press. Even the Protestant media asked how the number of Protestants in counties Mayo and Galway could decrease by 25 per cent when such huge resources were being spent to proselytise the area.[250] Between 1849 and 1861, the ICM had spent over £300,000 and had very little to show for it. The ICM continued to insist it was achieving its objectives. Zooming in on its west Galway parishes, it showed that the Protestant-to-Catholic ratio had improved, as in Omey (Clifden), where the percentage of Protestants had increased from 2.19 to 13.38 per cent between 1834 and 1861 and that membership of the Established Church had actually increased by

Table 4.2 Religious composition of mission parishes in Galway and Mayo, 1834, 1851 and 1861

| | Population | | | | | | | | Percentage | | |
| | 1834 | | | 1851 | | 1861 | | | 1834 | 1851 | 1681 |
	E.C.	Dis.	R.C.	E.C.	R.C.	E.C.	Dis.	R.C.	E.C.	E.C.	E.C.
Cong	108	0	8880	1187	5245	156	10	5587	1.20	18.45	2.71
Ballinakill	113	0	7604	495	4857	278	19	4289	1.46	9.25	6.06
Ballyovie	17	0	4303	125	2948	202	2	2633	0.39	4.07	7.12
Kilanin	94	0	9528	375	7601	169	4	7783	0.98	4.70	2.12
Kilcummin	138	0	10359	400	6552	287	107	8061	1.31	5.75	3.39
Moyrus	108	0	10381	256	7457	258	12	8288	1.03	3.32	3.01
Omey	157	0	7009	2235	7487	827	23	5332	2.19	22.99	13.38
Ballindoon	44	0	5612	incl. with Omey		305	1	3956	0.78	N/A	7.16
Total	779	0	63676	5073	42147	2482	178	45929			

Note: E.C. = Established Church, Dis. = Dissenter, R.C. = Roman Catholic

Source: (1834 and 1861 figures), *Irish Ecclesiastical Gazette*, 20 May 1864; (1851 figures), Edward Stopford, *A reply to Sergeant Shee on the Irish Church* (Dublin, 1853), p. 75.

Table 4.3 Religious composition of Ireland in 1834 and 1861

	Population		Percentage	
	1834	*1861*	*1834*	*1861*
Established Church	800,730	693,357	10.07	11.96
Catholic	6,436,060	4,505,265	80.91	77.69
Presbyterian	643,058	529,291	8.08	9.13
Other	74,312	71,105	0.93	1.23
Total	7,954,160	5,798,967		

Source: W. C. Plunket, *The Church and the census in Ireland* (Dublin, 1865)

approximately 1,500 in the missionary region (see table 4.2). It correctly argued that many Catholic children attended mission schools and were therefore brought under the influence of Protestantism. The ICM also argued that emigration had depleted convert numbers, stating that three-quarters of its converts had emigrated, due not only to persecution but also because

> The freedom of mind and thought resulting from Protestant teaching ... together with the gradual requirement of comfort which grows with Protestant customs ... motives for leaving the country are plainly more numerous and powerful with the convert than with the Roman Catholic ...[251]

In blaming emigration for depleted convert numbers, the ICM evidently forgot that it had reassured supporters, as late as 1863, that Connemara's converts were 'preserved from dispersion by English liberality'.[252] Venables' publication also nullified the emigration excuse by including a letter from Revd Ryder which stated that while his congregation experienced 'a very considerable emigration', its numbers were maintained by new accessions from Rome, whereas emigration had reduced Errismore's Catholic congregation by almost one half.[253] One publication even tried to claim that the percentage decline in Protestants and Catholics between 1834 and 1861 should have been equal (ignoring the obvious predominance of Catholic famine deaths) and that the difference, which amounted to tens of thousands, could only be explained by the emigration of converts.[254]

In fact low convert numbers were due to reversions to Catholicism, as had been observed elsewhere.[255] The Stopford census of 1851, taken in the immediate wake of the famine and at the height of mission activity, may be assumed to accurately reflect uptake of mission services at that time and is supported by other sources. In July 1851, 3,500 persons in Errismore and Errislannan were fed weekly by the mission but ten years later only 305 persons in that region returned themselves as Protestant (see chapter 5).

In Cong parish, location of longest-established Castlekerke mission, there were 108 Protestants in 1834, 1,187 in 1851 but only 156 in 1861.[256] Fickle converts reverted when better times returned. Evidence from Connemara 'remembers' how converts passing by a Catholic church would say 'Slán agat anois, a Dhia, go bhfásfaidh na fataí' [Goodbye God till the potatoes grow].[257]

Without doubt some emigrated, but the question regarding the absolute number of converts, both genuine and short-lived, remains unanswered. Numerous converts emigrated throughout the English-speaking world, where their descendants are still Protestant and have provided generations of Protestant clergymen. For instance, William Manning, bishop of George, Cape Town, South Africa (1978–87) was a grandson of convert mission teacher, Arthur Manning[258] and descendants of Thomas, Samuel, John and William King (figure 4.1), many of whom were clergymen, moved to England, the United States, Australia and to the north of Ireland.[259]

The ICM's 1864 annual report triumphantly reported the census results, informing supporters that the percentage decline in the Established Church between 1834 and 1861 was only 14.8 per cent whereas the decline in the Roman Catholic church was 30 per cent, and telling how over 2,000 persons in west Galway recorded themselves as members of the Established Church. It used the existence of church buildings as proof of conversions in west Galway, adding that similar advances had been made in Dublin.[260] In an article written by the ICM, readers of the *Irish Ecclesiastical Gazette* learned that 'unquestionable results' in Connemara confirmed the mission's advances and justified its continued support.[261]

Understandably, the Protestant community was not wholly convinced. The public's attention had been drawn to the activities of the ICM in Connemara when Thomas Plunket, bishop of Tuam, was accused in parliament of evicting tenants at his estate in Partry for refusing to send their children to ICM schools. Accusations of bribery and the outcry over the 'War in Partry' had alerted some to the ICM's questionable methodologies,[262] while the split from the Irish Society had exposed the ICM's controversial practices. Mr Briggs, a Protestant clergyman from Cork, alleged in June 1861 that most converts were 'aided in various ways, on condition of attending classes ... [but] were sure to go back to the only creed they every believed in – and we know that scores have done so'.[263] The census of 1861 resolutely confirmed their doubts and Protestant concerns over the ICM's methods and successes were publicly voiced.

The 1860s saw the publication of aggressive Protestant challenges to the ICM's advertised successes. When John Garrett's *Good news from Ireland* was published in 1863 to appeal for funds for the WCCES, the Englishman Sir Henry Stewart Cunningham penned a counter-publication *Is 'Good*

News from Ireland' true?, which protested at both the veracity of the mission's claims and at its methodologies.[264] This sceptical publication was answered in 1865 by George Venables in *The good news is true; or what an English clergyman saw in Connemara*, which insisted that Cunningham's work was 'a calumny ... by which the enemy would hinder the work'.[265]

In *Is 'Good news' from Ireland true?* Cunningham efficiently deconstructed Garrett's *Good news from Ireland*, asserting that the mission 'thrives tolerably well when funds are plentiful; that it dies away directly they run short'. He claimed that the public was becoming 'increasingly uneasy on the subject' and that the days of this 'monstrous scandal' were numbered, insisting that rather than becoming more Protestant, the Irish were 'already the hottest Ultramontanes in Europe' and were assuming a triumphant confidence which was justified by their numerical superiority.[266]

The same year as Cunningham's book appeared also saw the appearance of a second extremely critical publication, this time by a former mission-supporting 'Irish Peer', who was so enraged by the ICM's methodologies, as well as by its obvious lack of success, that he published a lengthy pamphlet which condemned the ICM's methods and outlined its lack of success in Connemara, saying that he had once hoped that 'an impression once made upon their adversary's ranks' would result in widespread conversions but now realised this was improbable.[267] He not only questioned the efficacy of the mission but bluntly accused them of causing 'much direct and indirect evil', pointing to the growth of Catholic convents and churches with large congregations. He directly attributed the increasing inter-confessional tensions to proselytising efforts and condemned the 'ill-judged' controversial methods and the calibre of some scripture readers, adding that 'Protestants would have been better reforming their own flocks'.[268] He contradicted the mission's assertion that 'there is a spirit of inquiry' among Catholics, saying those who remembered these expressions from years back 'must smile at the repetition of this language in the *present* day'.[269] The 'Irish Peer' concluded that the ICM was a total failure, and acknowledged that it was probably too much to expect that those who had given their lives to the cause would now admit themselves the victims of a 'life-long delusion'.[270]

Although the 1861 census results were largely responsible for the decline in support for the ICM, the census results did not themselves defeat the mission. They merely confirmed the absence of a significant convert community by 1861. This absence was a direct result of aggressive counter-missionary tactics of the Catholic church in the 1850s and the amelioration of extreme famine conditions. The low numbers of Protestants in the 1861 census reverberated outside the ICM and heralded the disestablishment of the Anglican Church in Ireland in 1869.

Few Irish Protestants saw the wisdom of continuing a futile crusade to convert Catholics while their own church was under severe threat. Irish support for the ICM, which had been in decline since the disassociation from the Irish Society in 1856, fell but did not altogether cease, as seen in table 4.5 (p. 156). Support for the ICM among Irish Protestants in the 1850s and 1860s ranged from those who strongly promoted the movement to those who were implacably opposed to both its aims and its method-ologies. The majority of Irish Protestants lay somewhere in between, with most agreeing to the ideology of bringing non-scriptural Catholics to the Protestant truth.

The support of Ireland's Anglican bishops was crucial to the success of the ICM. Despite the backing of some aristocrats of Ireland and England, the ICM lacked the support of Richard Whately, archbishop of Dublin (1831–63), who disapproved of proselytism and condemned it in his charge to his clergy 'On the right use of "national afflictions".[271] Recent scholarship has shown that in the 1850s, 'Only a minority of the Established Church's parsons were in favour of the movement ... and Whately forcibly opposed it'.[272] Whately, an Oxford theologian, was relatively unpopular with Dublin Protestants, especially among evangelicals, who considered his sermons too complex and who favoured popular preachers such as Charles Fleury and John Gregg, both of whom were ICM supporters.[273] John Gregg, later bishop of Cork, expressed his confidence in the ICM in its early years, stating 'If the friends of the Mission are able to go on supporting it as they have done for a few years, I am not sure that all the men on earth, and all the powers of Satan, will not be able to put it down.'[274]

Whately's biographer, William Fitzpatrick, described the evangelical Dublin clergy of the time as inoculated with the 'virus of Dr. Magee's retrospective view'.[275] Such proselytising tendencies were not universal among the Church of Ireland clergy. Whately was, of course, in favour of the conversion of Irish Catholics in principle but objected to the ICM's methods. Tensions regarding support for the ICM cause within the Irish Church were played out at micro-level in the Whately household. Richard Whately's criticism of the ICM contrasted with enthusiastic support given the venture by his wife and daughters, who were especially involved with Mrs Smyly in the ICM children's homes, as was Whately's son-in-law, Charles Wale.[276] Another daughter was secretary of the Priests' Protection Society, which aggressively sought out and aided convert-priests from Rome. This contrasted with her father's attitude to such men; convert ex-Maynooth priest L. J. Nolan was given no encouragement by Whately, who forbade him to preach in the diocese.[277] Donald Akenson argues that despite E. J. Whately's claims that her father approved of the missions, research has shown that he was very much opposed to their methods.[278] The fact that Alexander Dallas preached at the funeral of Mrs Whately is testament to her attachment to the mission and the ICM made great use of Mrs Whately's patronage, with frequent references in publicity literature to the 'deep and earnest sympathy actuating several members of the family of the Archbishop of Dublin'.[279] The variance between the views of the archbishop and his wife must have caused serious disharmony in the Whately household, as the ICM very publicly associated itself with the archbishop's family while the archbishop was repeatedly reiterating his opposition to its methodologies:

> Truth should indeed be earnestly recommended, but recommended as truth; and error censured because it is error, without any appeal to men's temporal wants, and sufferings and interests, or any other such motives as ought not in such a question be allowed to operate.[280]

Whately's opposition to the ICM stemmed from its giving inducements to convert, a practice he consistently denounced. He remained unconvinced of the ICM's separation from its relief charities. However, as Paul Cullen's intolerant attitude to Protestants became increasingly evident, Whately grew less antagonistic to the ICM and founded the separate Society for the Rights of Conscience (1856) to assist victimised converts but always objected to the duality of preaching and distribution of aid. Many other Protestants had similar reservations about combining aid and scriptural instruction.

In its early days, many Irish clergymen appealed to the ICM to establish missions in their districts. In 1854, the clergy of Cork city promised to 'give our hearty and active co-operation in the missionary work that is about to be carried on here by the ICM'.[281] Over 500 and 80 clergy met an ICM delegation in Dublin and Cork respectively the same year.[282] The ICM received applications for missionary services from the entire country but owing to insufficient funds was obliged to decline, concentrating on its direct missions in west Galway, Dublin and a few localised provincial towns. However, by the mid 1860s, especially after the publication of the 1861 census, support had considerably declined, and few applications were forthcoming. While many bishops supported the West Galway Church Building Fund in 1851, indicating support for newly founded convert communities, support for aggressive missionary work appears to have been lacking among Irish bishops.[283]

Although Irish support for the ICM was especially drawn from areas where Protestants were numerically strong, i.e. the cities of Dublin and Cork and sections of the north of Ireland, funds were also received from Protestants throughout the island and the ICM's profile was maintained by the *Christian Examiner*. Although this paper's content was mostly concerned with evangelical doctrinal argument, lengthy and supportive accounts of the ICM were published almost every month in the mid 1850s. In May 1857 it exclaimed: 'What hope for thankfulness is here! – what room for hope! – what field of exertion! – what need for prayer!' Readers heard that the minds of 'the most bigoted yield to the force of evidence which they can no longer resist' and were informed that the writer saw 'on all sides proofs of the Lord's blessing' on a recent tour of the Connemara missions.[284] Its editor, Charles Stanford, was satisfied the Society was worthy of public support and urged each reader to give thanks to God for the foundation of the ICM through which the 'long neglected Roman Catholics of Ireland ... [would be] gathered in so many to the fold of Ireland's ancient Church'.[285] Following the publication of *The only complete copy* in 1864, the *Christian Examiner* made a personal attack on George Webster. It described Webster's allegations of bribery as unfounded and as 'puerile and ridiculous ... and exhibiting the painful contractedness of the mind that created or invented them'.[286] Stanford challenged Webster's allegations that the ICM enticed conversions from the hungry, saying in language reminiscent of Marie Antoinette, that the mission had been accused of bribing converts with 'tarts and cheesecakes'. The paper reiterated its wholehearted support of the mission and its belief in ICM successes, writing that Dallas had earned 'the unfeigned gratitude of every Christian who loves his country' and praising 'the abundant success and prosperity of the Society for Irish Church Missions'.[287]

The content of the magazine suggests that the ICM commanded considerable backing from the more conservative element of Protestantism. The support of some rural Protestants is evident from an address presented to ICM missionary, Revd Dalton, when diminishing finances forced his removal from his County Roscommon parish, in which his former parishioners wrote glowingly of the 'value of direct mission among the Roman Catholics of Ireland'.[288] It should not be construed, however, that Revd Dalton's work among Catholics had the unanimous support of his Kilbryan parishioners, as a very different address appeared in the *Irish Ecclesiastical Gazette* which made no reference to missionary work among Catholics but congratulated Revd Dalton on building a new parish church.[289]

Evidence exists of sympathy among some clergy of the Down diocese. In 1864, Revd Archibald Gault, ICM missionary 1853–64, was presented with a lengthy address by his diocesan colleagues which expressed their appreciation for the 'general principles of the Society, of which you are an ordained Missionary ... by the blessings of God and your persevering efforts, the Roman Catholics around us have been sensibly stirred to anxious inquiry'.[290] In his reply, Revd Gault acknowledged that not all clergy supported the Society when it was 'wantonly assailed by its enemies', but asked 'has not the evil tide of Romanism been successfully stayed

– have not the Romish Priests been effectually silenced?' This address to Revd Gault is a rare example of overt Irish support for the ICM fifteen years after its inception; it should be noted that it originated in an area where Protestants were numerically strong. Despite Revd Gault's implication that some clergy had criticised the ICM, the address was signed by thirty-eight clergy from a total of 108 in the Down diocese, including the dean of Connor, the precentor of Connor and three prebendaries of the diocese, but not the bishop (table 4.4). However, signing an address need not imply unconditional or life-long commitment to the cause. One signatory, Edward Maguire, was missionary at Cushendall in 1857 but only briefly mentioned his ICM involvement in his memoirs, which he wrote in 1904. Perhaps, on reflection, he considered that it had not impacted on most of his clerical life.[291]

Table 4.4 Signatories of address to Revd Archibald Gault, 1864

	Signed	*Did not sign*
Bishop		1
Diocesan office holder	7	14
Rector/vicar	21	38
Curate	10	16

Irish Church Directory, 1864; Irish Ecclesiastical Gazette, 20 Apr. 1864

The influential book, *The only complete copy*, published by 'Four Rectors' systematically deconstructed the ICM's claim of support from within the Church of Ireland. As an example of the ICM's manipulation of facts, this book cites the ICM's circular to clergy in the Cork diocese which stated: 'The attention of the Irish clergy is asked to a memorial recently sent to the Lord Bishop of Limerick by several clergymen in the diocese.' This might suggest that a considerable number of Limerick clergy supported the ICM, whereas in fact 'several clergymen' amounted to five incumbents and five curates, or less than 5 per cent of the diocesan total of 105 rectors and 45 curates, although an effort was made to have everybody sign.[292] In spite of the bishop's negative response, the ICM had implied that the movement commanded substantial backing among Limerick clergymen, omitting to mention that the bishop had written that he would wish for 'the concurrence and support of a much larger number of the clergy – particularly the beneficed and senior members – than have subscribed their names in the present instance'.[293]

In 1854 the ICM had passed two resolutions thanking its supporters and asking for their continued support, but by 1863 the Society was slowly in retreat and was then willing to admit that some Protestants simply refused to help.[294] In 1868 it wished that Protestants would 'acquire an increased knowledge of Romish controversy ... it would be a most valuable help', and the following year it acknowledged that it had to contend 'with many Protestants opposing to our work, and with many more indifferent to it and with only a few warmly interested'.[295] John Garrett remarked how Revd Charles Seymour had endured serious opposition from 'brother-clergymen and laymen of the Church' who admired his love of the church but 'the wisdom they doubted'.[296] Richard Hobson, scripture reader at Ardee (1851–62), told of how many Anglican clergy kept entirely aloof and some even opposed the mission,[297] whereas one mission tourist suggested that many wished to support the missions but didn't feel free to do so.[298] Other Protestant missions in Ireland experienced similar apathy and antagonism; the pan-Protestant Evangelistic Mission encountered little Irish support and the Presbyterian E. M. Dill observed that it was distressing that 'our missionaries sometimes meet more hindrance from their own brother ministers, than from Popish priests'.[299]

Catholic clergy realised that not all Protestant clergymen or gentlemen supported the proselytising movement. Frs Daniel Cahill and James Maher were pleased to report that the gentry and Protestant clergy had 'the good taste to absent themselves'[300] and that not all the Protestant clergy of Ireland were 'guilty of these odious practices'.[301] As early as 1853 Clifden's Catholic community was informed that 'right-minded and honest Protestants are beginning to be ashamed'.[302] Connemara's Catholics differentiated between missionary and non-missionary Protestants, asserting that 'Protestantism, which is a gentlemanlike belief, usually leaves Catholics alone, getting respected in return'[303] and that the 'liberal Protestants of Connemara' disapproved of the 'nefarious devices resorted to ... in maintaining the vile system of souperism among the Catholic peasantry'.[304]

As already outlined, the expected mission successes were disappointingly absent in the returns of the 1861 census and instead the vulnerability of Irish Protestantism was highlighted. The (admittedly High Church) *Church Times* of June 1866 criticised proselytising societies which exaggerated their successes to increase their donations from England as 'one shameless defamatory, gigantic falsehood'.[305] The focus of attention of Irish Protestants shifted from the conversion of Catholics to maintenance of Protestants. In a series of detailed articles in the *Irish Ecclesiastical Gazette*, the unidentified 'Clericus' stated that missions to Catholics had not gained one-tenth of the number of Protestants lost to Rome through 'the apathy of the Protestant clergy during a long series of years ... Now we feel how much we need every Protestant. We shall yet lament every one we have lost.'[306]

Many members of the Church of Ireland questioned the wisdom of seeking new converts when existing impoverished Protestants were lost to Catholicism because of clerical neglect. Others, in contrast, felt that Protestant numbers would be even smaller were it not for the ICM.[307] Even the evangelical *Christian Examiner*, while remaining an ardent supporter until its demise in 1868, prioritised the defensive needs of the church above its missionary activities, saying

> And if we never succeeded in prevailing upon a Roman Catholic to enter the door of a house where the Gospel is preached, or to listen to the sound of it anywhere, still surely the very members of our own Church need to be reminded of the destructive falsehoods, from which they have been rescued, and warned against indulging in a more lenient or partial judgment of the Great Apostasy, than has already been pronounced upon it by the Word of God.[308]

As disestablishment loomed, Irish support for the ICM dissipated and Irish Protestants were increasingly concerned about safeguarding their own population. They gave little encouragement to those who wished to aggressively seek converts from Catholicism, as voiced in a letter to the *Galway Express*: 'What would we say to the farmer who, while his own flock were dying of starvation, was continually buying others?'[309] This should not be construed as a disinclination to receive converts from Catholicism but rather a dislike of controversial work and an appreciation of the insecurity and decreased status of their soon-to-be disestablished church. While clearly in favour of converting Irish Catholics, one Anglican clergyman considered that controversialism was counter-productive and direct missionary work had 'roused the activity of the Romish Church … [so that] the mass of the Roman Catholics are now animated with an earnest attachment to their Church',[310] while James Godkin considered that the 'aggressive nature of the mission produced results to be lamented, but which were inevitable'.[311] Recent scholarship has claimed that some churchmen partly blamed proselytism for disestablishment as it highlighted the Church of Ireland's neglect of the Catholic population prior to the formation of the ICM.[312]

Evidence exists that Protestant clergy in Ireland were irritated at the demands of supporters in England and Scotland that they become more missionary in character. When the Scotsman, John Campbell Colquhoun, urged a more active, aggressive approach at the mission's 1865 AGM in London, contrasting letters to the *Christian Examiner* illustrate opposing attitudes of clergy, both of whom were in favour of the conversion of Catholics. 'X' admitted that the ICM was unpopular but also claimed that Irish clergy were lazy and apathetic, while 'Z' on the other hand, thought that work among Catholics could only be successful if carried out 'in the quietest and unobtrusive manner', which ran contrary to ICM methodologies:

> The ICM is an unpopular society no doubt, but why? Simply because it stirs up a nest of hornets, who otherwise might sleep and keep quiet; and the sole cause of its being held in disrepute is, that the clergy as a body are unwilling to be forced out of the old jog-trot, humdrum mode of procedure which has been the bane and will be the ruin, unless God in his mercy averts it, of our Church.[313]

> Dublin and the West coast, with a few others, are exceptional cases ... in most other districts where the work was begun, missionaries and converts have been driven from the field, or, if permitted to exist, reduced to most insignificant dimensions. Nothing, in fact, can be effected, except in the quietest and most unobtrusive manner.[314]

The above letters illustrate the unspoken approval of the conversion of Catholics as a laudable objective. They differ merely on their opinion of the ICM's methodology and clearly illustrate that more Irish clergy would have supported the movement had it adopted a less controversial approach.

Although the ICM drew significantly more support from England than from Ireland (over 70 per cent of its annual income originated in England),[315] a significant number of Irish Protestants, both within and without the Established Church, supported efforts to convert the Catholics of Ireland. Missionary work of this nature was undertaken by all Protestant denominations in Ireland, including the Baptist, Wesleyan Methodist and Presbyterian churches, but operated on a smaller scale and, in some instances, for a shorter duration and in a less public manner. The Wesleyans concentrated their efforts in the more Protestant districts. Of the fifteen scripture readers and teachers engaged by the Primitive Wesleyan Missionary Society in 1860, eleven operated within the counties of Ulster and three were employed in the adjoining county of Leitrim. The remaining agent laboured at Turlough in County Mayo, where his progress was 'anything but encouraging'.[316]

Presbyterian missions in Connaught were maintained in a similar fashion to the ICM (see chapter 1) and experienced a similar decline from the 1850s. Their decline can be attributed, not only to a lack of success and a decline in income (as experienced by the ICM), but also to vicious infighting within the various strands of Presbyterianism. Tensions between the Scottish Ladies' Committee and the Presbyterian Church in Ireland resulted in an acrimonious sundering of the Connaught operations into Irish and Scottish missions. The Scottish Committee, originally founded as the 'Society to aid the Home Mission of the Presbyterian Church in Ireland', ceased to be a mere auxiliary and became the 'Scottish Ladies' Mission to Roman Catholics', thereby removing itself from the control of the General Assembly in Belfast.[317] The Scottish Ladies' secured ownership and control of the flagship Ballinglen institute in north Mayo in 1864, dismissing Robert Allen (superintendent) and Michael Brannigan (missionary). The Presbyterian Church of Ireland continued to manage its Ballina orphanage and mission schools at Ballycastle and Dromore West; from 1864 these were under the superintendence of Revd Brannigan. The Scottish mission functioned at Ballinglen until the 1870s, after which time the Scottish Ladies' remitted funds to the General Assembly for its Connaught mission, which was maintained into the early years of the twentieth century.

The Presbyterian Church in Ireland, while concentrating on its Connaught mission, operated an itinerating 'mission from Ulster' in the adjoining counties. It hoped in 1867 that it could make 'Longford, Galway, Roscommon, Mayo ... distinguished for intelligence, education, morality, progress', exclaiming that 'Were Ireland Presbyterian, instead of Romanist, oh what an Ireland it would be!'[318] These sentiments were shared by the Baptist Irish Society, which reminded supporters in 1858 of its 'great work' but admitted that its missions to Catholics were less successful than it had hoped, but were 'productive of an amount of spiritual good which would utterly forbid such an abandonment of the work there'.[319] The Primitive Wesleyan Methodist Missionary Society was more optimistic, reporting 'a spirit of enquiry awakened among thousands of our Roman Catholic brethren', and promised in 1860 that popery's days were numbered as it was evident that God was clearly 'pouring out his wrath upon her'.[320]

Irish Anglicans who supported the idea of converting the Catholic population donated to the ICM and to the Anglican IS in equal measure. Even after the dissolution of the merger between the ICM and the IS in 1856, the ICM continued to command a significant degree of support throughout Ireland; for instance, twenty-seven parishes in the Ferns diocese donated a total of £96 in 1861. As table 4.5 shows, donations to the ICM and the IS conformed to a similar pattern in the 1860s, with both Societies experiencing a 30 per cent reduction in Irish subscriptions over the decade. A number of lay persons lent their support to both the ICM and the IS; the earls of Mayo, Roden, Clancarty and Bandon were vice-patrons of both Societies in 1862. This dual patronage was not evident among the Irish bishops; in 1862 twelve Irish bishops were listed among the patrons of the IS,[321] while no Irish bishop was listed as an ICM patron at this juncture although they may have supported the organisation in a private capacity.

It is likely that the ICM's considerable income (which averaged £22,462 in the 1860s) was matched if not surpassed by the combined annual incomes of other societies founded with the same purpose. It has not been

Table 4.5 Subscriptions to the ICM and IS in 1860 and 1869

	ICM			IS		
	From Ireland	*From England*	*Total*	*From Ireland*	*From England*	*Total*
1860	5,052	20,171	25,223	5,271	3,511	8,782
1869	3,563	16,625	20,188	3,687	4,132	7,819
% decline	29.47	17.58	19.96	30.05	–17.69	10.97

Source: ICM, *Annual report*, 1860, 1869; IS, *Annual report*, 1860, 1869.

possible to source an exact income for every society engaged in mission work to the Romanists; where reports are extant, they are rarely available for the same year. Nevertheless, we can quantify the income of the more prominent societies and make allowances for others. A combined annual income of £18,000 can be verified for the Irish Society, Presbyterian, Baptist and Wesleyan Methodist missions in the early 1860s.[322] To this we must add the incomes of those societies whose reports have not been located (e.g. Scottish Ladies' Society) and those whose expenditure on specifically Irish missions was not itemised (Scottish Reformation Society, British Reformation Society).

In the case of the many societies which operated among both Catholic and Protestant populations, it is impossible to isolate the expenditure on missions to Catholics. Examples of this nature include the Hibernian Bible Society, whose workers were ordered to direct their efforts 'to every poor family, whether Protestant or Roman Catholic',[323] the Dublin Bible-Women's Mission, founded to assist poorer members of the Church of Ireland but whose 'aid shall not be withheld from the poor of any denomination who may be willing to avail themselves of it',[324] and the pan-Protestant Dublin City Mission, which stated that 'though Protestants are our first object, we do not neglect openings among Roman Catholics either'.[325] When we consider the expenditure of these various societies, quantified and un-quantified, it is reasonable to estimate that the total spent on mission work among the Catholic population was at least double the ICM's annual outlay. As these societies were more circumspect in their missionary objectives than was the ICM, couching their 'mission to Catholics' in a general philan-thropic discourse and operating without a tangible infrastructure, the extent of proselytising activities can be easily underestimated. It is equally fair to state that the Catholic depiction of proselytism tended to exaggerate its occurrence, as discussed in chapter 7.

Notes

1 Edward Stopford, *A reply to Sergeant Shee on the Irish Church* (Dublin, 1853), p. 75.

2 John Garwood, *The million-peopled city: or one half of the people of Lodond made known to the other half* (London, 1853), p. 297.

3 C. H. Seymour, *Late synod in Tuam: questions for the bishops, priests and people of the church of Rome* (Dublin, 1854), p. 2.

4 Ballinakill (1852), Aasleagh (1853), Errislannan (1853), Sellerna (1853), Bunlahinch (1853), Tourmakeady (1853), Moyrus (1855), Renvyle (1855), Ballyinahinch (c. 1855), Castlekerke (1865), Errismore (1865). Ballyconree church was consecrated in 1871.

5 E. M. Dill, *The mystery solved, or Ireland's miseries: the grand cause, and cure* (Edinburgh, 1852), p. 200.

6 CP, MS No. GRE/G3/2/22, Memorial to the late Mrs D'Arcy; MS No. GRE/G3/5/38, Mary D'Arcy to Elizabeth Copley, 18 Jan. 1858.

7 CP, MS No. GRE/G3/2/20, Fanny D'Arcy to Elizabeth Copley, 22 Mar. 1854. In this letter she stated that mission funds were plentiful but relief funds were more worrisome.

8 CP, MS No. GRE/G3/5/44, Mary D'Arcy to Elizabeth Copley, 30 Jan. 1858.

9 CP, MS No. GRE/G3/5/68, Mary Darcy to Elizabeth Copley, 9 Sept. 1858.

10 CP, MS No. GRE/G/3/3/1, Hyacinth D'Arcy to Elizabeth Copley, 4 Nov. 1853.

11 CP, MS No. GRE/G3/5/63, Mary D'Arcy to Elizabeth Copley, 23 June 1858.

12 'An Address to the kind English who visited Connemara in the summer of 1853 from the Clifden Male Model School', enclosed in CP, MS No. GRE/3/2/19, Fanny D'Arcy to Elizabeth Copley, 7 Feb. 1854.

13 CP, MS No. GRE/G3/5/34, Mary D'Arcy to Elizabeth Copley, 26 Dec. 1857.

14 [A. R. C. Dallas], *Proselytism in Ireland, the Catholic Defence Association versus the Irish Church Missions on the charge of bribery and intimidation* (London, 1852), p. 36.

15 ICM Archive, ICM agency books, 1856.

16 NAI, Dept. of Education files, application for Cleggan National School (NS), MS No. ED/1/35/25.

17 Marian Freyer, *Connemara, its social and religious aspects* (Galway, 1861), p. 49.

18 TCD, MS No. OLS X–1–531 no. 267, *Advice to the soupers*.

19 ICM Archive, ICM agency books, 1856–67.

20 Michael O'Sullivan to H. C. Eade, 29 Sept. 1854 in John O'Callaghan, *Society for Irish Church Missions and the Rev. J. O'Callaghan: Lough Corrib mission* (Dublin, 1855), pp. 41–2.

21 Thomas Plunket, *The West Galway Church Building Fund, an appeal from the bishop of Tuam* (Dublin, c.1860).

22 Ballycroy was formed by a combination of the General Irish Reformation Society and the Irish Society and was also assisted by the Island and Coast Society.

23 Original parishes were Roundstone, Clifden (Omey) and Ballinakill. There

is no evidence to suggest that Ballinahinch church, which was served by the Roundstone clergyman, was in receipt of separate WCCES funding nor is there evidence that Bunlahinch, County Mayo was ever aided by the WCCES.

24 F. D. How, *William Conyngham Plunket, fourth Baron Plunket and sixty-first archbishop of Dublin* (London, 1900), p. 43.

25 *Irish Ecclesiastical Gazette*, 15 Feb. 1860.

26 Gerard Moran, *The Mayo evictions of 1860* (Westport, 1986); Miriam Moffitt, *Soupers and Jumpers: the Protestant missions in Connemara, 1848–1937* (Dublin, 2008), pp. 80–4.

27 William Conyngham Plunket, *A book for tourists in Ireland. Sights to be seen in Dublin and Connemara … with an introd. by the Lord Bishop of Rochester* (n.p., 1863); W. C. Plunket, *A short visit to the Connemara missions. A letter to the Rev. John Garrett … from the Rev. W. C. Plunket, with a preface by the Lord Bishop of Rochester* (London, Dublin 1863); John Garrett, *Good news from Ireland. An address to the archbishops and bishops of the Church of England* (London, 1863).

28 *First report of the West Connaught Church Endowment Society 1861* (Dublin, 1861); *Second report of the West Connaught Church Endowment Society 1863* (Dublin, 1863); [West Connaught Church Endowment Fund], *The Church in Ireland: the speeches delivered at the Hanover Square Rooms, on Thursday, June 11, 1863 … in aid of the West Connaught Church Endowment Fund* (London, 1863); *Irish Ecclesiastical Gazette*, 20 May 1865.

29 *Irish Ecclesiastical Gazette*, 15 Feb. 1862.

30 Only twelve possible locations for missionary churches in counties Mayo or Galway have been identified: in the Achill mission (Dugort, Achill Sound and Inisbiggle), and in missions associated with the Irish Society in north Mayo (Bangor and Poulathomas), in Aughaval (Westport) parish in County Mayo (Knappagh, Ayle, Slingan, Kilmeena, Carrowholly) and Bunlahinch in Kilgeever (Louisburg) parish, County Mayo and the island of Aran (County Galway).

31 Moffitt, *Soupers and Jumpers*, pp. 114–23, 152–73.

32 Quoted in Desmond Bowen, *The Protestant crusade in Ireland, 1800–70* (Dublin, 1978), p. 244.

33 *Banner of the Truth*, Apr. 1868, pp. 28–9.

34 Edward Aurich, *Report made to the ICM Committee by the Rev. E. Auriol and the Rev. E. Bickersteth of their third visit of inspection to a portion of the missions of the Society* (London, 1868).

35 Bowen, *Protestant crusade*, pp. 224–5.

36 *Banner of the Truth*, Aug. 1869, pp. 17–18.

37 William Meagher, *Notices of the life and character of his grace, Most Rev. Daniel Murray, later archbishop of Dublin* (Dublin, 1853), p. 123.

38 For example, Margaret Aylward published a three-page list of 'Perils to the faith of Catholic Orphans' in Saint Brigid's Orphanage, Dublin, *Annual report*, 1859, pp. 17–19.

39 Jacinta Prunty, 'The geography of poverty: Dublin 1850–1900: the social mission of the church with particular reference to Margaret Aylward and

co-workers (Ph.D. dissertation, National University of Ireland, 1992), pp. 171–212.

40 LAC, *Annual report*, 1856, p. 6.

41 Ibid., 1856, p. 9; Sheridan Wayne Gilley, 'Evangelical and Roman Catholic missions to the Irish in London, 1830–1870 (Ph.D. dissertation, University of Cambridge, 1970), p. 108.

42 LAC, *Annual report*, 1856, p. 21.

43 Sarah Davies, *St. Patrick's armour: the story of the Coombe Ragged School* (Dublin, 1880), p. 16.

44 LAC, *Annual report*, 1852, p. 13; ibid., 1854, pp. 7–8.

45 Ibid., 1856, p. 6.

46 Ibid., 1852, p. 16.

47 William Marrable, *Sketch of the origin and operations of the Society for Irish Church Missions to the Roman Catholics* (London, 1853), p. 451.

48 Margaret Preston, *Charitable words: women, philanthropy and the language of charity in nineteenth-century Dublin* (London, 2004), p. 68.

49 LAC, *Annual report*, 1856, p. 9; ibid., 1855, p. 8.

50 SBO, *Annual report*, 1868, p. 3.

51 Ibid., 1858, p. 18; Jacinta Prunty, 'Margaret Louisa Aylward' in Mary Cullen and Maria Luddy (eds), *Women, power and consciousness in nineteenth-century Ireland* (Dublin, 1995), p. 69.

52 Quoted in Prunty, 'The geography of poverty', pp. 244–5.

53 SBO, *Annual report*, 1864, p. 28.

54 Quoted in Prunty, 'The geography of poverty', p. 245.

55 D. W. Cahill, *Second letter of the Rev. D. W. Cahill D.D. to the Right Hon. Lord John Russell* (Dublin, 1851).

56 Paul Cullen, *The pastoral letters and other writings of Cardinal Cullen, archbishop of Dublin etc., etc.*, edited by the Right Reverend Patrick Francis Moran, D.D. bishop of Ossony (3 vols, Dublin, 1882), i, p. 425. See also the writings of Daniel Cahill listed in the bibliography of this work.

57 Moffitt, *Soupers and Jumpers*, pp. 165–6.

58 See, for instance, SBO, *Annual report*, 1859, p. 12.

59 Quoted in Mary Purcell, *The story of the Vincentians* (Dublin, 1973), p. 109.

60 Anonymous, 'Them also', the story of the Dublin mission (2nd edn, London, 1866), p. 41; Alexander R. C. Dallas, *The story of the Irish Church Missions. Continued to the year 1869, etc.* (London, 1875), pp. 178–9.

61 PICA, MS No. KIR/NC/1/1857/15, Paul Cullen to Tobias Kirby, 14 Apr. 1857.

62 SBO, *Annual report*, 1863, p. 15; ICM, *Annual report*, 1872, p. 10.

63 Davies, *St. Patrick's armour*, pp. 26–7; Anonymous, 'Them also', p. 63; Myles V. Rowan, *An apostle of Catholic Dublin: Father Henry Young* (Dublin, 1944), pp. 265, 303.

64 SBO, *Annual report*, 1888, p. 16.

65 Anonymous, 'Them also', pp. 97–8.

66 *Catholic Directory*, 10 May 1859, p. 229; *The Telegraph*, 3 Dec. 1853, see also *The Telegraph*, 20 Aug. 1853; *Catholic Telegraph*, 17 July 1858.

67 Bearnárd Mac Uaid, 'Stair oideachas Bráthar Triomhadh Úird Riaghalta Sain Proinsias san naomhadh céad déag' [The history of education of the Third Order of Saint Francis in the nineteenth century] (MA dissertation, University College, Galway, 1956), p. 33.

68 Pius IX to John MacHale, 21 Oct. 1852, in Bernard O'Reilly, *John MacHale, his life, times and correspondence* (2 vols, New York, 1890), ii, p. 434.

69 NAI, Dept. of Education files, Application for Glann [sic] school, Kilcummin (Oughterard), MS No. ED/35/38, 16 Dec. 1861. This application stated that there were no other schools 'within limits', which contradicts the ICM agency books which maintain that Glan mission school was staffed until 1867.

70 Vincentian Archive, 'Life of Fathers Dowley and Lydon', p. 103.

71 Claddaghduff (1853), Aughrismore (1861) and Omey (1861). Claddaghduff Development Association, *To school through the years: a history of the people and schools of the Claddaghduff area, 1853–2003* (Claddaghduff, 2004).

72 Anonymous [Angelo Maria Rinolfi], *Missions in Ireland: especially with reference to the proseltizing [sic] movement; showing the marvellous devotedness of the Irish to the faith of their fathers, by one of the missioners* (Dublin, 1855), p. 68.

73 Hamilton Magee, *Fifty years in the Irish Mission* (Belfast, 1905), p. 98.

74 *The Times* (London) 14 Jan. 1859.

75 Desmond Bowen, *Paul Cardinal Cullen and the shaping of modern Irish Catholicism* (Dublin, 1983), pp. 106, 171; PICA, MS No. KIR/NC/1/1853/4, Paul Cullen to Tobias Kirby, Dublin, 28 Jan. 1853, Italian; Paul Cullen to Tobias Kirby, Dublin, 13 July 1852, in 'Irish College, Rome: Kirby Papers', edited by Patrick J. Corish, *Archivium Hibernicum*, xxxi (1973), pp. 43, 45, hereafter referred to as Kirby, *AH*.

76 PICA, MS No. KIR/NC/1/1852/37, Paul Cullen to Tobias Kirby, 13 June 1852; Paul Cullen to Tobias Kirby, Dublin, 13 July 1852, Kirby, *AH*, xxxi (1973), p. 43.

77 John MacEvilly to Paul Cullen, 12 July 1857, quoted in Liam Bane, *The bishop in politics: life and career of John MacEvilly* (Westport, 1993), p. 73.

78 John MacEvilly to Tobias Kirby, in Irish College, Rome, New Kirby Papers, quoted in Bowen, *Paul Cardinal Cullen*, p. 174.

79 Máire Ní Shúilleabháin, *An t-Athar Caomhánach agus an cogadh creidimh i gConamara* [Fr Kavanagh and the battle of the faith in Connemara] (Dublin, 1984), p. 51.

80 Letter from Fr Kavanagh, Oughterard, *The Tablet*, July 1853.

81 Ní Shúilleabháin, *An t-Athair Caomhánach*, p. 54.

82 PICA, MS No. KIR/NC/1/1852/53, Paul Cullen to Tobias Kirby, Dublin, 4 Nov. 1852.

83 James H. Murphy, 'The role of Vincentian parish missions in the "Irish counter-reformation" of the mid nineteenth-century', *Irish Historical Studies*, xxii (1984), 152–71.

84 Murphy, 'The role of Vincentian parish missions', p. 158; Vincentian Archive, 'Life of Fathers Dowley and Lydon'.

85 Ibid., p. 105.

86 PIRA, MS No. KIR/NC/1/1853/4, Paul Cullen to Tobias Kirby, 28 Jan. 1853,

Italian; MS No. KIR/NC/1/1853/13, Paul Cullen to Tobias Kirby, 24 Mar. 1853.

87 Anonymous, *Missions in Ireland*, pp. 72, 87–8, 252, 258, 266.

88 PIRA, MS No. KIR/NC/1/1853/4, Paul Cullen to Tobias Kirby, 28 Jan. 1853, Italian.

89 Vincentian Archive, 'Life of Fathers Dowley and Lydon', pp. 102, 104.

90 E. J. Quigley, 'Grace abounding, a chapter of Ireland's history, part VII', *Irish Ecclesiastical Record*, xxii (1923), 63; Freyer, *Connemara*, p. 61.

91 Mrs [Matilda Charlotte] Houstoun, *Twenty years in the wild west; or, life in Connaught* (London, 1879), p. 48.

92 Quigley, 'Grace abounding … part VII', 65.

93 See, for example, *The souper's petition*, TCD, MS No. OLS X–1–531/18a. This ballad was printed on the same sheet as *Ave Maris Stella, Hail Queen of Heaven*.

94 'Report of Clifden Petty Sessions', *Mayo Constitution*, 17 July 1860; for further examples see Moffitt, *Soupers and Jumpers*, pp. 108, 118.

95 E. A. D'Alton, *History of the archdiocese of Tuam* (2 vols, Dublin, 1928), ii, pp. 60–1; Moffitt, *Soupers and Jumpers*, p. 82.

96 Vincentian Archive, 'Life of Fathers Dowley and Lydon', p. 100.

97 Harriet Martineau, *Letters from Ireland* (London, 1852), p. 107.

98 Murphy, 'The role of Vincentian parish missions', pp. 168–70.

99 Vincentian Archive, 'Life of Fathers Dowley and Lydon', p. 109.

100 Freyer, *Connemara*, p. 42.

101 Robert Backhouse Peacock, *The reformation in Ireland. Notes of a tour amongst the Missions in Dublin and West Galway in … September 1852* (2nd edn, London, 1853) p. 40; Moffitt, *Soupers and Jumpers*, pp. 85–6.

102 *Banner of the Truth*, Apr. 1853, p. 57; Sept. 1853, p. 146.

103 Ibid., Sept. 1853, pp. 146–7.

104 *Banner of the Truth*, Apr. 1851, p. 55; Anonymous, *The Protestant in Ireland* (London, 1854), p. 137.

105 *Irish Missionary Record and Chronicle of the Reformation*, Dec. 1852. This publication includes other examples of violence at Kiltimagh (Feb. 1853), Ballyhean and Boyle (Mar. 1853), Doon and Castlekerke (Apr. 1853), Castlebar (May 1853), Tuam and Taughmaconnell (June 1853), Cong and Balla (July 1853), Kilkenny, Ennis, Ballyhean and Spiddal (Aug. 1853).

106 Anonymous, *Missions in Ireland*, passim.

107 Máirín Johnson, 'Priests and proselytism in the nineteenth century' in Vivian Uibh Eachach, *Féile Zozimus* (Dublin, 1992), pp. 61–6.

108 *Banner of the Truth*, Oct. 1859, pp. 151–4.

109 *Connaught Watchman*, 19, 26 Nov. 1851.

110 'Conversion and persecution in Ireland' in *The Dublin University Magazine*, xl (August 1852), 245.

111 For example, see earl of Roden, *Progress of the reformation in Ireland: extracts from a series of letters written from the west of Ireland to a friend in England in September 1851* (2nd edn, London, 1852), pp. 34–5; Peacock, *The reformation in Ireland*, p. 27.

112 *Banner of the Truth*, Ang. 1851, p. 136; Anonymous, *The Protestant in Ireland*, p. 140.

113 Freyer, *Connemara*, p. 71.

114 John MacHale, *Powerful letter of the Rev. Dr. M'Hale on its not yet being too late for the people of Ireland to exert themselves in behalf of their insulted religion ...* (Dublin, 1851), p. 12.

115 IFC Archive, S65: 357–9; Séamus Mac an Iomaire, *An Stoc* (Dublin, 1925), quoted in Cormac Ó Gráda, *An drochshaol, bealoideas agus amhráin* [The famine, folklore and song] (Dublin, 1925), pp. 56–8.

116 Johnson, 'Priests and proselytism', pp. 61–6.

117 Quoted in Lucy McDiurmid, *The Irish art of controversy* (Dublin, 2005), p. 134.

118 Society for Irish Church Missions, *Early fruits of Irish missions* (6th edn, London, 1852), p. 17.

119 Desmond Bowen, *History and shaping of Irish Protestantism* (New York, 1995), p. 264.

120 Quoted in 'Bible societies in Ireland, letter to the Rev. J. P. Garrett, Nov. 1858' in James Maher, *The Letters of Rev. James Maher, D.D. late P.P. of Carlow–Graigue, on religious subjects, with a memoir*, ed. by the Right Rev. Patrick Francis Moran (Dublin, 1877), p. 261.

121 'Bible Societies in Ireland, letter to the Rev. J. P. Garrett, Nov. 1858' in Maher, *Letters of Rev. James Maher*, p. 261.

122 'On proselytism in the west of Ireland, 11 June 1866' in Maher, *Letters of Rev. James Maher*, p. 407.

123 For instance, highly critical accounts of Protestant missions in Ireland were regularly featured in English Catholic journals, *The Tablet* and *The Month*.

124 D. W. Cahill, *Controversial letter from the Rev. Dr. Cahill in answer to seven Church of England ministers who have challenged him to a public discussion in Sligo* (Dublin, 1855) also published in *Freeman's Journal*, 9 May 1855.

125 Peadar MacSuibhne, *Paul Cullen and his contemporaries, with their letters* (5 vols, Naas, 1962–74), ii, p. 227. Cullen erroneously referred to proselytisers as agents of the Church Missionary Society.

126 R. V. Comerford, *Ireland* (London, 2003), pp. 59–61, 98.

127 'Confirmation at Partry', *Tuam Herald*, 7 July 1866.

128 'On the visit of the itinerant preachers to Carlow, 24 Aug. 1853' in Maher, *Letters of Rev. James Maher*, p. 197.

129 'On the same subject [proselytism], 4 Dec. 1851' in Maher, *Letters of Rev. James Maher*, pp. 149–50.

130 Freyer, *Connemara*, p. 49.

131 Anonymous, *Missions in Ireland*, p. 74.

132 *A much admired song in praise of the Rev. Dr. Cahill*. TCD, MS No. OLS X–1–531/116.

133 IFC Archive, S4: 219–20, told by Br Joseph of Clifden (86); S65: 246. The ICM operated schools at each of the above locations.

134 IFC Archive, S–66: 382–3. [Bhí na Protastúnaigh ag déanamh bóthar nua agus thugadís mín do aon duine a iompóchadh ina Protastúnach / The Protestants

were making a new road and they gave meal to anyone who would turn Protestant].

135 D. W. Cahill, *Letter from the Rev. D. W. Cahill on the souper government to the people of Ireland* (Dublin, 1856), p. 3; D. W. Cahill, *Letter from the Rev. D. W. Cahill, D.D., to his excellency, the earl of Carlisle* (Dublin, 1856), pp. 11–12.

136 Government-funded institutions which provided for Catholic children were listed in 'Perils to the faith of Catholic Orphans' in SBO, *Annual report*, 1859, 17–19.

137 See for example, *Dr. Cahill's letter to the soupers of Belfast* and *A new song written on the much-beloved Rev. Dr. Cahill*. TCD, MS Nos OLS X–1–531/117, OLSX–1–352/260.

138 'On the Society for Irish Church Missions to Roman Catholics, to His Grace, the Most Rev. Dr. Trench, 6 Feb. 1866' in Maher, *Letters of Rev. James Maher*, p. 393.

139 Ibid., p. 389; D. W. Cahill, *The first letter from the Rev. D. W. Cahill to the Roman Catholics of Ireland on the present menacing attitude of persecution which England has assumed towards the Catholics of Ireland* (Dublin, 1851), p. 8; D. W. Cahill, *Eloquent and impressive sermon of the Rev. Dr. Cahill in the Augustine Church, Limerick on St. Patrick's Day* (Dublin, n.d.); D. W. Cahill, *Eighth letter of the Rev. Dr. Cahill to his excellency, the earl of Carlisle* (Dublin, 1856), p. 8.

140 'Pastoral letter on proselytism, 1856' in Cullen, *The pastoral letters*, i, p. 418.

141 'Letters on the dangers to which the faith of poor children are exposed, 24 May 1860' in Cullen, *The pastoral letters*, i, p. 768.

142 *Banner of the Truth*, Feb. 1852, p. 21.

143 D. W. Cahill, *Twelfth letter from the Rev. Dr. Cahill to his excellency, the earl of Carlisle* (Dublin, 1856), p. 2.

144 'On the evils of proselytism, 7 Dec. 1867' in Maher, *Letters of Rev. James Maher*, p. 490.

145 D. W. Cahill, *Letter V from the Rev. D. W. Cahill to the Right Honourable Lord John Russell* (Dublin, 1852), p. 12; Cahill, *Most important letter … to … the earl of Carlisle affecting the Irish Catholics …*, p. 7.

146 'On the evils of proselytism, 7 Dec. 1867' in Maher, *Letters of Rev. James Maher*, p. 494.

147 'On the evils of proselytism, 7 Dec. 1867'; 'The bible-readers in Carlow, 31 Dec. 1856' in Maher, *Letters of Rev. James Maher*, pp. 494, 210.

148 *The Telegraph*, 6 Aug. 1853.

149 Cahill, *Twelfth letter … Dr. Cahill …earl of Carlisle*, p. 2; D. W. Cahill, *Letter of the Rev. D. W. Cahill, D.D., to the Right Hon. Lord Viscount Palmerstown* (Dublin, 1855), p. 12, also published in the *Freeman's Journal*, 30 Oct. 1855.

150 D. W. Cahill, *Important letter from the Rev. D. W. Cahill to the Rt Hon., the earl of Derby* (Dublin, 1852), p. 6.

151 Cahill, *Letter … D. W. Cahill, D.D … Lord Viscount Palmerstown*, p. 10.

152 D. W. Cahill, *Extract of a letter from the Rev. D. W. Cahill of this day* (Dublin, 1856), p. 3; D. W. Cahill, *Powerful address from the Rev. Dr Cahill to the tradesmen and labouring classes of Ireland* (Dublin, 1856), pp. 3–4.

153 *Daily Express*, Apr. 1857, quoted 'Letter to the Rev. Wm. J. Purdon, on the late meeting of the Carlow Bible Society, 4 Sept. 1860' in Maher, *Letters of Rev. James Maher*, p. 284.

154 'Anglican attempts at proselytism in Ireland, 20 July 1866' in Maher, *Letters of Rev. James Maher*, p. 426, see also *Saturday Review*, 15 Sept. 1866.

155 'The alleged "conversions" in Connemara, 21 June 1866' in Maher, *Letters of Rev. James Maher*, p. 418.

156 Kathleen Villiers-Tuthill, *History of Kylemore Castle and Abbey* (Connemara, 2002), p. 13.

157 Dallas, *Proselytism in Ireland ... the Catholic Defence Association versus the Irish Church Missions*, p. 9.

158 Ibid., pp. 6, 11.

159 Ibid., pp. 19–20.

160 John Wolffe, *The Protestant crusade in Great Britain, 1829–1860* (Oxford, 1991), pp. 198–289.

161 Theodore Hoppen, *The mid-Victorian generation, 1846–1886* (Oxford, 1998), p. 436; Wolffe, *Protestant crusade*, pp. 246–89.

162 ICM supporters Frewen, Hamilton and Mandeville supported Benjamin Disraeli, other supporters such as Ashley, Inglis and Plumptre backed the prime minister, Lord John Russell 1846–52, while yet others abstained.

163 Shaftesbury diary, 15 Jan. 1851, quoted in Wolffe, *Protestant crusade*, p. 261.

164 The Scottish Reformation Society (1851) and the Evangelical Alliance (1845–46) in particular suffered this fate, unlike Anglican organisations such as the National Club and Protestant Association.

165 Wolffe, *Protestant crusade*, p. 263.

166 Derby to M'Ghee, 21 Feb. 1855, quoted in Wolffe, *Protestant crusade*, p. 274.

167 Wolffe, *Protestant crusade*, pp. 277–8.

168 Edward Bickersteth (1850), duke of Newcastle (1851), Sir Digby Mackworth (1852), duke of Manchester (1855), Sir Robert Inglis (1855), George Kenyon (1855), Mortimer O'Sullivan (1858), earl of Winchilsea (1858).

169 Detailed breakdown of source of income does not exist for years before 1860.

170 CPAS, *Annual reports*, 1836–1940.

171 CMS, *Annual reports*, 1836–1940.

172 *The Times* (London), 15 July 1856.

173 *Kilkenny Moderator*, 5 Nov. 1856.

174 *The Rock*, 27 Oct. 1855.

175 *The Warder*, 26 Feb. 1856.

176 *The Rock*, 27 Oct. 1855.

177 *The Times* (London), 11 Mar. 1857.

178 *Catholic Telegraph*, 9, 16, 27 Jan., 3 Apr., 1 May 1858.

179 ICM Archive, Irish Society minutes, 19 Mar. 1850.

180 Plunket, *A short visit to the Connemara missions*, p. 66.

181 'Report of 38th annual meeting of Irish Society', *Irish Ecclesiastical Gazette*, May 1856.

182 ICM Archive, Irish Society minutes, 16 Dec. 1856; 1 Feb. 1859.

183 Irish Society, *Report of the Irish Society for promoting the scriptural and religious instruction of Irish Roman Catholics chiefly through the medium of their own language* (Dublin, 1862), p. 27.

184 Ibid., p. 15.

185 William Fitzpatrick in Charles Bullock, *What Ireland needs, the gospel in her native tongue* (London, c.1880), p. 36. William Fitzpatrick was the Irish Society's missionary at its successful colony at Doon, County Limerick.

186 Henry Ashworth, *The Saxon in Ireland* (London, 1851), pp. 73–4.

187 TCD holds a collection of over 400 handbills advertising controversial sermons of the ICM (2 vols, MS Nos Gall.6.m.71, 72).

188 Hermes, *Souperism and Romanism; being a reply to the editor of the Irish Quarterly Review, in his address to His Excellency the earl of Carlisle, entitled 'Soup and sanctification', 'The Irish Church Mission' 'Scripture Readers' etc. which he designates as a public nuisance, 'lest the people'* (Dublin, 1857), p. 41.

189 John Crawford, *The Church of Ireland in Victorian Dublin* (Dublin, 2005), p. 61; Bowen, *History and shaping of Irish Protestantism*, p. 302.

190 Thomas Andrews, *The Church in Ireland, a second chapter of contemporary history* (London, 1869), pp. 62–3.

191 Houstoun, *Twenty years in the wild west*, p. 127.

192 Ibid., pp. 194, 130, 48.

193 Digby Neave, *Four days in Connemara* (London, 1852), p. 73.

194 James Godkin, *Ireland and her churches* (London, 1867), p. 200.

195 Alan Acheson, *A history of the Church of Ireland, 1691–1996* (Dublin, 1997), p. 198.

196 Godkin, *Ireland and her churches*, pp. 399–400.

197 George Venables, *The good news is true; or what an English clergyman saw in Connemara … with a preface by the Rev. W. C. Plunket* (London, 1865), pp. 24, 35.

198 Ibid., pp. 11–12, 70.

199 William McIlwaine, *Irish Church Missions to the Roman Catholics: supplement to correspondence* (London, 1861), pp. 16–17.

200 Freyer, *Connemara*, p. 64.

201 *Banner of the Truth*, July 1862, p. 97.

202 Ibid., June 1863, p. 81; ICM, *Annual report*, 1866, p. 39.

203 *Banner of the Truth*, June 1863, p. 81.

204 *Christian Examiner and Church of Ireland Magazine* (hereafter *Christian Examiner*), Mar. 1864.

205 E. Broderick, 'Waterford's Anglicans: religion and politics, 1819–1872' (Ph.D. dissertation, University College, Cork, 2000), p. 317, quoted in Crawford, *The Church of Ireland*, p. 65.

206 *Belfast Newsletter*, 8 Jan. 1847.

207 Ibid.

208 *Hansard's Parliamentary Debates*, third series, 1847, lxxxix, 502.

209 *Northern Whig*, 13 Feb. 1847.

210 *Hansard's Parliamentary Debates*, 3rd series, 1847, lxxxix, 502.

211 *Banner of Ulster,* 8 Jan. 1847.

212 Marrable, *Sketch of the origin,* pp. 42–3.

213 Quoted in Arthur G. Dann, *George Webster: a memoir* (London, 1892), p. 50.

214 Stuart A. Moody, *Ireland open to the Gospel* (Edinburgh, 1847), p. 60.

215 Anonymous, 'Them also', p. 50.

216 William John Fitzpatrick, *Memoirs of Richard Whately ... with a glance at his contemporaries & times* (London, 1864), ii, 206–8, 218; Donald Akenson, *A Protestant in purgatory* (Connecticut, 1981), pp. 213–14.

217 Dann, *George Webster,* p. 54.

218 Ibid., p. 48.

219 Wolffe, *Protestant crusade,* pp. 186–7.

220 Dann, *George Webster,* pp. 48–9.

221 LAC, *Annual report,* 1856, p. 9.

222 Henry Cory Eade, *Irish Church Missions, are the converts bribed?: a correspondence between the Rev. Henry Cory Eade ... and the Rev. George Webster* (Dublin, 1864).

223 Four Rectors (eds), *The only complete copy of the correspondence between G. W. and H. C. Eade and A. R. C. Dallas, relating to the charge of bribery against the Society ...* (Dublin, 1864).

224 John Campbell Colquhoun, *Irish Church Missions. Reply ... to certain charges against the Society made by the Rev. George Webster, M.A., Chancellor of Cork* (n.p., c.1864).

225 Eade, *Irish Church Missions, are the converts bribed?,* pp. 12, 21.

226 Joseph Denham Smith, *Connemara, past and present* (Dublin, 1853), pp. 127–8.

227 Quoted in ibid., p. 128.

228 Dann, *George Webster,* pp. 50–1.

229 Ibid., p. 49.

230 Marrable, *Sketch of the origin,* pp. 42–3.

231 Dann, *George Webster,* p. 50.

232 IFC Archive, A77:238, spoken by Micheál O'Maoláin, Baile Nua, Cleggan, Ballinakill; testimony of Colm Ó Ceallaigh in Raymonde Standún and Bill Long, *Singing stone, whispering wind: voices of Connemara* (Dublin, 2001), pp. 119–20.

233 Quoted in Ní Shúilleabháin, *An t-Athair Caomhánach,* p. 52.

234 Marrable, *Sketch of the origin,* pp. 42–3.

235 CP, MS No. GRE/G3/2/12.

236 Arthur W. Edwards, 'Historic sketch of the Church of Ireland' in J. Byrne, A. W. Edwards, W. Anderson and A. Lee (eds) *Essays on the Irish Church by clergymen of the Established Church in Ireland* (London, 1866), pp. 286–7. Revd Edwards was described as 'a writer who was very friendly to the missions' in G. Locker Lampson, *A consideration of the state of Ireland in the nineteenth century* (London, 1907), pp. 277–8.

237 John Forbes, *Memorandums made in Ireland in the autumn of 1852* (2 vols, London, 1853); Mr and Mrs Hall, *The west and Connemara* (London, 1853);

Sidney Godolphin Osborne, *Gleanings in the west of Ireland* (London, 1850).

238 Forbes, *Memorandums*, i, pp. 245, 252–3; Osborne, *Gleanings in the west of Ireland*, p. 242.

239 Ibid., i, pp. 245–56.

240 Hall, *The west and Connemara*, pp. 55–6.

241 Ibid., p. 56.

242 *Free Church Magazine*, 1851, p. 42; A. R. C. Dallas, 'The present position of popery and Protestantism in Ireland. A lecture, etc.' in Church of England Young Men's Society, *Six lectures on Protestantism Delivered before the north of London auxilliary to the Church of England Young Men's Society in October, November and December 1851* (London, 1852), pp.193–4; Roden, *Progress of the reformation*, p. 33; Garwood, *The million-peopled city*, p. 297.

243 Stopford, *A reply to Sergeant Shee*, p. 75.

244 Ibid., p. 71.

245 Quoted in Hermes, *Souperism and Romanism*, p. 16.

246 G. W. Dalton, *Irish Church Missions ... Lecture delivered in Dundalk ...* (Dundalk, 1859), pp. 14–15.

247 'Letter by W. T. T.' in *Church Examiner and Church of Ireland Magazine*, June 1862.

248 W. C. Plunket, *The Church and the census in Ireland* (Dublin, 1865), p. 3.

249 Ibid., p. 3; Venables, *The good news is true*, pp. 54–5.

250 *The Times* (London), 30 June 1863. The Protestant population of counties Mayo and Galway fell from 22,763 in 1834 to 17,156 in 1861.

251 *Irish Ecclesiastical Gazette*, 18 Mar. 1864 (article written by ICM).

252 Plunket, *The Church and the census*, pp. 26–7; *A book for tourists in Ireland*, p. 46.

253 Roderick Ryder, Errismore, to W. C. Plunket, 21 Mar. 1864 in Venables, *The good news is true*, p. 88.

254 A[braham] Hume, *Results of the Irish census of 1861, with a special reference to the condition of the Church of Ireland* (London, 1864), p. 41.

255 William O'Brien, *Dingle: its pauperism and proselytism*, pp. 11–26 quoted in Thomas O'Neill, 'Sidelights on souperism', *Irish Ecclesiastical Record*, lxxi (1949), p. 63. Unfortunately it has not been possible to locate O'Brien's work.

256 Stopford, *A reply to Sergeant Shee*, p. 75.

257 Testimony of Fr Tomás Ó Cadhain in Standún and Long, *Singing stone*, p. 31.

258 J. B. Leslie, *Clergy of Tuam, Killala and Achonry, biographical succession lists*, compiled by Canon J. B. Leslie and revised, edited and updated by Canon D. W. T. Crooks (n.p., 2008), p. 471. Moffitt, *Soupers and Jumpers*, pp. 38–40.

259 By email, Anne Montague, Cincinnati, US (great-great-grand-daughter of John King) to author (18 Oct. 2008); Roseleen Love, Melbourne, Australia (great-great-grand-daughter of Michael King) to author (18 Oct. 2008).

260 ICM, *Annual report*, 1864, pp. 14–21.

261 *Irish Ecclesiastical Gazette*, 18 Mar. 1864.

262 Moran, *Mayo evictions, passim*; Moffitt, *Soupers and Jumpers*, pp. 80–4.

263 Quoted in E. J. Quigley, 'Grace abounding, part XI', *Irish Ecclesiastical Record*, xxii (1923), 608.

264 Garrett, *Good news from Ireland*; Henry Stewart Cunningham, *Is 'Good news from Ireland' true? Remarks on the position and prospect of the Irish Church Establishment* (London, 1865).

265 Venables, *The good news is true*, pp. v–vi, 47–8.

266 Cunningham, *Is 'Good news from Ireland' true?*, pp. 23–4, 30.

267 An Irish Peer, *A letter to His Grace, the archbishop of Dublin on proselytism, by an Irish Peer* (Dublin, 1865), p. 31.

268 Ibid., pp. 21, 8, 10–11, 23, 34.

269 Ibid., p. 8.

270 Ibid., p. 41.

271 Fitzpatrick, *Memoirs of Richard Whately*, i, pp. 4–5.

272 Akenson, *A Protestant in purgatory*, p. 137.

273 Fitzpatrick, *Memoirs of Richard Whately*, i, pp. 118, 228–9.

274 *First report of the Society for Irish Church Missions to the Roman Catholics* (London, 1850), p. 3.

275 Fitzpatrick, *Memoirs of Richard Whately*, i, p. 149. Archbishop Magee is credited with initiating the Second Reformation in 1828. Attempts at introducing the scriptures to the people had already been in place via the Irish Society (1818) and the Hibernian Bible Society, but with the backing of Archbishop Magee, a more aggressive approach was adopted.

276 Akenson, *A Protestant in purgatory*, pp. 208–9.

277 Fitzpatrick, *Memoirs of Richard Whately*, i, p. 274.

278 Akenson, *A Protestant in purgatory*, p. 250. fn. 9; E. J. Whately, *The life of Archbishop Whately* (2 vols, London, 1866), i, pp. 227–30.

279 Garrett, *Good news from Ireland*, p. 12.

280 Fitzpatrick, *Memoirs of Richard Whately*, ii, p. 61.

281 ICM Archive, ICM minutes, General Committee, No. 1660.

282 *Report or general summary of information communicated by the Hon. Sec. for missions to the committee, upon his return from a journey in Ireland, undertaken for the purpose of meeting a number of clergy, and of arranging various matters in connection with the missions; occupying from 28th April to 3rd June, 1854* (London, 1854).

283 Thomas Plunket, *The West Galway Church Building Fund, an appeal from the bishop of Tuam* (Dublin, [c.1860]). Contributions were received from the bishop of Tuam (£100), Lord Primate (£100), archbishop of Dublin (£50) and the archdeacon of Killala (£100).

284 *Christian Examiner*, Apr. and Oct. 1860.

285 Ibid., July 1861, Dec. 1860.

286 Ibid., Mar. 1864.

287 Ibid., Mar. and June 1864.

288 Ibid., Feb. 1858.

289 *Irish Ecclesiastical Gazette*, Dec. 1857.

290 Ibid., 20 Apr. 1864.

291 Edward Maguire, *Fifty eight years of clerical life in the Church of Ireland* (Dublin, 1904), p. 26.
292 Four Rectors (eds), *The only complete copy*, p. 10.
293 Henry, bishop of Limerick, to Revd J. T. Waller, Monday, 4 Aug. 1863, quoted in Four Rectors (eds), *The only complete copy*, pp. 10–11.
294 ICM Archive, ICM minutes, Executive Committee, Nos, 1835, 1836; Crawford, *The Church of Ireland in Victorian Dublin*, p. 66.
295 ICM, *Annual report*, 1868, p. 43; 1869, p. 49.
296 Garrett, *Good news from Ireland*, p. 21.
297 Richard Hobson, *What hath God wrought, an autobiography. Richard Hobson. With an introduction by Right Rev. F. J. Chevasse* (London, 1913), p. 19.
298 David Alfred Doudney, *A run through Connemara. By the editor of the 'Gospel Magazine' and 'Protestant Beacon'* (London, Dublin, 1856), p. 48.
299 John Ross, *The Irish Evangelistic mission of August, 1853, in three letters relating to its operation, fruits and lessons* (London, 1853), p. 3; Dill, *The mystery solved*, p. 292.
300 'Letter to the Rev. Wm. J. Purdon, on the late meeting of the Carlow Bible Society, 4 Sept. 1860' in Maher, *Letters of Rev. James Maher*, p. 285.
301 Cahill, *Most important letter ... to ... the earl of Carlisle affecting the Irish Catholics ...*, p. 7.
302 'Address to the inhabitants of Clifden from the Rev. Fathers Rinolfi and Lockhart, Missionary Priests of the Order of Charity' quoted in Anonymous, *Missions in Ireland*, p. 96.
303 Letter from 'Pereginus', *Galway Vindicator*, 18 July 1877.
304 *Galway Vindicator*, 16 June 1877.
305 *Church Times*, June 1866.
306 *Irish Ecclesiastical Gazette*, 15 May 1863.
307 Letter from 'An occupant of a back pew', *Galway Examiner*, 25 Nov. 1865; letter from 'A Protestant layman', *Galway Examiner*, 27 Jan. 1866.
308 *Christian Examiner*, Oct. 1863.
309 Letter from 'An occupant of a back pew', *Galway Express*, 25 Nov. 1865.
310 James Byrne, 'On the general principles of the establishment and endowment of religious bodies by the state with special reference to Ireland. – The influences exerted on the Irish Church Establishment' in J. Byrne, A. W. Edwards, W. Anderson and A. T. Lee (eds), *Essays on the Irish Church by clergymen of the Established Church in Ireland* (London, 1866), p. 289.
311 James Godkin, *Religious history of Ireland* (Dublin, 1873), p. 268.
312 Donald Lewis (ed.), *The Blackwell dictionary of evangelical biography* (2 vols, Oxford, 1995), i, p. 288.
313 Letter from 'X', *Church Examiner*, June 1865.
314 Letter from 'Z', *Church Examiner*, July 1865.
315 ICM, *Annual report*, 1860–1937. Breakdown figures not available outside these years.
316 Primitive Wesleyan Methodist Missionary Society, *Report of the committee for the year ending June 1860* (Dublin, 1860), pp. 10, 15.
317 *Reply to Review of Charges brought by a Free Churchman against the Scottish*

Ladies' Association, in aid of the Irish Presbyterian Mission to Roman Catholics (n.p., c.1864).

318 Presbyterian Church in Ireland, *Mission to the Roman Catholics* (n.p., 1867), pp. 2–3.

319 *Irish Chronicle*, March 1858, pp. 194–5.

320 Primitive Wesleyan Methodist Missionary Society, *Report … 1860*, p. 7.

321 Bishops of Tuam, Meath, Cashel, Ossory, Down, Kilmore, Killaloe and Cork. Irish Society, *Report of the Irish Society for promoting the scriptural and religious instruction of Irish Roman Catholics chiefly through the medium of their own language.*

322 Baptist Irish Society, £3,001 in 1862; Primitive Wesleyan Methodist Missionary Society, £3,769 in 1860; Presbyterian Church in Ireland Home Mission, £3,000 in 1859; Irish Society, £9,303 in 1862. *The Primitive Church Magazine*, July 1862, p. 167; Primitive Wesleyan Methodist Missionary Society, *Report … 1860*; John Logan Aikman, *Cyclopaedia of Christian Missions* (London, 1860), p. 194; Irish Society, *Report … 1862*.

323 Dudley Levistone Cooney, *Sharing the word: a history of the Bible Society in Ireland* (Dublin, 2006), p. 57.

324 *Report and statement of accounts of the Dublin Bible-Woman Mission, in connection with the Church of Ireland* (Dublin, 1877), p. 15.

325 Dublin City Mission, *Annual report* (Dublin, 1873), p. 7.

Chapter 5

Errislannan and Errismore missions, 1848–1919 (case study)

The Irish Church Missions targeted its activities at the Irish poor, both in the Dublin slums and in the famine-stricken region of west Galway. Most of the ICM's western operations were located in the Clifden poor law union where, at the height of the famine in 1847, 86.62 per cent of the population was dependent on 'soup rations' distributed by the Relief Commissioners.[1] 'Lucht na bhfataí' [the potato-people] of the western seaboard were without question among the poorest in the entire country during the famine era, following the failure of their food crop for four consecutive years, 1845–48.[2]

The scale of ICM activity in Connemara precludes an in-depth study of its entire operations. The neighbouring missions of Errislannan and Errismore are examined as they accurately represent the experiences of the ICM in Connemara. Errismore was arguably the most successful of all Connemara missions, with Sellerna as a possible second, whereas Errislannan, after the initial successes of the famine years, fell into the doldrums somewhat. Although the experiences of Errismore mission mirror those of Errislannan, there are two significant differences between the two. Firstly, Errismore lacked resident gentry supporters, and secondly, it operated on a far greater scale, probably because of its mission colony at Daly Hill.

Errislannan mission

The ICM began its mission work in the Errislannan district in January 1848 and was immediately invited to establish schools in Errismore.[3] By this time the worst of the famine had passed but was followed by 'cholera, pestilence and sad diseases', resulting in a continued demand for mission relief.[4] As happened at Castlekerke, mission schools were established, houses were visited by scripture readers and Irish teachers were recruited among the converts and older schoolchildren.

In the early years, mission publications abound with stories of great success in Connemara, with estimations of attendances at mission services where relief was distributed (invariably depicted as devout converts). William Kilbride, a deacon awaiting ordination, and Revd John Gregg (later bishop of Cork), observed eighty adults and ninety children in Errislannan schoolhouse.[5] Gregg commented that thirty young persons had recently been confirmed and that over 100 children attended school. The scale of the mission can be gauged from table 5.1, which shows that almost 1,500 persons were fed in Errislannan and Ballinaboy schools in a single week in 1851 by the Fund for the Relief of Converts and Children of Connemara, which was established in early 1848.[6] This relief fund went unmentioned in *The Banner*, readers being told instead that locals were interested in doctrinal issues such as why Protestants did not honour the Blessed Virgin; supporters were assured of the hunger of Errislannan's Catholics for the scriptures, quoting one convert as saying, 'I now see no man is anything who does not know the Bible.'[7]

Table 5.1 Attendance at mission schools in Errismore
and Errislannan, 19–26 January 1851

	Present	*Sick*	*Fed*
Errislannan mission			
Errislannan	734	–	721
Ballinaboy	693	92	759
Total	1427	92	1480
Errismore mission			
Derrygimla	860	30	82
Duholla	839	72	703
Aillebrack	566	9	483
	2265	111	1268

Source: Fanny Bellingham, *Fourth account of the fund entrusted to Miss Fanny Bellingham ... for the Relief of the Converts and Children of Connemara* (Wonston, 1851)

The support of Revd Dr Richard Wall, Errislannan's principal landowner, was crucial to the progress of the mission. Revd Wall, a fervently evangelical clergyman, had purchased an estate on the peninsula in 1842 and maintained a strong interest in the ICM's work. After acquiring his Errislannan property, Revd Wall redirected the public road from the north (rear) of the manor to the south, enclosing the area around the house, thereby cutting off the locals from their medieval church of St Flannan and nearby holy well. He also reorganised landholdings on his estate, removing the rundale division of good and bad lands, sequestering the fertile land near the manor for himself and dispatching his tenants to the stony land near the shore. Having separated the Catholic peasantry from the good land on the one hand, and from their church on the other, Revd Wall then began to promote the most aggressive nineteenth-century proselytising mission. He actively sought funds for mission work and for the building of Errislannan mission church, which he promised would bring the blessings of 'CIVILISATION, INDUSTRY, CONTENTMENT, LOYALTY AND PEACE' (his capitals). Initially Revd Wall and his wife divided their time between Errislannan and Dublin, where he was chaplain of the Chapel Royal in Ringsend, but soon settled in full-time in Errislannan.[8] Until his death in 1869, Revd Wall received over two hundred pounds a year from his Dublin appointment but the parish which he deserted, without even supplying a curate, was 'a poor and populous district', so concern for the religious welfare of the poor appears not to have been his priority.[9] Apart from the spiritual well-being of his tenantry, he may have been influenced by the ICM's provision of temporal relief, especially during the famine years.

Revd Wall was unpopular, described by his great-grand-daughter as the 'terror of his family' and was so hated locally that his bones were dug up and scattered around the graveyard during the extreme animosity of the Land War.[10] Although he championed the building of Errislannan mission church, the resulting building bore a great resemblance to an estate church and was sited almost opposite the gate of Errislannan manor. It was strategically located on high ground, visible from out at sea, and also visible from the road that approached Clifden from Galway.[11] From the description of the church in the 1920s, it is obvious that it was built more for the comfort of the Walls (and their descendants, the Heathers) than to serve the local convert community:

> The Heather family sat in one of the three square pews at the west end, with a fire behind us, two comfortable armchairs, and plenty of cushions and musty floorstools … Between him [the rector at the east end] and us stretched a vast sea of empty pews that had once seated two hundred people.[12]

The Banner reported that a collection was taken up among the converts for a new stove; it appears this stove found its way inside the Heathers' pew while the converts sat on pews in the cold.[13] This demonstrates how the ICM supported the class structure of its localities and was concerned to keep the local gentry on-side. As observed of evangelical home missions in England, 'the crucial distinction was between spiritual equality and social subordination'.[14]

Errislannan manor was a deeply evangelical household, with nothing to read 'except for large leather-bound tomes teaching the Protestant to floor the Roman Catholic in argument', where drink and cards were 'the

Devil's Visiting Cards' and where nobody was allowed to ride, drive, swim, dance or read books on Sundays. Scriptural Protestantism ran deep in the Heather/Wall families, with family prayers twice a day and one daughter, Eva Heather, working as a missionary in India.[15] Errislannan church was deeply evangelical in its focus, no cross being allowed on the communion table. As late as the 1920s, when Alannah Heather hung a cross of lilies from the pulpit, she found it thrown in the churchyard the following morning.[16]

One aspect of the ICM's work was the establishment of orphanages at Glenowen and Ballconree. These served the dual purpose of the philan-thropic feeding and clothing of destitute children and also for their rearing in the biblical truth. During and immediately after the famine Mrs Sarah Wall (wife of Revd Wall) and Fanny D'Arcy went round stricken houses collecting destitute children, which was not always appreciated by the locals who 'kidnapped' or 'rescued' children from the side-car.[17] *Erin's Hope* is full of heart-rending stories of these children, and also of children being punished by their parents for attending the mission schools. One mission agent told of a child who pleaded for a night's lodging when her father cast her out for refusing to leave Errislannan mission school.[18] The persecution meted out to those who converted or availed of the ICM's education or relief was recounted in annual reports and in *The Banner*, reporting that mission pupils were beaten by their parents, although it is possible they were *sent* by their parents in order to be fed. The 1854 report stated that thirty pupils of Ballinaboy school were driven from their houses by a Catholic landlord, twenty of whom were 'scattered about the country or obliged to take refuge in the poorhouse; the remainder succeeded in procuring homes sufficiently near and still continue to attend school'.[19]

The destitution of the area is reflected in statements such as 'Many would attend the school but for their nakedness', and the early progress of the mission was undoubtedly due to the distressed state of the district.[20] The mission's ability to distribute food and relief was greatly resented by the Catholic clergy, as when Patrick MacManus, parish priest of Clifden, reported in 1853 that the district was 'infested with hordes of auxiliary soupmakers'.[21] Aggressive Catholic counter-mission halted the uptake of the ICM's services, most especially after the 1853 mission of the Rosminian Fathers Rinolfi and Lockhart, and the establishment of Errislannan national school. Many former converts reverted at this time; the *Irish Catholic Directory* reported that 'sixteen unfortunate perverts [were] received back into the Church at Clifden, by Rev. P. M'Manus' in September 1853.[22] The Franciscan Brothers were also pivotal in combating the ICM; they provided male schools at their Roundstone and Clifden monasteries and toured the district catechising the poor.[23]

The ICM reassured its supporters, however, that there was 'hardly a house in which the reader is not welcome, and *not one* where he is not at least civilly received'.[24] By the consecration of Errislannan church in 1855, in spite of the immense support of the Wall family, the mission was on the wane and attendances at Sunday service were in decline. The following year, the mission admitted that no adult 'cast off the shackles of Rome' during the previous twelve months and that converts were greatly outnumbered by those 'still enslaved'.[25] From this time, stories of individual converts rather than a surge of communal conversions are commonplace in mission publications. In 1857, supporters learned of a young convert, a former pupil of Errislannan school, who had served in the Crimea and was now an 'earnest probationary reader at Errislannan'.[26] Assurances were given that many had openly professed Protestantism and that others were Catholics 'only in name'.[27] The association of large numbers of young persons with the mission was regularly reported and supporters regularly learned of the marriage of converts:

> There have been two marriages in Errislannan church since it was consecrated where all parties were converts. One of the young women had been baptised eighteen years before by Mr Burke, then Roman Catholic priest; and it was he who now, as a Protestant clergyman, married her to a young man who has been a steady convert for years.[28]

Regular encouraging accounts of the mission appeared in *The Banner*; supporters learned how 'scripture-readers, generally speaking, are well received', which may have misled the reader, as at this time there was only one scripture reader in the mission (James Lyden).[29] This application of the plural where only one person was employed was commonplace. When the 1867 annual report stated that 'The Readers often meet with opposition', there was only one reader (Michael O'Toole) stationed at Ballinaboy and none at Errislannan. The mission admitted that it encountered opposition, and that the 'dread and scorn and persecution of neighbours' deterred many who stood 'on the very brink of that river of the sanctuary that is to separate them forever from the Church of Rome'.[30]

The ICM deemed that Catholic opposition, in the shape of nearby Errislannan national school, was a failure, reporting that no pupils were withdrawn from the mission school, and that the combined attendance in Errislannan and Ballinaboy mission schools was eighty, where pupils were raised 'to a scale of intelligence far above their besotted and ignorant neighbours'.[31] The location of national schools was calculated to cause maximum harm to ICM schools.[32] Errislannan NS, established in the mid 1850s, was relocated to a new building in 1863 on the piece of land nearest the mission school and, crucially, not owned by Revd Wall.[33] This practice was replicated throughout Errismore and Errislannan; Ordnance Survey maps indicate that only a few hundred yards away separated Ballinaboy NS from Ballinaboy mission school, Aillebrack NS from Aillebrack mission school, and Calla NS from Duholla mission school (see figure 5.1).

Throughout the 1860s the mission maintained its presence in Errislannan, with attendances of around twenty-five in Errislannan school and ten in Ballinaboy, but after the 1850s it appears that there were few enrolments of younger children.[34] It is possible that the five children of Ballinaboy school in 1868 were from the same family, maybe even children of ICM agents (Michael O'Toole, scripture reader and his teacher wife, Eliza), who had at least two children of school-going age.[35] Decreasing attendances at Ballinaboy and Errislannan schools at this time were explained by a change of teachers, caused partly by the death of Charles Hawkshaw, who was described as having been chiefly instrumental in training a 'very nice class of Irish-teachers', who were 'a most important branch of the agency'.[36]

Two marriages were performed in Errislannan church in the 1870s compared with twelve in the 1860s. This may be partly due to the opening of nearby Errismore church in 1865,[37] but the continued decline in marriages (only three in total after the 1870s, in 1880, 1891 and 1900) indicate little mission involvement by younger generations. Although research clearly suggests otherwise, supporters were reassured that the mission was successful, that its congregation grew by one-fourth in 1866, that, for example, three adults openly converted in 1868, and the number of pupils of Irish teachers had nearly doubled.[38]

The building of Errislannan parsonage in 1868 saw the appointment of a resident clergyman, Charles Campbell 1866–69, succeeded by Benjamin Irwin 1870–85. These were assisted by two scripture readers, two teachers in Errislannan school and one or two teachers in Ballinaboy school; Jane Heather from the manor also taught in Errislannan school. A third school functioned briefly at Derryeighter (1872–74), when parents requested that the mission 'send a schoolmaster to teach their children'. Revd Wall provided a house free and Pat Corbet, a former pupil of Errislannan school, was appointed teacher. ICM publications reported intense Catholic opposition to Derryeighter school, the priest prayed that its pupils might be withdrawn 'before they be lost forever' and warned parents not to place their children 'on the Devil's roll'.[39] As no schoolhouse has been located in the records of the Valuation Office, school was probably held in a house, as happened in Tourmakeady where a convert was badly beaten for lending his cabin for a mission school.[40] Informal schools also existed in nearby Errismore, where no evidence of schools at Dolan (1873–74) or Mannin (1868–75) can be found. Other 'missing' or 'informal' mission schools in Connemara include Claddaghduff (1850–64), Patches (1870–80) and Russadillisk (1864–92). This suggests that the ICM applied a lower standard of school accommodation in Connemara than in Dublin, which was also true of teaching standards.[41] Whereas all Dublin teachers had passed through the ICM's Dublin Training School, untrained teachers like the above Pat Corbet were to be found throughout Connemara.

It was noted in 1872, after twenty years of mission work, that the parents of five-sixths of Errislannan's pupils were still Catholic, availing of the mission's education without actually converting. This was also found in Errismore mission. Since success was invariably measured in numbers of converts, it was necessary to reassure supporters that 'it would be a great mistake to infer from this that the missionary work has been at a standstill'. Readers of *The Banner* and the mission's annual reports learned of cottage meetings, weekly Irish classes and controversial discussions and were informed that over 200 Catholics heard or read the scriptures each month and that service was celebrated in Errislannan church and Ballinaboy schoolhouse each Sunday. Over the following decade they were assured that Errislannan's Catholics were avidly interested in doctrinal issues and that the mission continued to attract new inquirers, opening a weekly class in 1875 for those who were too old for the mission school; in 1877, they learned that Irish teachers had attracted new pupils and that three Catholics had openly converted.[42]

The 1875 *Report of the Tuam Diocesan Synod* gave the Protestant population of Errislannan as sixty-eight.[43] When allowances are made for the Heather family in the manor, the Irwins in the rectory, Geoffrey and Mrs Heanue and family (Ballinaboy teachers), Patrick and Mrs McNamara and family[44] (Errislannan teachers) and the Gorham family (church sexton), it is obvious that the mission had only a small 'native' community who did not depend on it for their livelihood. It has not been possible to identify the Irish teachers, who were also maintained by the mission. The ICM explained that emigration reduced its convert community by telling that some converts had moved to 'Australia, New Zealand and California … others in the army and navy …'. They also claimed that more Catholics might attend the school were it not for the priests who, in 1882, were described as 'more enraged and more reckless'.[45]

An extremely aggressive campaign was carried out against the mission and its convert community between 1878 and 1883, with frequent violent attacks against mission personnel and property.[46] This 'anti-jumper' crusade, which coincided with the violence and social upheavals of the Land War, had its origins in Catholic resentment at the mission's distribution of assistance to those who converted or sent their children to mission schools. The close connection between the ICM in Errislannan and families such as the Walls/Heathers contributed to animosity as the locals vented their anger on unpopular landlords. Intimidation of the convert and mission community forced most 'nominal' converts to dissociate from the mission at this juncture. After these turbulent years, the mission continued as before, although in a less arrogant fashion.

Without warning, Errislannan mission was closed in 1885, a direct result of a split between Revd Cory, ICM superintendent in Clifden, and the London committee, who felt that Connemara parishes had become more parochial and less actively missionary in character. This resulted in the closure of Clifden, Ballyconree and Errislannan missions; when 'the school was broke up; the faithful reader who had spent his life in the work was turned adrift …'.[47] Revd Cory, being in receipt of a reasonable diocesan stipend, remained in Clifden and Revd Brown of Ballyconree, having independent means, stayed at Ballyconree. The public appeal for funds to maintain these 'abandoned' missions must have been fruitless.[48] Revd Irwin, with no income and a family to maintain, left Connemara at this time but returned to Ballinakill later in life. In a letter to the *Irish Ecclesiastical Gazette*, Revd Irwin stated that he had been 'shamefully treated' but admitted that he 'could not pretend to say that the Missionary work had succeeded according to my desires and hopes'.[49] Following the death of Revd Cory in 1887, Errislannan and Ballinaboy stations re-opened as part of the united mission of Errismore and Errislannan, under the direction of Revd Thomas Nee of Errismore. Text teachers were reappointed and both schools re-opened, but attendances were small and active missionary work was minimal.[50] As Ballinaboy school was closed in 1880, the ICM's presence was maintained by scripture reader William Manning (senior), but closed entirely in 1892. In 1932, the ICM sold its nine acres of land at Ballinaboy, including the former schoolhouse, to a person unconnected with the mission.

Conversions, especially during times of want, were frequently insincere. Many considered it best to live a Protestant but die a Catholic. Stories of death-bed reversions to Catholicism are to be found in the Irish Folklore Commission's Schools' Survey (1937), with many instances of dying converts attempting to send for the priest and being impeded by Protestants. One story from Errislannan recorded how 'a local man and woman changed their religion to impress the people in the big house. The man died, and when the woman was dying, the lady in the big house wouldn't get the priest.'[51] Similar stories are found in the schools' collection for other mission locations, especially in the Ballinakill region.[52] Almost eighty years later (2004), a similar story was told by Christy Butler regarding a convert called Connors at Castlekerke. Christy's father was working in a field next door to the Reynolds' house (also converts) with whom Matt Connors lived at the end of his life. Mr Butler could hear Matt Connors calling him throughout the day before he (Connors) died, but the Reynolds family refused to admit Mr Butler in case he would get the priest.[53] Death-bed reversions were also recounted in street-ballads; the following tells of the repentance of a mother when faced with the imminent death of her child:

> True, we strayed from thy fold, Sagarth Aroon,
> Lur'd by their wretched gold, Sagarth Aroon,
> When dying with want and woe, knowing not where to go,
> Oh! Famine's a deadly woe, Sagarth Aroon.[54]

It was claimed that mission agents prevented dying converts from accessing Catholic clergy. Revds Campbell and Fleming were attacked by a mob of 300 persons for preventing Fr Patrick Walsh's access to the death-bed of Myles Burke of Ballinaboy. At the ensuing Clifden Petty Sessions both parties were fined a farthing and each party had to meet its own costs.[55] The ensuing campaign to raise funds for Fr Walsh's legal costs shows the strong support for the anti-souper movement throughout the west of Ireland.[56]

An examination of the manuscript returns of the 1901 census for those townlands which comprised the Errislannan mission reveals that the only Protestants in Errislannan were the Heathers (original Protestants), John Conry and family, Ballinaboy (scripture reader), James Lyden and family, Errislannan (scripture reader), Margaret Trelford and daughter, Errislannan (original Protestants, brought in as farm workers when Connemara was 'settled' in the early nineteenth century) and Pat Gorham and family, Errislannan (sexton, convert). A note in the preacher's book in 1916 gave the church population as sixteen, reflecting an 82.35 per cent decrease since 1875.[57] After the closure of Errislannan mission school in 1904, which marked the end of the ICM's involvement in Errislannan, the national school opposite was relocated to the more convenient position nearer the main road in 1910.

In the 1920s the Heathers and the Gorhams were the only Protestants in Errislannan. After the death of Pat Gorham, once again, the only Protestants in Errislannan were the owners of the manor.[58] The experiences of Errislannan mission confirm that it succeeded in attracting converts during and immediately after the famine, but that despite the availing of the mission schools, few children of later generations embraced the Protestant faith.

Errismore mission

Missionary work began in Errismore in 1848 when the inhabitants of Derrygimla petitioned Revd Dallas to provide a school so that 'their children might be taught as those in Clifton [sic] were'. When Revd Dallas first visited Derrygimla, he was mistaken for the Relieving Officer. On addressing the assembled crowd, the people of Derrygimla told him that they wanted relief.[59]

It should be noted that Derrygimla's inhabitants asked for education and relief; they would not have considered themselves lacking in religion. Douglas Hyde described Connaught's Catholics as a very pious race, with prayers for every occasion, to keep the fire lit overnight, against toothache, whooping cough, stopping blood, back ache, to protect against the good people (fairies), etc.[60] Errismore had a resident priest and a Catholic chapel.[61] The existence of St Caillin's chapel and holy well on Chapel Island; Tobercaillin at Keerhaunmore; the holy well of the seven daughters at Aillebrack; a medieval parish church at Bunowenmore; and a holy well on Daly Hill, Derrygimla (where the mission would later establish a colony) demonstrates that Christianity was deeply rooted in Errismore, albeit not of a scriptural type.[62]

After deciding to establish a mission at Errismore, the ICM dispatched Clifden schoolteacher, Thomas Moran, who was ambushed and beaten at Ballinaboy. On arrival in Derrygimla, he found 430 children waiting for him. These were divided according to their location and schools opened at Derrygimla, Aillebrack, Duholla and Ballinaboy.[63] Derrygimla, close to the village and chapel of Ballyconneely, was chosen as the focal point of the mission and the eventual site for its church. *The Banner* reported in 1850 that scripture readers were well received, and that many considered the missionaries were a blessing to the country.[64] In early years, Errismore and Errislannan missions were served by William Kilbride, an Irish-speaking clergyman, and the ICM considered that widespread conversions were possible if scripture reading in Irish were extended to the entire population.[65] As in Errislannan, large numbers availed of mission relief immediately after the famine; Table 5.1 shows that over 2,000 persons were fed at Errismore in a single week in 1851. In the early 1850s, mission schools were 'very well attended ... Derrygimla, Duholla and Aillebrack ... comprising about 150 children, join in one on Sunday, for Sunday-school and service'.[66] The ICM interpreted and portrayed these large attendances at 'feeding' schools and services as proof of deeply held doctrinal conversions.

Revd Kilbride drew the attention of mission supporters to the destitution of the area, having even to provide coffins for converts who died of starvation. Although he stressed that the mission offered no temporal assistance, he appealed for donations to Miss Bellingham of Dublin (later Mrs Hyacinth D'Arcy) 'to convey assistance in every way to the starving converts' through the Fund for the Relief of Converts and Children of Connemara.[67]

In 1852 Revd Roderick Ryder took charge of Errismore mission, where he remained until his death in 1884. This former Catholic priest from Craughwell in east Galway had converted to Protestantism following a

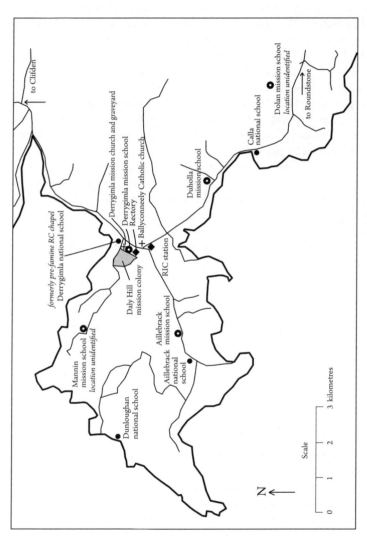

formerly pre-famine RC chapel
Derrygimla national school

Derrygimla mission church and graveyard
Derrygimla mission school
Rectory
+ Ballyconneely Catholic church

Daly Hill
mission colony

RIC station

to Clifden

Duholla
mission/school

Calla
national school

Dolan mission school
location unidentified

to Roundstone

Mannin
mission school
location unidentified

Aillebrack
mission school

Aillebrack
national
school

Dunloughan
national school

N ←

Scale

0   1   2   3 kilometres

5.1 Errismore mission

dispute with his bishop.[68] After a time of training with Revd Dallas in Wonston, he was sent back into his former parish as a missionary and was removed to Ballyconree in 1850, where he married Sarah Bailey, matron of the ICM's orphanage. He was described as 'a robust, middle aged man, with a clear eye, a hearty manner, and a frank genial expression of face'.[69] He had suffered the same social consequences as Connemara converts, having 'lost the society and friendship of all that were dear to me on earth',[70] and could therefore 'sympathise with and direct others in their doubts and fears, their conflicts and their conquests;'[71] his fluency in Irish was also essential. Revd Ryder wrote that, on hearing of his transfer to Derrygimla, the local priest Fr Edward Gibbons prayed that 'if any man raised his hand to recognise or salute, that hand might rot or fall from the shoulder', leading Revd Ryder to publicly pray for 'Fr Gibbons and the souls he was leading astray'.[72]

The oral tradition of Revd Ryder in the Ballyconneely community of today is telling. It was believed locally that his son, Alexander, went to America because life was so unpleasant for him.[73] The facts are rather different. Alexander Ryder was ordained a Church of Ireland clergyman in 1877 and served in the Down diocese until his death in 1919.[74] A locally held story relates that Mrs Ryder had been unaware of her husband's life as a Catholic priest. It is told that she put on a set of Catholic vestments she found in the parsonage and that Roderick came in while she was wearing them and was furious at her discovery.[75] It is inconceivable that Mrs Ryder would be unaware of her husband's former life, given her own association with the mission prior to her marriage and the publicity which the ICM gave to its priest-converts. It is also inconceivable that Revd Ryder would have kept a set of vestments. The story may infer a desire on the part of the local Catholic population to believe that Revd Ryder had not *totally* left the Church of Rome. It can be difficult to disentangle local myth-making and inherited moralising tales from fact, as authoratative voices on both sides tapped into existing prejudices, fears and ignorance.

Errismore mission was much more successful than Errislannan and also more long-lived, although it petered out in the early twentieth century. Unquestionably, it gathered many converts, but not nearly as many as was inferred in mission publications. It was claimed that many steadfast converts had once been fierce opponents, such as J. Mannion, who was 'in the habit of standing at the door, pitchfork in hand, to keep out the readers'. The mission experienced intense opposition, its agents and property coming under attack; the windows of Derrygimla and Ballinaboy schoolhouses were broken by a man who claimed his actions had been imposed on him in the confessional by Fr Gibbons which, according to the mission, was 'the best specimen … of what Popery makes her sons'.[76]

Mission publications frequently told of persecutions endured by converts. *The Banner* told of Widow O'Donnell of Errismore, one of Connemara's first converts, who was evicted despite owing no rent. Her landlord told Revd Ryder that he would meet the cost of ten such evictions rather than have a 'jumper' on his property.[77] Supporters heard how converts would be employed by 'Romish landlords' if they agreed to attend mass.[78] Inter-confessional animosity escalated to the extent that five attempts were made in the early 1850s to burn converts' houses; two houses were totally burnt, one of which belonged to the previously evicted Widow O'Donnell. She may have been singled out because scripture reader Michael McNiffe and his wife lodged with her. Four bushels of potatoes, the winter's stock of food, and the reader's supply of books were lost. An appeal to help this 'houseless, homeless ... penniless' woman raised £18 2s. and enabled the rebuilding of her house.[79] When Widow O'Donnell's daughter, Anne, died two years later, *The Banner* reported her burial in Clifden Protestant cemetery which was 'the last testimony she could give of her dying trusting in Jesus' and told that Ballyconneely's priests

> cursed them all, and poor Anne after her death ... They quenched the candles at mass, rang the bell and told them she was burning in the fires of hell; and then cursed anyone who would sell to, or buy from the mother, brother, or any of her family, or any of the 'jumpers' who accompanied her.[80]

In 1859, the Clogherty family was evicted for sending their children to an Aillebrack mission school. An appeal was launched, following a report in *The Banner* where Mrs Clogherty was quoted as saying: 'say that I love the Bible, my children love it, my husband loves it ... Tell my landlord that he can throw down this old house, and throw us and our children on the road; but, by God's grace, we will not give up our Bible, nor the Bible-school.'[81] The appeal raised ten pounds, five pounds of which was donated by Mrs Whately of Dublin with a note of 'deep sympathy at this sorely tried family'.[82] The parish register of Clifden Catholic church triumphantly recorded the return of the Clogherty family thirteen years later, when Dean Patrick MacManus recorded the baptism of six family members who 'were making with the lying, heartless jumpers but when hunger and want had somewhat abated they left the soup dens & left instead of their souls & bodies their heaviest crime. These were a true example of all who went to by [illegible word] dens from the pressure of dire want ... This record will be a lasting testimony of the villainous hypocrisy of the soupers.'[83]

Mission supporters were frequently told of assaults on its staff, although sometimes the mission workers brought trouble on themselves, as when readers approached Catholics at the annual pattern-day at St Caillin's well near Aillebrack.[84] Priestly opposition to the missions was intense; 'vigorous' priests entered houses and physically attacked those who admitted scripture readers or sent children to mission schools.[85]

Persons accommodating orphans attending mission schools were forced to expel these children, such as Tom C. and Tim Cl. whose stories were told in *Erin's Hope*. It is thought that Tim Cl. refers to Tim Clesham, a child-convert who later became a scripture reader and subsequently an ICM clergyman.[86] As a child he was the only son of a widow who for years lived in her brother's house. Although his uncle was very fond of him and listened to his reading of the scriptures, he was forced to cast the child from his house when they [Tim's uncle and mother] were reportedly excommunicated 'as the neighbours would not speak to them while under excommunication they had no choice but to obey the priest'. ICM supporters were reassured that both boys were now 'more determined than ever against popery', and refused to yield, although no longer allowed home.[87]

'Excommunication' extended to excluding converts from fishing parties, a vital means of livelihood in this coastal parish, and details of the dangers to which convert fishermen were exposed were regularly published in *The Banner*. When this happened to nine convert families in Errismore, the Rights of Conscience Society granted Revd Ryder money 'to provide three boats for these nine families, paid by them next harvest out of the profits'.[88]

Table 5.2 Protestant population of Errismore, 1854 and 1856

	1854	*1856*
Original Protestants	22	30
Adult converts	74	76
Irish teachers over 16 years	24	18
Children in school under 16 years	176	120
Total	296	244

Source: ICM, *Annual report*, 1857, p. 69.

Despite physical assaults, some parents continued to send their children to mission schools. Most families remained Catholic, thereby availing of the mission's education without actually converting, mirroring the pattern in Errislannan.[89] Table 5.2 shows that attendance at mission schools declined markedly once national schools were established in the mid decade. It took almost a decade for purpose-built national schools to be erected throughout Connemara;[90] in Errismore, school was held in Ballyconneely chapel in the interim.[91]

Attendance at mission schools while remaining Catholic was common throughout Connemara, as was the practice of availing of mission relief without actually converting. This was repeatedly mentioned in folklore, often telling of how locals took advantage of the ICM for educational and other temporal reasons, although occasional conversions were noted. It was reported in Ballinakill that

> Chuaigh daoine chun na scoileanna sin ach níor iompuigh said. Fuair daoine oideachas maith ón na scoileanna seo. Fuair daoine obair maith i dtíribh eile agus is tré oideachas na scoil seo a fuair said é, ach níl an scéal mar sin ag gach duine, caith daoine áiriththe a gcreidimh uathu.[92]

> [People went to those schools but didn't convert. People got good education in those schools. People got good jobs in other countries and it's through the education from those schools they got them, but it wasn't like that for everyone, some people discarded their faith]

> All the people that went got a cup of soup at noon daily. The first day they went they got a flannel coat. One man whose name was Tommy Heaney went two day[s], as soon as he got the flannel coat he never went to it again.[93]

Unlike Errislannan, a reasonable number of these converts persevered, although not nearly as many as missionary publications suggest. Errismore's relative success may be due to the presence of cottages for converts, as discussed below. As in nearby Errislannan, Errismore mission performed best in periods of want. Even after the 'hungry years' had passed, Sunday services were well attended and the mission claimed numerous conversions in the 1860s, reporting over 200 converts in the district, that 200 Catholic families were visited weekly and that over twenty persons converted in a single year.[94] It should be noted that Connemara experienced extreme distress during the early 1860s and again in the early 1870s caused by bad weather resulting in a lack of fuel and disappointing harvests. In 1863, at the height of this time of hardship, Revd Ryder told that he had 'seven new adult converts present for the first time last Sunday. I had three new adult converts the previous Sunday and nearly every Sunday I have some.'[95]

The region was romantically portrayed in mission publications, capitalising on the wildness of the region, the potential for missionary success and temporal needs of its inhabitants:

> The country is very wild and poor and the cabins most miserable … Yet this country, so poor to our eye, is a rich harvest field for Jesus … More than four hundred converts have passed away from Derrygimla, many of whom are known to be earnestly labouring for the conversion of souls to the Lord.[96]

Revd Ryder outlined the necessity of the mission's feeding programme in Errismore to the supporters of the Fund for the Relief of Converts and Children of Connemara:

it would be sad, indeed, if the usual supply of Indian meal for the poor and fatherless and persecuted children should cease at so critical a crisis ... We now have twelve orphans in Errismore schools, others with one parent, equally destitute; some whose parents are very poor, and who are denounced each Sabbath by the Priest for sending them to us, and also persecuted by their Romish neighbours.[97]

The parcels of clothes you sent for our school-children proved a very great blessing indeed. We cannot find words to express our deep gratitude to you and to the kind friends ... Many of the children were very naked. Some were unable to attend school for some time.[98]

In spite of appeals such as the above, *The Banner* insisted that conversions were doctrinally based. It asserted that Errismore mission had 'no inducement to give either parents or children but that of a sound scriptural and secular education. We have neither meat, nor money nor clothes to offer'[99] and readers learned that when converts approached Revd Ryder for some place where they might be safe from Catholic neighbours, landlords and priests, he told them that he had 'no houses, nor money, nor land'.[100] This contradicts the records of the Valuation Office, which confirm that Revd Dallas owned land and five cottages at Daly Hill, Derrygimla from 1855. The number of cottages, which were constantly occupied, had grown to eleven by 1873, as discussed below. Apart from distribution of temporal relief, employment of converts as Irish teachers provided a steady flow of income. Agency books only identify Irish teachers by name from 1904, but the importance of this income in earlier years should not be overlooked.

In common with the Catholic population, the mission had to contend with the two scourges of nineteenth-century Connemara; consumption and emigration. *The Banner* and *Erin's Hope* are peppered with stories of converts dying a lingering (but always joyful) death, as in the case of trainee scripture reader, Val Conneely of Derrygimla.[101] Intense pressure to bury the dead with their Catholic relatives led to the consecration of Derrygimla burial ground in 1863. The first person interred was an elderly convert, whose unlikely last words were quoted in *The Banner*: 'I renounced the wafer to follow Him, the type for the antitype, the shadow for the substance. He is my all in all.'[102] Regardless of the sentiments expressed, it is doubtful whether an elderly man, probably illiterate, whose first language was undoubtedly Irish, would have possessed such a sophisticated theological vocabulary.

The missions continued throughout the 1860s, bolstered by the consecration of Derrygimla church in April 1865. In 1862, attendances at Sunday services were reported as 120 in Derrygimla and 54 in Duholla, with 138 children on the schools' rolls. Supporters were told that 'Romanism is losing its hold on the minds of the people' and informed that over 220 attended service in Derrygimla during Mr Dallas' visit.[103] It has been reliably

ascertained that an illustration of Derrygimla church which appeared in
Erin's Hope did not in any way resemble the actual building.[104] In reality,
the church was similar to Errislannan church (still extant), a nave with no
transepts, although it was portrayed as a more substantial building in the
missionary publication.[105]

An episode in 1866 reveals the actual extent of the ICM's success in
Errismore. Having toured the missions and attended the consecration
of Castlekerke and Derrygimla churches, Richard Trench, archbishop of
Dublin, informed readers of *The Times* that he had witnessed widespread
conversions in Connemara, had encountered 'enquiring Romanists', and
stated that the Protestant population of Errismore consisted of seventy-six
original Protestants and 206 converts, ninety-six of whom were scholars
under fifteen years of age.[106] This sparked a newspaper dialogue in which
the archbishop's observations were disputed by Connemara's Catholic
clergy. Patrick MacManus, parish priest of Clifden, asserted that Errismore
comprised 3,008 Roman Catholics, eighteen original Protestants, twenty-
nine 'so called converts' plus an additional twenty-four families in the
mission colony and that the entire Protestant population of Connemara,
exclusive of mission staff and Irish teachers, did not number sixty
persons.[107] Dr Trench's estimate of Connemara converts was also refuted
by James W. Kavanagh, head inspector of schools, whose work provided
him with intimate knowledge of all educational establishments in County
Galway. Kavanagh asserted that converts were 'very few' and that 'most
of the children and some of the adults' did not belong to the locality.[108]
The ICM insisted that the archbishop's observations were factual and that
the only 'imported' Protestants were mission agents and a small number
of children in its orphanages and insisted that, while the Protestant
population had been diminished by emigration, substantial congregations
remained.[109]

The archbishop's observations were widely discredited in the nationalist
press.[110] The *Dublin Evening Post* took a great interest in the extent of
conversions in Connemara and claimed in an editorial of 21 May 1866
that the ICM was 'a fraud upon English credulity and a persecution of
Irish misery',[111] saying on another occasion that its converts were
'nothing but the miserable victims of poverty'.[112] It sent a reporter called
O'Farrell to ascertain the actual extent of conversions in Errismore. On
visiting Derrygimla school, he found thirty-one children *in situ*, not the
146 pupils viewed by Archbishop Trench and was told by ICM teacher,
Robert Stephenson, that few Catholic pupils attended the school. In a
long detailed article, O'Farrell described how, during the archbishop's
mission tour, persons were transported around mission stations by
eleven Catholic car-men who were engaged by the ICM and that these

car-men had constituted the body of 'enquiring Romanists' observed by the archbishop.[113] He stated that convert numbers in no way approached Dr Trench's estimates, a claim confirmed by Catholic clergy who asserted that the convert community was comprised solely of those who benefited directly by mission involvement.[114]

The ICM explained that its subsequent dismissal of the school-teacher Stephenson hinged on a dispute over payment for turf, while Stephenson insisted that he was victimised for revealing the truth about attendances and brought a case against the mission. At the ensuing court case, held before Chief Justice Monaghan on 15 September 1866, Stephenson asserted that only three or four pupils of Catholic parentage attended the school and a deposition from O'Farrell stated that of the thirty-one children present when he visited, '5 are the children of a reader, 4 of the schoolmaster, and 6 the children of a pensioner from Cork, all Protestants; making a total of 15'.[115]

In the extensive newspaper dialogue pertaining to the above episode, Catholic sources insisted that missionary successes in Connemara were in severe decline and that conversions had been negligible since the extreme famine years. Fr Hosty asserted that there had not been 'a single pervert' in the Castlekerke district since 1849 and that the archbishop's mission tour was undertaken to publicise and bolster a 'tottering system'.[116] If this was the case, the entire episode merely publicised the exaggeration of the ICM's claims, which had been under inspection since the publication of the results of the 1861 census in 1863.

The entire episode passed almost un-noticed in the Protestant media. The ICM fought a weak campaign to contradict the above allegations; the Protestant *Saunder's Newsletter* insisted that testimonies of Dr Trench and Revd Henry Cory, ICM clerical secretary, proved that the mission was 'an accomplished fact'.[117] In addition to protesting the existence of converts, the ICM argued that local hostility forced many to emigrate; the extent of which cannot be accurately ascertained.

Armed with an education and the use of English, converts emigrated in considerable numbers to English-speaking countries and throughout the empire. Widow O'Donnell's son settled in Cincinnati, as 'librarian over the Sunday school books'.[118] Persecuted by their Catholic neighbours, other emigrating converts joined the military.[119] The mission explained its apparent lack of success in the 1861 census by emphasising the forced emigration of converts, arguing that its influence was ongoing and global, as its converts were 'brought out of the darkness of Rome to the marvellous light of the Gospel through the instrumentality of the Irish Church Missions … They are His, although removed from this part of His vineyard.'[120]

Although there was some truth in this, it is probable that the emigration of converts was not as widespread as portrayed by the ICM. Persecution and emigration of converts had been a part of mission experience from its early days. In 1860 it was remarked that the mission was exposed to 'daily annoyances and petty persecutions' which forced converts to move abroad. The emigration excuse was frequently contradicted in ICM publications, as in two consecutive annual reports, the first of which told how losses from emigration and death were balanced by immigration of Protestant families and by successes from Rome; the next year supporters heard how converts had gone to Scotland, England and America, where 'All the boys and girls from Errismore – and they are many in Boston, Toronto and Manitoba – are faithful and zealous for the truth.'[121]

Errismore's converts were frequently employed as Irish teachers; these taught their Catholic neighbours to recite scriptural texts and read the bible in Irish. Mary D'Arcy (sister-in-law of Hyacinth) outlined how converts could be 'the means of diffusing the light' among their neighbours and suggested that economic reasons could also have played a role in convert emigration.[122] The pervasive efforts of Irish teachers were observed by Revd Conerney of Sellerna, who wrote that 'the converts are teaching their ignorant neighbours by a holy walk and conversation'[123] and it was reported that priests feared Irish teaching more than any other agency because Catholics 'are united to them by blood and relationship'.[124] It has been argued that the system of paying converts for Irish teaching was in fact merely a method of bribing them to remain Protestant and that many, being illiterate, were unfit to teach. The presence of thirteen Irish teachers in Errismore in 1887 confirms this, as by then conversions from Catholicism had practically ceased.[125]

Social ostracism of converts was part of the counter-missionary effort, with any contact between converts and Catholics being suspect. In addition to exclusive dealing, boycottings and isolation, converts were the butt of taunts, insults and gibes. Francis Costello, a Franciscan Brother, was particularly skilful at penning satirical songs, as is evident from the following extract from his ballad 'The Souper's Song':[126]

> Then hasten to that fold in time,
> Where victuals, clothes and tracts combine,
> To form the saving flood,
> And quit that wretched Godless throng,
> Whose feasts are few, and fasts are long,
> Whose souls are in the mud.

Amhrán grinn, or mocking verse ridiculing the missions, sung to Connemara converts, was known by several persons when the Folklore Commission visited the region in 1936–37, demonstrating the longevity of mission memories.[127] Douglas Hyde collected similar songs denouncing mission involvement, one of which illustrates the mistaken perception that missionary activity was government led.

> Diúltaigh do na h-acair sin, agus séan an creideamh Gaídhealach,
> Agus iompaigh leis na Protastúin, agus léigh do recantation
> Béidh fíuntar an do family agus buadhactáil agad t'réir sin,
> Gheobhaidh tú deire o'n Government, ní h-ionnann a'r lucht na déirce.[128]

> [Betray yourself to this territory and give up the Gaelic faith
> And turn with the Protestants and read your recantation
> Your family will prosper and benefit from this
> You'll get a grant from the Government that won't be given to the
>   mournful.]

A hymn composed by Brother Costello to commemorate the consecration of the new Catholic church in Clifden combines the memory of the suppression of Catholicism with triumphant assertions that Protestant missions had been defeated.[129]

I

> Hail Faith of our Fathers! shine gloriously on,
> Oppression but knits thee to Erin's green soil;
> Thou art blooming in verdure, while withered and gone,
> Are hands that again would thy altars despoil.
> How often the stranger, all red with our gore,
> Chased the Priest, like the wolf over mountain and wold
> Yet the bright light of Faith burns on as before,
> While the shrines of the stranger are lifeless and cold.

II

> Even here in our lonely retreats of the west,
> Has the wealth of an empire been squandered in vain,
> To uproot the old Faith from the Irishman's breast,
> And revive the dry bones of the sasanagh fane.
> But vain as the spray on our rock-guarded shore,
> Or the zephyrs that play on the thunder-proof hill,
> The church of the saxon is dead at the core,
> And the Faith of our Fathers is flourishing still.

Mission schools were the most effective method of inviting Catholic involvement, owing to the scarcity of national schools. Information regarding pupil numbers for the first two decades of mission has not survived, the first objective evidence being the census of education in 1868.[130] Unfortunately some mission schools were closed on the day of the census. This parliamentary report indicated that 340 children of the Established Church and 115 Roman Catholic children were present in mission schools in west Galway on the specified day, but Derrygimla male and female schools, Errislannan school and Derryeighter school and many others were closed. Of the twenty-five children present in mission schools of Errismore and Errislannan, ten were from the Established Church and fifteen were Roman Catholic. It was found that only Catholic children attended Duholla school in 1868; Aillebrack school had four Protestant children out of a total of six pupils, which can be explained by the nearby coastguard station. (As coastguards were drawn from the British Navy, their children were more likely to be Protestant.) Although its attendance of six pupils appears small, Revd Ryder was optimistic about this school (see below) and also about the Mannin school (four pupils), which he said was continuing in spite of priestly opposition and that many had promised to send their children when the 'cursing and altar denunciations shall be over'. His comment that 'Bunowenbeg [Aillebrack] is doing better than in past years' conveys to subscribers an impression of a school with more than six pupils.[131] Although Mannin school certainly existed (being listed in the 1868 educational census), it must have been held in a private house as it does not appear in the records of the Valuation Office and although mission publications suggest otherwise, no 'schoolhouse' existed. These small attendances emphasise the insecurity of the mission schools: Aillebrack and Mannin schools closed within ten years of the 1868 census.

The same ICM annual report (1868) claimed that mission schools were gradually gaining ground when compared with the earlier years when 'consequent on the very violent opposition of the priests ... schools were decimated'. The priest reportedly succeeded in removing the children of three 'Romish' parents and of one 'nominal convert' from Duholla but these had promised to return. Revd Ryder told that he had recently received four adult converts, and that fourteen original Protestants (including children) had recently come to live in the area.[132] These probably occupied the six new cottages in the Daly Hill colony, as discussed below. Numbers prior to 1868 must have been very small indeed, if attendances of six and four children represent an improvement, a fact not revealed to the ICM's supporters in England. Readers were told that the work was 'encouraging and advancing favourable and steadily' and that 'our schools maintain their numbers, and many new scholars come from time to time'.[133] As late as 1894–95 twenty-seven children from Errismore and seven from Errislannan were awarded prizes by the Diocesan Board of Education.[134] The number of prizes in Errismore school greatly exceeds that of any other day school but even an apparently healthy population did not ensure the continuance of the mission. The decrease in pupils from fifty-six to sixteen over an eleven year period must have continued, as the school closed in 1919.

Analysis of the names of prize-winning children in Errismore and Errislannan shows that some families had no connection with the parish vestry. This may suggest that they were Catholic children, Protestant children of another denomination, that their fathers were dead or that they were children of coastguards and not part of the long-term parish community.[135] The sharp decline in pupil numbers in Errismore school between 1898 and 1909 (fifty-six to sixteen over eleven years), and the catastrophic decrease in parish populations (310 to 28 between 1875 and 1916) deserve some consideration; it is clear that this represents an ageing population.[136] Although some parish registers for the 1860s were destroyed in the Public Record Office fire, there were 290 baptismal entries in the extant registers of the Connemara parishes during the decade. In the 1890s, after forty years of missionary work, and in a period for which all the registers survive, there were only 118 baptismal entries.

As late as the 1890s, mission agents claimed that theological discussions were held with 'enquiring' Catholics and bibles distributed throughout Errismore and, despite intense priestly opposition, there was not 'a creek or corner where we are not received'.[137] With such confident reports emanating from the ICM, unsurprisingly English supporters believed in a thriving convert community, whereas in reality school numbers were augmented by children of coastguards, lighthouse keepers and other 'servants of the state', such as police and land commission officials. English supporters were unaware that these, and not Irish Catholics, were the main recipients of the ICM's education, especially after 1880 (see table 5.3). Many supporters presumed that Connemara had become increasingly Protestant after decades of mission. As late as 1884, readers were told that 'our congregations maintain their numbers by new accessions from the Romish Church ... We have work for four scripture readers instead of two, the people are ready to receive them.'[138] This portrayal of a thriving mission does not stand up to scrutiny. It can be shown that even as the mission was boasting numerous conversions, few persons were becoming Protestant, that a considerable number had returned to Catholicism between 1871 and 1881, and that many more would follow. The success of Catholic counter-missionary activities is best illustrated by the removal of all Catholic children from mission schools between 1871 and 1881, the years of the violent 'anti-jumper' crusade, when the attendance of Catholic children fell from 168 to zero.

Errislannan and Errismore missions together comprised the civil parish of Ballindoon, enabling population trends to be monitored from 1861–1911 (see table 5.4).[139] The erection of extra cottages at the ICM colony of Daly Hill, Derrygimla, was reflected in an increase in the Protestant population of Ballindoon from 305 to 353 and in a slight increase in the percentage of Protestants in Errismore between 1861 and 1871. This increase was short-lived and the number of Protestants declined sharply in the early

Table 5.3 Attendance by religion at national and mission schools in Errismore, 1871–1911

	Catholic national schools					Mission schools				
	1871	*1881*	*1891*	*1901*	*1911*	*1871*	*1881*	*1891*	*1901*	*1911*
Number of schools	4	4	5	5	5	4	4	3	2	1
RC pupils	244	315	307	291	305	168	0	7	0	0
EC pupils	0	0	2	6	0	74	69	34	42	12
Presbyt./Methodist	0	0	0	0	0	3	3	1	0	0

Source: Census reports, 1871, 1881, 1891, 1901 and 1911.

Table 5.4 Population of Ballindoon parish, County Galway (Errismore and Errislannan missions), 1861–1911 showing religion and literacy

	1861	1871	1881	1891	1901*	1911*
C of I population	305	343	197	159	113	94
RC population	3956	3634	3337	2632	2287	2067
C of I as % of total population	7.06	8.59	5.56	5.67	4.70	4.34
C of I population < 5 years	56	59	22	22	15	N/A
% of C of I population < 5 years	18.36	17.20	11.17	13.84	13.27	N/A
C of I population, 5 years & up	249	284	175	137	98	N/A
C of I population, 5 years & up, illiterate	73	65	20	30	10	N/A
% C of I population, 5 years & up, illiterate	28.91	22.89	11.43	21.9	10.20	N/A
% RC population, 5 years & up, illiterate	77.72	72.25	62.50	53.38	38.66	N/A

* 1901 & 1911 census conducted on basis of Electoral Districts not civil parishes. In 1911 literacy measures on basis of 9 years and upwards; C of I = Church of Ireland; RC = Roman Catholic .

Source: reports of the 1861, 1871, 1881, 1891, 1901 and 1911 census.

years of the 'anti-jumper crusade' of 1878–1883. Table 5.4 shows that the number of young Protestant children in 1881 (22) was less than half the 1871 figure (59), a further indication of the return of entire convert families. Analysis of the literacy levels of the two communities illustrates the benefits of conversion: in 1861 only 28.91 per cent of Protestants were illiterate compared with 77.72 per cent of Catholics, while the reality of a convert population is proven by the existence of 73 illiterate Protestants in Ballindoon in 1861, which declined markedly to 20 in 1881.

The ICM acknowledged that opposition national schools had been established in Errismore in the 1860s[140] and folklore evidence indicates that national school facilities were inferior to those in mission schools:

> Do bhí leabhair ag na páisdíbh i gcomhnaidhe ins na scoileanna protastúnach ach ní bhiodh seaid i gcomhnaidhe ag na páisdibh ins na scoileanna eile … Do bhíodh suideacháin aca ins na scoileanna protastúnach ach do shuidheadh said ar cloiche agus ar bhoscaí ins na scoilleanna eile.[141]

> [Children in Protestant schools always had books but those in other schools didn't always have them … There were seats in Protestant schools but they sat on stones and boxes in the other schools.]

Although national schools were generally located adjacent to mission schools, the decrease in Catholic children in mission schools was not accompanied by a significant increase in numbers in national schools and was reflected in a significantly lower school attendance among Catholics than Protestants, especially during the decade 1871–81, when Catholic schoolchildren as a percentage of the total Catholic population fell from 11.3 to 9.4. Surprisingly, there is no folklore evidence of Catholic resentment at being forced to raise their children in ignorance.

> Bhí sean sgoil produstúnach i mBéal-an-hÁtha fadó agus bhí máighistir ann ó Béal Feirsde ach níor thaithnigh an sgoil seo leis an sagart agus chuir sé cosp leis gan moill agus ní raibh sgoil ar bith ann ar feadh i bhfad.[142]

> [There was a Protestant school in Beal an Atha a long time ago and the master was from Belfast but the priest didn't approve of it and he soon put a stop to it and there was no school at all there for a long time.]

The number of Irish teachers employed by the ICM in Errismore and Errislannan decreased sharply after 1880. This trend is found throughout the Connemara missions (see figure 5.2). The striking concurrence of reversions to Catholicism and decline in number of Irish teachers substantiates the charge that the employment of converts as Irish teachers was merely a means of bribing them to remain Protestant. Errismore's Protestant population of 310 in 1875 compares favourably with that of 270 in 1866; the increase can be explained by the growth of the Daly Hill colony, as discussed

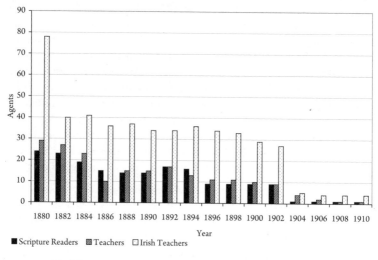

5.2 Mission agents in Errismore and Errislannan, 1880–1910

below. Since there is no reason to expect a change in the composition of Errismore Protestants in the interim, apart from the in-migration of six families for the new cottages, it is assumed that families identifiable in the listing of vestrymen available from 1870–1919 reflect families of the preceding decade.[143] Research identifies only fourteen resident vestrymen of long standing in Errismore. All but four of the vestrymen were probable converts (John Trelford, William Young, Timothy McNiffe and William McNiffe). John Trelford was an original Protestant; William Young was a man of substantial means and a justice of the peace and the McNiffes were descendants of scripture reader, Michael McNiffe. Tim McNiffe's school-teacher daughters, Fanny, Laura, Edith and Alice, provide the sole example of third generation mission employment.

Seven of the remaining ten vestrymen were employed by or housed by the mission (Thomas Burke, John Conry, Stephen Coursey, Patrick Gorham, John Lavelle, James Lyden and John Mullen). Thomas Naughton, James Burke and Andrew Shiels are the only exceptions, possible life-long converts who may or may not have received recompense at some stage.

Without doubt the ICM had considerable success in Errismore in its early years, but it can be shown that mission involvement did not generally exceed one generation, with most persons reverting once the hungry years had passed or when social pressure to revert outweighed mission benefits. Catholic clergy admitted the existence of twenty-nine converts plus twenty-four convert families at Daly Hill in 1866,[144] but from the mid 1860s there is substantial evidence of reversions to Catholicism. In a letter to the *Dublin Evening Post* in 1866, Patrick MacManus, parish priest of Clifden, told how two families (Daniel Mulkerin and Patt Goolde), consisting of twenty-nine persons were 'restored to the peace of conscience, for their hearts had no rest since they left the Ark'.[145]

One of the first recorded reversions took place in Clifden Catholic chapel in 1862 when two Hodgins children from Derrygimla, Errismore were re-baptised and their parents Patrick and Anne (neé Conneely) noted as 'jumpers'.[146] These children had been previously baptised as Protestants; their parents may not have been dependent on mission relief as this reversion took place during the distress of the early 1860s.

Thomas Gorham and Margaret Connolly, both from Salruck about twenty miles north of Errismore, had been married in the Protestant church in Clifden in 1864.[147] The following year their daughters, Margaret and Mary, were baptised in Ballyconneely Catholic church and noted as 'jumpers', their address given as Daly Hill. In 1873 another daughter, five year old Brigid, was also baptised Catholic and again noted as a 'jumper'.[148] In contrast to the Hodgins family, the Gorhams remained Protestant until the hardship of the early 1860s had passed.

A considerable number of parents who baptised children in the Catholic church in the 1860s opted for Protestant baptisms for later children, possibly prompted by the harsh state of agriculture in Connemara, and many 'converts' showed remarkable fluidity regarding religion.[149] In 1872 – a time of great hardship in Connemara – Revd Ryder described an influx of converts to his congregation and new pupils in his mission schools.[150] He was clearly speaking the truth as many parents sought Protestant baptisms for their children at this time; the majority of these would later return to Catholicism. For instance John and Mary Conneely (née Mannion) of Daly Hill baptised two children as Protestants (Patrick and Ellen, 1859), baptised their next child a Catholic (Anne, 1865) but brought the next three children to Revd Ryder's mission church (William, 1867; John, 1868; Thomas, 1872). In 1873 they returned to Catholicism, when Margaret and Jane were baptised by Fr Brennan, who remarked in the baptismal register that 'he, his wife and 6 children, converts, baptised after being baptised by Rev. Mr. Ryder'.[151]

Refusal to church mothers whose children attended mission schools was a tactic commonly employed by the Catholic church, a very effective strategy as 'unchurched' women were traditionally debarred from food preparation. 'Not churched, children jumpers' was recorded beside the baptismal record of two children from Boatharbour, Errislannan in 1876: Peter, son of Pat and Catherine Joyce (neé Brennan) and Helen, daughter of Owen and Mary Gorham (neé O'Neill).[152] These families may have only recently become involved with the mission as four siblings of Helen

Gorham had been previously baptised without comment in the Clifden Catholic church between 1861 and 1872.[153]

The truth of the mission's claims of a substantial convert community in Errismore in early decades is borne out by the extent of the reversions to Catholicism.[154] Since many elderly persons and widows availed of mission relief, it is likely that these families with young children represent only a portion of the ICM's converts. Former converts, who had been baptised in the Protestant church, were re-baptised on their return to Catholicism and although a charge of 3s. 6d. was universally levied on normal baptisms, no charge was made for re-baptisms.[155]

The practice of paying converts as Irish teachers might have been expected to result in ongoing family loyalty to the mission, but this was not the case. Detailed genealogical analysis of converts clearly shows that involvement with the mission rarely persisted even into the second generation, evident from the following exploration of the Burke and Mullen families. This also shows the ease of movement between the denominations which persisted until the start of the twentieth century.[156]

The Burke family of Daly Hill

During the years of the 'anti-jumper' violence (1878–83), many converts and children of converts adopted the Roman religion, especially during 1880 and 1881. Perhaps the most revealing of these were the Burke girls, daughters of Irish teacher Tom Burke and his wife, Bridget Ward. Jane and Kate Burke were baptised in Ballyconneely Catholic church on 1 August 1880, followed one week later by their sister, Anne. These girls were adults acting independently of their parents. Jane was nineteen years old when she changed her religion and her parents were then twenty-five years married.[157] Her parents, who represent the first generation of child-converts, remained Protestant until death and were buried in the mission graveyard at Derrygimla (Bridget in 1900 and Tom in 1916) with addresses given as Daly Hill, where they had lived in a mission cottage.[158]

The reversion of children of converts was reflected in the severe drop in the Protestant population as original converts died without being replaced in significant numbers by subsequent generations. When Tom died in 1916, his funeral was boycotted by Errismore's Catholics, who would have been forbidden to enter a Protestant church. It was admitted that it was difficult to gather enough men to carry his coffin, as by then the Protestant population comprised a mere handful of elderly persons.[159] In common with most Connemara families, both Catholic and Protestant, almost all Tom Burke's children and grandchildren were in America, while one grandson – a staunch Protestant – had been wounded in France.

Reversions to Catholicism were not always permanent. Jane Burke, whose conversion to Catholicism we have already noted, remained Catholic for a time. The baptisms of four children of Jane Burke and Matthew Early are recorded in Ballyconneely Catholic church: Michael (1884), Thomas (1885), Margaret Jane (1888) and George (1890). In spite of Catholic baptisms, Michael and Thomas Early, with another sister Katie, attended Derrygimla mission school in 1894–95. By the 1901 census, the family had reverted to Protestantism, with Jane Early living with her father in a mission cottage. She described herself as a widow and listed her religion and that of her children as Church of Ireland.[160] Local knowledge attributes her change of abode and of religion to marriage difficulties. In 1911, Jane, together with her father and her daughter Norah, were still listed as Church of Ireland and still in a mission cottage. There is no further record of this woman or any of her children in the Connemara parish registers.

The reversion of daughters of an Irish teacher must have caused considerable damage to the morale of Errismore mission and would have been a great cause of triumph among Catholic clergy, signified by the comment beside the baptismal entry of the Burke girls: 'Protestants before this baptism, neutralising jumper [illegible word]'.

The Mullen family of Daly Hill

John Mullen and his wife Catherine Conry could never be described as steadfast converts. They were married in Clifden Catholic church in 1888 and baptised their first two children as Catholics, Patrick (1889) and Mary (1892) and the next two as Protestants, Martin (1893) and Anne (1895). Three years later, in 1898, they came back to the Catholic church when Catherine was baptised and Anne, already baptised Protestant, was rebaptised a Catholic, when it was noted in the Catholic register that they had 'joined the Dalyhill Jumpers for the past five years and continue there'. Their next three sons were baptised as Protestants, Thomas (1900), John (1902) and James (1904). The mission paid John Mullen 10s. a week from 1904, with a comment that he had previously been employed as an Irish teacher. In spite of such mission advantages, the next three children were baptised in the Catholic church, Margaret Ellen (1905), Alice (1908) and Bridget (1911), when John Mullen was noted as an 'acatholicis'. Although Catherine came from a convert background (her parents had married in Clifden Protestant church in 1862),[161] it appears it was she who drew away from the mission. She may not have attended a mission school as she was listed as unable to read or write in the 1901 census, where the entire family was listed as Church of Ireland. In 1911 Mrs Mullen and her two youngest daughters gave their religion as Catholic while Margaret, now old enough to attend school, was returned as Protestant. The mission continued to pay John Mullen until Errismore mission closed in 1919 and allowed the family to remain in Daly Hill until they received a county council cottage in 1918.

The identification of reversions such as outlined above should not lead to the conclusion that no Protestants remained in Errismore and Errislannan. It would appear that the Burke families, and some of the Mullens, along with about ten other persons remained Protestant until death. Where possible, the age of Errismore's converts has been calculated using a combination of the 1901 census and burial records. It was found that most long-term converts were of school age when the mission was established in Errismore, the favourite age of an Irish teacher. This cohort of child-converts was the most fruitful for the mission. At the outset of mission, Revd Ryder explained that 'these boys and girls will soon be the fathers and mothers of another generation' and would therefore perpetuate the Protestant influence.[162] This generation of child-converts provided most of the mission's successes; their children, however, would either convert to Catholicism or emigrate.

Of the twenty-six Church of Ireland households identified in the Errislannan, Doonlaoughan and Bunowen District Electoral Divisions in 1901 (almost equal to the missions of Errismore and Errislannan), only two were possible convert families not maintained, at least in part, by the mission. After more than fifty years of effort, the mission's possible 'independent' conversions amounted to two families: James Burke of Emloughmore and Thomas Naughton of Duholla. Even one of these (James Burke) may have been an Irish teacher.

Daly Hill mission colony

The general tenement valuation (Griffith's) of 1855 shows that Alexander Dallas rented cottages in Derrygimla to five persons; the parish priest of Clifden claimed that this land was given free by the Law Life Assurance Company.[163] The next listing of occupiers is found in the Valuation Office records for 1873, when the number of cottages had increased to eleven. These were extremely poor houses, most valued at only three shillings and in 1873 three out of eleven were occupied by widows. In 1911, Sarah Parsons lived in a one roomed, class 4, mission cottage, all other cottages being class 3 houses. A small amount of land accompanied each cottage, the largest plot was three and a half acres, valued at £1 6s. 0d., the six smallest plots were about one acre each, valued at approximately 10s. 0d. each. By 1904 most of the mission cottages were 'down'; Delia Molloy's was the last occupied but was 'in ruins' in 1920.

The 1901 census lists ICM school-teacher, Patrick Burke, living in a mission house. According to the Valuation Office lists, he occupied a house valued at two pounds, whereas the rectory was valued at six pounds, compared with the cottages valued at two or three shillings, which underscores the social differences between the providers and recipients of mission.

After the disestablishment of the Church of Ireland in 1869, parishes were expected to contribute to their upkeep. As parishes were under pressure to make their assessments, all parishioners were obliged to contribute. Therefore annual subscription lists may function as surrogate household lists. Examination of these lists reveals a lack of support among persons native to the area but not associated with the mission, i.e. not mission agents, RIC or coastguards.[164] The low level of local support in Errismore and Errislannan should be interpreted, not as an unwillingness to contribute on the part of converts, but rather as a lack of any significant enduring convert community.

With almost all their converts lost to them, continuing ICM involvement in Errismore was untenable. The ICM severed its connection with the parish in 1919, following the death of Revd Thomas Nee. Table 5.5 shows the inevitable decline of Errismore's ageing convert population between 1900 and 1917.

Table 5.5 Church of Ireland population, Errismore, 1900–17

Year	Population	Year	Population
1900–01	118	1909–10	52
1901–02	114	1910–11	56
1902–03	N/A	1911–12	51
1903–04	N/A	1912–13	43
1904–05	N/A	1913–14	41
1905–06	N/A	1914–15	N/A
1906–07	57	1915–16	35
1907–08	52	1916–17	28
1908–09	42		

Source: RCBL, MS No. P. 168/8/1/5, Errismore preacher's book.

These stark figures mask the existence of approximately twenty persons associated with the Marconi Radio station and the coastguard service, who departed in 1921–22. Service was held bi-weekly in Errismore church until 1952, but congregations were small (five to ten persons). The final service was held in Derrygimla on 26 October 1952 and the church demolished shortly after. It had functioned for eighty-seven years.

This decline in convert numbers was mirrored throughout west Galway, where the ICM merely maintained its ageing workers. Active mission work had long ceased: the occupation of the elderly John McClelland was listed as farmer in the baptismal record of his daughter, Christina in 1935, although the ICM paid him £65 as a scripture reader in that year; the ICM's involvement in west Galway ceased with his death in 1937. The recording of his occupation as farmer may also suggest that Clifden parish wished to obliterate the existence of mission agents.

Errismore's experience of a single generation of converts, the school-going cohort of the 1850s, is found throughout Connemara. In all of Connemara, century-long adherence to Protestantism was observed in just one instance: Thomas Mullin of Moyard (1870–1959), son of Matthias (d. 1903) and Bridget (d. 1919) and grandson of labourer-converts Patrick and Peggy Mullin of Cleggan.

The bitter legacy of mission work in Errismore may be gauged by the omission of any reference to proselytism in the IFC schools' questionnaire of 1937–38. The topics of 'an droch-saol' [bad times or famine] and 'sean-scoileanna' [old schools] were not covered in any school in the Errismore region, where the ICM was most likely to feature. This may have been due to the recent functioning of the mission, which was less than twenty years closed at this time. The missions of Ballinakill, Renvyle and Clifden, where information regarding sensitive topics such as the mission and the famine was gathered, had closed considerably earlier. It is likely that it was parish policy to exclude all mention of the proselytising activities since all national schools in Errismore sidestepped any discussion of both the ICM and the famine.[165] It is probable that the memories gathered for the schools' survey in Ballinakill, Renvyle, Clifden and Moyrus parishes were replicated in Errismore and therefore are included in this case study.

In 1937, the local perception and folk memory of mission workers were not favourable: 'Droch-dhaoine a bhí iontu' [they were bad people][166] and their contempt for the Irish people and their heritage was repeatedly outlined: 'Bhí droch-mheas ag na múinteóirí ar na Gaedhil agus ar cultúr na n-Éireann' [the teachers had contempt for the Irish and Irish culture].[167] The survey reported many handed-down stories of the mission and its feeding programme: 'scoileanna brocáin an t-ainm a bhí othra agus atá ortha fós' [They were known as stirabout-schools and they still are].[168] Interviewees told how

Thug said anbhruith do dhaoine na h-áite seo. Bhí pota mór ins an páirc agus do bhíodh na daoine thart timpeall an phota sin agus spúnóga aca … Bhí go leor daoine a diompaidh leis na protastúnaigh le h-aghaid airgid.[169]

[They gave soup to the local people. There was a big pot in a field and people would be around that pot with spoons … A lot of people converted to Protestantism for money.]

Bhí cuid dos na Sasanaigh ag roinnt an mín-bhuidhe agus an t-éadach ar na daoinidh bochta. B'fhearr de cuid de na daoine bás a fhághail les an ocras

nó an mín bhuidhe agus an t-éadach a ghlacadh ach diompuigh cuid dos na
daoine les na Sasanaigh.[170]

[Some English were giving yellow meal and clothes to the poor. Some people
would prefer to die of hunger rather than take the yellow meal but some
converted with the English.]

These clearly show that conversions in Connemara stemmed from the
provision of relief rather than from a doctrinal inclination to Protestantism:
'During the times of the famine the protestant [sic] people gave money
to the catholics [sic] to turn over, so they did rather than starve with the
hunger'.[171] The veracity of these 'memories' is confirmed by the detailed
identification of mission personnel; many persons correctly recalled names
of ICM teachers:

Bhí said ag íarraigh Caitlicigh a mheallagh chun scoile díobh agus thugaidis
éadaighe agus biadh dóibh muna ghlacadh na Caitlicigh iad. Bhi fear darbh
ainm Millea agus fear darbh ainm Ó Conaill ag múineadh ins an ceann a
bhí sa mBaile Nua ... fear darbh ainm Booth agus fear agus a iníon darbh
ainm Mc Cártaigh ... i mBarr na hAille; ... fear darbh ainm Crusheen ag
múineadh ... i nOileán Iomaidh.[172]

[They were trying to tempt Catholics to the school and they gave food and
clothes to them if they would. There was a man called Millea and a man
called O'Connell teaching in the one in Ballynew ... a man called Booth
and a man and his daughter called McCarthy in Barnahalia ... a man called
Crusheen teaching ... on Omey Island.]

The apparent obliteration of mission memory in Errismore, evident from its
omission in the 1937 schools' survey, was continued by the demolition of
Derrygimla church in the 1950s to complete the eradication of the mission
from local consciousness. The mission has been effectively air-brushed
from memory. Few relics remain on the Connemara landscape, its schools
are mostly in ruins and its churches demolished. In a telling comment,
suggestive of deep sensitivity regarding the history of proselytism in
Connemara, Ballinkill vestry decreed in 1926 that the disused mission
church at Sellerna should not remain on the landscape, but should be
demolished and its stones removed lest anyone have 'an opportunity for
pointing the finger of scorn'.[173]

Errislannan and Errismore missions had showed great promise in their
early years when numerous 'conversions' were undoubtedly achieved. In
1851, over 3,500 persons availed of mission relief in a single week in
Errislannan and Errismore alone, yet by 1875 the parish populations stood
at a mere 68 and 301 respectively. Forty years later, after almost seventy
years of aggressive mission, these populations had fallen to sixteen and
twenty-eight, most of whom were employed, housed or maintained by

the ICM. The promising harvest of conversions from Catholicism had obviously not materialised.

So what had gone wrong? Did the ICM ever gain conversions, or was the enterprise a failure and pretence from the start? It would appear not. Although advertisements of thriving congregations portrayed by the ICM have been shown to have been 'managed', it would appear that the mission enjoyed a reasonable degree of success in the 1850s, which declined as the Catholic church provided education and relief and organised counter-missionary social action. The extent of the reversions confirms that a substantial convert community had actually existed, but briefly.

Despite the ICM's protestations that doctrinal conviction secured conversions to Protestantism, conversions in Errismore and Errislannan resulted from material want in famine times: 'sin é an tam ar diompuigh na Caitleachaí' [that was the time when the Catholics turned].[174] A retired Catholic schoolteacher from Errismore recalled that the starving people knew that 'to profess the reformed religion was to get money down' and described how he watched 'the general sapping of morality as first one family, then another, conformed outwardly'.[175]

Many of the ICM's conversions, contrary to depictions in mission literature, have been shown as fickle, short-lived and influenced by material gain, but not all of Connemara's converts reverted. Some emigrated or moved to other areas, in many cases to work in Protestant missions.[176] In 1923, Fr Quigley informed readers of the *Irish Ecclesiastical Record* that 'The Soupers removed their captives to Ulster and got them small jobs, gardeners, land stewards, bailiffs, railway porters. And in Dublin, the Bench was Souper almost to a man, and the doorkeepers, etc., in the Four Courts were Souper Birds'.[177]

Conversions obtained under famine duress were to prove short-lived, as had been observed as early as 1828, regarding the converts of Dingle and Kingscourt: 'The converts are like birds, which visit milder climates at intervals – but their coming is a proof of a great severity in their native country, and they return when the iron days are passed, and the sun cheers them from home.'[178]

Although the ICM presented to its supporters that a willingness to converse with mission agents signified an inclination to convert, the Catholics of Errismore and Errislannan were 'not for turning'. Revd Irwin, with fifteen years' experience of Errislannan mission, explained in 1885 that:

> It requires a good deal of gushing enthusiasm, or artistic painting, to say that the undoubted facilities for conversing with the people mean a readiness on their part to embrace the purer faith and form of worship which we can offer them. Traditional and current influences bind their religious sentiments.

Family, social and political ties account for what we should otherwise call marvellous insensibility and indifference. They are not insensible and not indifferent to real earnest conversation on religion; but they do not see their way to act upon what they hear.[179]

Revd Irwin's apt use of the terms 'gushing enthusiasm' and 'artistic painting' describes well the tone of mission publications but his optimistic interpretation of the perceived desire of Catholics for a scriptural faith remained unfulfilled. It would appear that Catholicism was deeply embedded in Errismore and that a scriptural form of religion lacked the appeal of the ritualistic popular religion. In times of want, their material needs understandably took precedence, but once the Catholic church had admitted national schools into the area, and once the 'hungry years' had passed, Protestantism had nothing to offer the Catholics of Errismore except social exclusion and communal contempt. Those who received more, in the form of housing and income, persisted only for one and occasionally two generations. Mission workers were only welcome if they represented a well-endowed mission, otherwise Protestantism was of little benefit, while the ferocity of the counter-mission ensured few braved the beatings, house-burnings and social exclusion meted out to converts.

It is not the origin, lifespan and demise of these missions that is most interesting, but rather the persistence of the myth of real success. Miss Barbour, an English traveller, was so appalled at the lack of scriptural religion in Connemara in 1893–94 that she returned the following year with a friend and a box of bibles to relieve 'the dire need of Roman Catholics, in Ireland, spiritual and temporal'.[180] By this time the ICM was clearly not engaging in active missionary work such as visiting the peasantry in their 'degrading surroundings'. Miss Barbour was told that 'you would never get a Protestant to squat down in one of those cabins'.[181] In her book, she refers to the ICM in a single footnote, which clearly states that the mission had long since been spent:

I would like to bear testimony to the work of the Irish Church Missions … it was in the west that Mr Dallas first commenced his noble work fifty years ago. But it is sad to visit those places which were once the scenes of his unwearied and indefatigable efforts, and to find schools closed and churches half empty.[182]

In spite of this obvious lack of success, the ICM's annual report of 1906 informed supporters that mission work in Connemara was 'quietly carried on during the years',[183] although we have seen that, even in its most successful mission, conversions had long ceased, while the 1910 report told how 'One of our Western Missionaries has had very distinct encouragement in his work, which has been much blessed'.[184] In reality, the original convert community was dying off, their places unfilled by upcoming generations.

It must be remembered that the readers of *The Banner* and the mission's annual reports were committed ICM supporters. When they accepted the portrayal of thriving missions in the ICM's publications, they did so because this is what they wanted to believe. When the ICM published a letter from a Connemara convert in 1913 which gave thanks that 'the Lord was pleased to use you for bringing me into the light of the Gospel, and out of the darkness by which I was surrounded',[185] mission supporters had no reason to question the current state of Connemara's missions or suppose that its most successful mission at Errismore was almost closed. By appealing to the ultra-Protestants of England, and by telling them what they wanted to hear, exposure of the ICM's failure in Connemara was unlikely.

It is possible that English supporters never realised the lack of administrative infrastructure in Connemara or the geographical expanse of the region. When English parish administration is contrasted with that which existed in Ireland, even after the advent of the ICM, an enormous disparity is evident between an intensely policed English people and a large Irish population scattered over vast expanses, with little contact with authority figures except possibly with the Catholic clergy. English civil parishes are substantially smaller than in Ireland; for instance in 1851 Hampshire consisted of 348 parishes, each containing an average of 2,335 acres and 1,042 inhabitants, whereas the civil parish of Ballindoon (Errislannan and Errismore missions) contained 20,033 acres and 4,435 inhabitants. In England, a subdued and much-watched population resulted from the existence of hundreds of minute parishes, each with its vestry, clergyman and parish constable, where justice had been administered in a self-sufficient manner for centuries, resulting in a tightly controlled society which starkly contrasted with Connemara where neither the Catholic nor Protestant churches could ever have envisaged delivering such intense control into the hands of the clergy.[186] It is likely that when English supporters read of church attendances of one or two hundred, they had no idea that in reality this represented a small percentage of the very large native populations, supplemented in many cases by 'servants of the state', superimposing mission information on their English conception of parish life.

So was there ever a prospect of a viable, successful mission in Connemara? It would appear not. With the benefit of hindsight, it is clear that there were many reasons why the missions failed. Firstly, the ICM was handicapped by its association with the landlord class. In the west of Ireland, feelings of an anti-British, anti-landlord and anti-Protestant nature ran high, with distinctions rarely made between the three. By identifying itself with much-hated landlords such as Revd Wall, the mission placed itself at a disadvantage and supplied ammunition to its opponents. This was also to set the scene for the dreadful treatment meted out to the mission during the years 1878–83.

A second reason lay in its public denigration of the popular religion of the people. Christianity was deeply embedded in Errismore and Errislannan, proved by the presence of two medieval churches and numerous sites of religious significance. The mission's perception that Christianity as professed in the Roman Catholic tradition in Connemara was not Christianity at all, seems to have conferred on it the right to insult and offend Connemara's Catholics and their traditions, as in Renvyle where they built a schoolhouse on top of a ring fort. By mockingly vilifying Roman Catholicism and its long-established practices and much-cherished beliefs, the Protestant missionaries deeply offended the host community who, although not scriptural, possessed their own strongly embedded Christian beliefs and practices, to which they were fervently attached.

Above all, the missions failed because they did not appreciate that, in Ireland, religion and ethnicity were intrinsically intertwined, largely consequent on the penal suppression of Catholicism. What developed in other countries as a class struggle had evolved in Ireland into a nationalist and religious crusade, bolstered by the Catholic counter-missionary tactic of identifying love of Ireland with allegiance to Catholicism. Nineteenth-century Connemara, with its emerging Catholic and national confidence, its deeply held concept of religion and its close network of inter-family ties, was an unwise location for a Protestant mission, especially one as aggressive and controversial as the ICM. As a venture, it could not but fail.

Notes

1 Christine Kinealy, *This great calamity: the Irish famine 1845–1852* (Dublin, 1994), pp. 5, 151.

2 Kathleen Villiers-Tuthill, *Patient endurance: the great famine in Connemara* (Dublin, 1997).

3 Mrs A[nne] Dallas, *Incidents in the life and ministry of the Rev. Alexander R.C. Dallas A.M.* (London, 1871), p. 391.

4 Alexander Dallas, *The story of the Irish Church Missions, part 1* (London, 1867), p. 153.

5 John Gregg, *A missionary visit to Connemara and other parts of the county of Galway* (Dublin, c.1850), pp. 23–4.

6 Fanny Bellingham, *Fourth account of the fund entrusted to Miss Fanny Bellingham ... for the Relief of the converts and children of Connemara* (Wonston, 1851).

7 *Banner of the Truth*, Nov. 1850, p. 21.

8 Alannah Heather, *Errislannan: scenes from a painter's life* (Dublin, 1993), p. 13.
9 James Godkin, *Ireland and her churches* (Dublin, 1867), pp. 219–20.
10 Heather, *Errislannan*, pp. 28, 75.
11 William Conyngham Plunket, *A short visit to the Connemara missions. A letter to the Rev. John Garret* (London, Dublin, 1863), p. 41.
12 Heather, *Errislannan*, p. 74.
13 ICM, *Annual report*, 1865, p. 51.
14 L. Davidoff and C. Hall, *Family fortunes: men and women of the English middle class, 1780–1850* (London, 1987), p. 113.
15 Heather, *Errislannan*, pp. 33–4.
16 Ibid., p. 75.
17 Ibid., p. 17.
18 *Erin's Hope*, 1853, p. 44.
19 ICM, *Annual report*, 1854, pp. 65–7.
20 *Banner of the Truth*, Feb. 1851, p. 21.
21 Letter from Patrick MacManus, *The Tablet*, 4 June 1853.
22 *Irish Catholic Directory*, 1854, p. 333.
23 Bearnárd Mac Uaid, 'Stair oideachas Bráthar Triomhadh Úird Riaghalta Sain Proinsias san naomhadh céad déag' [The history of education of the Third Order of Saint Francis in the nineteenth century] (MA dissertation, University College Galway, 1956), p. 168.
24 ICM, *Annual report*, 1854, pp. 65–7.
25 Ibid., 1856, pp. 57–9; ibid., 1857, p. 68.
26 Ibid., 1857, p. 68.
27 Ibid., 1858, pp. 64–5.
28 Ibid., 1858, pp. 64–5.
29 *Banner of the Truth*, 1 Mar. 1863, pp. 44–5.
30 Ibid., 1 Mar. 1863, pp. 44–5.
31 ICM, *Annual report*, 1862, pp. 54–5.
32 This practice was common throughout Ireland. In Dublin, St Brigid's schools and the Christian Brothers' schools were always strategically placed as close as possible to mission schools.
33 NAI, Dept. of Education files, MS No. ED/35/11/112.
34 ICM, *Annual report*, 1866, p. 68.
35 *Educational census: Return showing the number of children actually present in each primary school 25th June 1868; with introductory observations and analytical index*. H.C. 1870 [C.6v] XXVIII, Part v.1.
36 *Banner of the Truth*, 1 Jan. 1869, p. 15.
37 Four marriages were performed in Errismore 1865–69.
38 ICM, *Annual report*, 1868, pp. 64, 68.
39 Ibid., 1872, p. 54.
40 Earl of Roden, *Progress of the reformation in Ireland* (2nd edn, London, 1852), p. 34.
41 Valuation Office, Cancelled books, County Galway, Errislannan E.D.; townland Derryeighter, Derryloughan E.D., townland Manninmore and Bunowen E.D., townland Dolan.

42 ICM, *Annual report*, 1871, p. 50; ibid., 1872, pp. 54–5; ibid., 1873, p. 65; ibid., 1875, p. 56; ibid., 1877, p. 61.

43 *Report of the Tuam Diocesan Synod*, 1875, p. 36.

44 Patrick McNamara had at least two children; George (1864) and James (1865). RCBL, MS No. 518/2/1, Killanin baptismal register, entry No. 150; MS Nos P 491/2/1, Omey baptismal register, entry No. 112.

45 ICM, *Annual report*, 1876, p. 62; ibid., 1877, p. 47; ibid., 1882, p. 43.

46 Miriam Moffitt, *Soupers and Jumpers: the Protestant missions in Connemara, 1848–1937* (Dublin, 2008), pp. 136–51.

47 Letter from Benjamin Irwin, *Irish Ecclesiastical Gazette*, 4 June 1887.

48 'Urgent Appeal' from Revds Cory, Brown and Irwin for funds to enable maintenance of work among 'isolated convert families', *Irish Church Advocate*, Sept. 1885, p. 165.

49 *Irish Ecclesiastical Gazette*, 4 June 1887.

50 ICM, *Annual report*, 1887, p. 34.

51 IFC Archive, MS No. S4:95–6.

52 For example, IFC Archive, MS No. S6:121, told by Mrs Acton, Moyard.

53 Personal communication, Christy Butler, Oughterard, Aug. 2004.

54 TCD, MS No. OLS X–1–531 no 18a, *The souper's petition*.

55 'Archbishop Trench's converts' (editorial), *Dublin Evening Post*, 18 June 1866; ICM, *Annual report*, 1866, p. 68.

56 'Catholic Defence Fund for Father Walsh or rather Catholic Defence Fund against the souper raiders in Connemara', *Connaught Patriot and General Advertiser* (hereafter referred to as *Connaught Patriot*), 1 Sept. 1866; see also ibid. 28 Aug., 15 Sept. 1866.

57 RCBL, MS No. P. 167/8/3, Preacher's book, Errislannan.

58 Heather, *Errislannan*, p. 33.

59 Dallas, *Incidents in the Life*, p. 391.

60 Douglas Hyde, *Abhráin diada chúige Connacht or the religious songs of Connaught: a collection of poems, stories, prayers, satires, rarins, charms, etc* (Dublin, 1906), pp. 49, 59, 63, 225, 381, 389.

61 William M. Thackeray, *The Irish sketchbook* (Dublin, 1990, first published 1843), p. 211.

62 Office of Public Works, *Archaeological inventory of county Galway, west Galway including Connemara and the Aran Islands*, pp. 91, 94, 117, 118–19, 124.

63 Dallas, *The story of the Irish Church Missions, part 1*, pp. 163–4.

64 *Banner of the Truth*, Dec. 1850, p. 39.

65 Ibid., Mar. 1850, p. 39; ibid., Jan. 1851, p. 13.

66 Anonymous, *Two months in Clifden, Co. Galway, during the summer of 1855* (Dublin, 1856), p. 23.

67 *Banner of the Truth*, Jan. 1851, p. 13; Feb. 1851, p. 21; Apr. 1851, p. 61; May 1851, p. 82; July 1851, p. 108; Oct. 1851, p. 156.

68 Moffitt, *Soupers and Jumpers*, pp. 58–60.

69 Anonymous, *A day at Clifden* (London, 1853), p. 13.

70 Roderick Ryder, *Transubstantiation – the confessional. A letter … to … Dr. French, Roman Catholic bishop at Gort, etc.* (Dublin, 1846), p. 2.

71 Thomas Kerns, *Connemara past and present, occasional paper of the Irish Church Missions to the Roman Catholics* (n.p., 1859), p. 3.

72 *Banner of the Truth*, July 1852, pp. 109–10.

73 Máire Ní Shúilleabháin, *An t-Athair Caomhánach agus an cogadh creidimh i gConamara* [Fr Kavanagh and the battle of the faith in Connemara] (Dublin, 1984), p. 105.

74 James Leslie, *Biographical succession lists of the clergy of the diocese of Down* (Enniskillen, 1936), p. 69.

75 Personal communication, Paud Kennelly, retired national school-teacher, Aillebrack, Ballyconneely (Oct. 2004).

76 *Banner of the Truth*, Sept. 1852, p. 142; ibid., Sept. 1853, pp. 131–2.

77 Ibid., Sept. 1853, pp. 143–4.

78 ICM, *Annual report*, 1854, p. 110.

79 Robert Backhouse Peacock, *The reformation in Ireland. Notes of a tour amongst the missions in Dublin and west Galway in … September 1852* (2nd edn, London, 1853) p. 38; *Banner of the Truth*, Apr. 1854, pp. 55–6; ibid., Aug. 1854, p. 132.

80 Ibid., June 1856, p. 99; ibid., 1 Sept. 1860, p. 147.

81 Kerns, *Connemara past and present*, p. 3; *Banner of the Truth*, Apr. 1859, pp. 55–6, 132; ibid., Mar. 1860, p. 48.

82 CP, MS No. G/18/1/76, Donations to 'Cloghtery's land, Errismore' in balance sheet of *Thirteenth account of the Fund for the Relief of Converts and Children of Connemara from 3rd April 1859 to 3rd April 1860* (n.p., n.d.), pp. 11–12, 17.

83 Clifden parish office, Baptismal register No. 4.

84 ICM, *Annual report*, 1854, p. 109.

85 *Banner of the Truth*, 1857, p. 188.

86 Ibid., Sept. 1860, p. 147; ibid., Jan. 1894, p. 13.

87 *Erin's Hope*, 1855, pp. 115–19.

88 *Banner of the Truth*, 1 July 1862, p. 105; ibid., 1 June 1859, p. 93.

89 *Erin's Hope*, 1861, p. 85.

90 NAI, Dept. of Education files contain applications from the following schools: Cleggan, 19 Oct. 1861, MS No. ED1/35/30; Claddaghduff, 29 Oct. 1861, MS No. ED1/35/25; Omey Island, 26 Mar. 1862, MS No. ED1/35/39; Errislannan, 29 Jan. 1863, MS No. ED1/35/112; Derrygimla, 14 Nov. 1863, MS No. ED1/35/93; Tully, 28 Nov. 1864, MS No. ED/35/73; Aillebrack, 21 June 1866, MS No. ED1/36/2; Carna, 4 Sept. 1865, MS No. ED/35/51.

91 ICM, *Annual report*, 1864, p. 55.

92 IFC Archive, MS No. S4:309, told by Brighid Bean Uí Thuathaith, Sellerna.

93 IFC Archive, MS No. S6:121. This story naming Tommy Heaney was repeated many times in the Folklore Collection.

94 ICM, *Annual report*, 1861, p. 75. See also ibid., 1860, p. 147; ibid., 1862, p. 115; ibid., 1862, p. 58; ibid., 1863, p. 51; ibid., 1864, p. 58.

95 *Banner of the Truth*, July 1863, pp. 110–12.

96 *Erin's Hope*, 1861, p. 83.

97 CP, MS No. G/18/1/76. *Thirteenth account of the Fund for the Relief of Converts and Children of Connemara from 3rd April 1859 to 3rd April 1860*, p. 10.

98 Letter from Revd Ryder, Errismore, *Erin's Hope*, 1862, pp. 75–7.

99 *Banner of the Truth*, Jan. 1867, p. 16.

100 Ibid., May 1861, p. 75.

101 *Erin's Hope*, 1864, pp. 93–6.

102 *Banner of the Truth*, Feb. 1863, p. 19.

103 ICM, *Annual report*, 1862, p. 58 (report of Errismore mission); *Banner of the Truth*, Feb. 1863, p. 27; Sept. 1863, p. 138.

104 *Erin's Hope*, 1 October 1870, p. 33.

105 Personal communication (1) Charlie McClelland, Duholla, who attended service in Derrygimla church as a child and (2) Paud Kennelly, retired national school-teacher, Aillebrack, Ballyconneely, both October 2004.

106 Letter from Richard Trench, Archbishop of Dublin, *The Times* (London), 10 May 1866, reproduced in *Galway Express*, 19 May 1855.

107 Letter from Patrick MacManus, *Freeman's Journal*, 7 June 1866, see also letters from Patrick MacManus, *Freeman's Journal*, 21 May, 11 June 1866; in *Dublin Evening Post*, 18, 24 May, 1, 6, 22 June 1866. See also letters from Fr James Maher, *Freeman's Journal*, 14, 29 June 1866.

108 Letter from James W. Kavanagh, *The Times* (London), 19 May 1866, reproduced in *Freeman's Journal*, 21 May 1866, *Dublin Evening Post*, 22 May 1866 and *Galway Vindicator*, 23 May 1866.

109 Letter from Henry Cory, ICM, *The Times* (London), 21 May 1866, reproduced in *Galway Express*, 26 May 1866.

110 For example, see letter from Clifden curate, Fr Patrick Walsh, *Connaught Patriot*, 26 May 1866, 'The west Connaught proselytisers' in ibid., 2 June 1866; 'The conversions in Connemara' (editorial) and 'Dr. Trench and the Irish Church Missions' in ibid., 16 June 1866; 'Proselytisers challenged to a public enquiry in Connemara' in ibid., 7 July 1866; 'More tidings from Connemara' in ibid., 28 July 1866; 'The parson's impious assault on Father Walsh' in ibid., 18 Aug. 1866; 'Catholic Defence Fund for Father Walsh or rather Catholic Defence Fund against the souper raiders in Connemara' in ibid., 1 Sept. 1866; 'Dr. Trenche's [sic] Connemara tour' (editorial) in *Galway Vindicator and Connaught Advertiser*, 26 May 1866; 'Connemara missions' in ibid., 20 June 1866; 'The mission work in Connemara' in *Tuam Herald*, 16 June 1866.

111 See also 'The proselytising system' (editorial), *Dublin Evening Post*, 22 May 1866; 'Dr. Trench's statistics' (editorial) in ibid., 7 June 1866; 'Archbishop Trench's converts' (editorial) in ibid., 18 June 1866.

112 'Converts to Protestant proselytism in west Connaught', *Dublin Evening Post*, 10 Sept. 1866.

113 'The alleged conversion in west Connaught, by our special correspondent', *Dublin Evening Post*, 4 June 1866. O'Farrell is not identified here, but Godkin names him in his treatment of the episode, see Godkin, *Ireland and her churches*, pp. 410–12.

114 Letter from Richard Hosty, *Dublin Evening Post*, 4 June 1866. See also letter from Richard Hosty in ibid., 27 June 1866.

115 Godkin, *Ireland and her churches*, pp. 410–12.

116 *Dublin Evening Post*, 4 June 1866.

117 *Saunder's Newsletter and Daily Advertiser*, quoted in *Galway Express*, 9 June 1866. See also letter from Abraham Jagoe, missionary at Castlekerke, *Dublin Evening Post*, 11 June 1866; letter from Revds Hyacinth D'Arcy, Clifden, George Shea, Sellerna, Roderick Ryder, Errismore, in ibid., 19 June 1866.

118 ICM, *Annual report*, 1866, pp. 71–2.

119 Ibid., 1875, p. 24.

120 Ibid., 1883, p. 42; ibid., 1884, p. 38.

121 Ibid., 1860, p. 60; ibid., 1883, p. 40; ibid., 1884, p. 38.

122 CP, MS No. GRE/5/10, Mary D'Arcy to Elizabeth Copley, 11 Feb. 1856.

123 Society for Irish Church Missions to the Roman Catholics, *Information respecting the progress of the Society of the Irish Church Missions to the Roman Catholics* (London, 1850), p. 10.

124 ICM, *Annual report*, 1868, p. 64.

125 Ibid., 1887, p. 34.

126 Quoted in Mac Uaid, 'Stair oideachas Bráthar Triomhadh Úird Riaghalta Sain Proinsias', p. 179.

127 IFC Archive, MS No. 237:233–5.

128 Hyde, *Abhráin diada chúige Connacht*, pp. 169–71.

129 Franciscan Archive, 'New Church of St. MacDara, parish of Clifden, consecrated by His Grace, the archbishop of Tuam' in Francis Costello, *Hymns for the festivals of the Blessed Virgin Mary for the whole year* (Cork, n.d.).

130 *Educational census*, H.C. 1870 [C.6v] XXVIII, Part v. 1.

131 *Banner of the Truth*, 1 April 1868, p. 31.

132 Ibid., 1 Jan. 1867, p. 16.

133 Ibid., 1 Jan. 1869, 1 Apr. 1871, p. 31.

134 *Report of the Tuam Diocesan Board of Education*, 1894 and 1895.

135 RCBL, MS No. P. 168/6/1, Register of vestrymen, Errismore.

136 *Report of the Tuam Diocesan Council*, 1875, p. 36 and RCBL, MS No. P. 167/8/1, Preachers' book, Errislannan, note inside cover.

137 ICM agent, John Lavelle, quoted in *The Banner of the Truth*, Oct. 1892, p. 7.

138 ICM, *Annual report*, 1884, p. 38.

139 Precise comparison between 1901 and 1911 is impossible, since electoral districts replaced civil parishes as units of measurement. The electoral districts of Bunowen, Doonloughan and Errislannan approximate to the civil parish of Ballindoon.

140 ICM, *Annual report*, 1860, p. 13.

141 IFC Archive, MS No. S4:306–7, told by Brighid Bean Uí Clochartaigh, Muirnín, Cleggan.

142 IFC Archive, MS No. S10.273.

143 RCBL, MS No. P. 168/6/1, Register of vestrymen, Errismore.

144 Letter from Patrick MacManus, parish priest of Clifden, *Freeman's Journal*, 7 June 1866.

145 *Dublin Evening Post*, 22 June 1866.

146 RCBL, MS No. P. 491/2/1, Omey baptismal register, entry Nos 75, 136; Clifden parish office, parish register 2, p. 384.

147 RCBL, MS No. P. 491/3/1, Omey marriage register, entry no. 32.

148 Ballyconneely, Ballyconneely parish register No. 1, Margaret and Mary, 19 Aug. 1865; Bridget, 12 July 1873, parish register 1, pp. 7, 61.
149 For a detailed account of inter-faith migration see Moffitt, *Soupers and Jumpers, passim.*
150 *Banner of the Truth,* Apr. 1872, p. 31.
151 RCBL, MS No. P 491/2, Omey baptismal register, entry Nos 102, 103, Patrick and Ellen, 1859; Ballyconneely, Ballyconneely baptismal register No. 1.
152 Clifden parish office, parish register No. 4, 8 July 1876, p. 61.
153 Clifden parish office, parish register Nos 2, 4, John, 1861, Anne, 1864, Patrick, 1867, Cecily, 1872.
154 For a detailed account of the reversions of converts see Moffitt, *Soupers and Jumpers,* pp. 108, 124–7, 159–62, 164–9.
155 This seems quite a high price but was paid at almost every baptism. Baptism was only very rarely administered at no charge; occasionally 'pauper' is noted and no payment recorded. Consequently, it cannot be presumed that all free baptisms were returning converts.
156 See Moffitt, *Soupers and Jumpers,* for further details of reversions to Catholicism.
157 RCBL, MS No. P. 491/2/1, Omey baptismal register, entry 161.
158 RCBL, MS No. P. 491/3/1, Omey marriage register, entry 82; MS P. 168/4/1, Errismore burial register, entries 11 and 20.
159 *Banner of the Truth,* Apr. 1917, p. 18.
160 NAI, 1901 census, manuscript return on microfilm, Omey parish, Errislannan D.E.D., Katie (14), Margaret (13), George (11) and Norah (6).
161 RCBL, MS No. P. 491/3/22, Omey marriage register, entry 22.
162 CP, MS No. GRE/G18/1/64, *Eleventh account of the Fund for the Relief of Converts and Children of Connemara, 3 April 1857–3 April 1858,* p. 11.
163 Letter from Patrick MacManus, *Freeman's Journal,* 7 June 1866.
164 Moffitt, *Soupers and Jumpers,* pp. 103–4.
165 Ballinaboy NS, Ballyconneely NS, Aillebrach NS, Dunloughan NS and Calla NS.
166 IFC Archive, MS No. S4:307, told by Brighid Bean Uí Thuathaith, Sellerna.
167 IFC Archive, MS No. S5:310, told by Máire ní Gharabháin, Ballinakill. Sellerna mission was located at Imloch or Emlagh.
168 IFC Archive, MS No. S5:310, told by Máire Ní Gharabháin, Ballinakill.
169 IFC Archive, MS No. S4:308, told by Brighid Bean Uí Thuathaith, Sellerna.
170 IFC Archive, MS No. S10:251. This story was collected in Ballinafad NS, close to Ballinahinch station in Roundstone mission.
171 IFC Archive, MS No. S6:121, told to Francis King, Rockfield by his father.
172 IFC Archive, MS No. S4: 304.
173 RCBL, MS No. P. 741/5/1, Vestry minutes, Ballinakill, 28 Oct. 1926.
174 IFC Archive, MS No. S10:251. This story was collected in Ballinafad NS, close to Ballinahinch station in Roundstone mission.
175 Stephen Lucius Gwynn, *A holiday in Connemara ... with sixteen illustrations* (London, 1909), p. 282.
176 For example the following ICM agents emigrated to Protestant missions

abroad: Laura Mellett from Roundstone to Alaska with the CMS (daughter of convert ICM agent, John Mellett); convert William Hogan and his wife to Caledonia; Lillian McClean from Castlekerke to South America and Thomas Woods from Sligo to unidentified location with the CMS, *Banner of the Truth*, 1 Jan. 1894, p. 2; ibid., Apr. 1894, p. 4; ibid., Jan. 1897, p. 4.

177 E. J. Quigley, 'Grace abounding, a chapter of Ireland's history', *Irish Ecclesiastical Record*, xxii (1923), 613.

178 G. Ensor, *Letters showing the inutility and showing the absolute absurdity of what is rather fantastically termed 'The Second Reformation'* (Dublin, 1828), quoted in David Hempton, 'Evangelicalism in English and Irish society, 1780–1840' in M. A. Noll, D. W. Bebbington and G. A. Rawlk (eds), *Evangelicalism: comparative studies of popular Protestantism in North America, the British Isles and beyond, 1700–1990* (New York, 1994), p. 169.

179 *Irish Ecclesiastical Gazette*, 4 June 1885.

180 A. M. Barbour, *Connemara, on the eve of the twentieth century* (London, 1899), p. vii.

181 Ibid., p. 11.

182 Ibid., p. 60.

183 ICM, *Annual report*, 1906, p. 15.

184 Ibid., 1910, p. 17.

185 Ibid., 1913, p. 19.

186 The civil parishes of Omey and Ballindoon extended to 20,835 and 20,033 acres respectively, while their populations in 1851 were 4,296 and 4,435.

Chapter 6

The later years of mission, 1870–1950

The years 1870 to 1950 marked a dramatic shift in the political status and location of power in Ireland, with authority moving from the Protestant ascendancy to the Catholic majority throughout most of the island. This was most marked in the fifty years prior to the development of the Irish Free State and resulted in a shift of focus within the Irish Church Missions as it came to serve the preservation of Irish Protestant interests in the face of increasing Catholic power, while still maintaining its core mission to Catholics. At the same time, the ICM shifted its principal area of operation from rural west Galway to more urban locations. This chapter will consider the logistics and consequences of this dual refocusing, and will outline the changing role of the ICM in the rapidly altering political and social world of late-nineteenth-century and early-twentieth-century Ireland. It will demonstrate how the ICM portrayed itself, at this critical juncture, as the defender of Irish Protestant interests in the face of impending Home Rule and Catholic ascendancy. It first outlines how the ICM coped with change from 1870 to 1922 and then covers the years from 1922 to 1950.

Mission work among Irish Catholics, 1870–1922

Chapter 4 has shown that by the disestablishment of the Church of Ireland and the death of Alexander Dallas in 1869, the ICM had lost most of its Irish support and was attracting fewer converts. In 1868, Reverends Auriol et al. advised the ICM to concentrate on urban areas where community and family ties might be less obstructive to conversion. In spite of strong opposition from Revd Dallas, the ICM gradually withdrew from rural west Galway and established new missions in larger provincial towns, while maintaining a presence in Connemara. The mission's decreasing income, coupled with increasing salary costs, necessitated a severe reduction in staff numbers. The annual cost of a male teacher increased from £39 in 1860, to £65 in 1900, and to £118 in 1930, with salaries of female teachers, scripture-readers and bible-women increasing accordingly.

Table 6.1 Persons employed by ICM in active missionary work,
by region, 1860–1950

	1860	1870	1880	1890	1900	1910	1920	1930	1940	1950
Western missions	165	104	92	61	45	13	9	2	0	0
Dublin	92	47	96	91	107	69	52	39	52	22
Rest of country	133	66	36	31	47	17	10	4	1	1
Total	390	217	224	183	199	99	71	45	53	23

Source: ICM Agency books, 1860–1950

Table 6.1 shows the decline in the agency of the ICM, initially in Connemara and eventually nationwide.[1] This section will describe firstly the ICM's experiences from 1870 to 1922, starting with its Dublin operations, and will then outline its work outside Dublin and its increasing use of itinerating missions which brought the ICM into transient contact with larger numbers of people.

The Dublin mission, 1870–1922

By the last quarter of the nineteenth century the ICM acknowledged Dublin as the only city in Ireland where missionary work among the masses of Roman Catholics had been fully tried and its Dublin mission experienced the least change of all missionary locations.[2] The ICM's operations in the capital were its most successful and long-lived although decreasing income forced periodic reductions in numbers of trainee agents, as in 1889, when the London Committee ordered that 'All in training may be passed as probationers but no new candidates whatsoever to be invited'.[3] It should be acknowledged that, even in a reduced state, the mission operated on an impressive scale, especially in Dublin.

In 1892, over 2,000 pupils attended the ICM's fifty-six day schools and over 1,500 attended its thirty-one Sunday schools, while another 2,000 lived in the various homes associated with the mission.[4] It was claimed that two-thirds of pupils were of Roman Catholic parentage, which is true only if children of converts and mixed marriages were included, as discussed below.[5] Most children attended ICM schools to obtain relief since Catholic education was widely available both in Dublin and Connemara by the 1880s.[6] The ICM was highly critical of the teaching imparted in Catholic national schools, claiming that national school pupils would be able to 'tell you the exact measurement of almost every saint in heaven, and yet they cannot count the change of a two shilling piece, and a man's circumstances are such that he cannot plant independence in the mind of his children'.[7]

In spite of the diminishing appeal of ICM schools in Connemara and the reduction in its western operations, the London Committee introduced a mandatory Irish examination for all candidates from the west of Ireland entering its Training School as it considered it 'essential that the supply of workers able to speak the Irish language be maintained'.[8] Pupils in the Connemara mission schools were not taught Irish, which appears short-sighted; in 1908, it was reported that Edith McNiffe of Errismore, the daughter and grand-daughter of scripture readers Michael and Timothy McNiffe had no Irish.[9] Students were paid while in training and promised five years' service to the ICM, which was impossible to enforce. When three teachers left in 1900 without completing their five years, the Training School Committee asked that a legally binding agreement be drawn up in future. Even with this legal safeguard, trained agents did not always fulfil their obligations.[10]

The very anonymity and mobility of city dwellers which provided the ICM with some measure of success precludes such reconstruction of family and mission histories at a local level, as is feasible in Connemara. Unlike west Galway, Dublin converts were not easily identified; however, one convert's life-story was published in *The Banner*. This told of Henry Bonham, of North Circular Road, Dublin who died in February 1902. Formerly a zealous Catholic, Bonham's interest in Protestantism was awakened by handbills distributed outside the mission building. He attended Townsend Street controversial meetings and eventually openly converted in 1871. For his remaining thirty-one years, he attended the mission church and was elected as churchwarden and representative to the diocesan synod. His three daughters, Hannah, Mary and Anne, taught in ICM schools between 1877 and 1924.[11]

The ICM's Dublin mission prospered, in spite of strenuous Catholic opposition, which included social exclusion and boycotting of converts and agents.[12] Table 6.2 gives an idea of its extent in 1892 but excludes 'Sewing Classes' for mothers, bible classes for mission workers, children's meetings and Temperance Meetings. Schools, which also served as the location of missionary activities such as discussion classes and controversial lectures, were located at Coombe Male and Female (1850–1940+), Barrack Street Mixed (1870–82), Elliott Home (1887–1940+), Grand Canal Street Male and Female (1860–1940+), Kingstown (1861–1964), Luke Street, later Rath Row, later Townsend Street (1860–1940+) and Lurgan Street (1871–1940+).[13] Pupils not only received a scriptural education but also obtained food and clothes supplied through various committees of 'kind ladies' of Dublin, while the mothers of Grand Canal Street pupils were paid 1s. 6d. weekly for attending a sewing class.

Table 6.2 Weekly mission activities in Dublin, in 1892

Sun.	10.00 am	Meeting, Rath Row
	11.30 am	Church Service in Mission Church
	3.00 pm	Seven Sunday Schools for Adults and Children
	4.00 pm	Meeting in Kingstown
	7.00 pm	Service in Mission Church
	7.30 pm	Meeting at Coombe for Non-Church-goers
	8.30 pm	Meeting at Rutland Street Mission Hall
	4.00 pm	Open air meeting at Custom House
	7.00 pm	Meeting at Kingstown for Non-Church-goers
Mon.	7.30 pm	Gospel Meeting, Rath Row
	7.30 pm	Controversial Meeting, Lurgan Street
	7.30 pm	Controversial Meeting (occasional) Kingstown
	7.30 pm	Meeting at Kingstown
Tues.	7.30 pm	Meeting at Kingstown for Children
	7.30 pm	Meeting in Townsend Street, Controversial
Wed.	7.30 pm	Meeting at Kingstown
	7.30 pm	Meeting at Mission Building, Townsend Street
Thurs.	7.30 pm	Meeting at Kingstown
	7.30 pm	Controversial Meeting, Coombe
	7.30 pm	Controversial Meeting, Rutland Street Mission Hall
Fri.	7.30 pm	Meeting, Grand Canal Street
	7.30 pm	Controversial Meeting, Mountjoy Street
	7.30 pm	Meeting for Men Only at Coombe

Source: ICM, *Annual report*, 1892–93, p. 21.

Evidence exists that those who funded the ICM's feeding and relief programmes may have been unaware of its missionary objectives and methodologies. Stories of ICM homes, their origins and aims, with appeals for funds, were related by Sarah Davies, editor of *Erin's Hope*, in her many publications. As in earlier years, the ICM targeted the very poor; Townsend Street school-boys were described as the 'very refuse of the earth'.[14] Even in Dublin, the Irish language was employed where necessary; two Sunday classes for Irish speakers were held in the Coombe School.[15] Meetings were held for homeless persons, at which addresses were given and tea and bread distributed. These were so popular that for hours beforehand the poor stood 'patiently outside the door',[16] suggesting the hungry may have queued for food. Although the practice of distributing food at Townsend Street Sunday School had been discontinued by 1898, a former mission pupil remembers meetings where tea and bread were given to mothers of pupils in the Coombe mission school in the 1930s.[17]

The work of the ICM mirrored efforts of other Church of Ireland missionary societies which also operated in central Dublin. The Strand Street Institute (established in 1868) operated ten separate clubs, including a breakfast club and a women's sewing class, while the nearby Fishamble Street Mission (established in 1862) comprised eighteen different elements.[18]

The introduction of ICM bible-women in 1898 provided a new sphere of activity for females; by 1901, sixteen bible-women worked alongside eighty-nine scripture readers. The ICM's operations may possibly not have been as Dublin-centred as statistics would suggest as many Dublin workers were engaged in itinerating missions to fairs and markets (see below). Meetings specifically targeting cab-men and sailors were held in Dublin and mission bookshops operated in Dublin, Belfast and Galway, until decreasing finances forced the closure of all but the Dublin shop in 1906, replaced by a postal mission by which 'thousands of parcels of tracts and portions are being sent all over the land'.[19]

The missionary impact of schools and house-visiting was supplemented by street preaching and distribution of handbills; in 1892 over £300 was spent on handbills and placards. The ICM described Foster Place, opposite Trinity College as its 'Open-air Cathedral'[20] where street preaching took place two evenings a week from March to November.[21] The mission's 'Moveable Hall' was erected throughout the Dublin's suburbs. In 1899 it was placed in Drumcondra between the 'great Church of the Jesuit fathers' (Gardiner Street) and 'the residence of the Roman Catholic Archbishop', after which it was moved to Rathgar. In 1906 itinerants held 100 lantern meetings, which were attended by 2,000 Catholics and 3,000 Protestants.[22] In 1908, over 3,000 Catholics and almost 10,000 Protestants attended these meetings.[23] Although the ICM functioned at a reduced scale in comparison to its initial years, it should not be presumed that the scope and impact of its work were insignificant.

Catholic opposition to the ICM continued apace, with parents of mission pupils subjected to abuse from work comrades.[24] Paul Cullen continued to preach against the ICM, as did his successor, Edward McCabe (archbishop of Dublin 1878–85), previously parish priest of Francis Street, who had an intimate knowledge of ICM activities in the Coombe and had been instrumental in the foundation of Saint Brigid's Orphanage.[25] One of Edward McCabe's first tasks on appointment was to designate a priest in every slum parish to combat proselytism. As the ICM's relief programme underpinned its attraction for Dublin's poor, he condemned drunkenness as the cause of the underlying poverty which gave rise to 'proselytising dens where holy ladies carry on an unholy traffic in immortal souls'.[26] The advent of William Walsh to the archbishopric of Dublin (1885–1921) saw the recommencement of aggressive counter-mission, particularly targeting the residential care of destitute children. In 1886 he established the Sacred Heart Home in Drumcondra and the Catholic Boys' Home in Abbey Street for children rescued from proselytising homes, especially from the Birds' Nest. In a thinly veiled criticism of his predecessors, Dr Walsh observed that it was all but incredible that 'a traffic so disreputable should not long ago have been put down'.[27] As in earlier years, the ICM's presence ensured increased Catholic attention, a fact acknowledged by the mission.[28]

Catholic opposition usually focused on child-centred proselytism as 'the leakage ... is a perpetual running sore on the Catholic body' and claimed that apathy allowed the yearly 'Protestantising' of over a thousand children in the Birds' Nest Home.[29] Dr Walsh's criticism of mission schools where 'hundreds of Catholic children ... [were] imbued with a spirit of hatred of the Catholic faith and teaching'[30] was criticised in the *Church of Ireland Gazette* as 'rude, ungentlemanly and unworthy of a Christian prelate' while the *Belfast Newsletter* regarded it as 'a tribute to their usefulness and a proof that they deserve increased support'.[31] The ICM reported an organised opposition of priests and nuns and that, as in its earlier years, a regular band of agents hovered near its schools offering 'money, food, situations, and various other inducements' to remove their children from ICM schools where they were 'damning their souls' and 'selling their faith'.[32]

Catholic newspapers warned of considerable conversions to Protestantism, reporting that between 1885 and 1913 'probably 30,000 Catholic children and adults ... [converted] in Dublin alone'.[33] This estimate appears outrageously high as ICM sources indicate that 'over 230' adults were publicly received in the Mission Church between 1898 and 1910,[34] but may reflect the intake of Catholic children in ICM homes, although many Protestants were also admitted, evident from an analysis of children's surnames in the 1901 census. Conversions were frequently reported in mission publications; annual reports told of the conversion of twenty-one persons in 1911, thirty-seven in 1924 and forty in 1925, some of whom were said to be in training 'for missionary work among their fellow countrymen'.[35]

Fixed mission stations outside Dublin, 1870–1922

City missions outside Dublin generally targeted adults, frequently by means of night schools, although a Ragged School briefly operated in Cork in 1900, attended by twenty-six children. The *Irish Ecclesiastical Gazette* spoke approvingly of the ICM's Cork mission where, in spite of concerted opposition, 'Roman Catholics have been found willing and glad to attend'.[36] As in Dublin, the ICM's Cork operation targeted the poor, running a wood-chopping industry for destitute men, several of whom attended its bible class. Nearly forty women attended Cork's weekly sewing class; similar gatherings were held on other nights and meetings were held in two locations on Sundays. Supporters heard how Cork's Catholics 'read the Word and are giving up praying to their patron saints and even to the Virgin'.[37] In 1900, the ICM assumed responsibility for the entire missionary work among Belfast's Catholics when the Belfast Parochial Mission handed over its operations, after which three ICM scripture readers held controversial sermons and discussion lectures in the mission's moveable hall.[38]

By 1900, the ICM was working in Dublin, Connemara and twelve other locations. As the Appendix demonstrates, the city missions of Belfast, Limerick, Cork and Waterford were started, or in the case of Cork and Belfast, restarted in the 1880s, in line with the policy of increased urban operations which were considered to provide greater anonymity to prospective converts unencumbered by 'family, social and political ties'.[39]

In 1898 the ICM embarked on an entirely new method of evangelising when it opened the Limerick Medical Mission, where Dr Long and his nursing staff attempted to 'cure the soul and body by dispensing the Gospel along with medicine'.[40]

Dr Long, son of archdeacon Long of Cashel, had been warned by Limerick Protestants that it would be dangerous to 'speak about the bible' as at that time Limerick had communities of the most distinguished and experienced Catholic missioners: Jesuits, Redemptorists, Augustinians, Franciscans and Dominicans. He was welcomed by only two Limerick Protestant clergymen. Initially he encountered little opposition, but after a few months the Redemptorist priest, Fr Tierney, burst into the waiting room declaring, 'The doctor is a souper doctor. No Catholic is to go in there.'[41] Dr Long was denounced in all Catholic chapels in Limerick the following Sunday, necessitating police protection for mission staff. Tactics employed against the Limerick mission closely resemble those used in the 'anti-jumper' crusade in Connemara twenty years earlier.[42] Nationalist newspapers such as the *Munster News* and the *Limerick Echo* advised Limerick's Catholics to shun the mission. Bishop O'Dwyer made it a reserved sin to attend the dispensary and Fr Tierney told people to 'come to me with the names. I beg of you to help me stamp out this vile proselytism.'[43]

The frequent attacks on the Limerick dispensary and its staff were regularly reported in *The Banner*, where readers learned of priestly assaults on those who attended, such as the woman who was beaten 'black and blue with the knob end of an umbrella'.[44] Dr Long regarded such opposition as 'a Satanic attack to prevent the spread of Gospel Truth and the circulation of God's word'. One Limerick priest reportedly said 'the blood is up – I will not be answerable for the peace of the city'.[45] Violence against the mission escalated in a manner reminiscent of the Connemara outrages of

1878–83, resulting in two parliamentary debates on 18 and 28 June 1901. Parliamentary support for the Limerick mission was confined to MPs from the north of Ireland,[46] while it was denounced by the nationalist Limerick representatives.[47] Many persons in authority felt that the ICM was at least partly culpable for Catholic hostility. W. E. H Lecky, MP for Trinity College, Dublin, while 'disassociating himself from the mission', condemned the violence against mission personnel.[48] Mr Wyndham, Chief Secretary for Ireland, said that Dr Long's insistence on proselytism was undesirable[49] and that it was to be regretted that the ICM 'should conscientiously think it right to afford gratuitous medical attendance, with the avowed object of making converts in the midst of a Roman Catholic population'.[50]

The success of the Limerick mission, if measured in numbers of converts, was negligible although two-thirds of its average annual attendance of 500 were Catholic.[51] In his history of the mission, Dr Long identified converts by name; many of these were original Protestants who had previously converted to Rome on marrying a Catholic. In spite of few accessions from Rome, mission supporters were assured of its progress, as in 1907 when Dr Long told how 'The priests, though quietly exercising great power over the minds of the people, are losing it every day.'[52]

After the departure from the district of Fr Tierney, the instigator of the violence, the Limerick mission appears to have enjoyed a period of reasonable peace. Interestingly, the duration of the 'Limerick Pogrom' of 1904, a period of intense violence against its Jewish population also instigated by Redemptorists, appears to have been relatively peaceful for the medical mission.[53] Limerick Medical Mission continued into the 1930s until its ageing workforce was retired to the mission's Annuitants List. By then the ICM's activities were almost entirely centred in Dublin, although this may mask the operations of itinerant missions, as discussed below.

Itinerating missions and lantern lectures, 1870–1922

The Irish Church Missions altered its mode of operation in the late nineteenth-century, placing more reliance on itinerating missions. These were based in Dublin but travelled to fairs and markets throughout the country, where they erected their stalls, sold books, preached and sang. Catholic parish missions also toured the country, comprising parties of missioners who preached and catechised, accompanied by stalls selling religious goods such as statues, scapulars and rosary beads. Church of Ireland parish clergy regularly asked for ICM help in counteracting Catholic missions. For example, ICM agents attended an Oblate mission in County Kildare and aggressively argued with the Oblates, visited stalls, explained the superstitious nature of the merchandise and suggested that copies of the scriptures be sold instead.[54] Itinerating missions had formed

6.1 Itinerant evangelists preaching at a fair.
Source: *The Banner of the Truth*, October 1909

part of the ICM's operations from its inception but took on an increasingly important role after the downsizing of its Connemara missions in the 1880s. Initially their work was described as 'tentative' until funds would permit a 'more permanent and expansive machinery'. An expansion of itinerating missions was noted in 1889, when it was rather vaguely reported that 'Itinerating tours have been carried out to an increasing extent in different localities'.[55]

Following the Society's reappraisal of its operations in 1893, itinerating missions were to fulfil an important and increasingly political role, as discussed later. Although the Society had engaged in open-air mission since the mid 1880s, it announced a new mission plan at its 1893 annual meeting, to use 'methods more suitable to the altered circumstances' of the time. Supporters heard that fixed stations had recently been established in urban districts but that it was especially the 'itinerants' who would 'speedily and effectively reach these vast areas still unevangelised'. The ICM acknowledged that its work was hampered by the establishment of successful national schools beside western mission schools but added that its Dublin schools were still 'a most effective Missionary Agency'.[56]

This refocusing of attention was expected to free Connemara workers to work in other parts of the country which would be 'no retrograde step' as

Connemara's converts would be roused to undertake mission work among their neighbours.[57] In addition to public preaching, itinerant scripture readers made house-to-house visits throughout Ireland, speaking to 'rough town and country Roman Catholics', occasionally preaching in Irish.[58] It is clear from ICM literature that they encountered considerable opposition, although Archdeacon Long, father of Dr Long of Limerick, reported that ICM itinerants working in Templemore received 'not a disparaging look or word'.[59] The ICM's 1893 announcement of increased open-air work coincided with the impending threat of Home Rule following Gladstone's return to power. By then unambiguous links had already been forged between street preaching and resistance to Home Rule in locations such as Arklow, as discussed later.

As itinerating missions were without a focal point of operation, their work could be 'ambitiously' related. For example, in 1884 the four scripture readers of Ossory mission covered the counties of Kilkenny and Wexford and parts of Carlow and Waterford.[60] Over the next decade, annual reports told of the work of the 'Ossory mission', not disclosing that it had been reduced to one elderly scripture reader. By 1894, it comprised the single station of Knocktopher, manned by John Ennis until his death in 1904 aged seventy-seven,[61] after which the already retired Anthony McGinley was re-employed until 1925.[62] It is likely that John Ennis was employed part-time as, in 1910 with fifty years' service, he was paid five pounds per month, the same rate as in 1856.[63] His successor, Anthony McGinley, was paid a mere £70 per year in 1920. Analysis of the surnames and occupations in Knocktopher parish registers suggests that no conversions from Catholicism were effected, contrary to the impressive reports of the 'Ossory mission' in ICM publications.[64] Just as emigration was blamed for the scarcity of Connemara converts, the ICM claimed that results of itinerating missions were not readily evident as many left their rural homes to avoid detection and persecution,[65] an observation verified in a significant number of cases by correspondence in the ICM archives.[66]

As well as street preaching, the ICM held lantern missions in winter evenings. In 1900, 273 lantern meetings were held in ninety-two locations, attended by 9,575 Catholics and 13,423 Protestants.[67] It should be noted that by now the ICM's activities increasingly drew Protestant audiences. The mission had long considered that persons were more amenable to discussion when removed from their home surroundings. The ICM's 'Movable Wooden Hall' was sited in suitable locations; it was placed at the sea-side resort of Kilkee, County Clare in the summer of 1899 where 'very successful open-air meetings' were held on the beach.[68]

It is evident that the itinerating missions carried out substantial work among the Catholic community; it is equally evident that this was greatly resented by the majority population. Fr Ambrose Coleman, a Sligo Dominican, criticised proselytising missioners who, although largely ineffective, 'exercised the right to free speech for a number of years and they have exercised the right to offensive speech as well'.[69] While Fr Coleman may have viewed the ICM's work as ineffectual, not all Catholics were so complacent. The *Irish Catholic* of 26 April 1913 considered that the ICM's 'pious subscribers' got good value for their money, as most mission pupils became 'fully fledged Protestants' when adults, adding that the yearly loss through mission schools could not be quantified.

The elderly profile of ICM agents at the turn of the century may have hampered mission success. The salaries of experienced scripture readers and teachers, most of whom were employed full-time and spent their evenings conducting discussion lectures and controversial classes, compare extremely unfavourably with salaries paid to the ICM's fundraising deputation secretaries in England. Deputising secretaries, usually incumbents of English parishes, were paid £250 per annum plus expenses in 1866, a rate which remained constant for the next sixty years.[70] Agents engaged in full-time mission work were paid substantially less; in 1900 the average salaries for male and female lay-workers were £65 and £47 respectively, while ordained missionaries in Connemara were paid £84.

In the late nineteenth and early twentieth centuries, death and retirement were frequent occurrences among the ICM's ageing workforce and at least forty-seven elderly agents died between 1890 and 1924, many of whom belonged to the original cohort of 1850s converts.[71] Obituaries in *The Banner* and annual reports related the deaths of long-serving agents, some of whom had given fifty years' service such as the three Dublin teachers, Miss Emily Reilly, Miss O'Malley, and Miss McKenna, who retired in 1928. On retirement, these agents were paid from the Annuitants' Fund and the Dallas Memorial Fund, but since details of these funds are not extant, it is not possible to estimate their probable standard of living; they would have received an old-age pension from the state after 1908.

Not only were mission workers ageing and dying, so also were its original supporters and new helpers were 'sorely needed to take the place of those who are gone from us'.[72] Annual reports regularly told of the death or resignation of life-long advocates. In 1908, supporters heard of the resignation of Mrs Riddell, over fifty years honorary secretary and treasurer of the Leamington Association and the 1910 report told of the death of Miss Gertrude Newton of Derby, who was 'the last survivor of the little band of seven who knelt, in January 1846, with the Rev. A. R. C. Dallas, and commended to God the 20,000 letters to Ireland which led to the foundation of the society'.[73] With the death of her sister, Emily, in 1922, *The Banner* acknowledged that 'the last link with the early days of the ICM is broken'.[74]

In England, as in Ireland, support for the ICM waned from the late nineteenth century. *The Banner* admitted the difficulty of interesting English congregations, who were weary of Irish problems and apathetic to distinctly Protestant causes, asking evangelical clergy to 'lend their pulpits', promising that 'Ireland won for Christ will mean blessings untold for England'.[75] The ICM's colonising influence was reiterated, telling, for instance, that when mission work began in Connemara, the people were 'a band of savages ... [but now] are a civilised, law-abiding, and loyal community'.[76] In spite of this, each issue mourned the passing of life-long fundraisers, whose deaths left voids not filled by subsequent generations.

The preservation of Irish Protestant interests, 1870–1922

Political changes in Ireland caused the ICM to assume new self-appointed responsibilities. In the late nineteenth century, it emphasised an additional *raison d'etre*: that of safeguarding the Protestant population from the dangers of Rome and from the increasingly politicised Catholic majority. Although this had occasionally been mentioned in previous years, it was presented as being urgent from the mid 1880s as Home Rule threatened. In 1887, readers were told that it was 'becoming increasingly necessary to warn our people against Romish errors and to fit them, if possible, [for] Mission work among friends and acquaintances holding such views',[77] and in 1890, when the ICM presented controversial classes at the Young Women's Christian Association in Dublin and lectures in the Orange Hall in Rutland Square, supporters were asked to 'pray that these efforts may be much blessed to awakening Protestants to the danger of Catholicism'.[78] The mainstream Church of Ireland had lost interest in converting Catholics following the publication of the 1861 census, becoming more defensive in character and more concerned with preventing losses from Protestantism than with effecting gains from Catholicism. Three decades later, the ICM began to move in the same direction, explaining that children of mixed marriages and original Protestants should be well grounded 'not only in the truths of the Gospel, but well informed respecting the errors of Romanism. They are thus enabled ... to do the work of the Irish Church Missions, instead of falling prey to Roman cunning.'[79]

Although the ICM claimed in 1892 that two-thirds of its pupils were of Catholic parentage, statistics published for Dublin in 1885 show this was not strictly the case.[80] In 1885, two-thirds of pupils came from Catholic, convert and mixed-marriage parentage combined, with one-third being original Protestants. Although almost 500 Catholic children in Dublin were open to the ICM's missionary efforts, six out of every ten pupils had at least one Protestant parent. However, as children of Catholic parents in mission homes were probably returned as Protestant, this may underestimate the ICM's success.

The ICM reached even fewer Catholics in Galway. The earliest available statistics (1898–99) show that over half its pupils were original Protestants and that only 17 per cent came from convert backgrounds. Interestingly, they show that as late as 1892, almost 100 Catholic children attended west Galway mission schools. The ICM justified the attendance of Protestant children at its schools where they were 'kept from the influence of the priests' schools'.[81] However, the safeguarding of Protestant children did not necessarily justify the continuance of a mission school; funding for Oughterard mission school was withdrawn in 1900 'owing to there being only Protestant pupils'.[82]

Organisations such as the ICM, which not only attacked the errors of Rome but also safeguarded Protestant privileges, received increasing publicity as the threat of Home Rule loomed menacingly after Gladstone's return to power in 1886. In the 1890s, Protestant street preaching resulted in violent clashes between preachers and hostile Catholics which often degenerated into riot.[83] The chief agencies involved were the ICM, the Open Air Mission and the Evangelical Alliance. The ICM's allocation of £35,000 out of Mrs Hopper's legacy of £51,000 in 1890 to its 'Itinerating Evangelistic Fund' ensured that the mission was at the forefront of Irish street preaching.

From the early 1890s, preaching followed by violence was an almost weekly occurrence at Arklow, Cork, Athlone, Galway and Sligo, with less frequent episodes at Clara, Tullamore, Armagh, Cookstown and Bray. Tensions reached a crescendo in the mid 1890s. Ignoring police warnings, preachers persisted in holding street meetings, employing language which invariably provoked Catholics into behaviour which reinforced the unionist conviction that Home Rule could not be tolerated. The reporting of disturbances demonstrates the lack of support given to the preachers by middle-class Protestants. The *Cork Examiner*, a nationalist newspaper in Protestant ownership, while agreeing the right to free speech, considered that street preaching was 'an effort to introduce sectarian discord in the city'.[84] The lack of support for the ICM on the part of Robert Gregg, bishop of Cork 1878–93, confirms this view. As violence escalated, this newspaper insisted that steps be taken to prevent preaching but equally could not justify the crowd which gathered 'in expectation of excitement and disturbance'.[85] The intersection of politics and religion at this popular level was clearly evident, when Protestant evangelicalism was aggressively challenged by Irish nationalism with the singing of 'The gospel of thy grade' drowned out by verses of 'The boys of Wexford'.[86] Doherty's exploration of

the underlying anti-Home Rule agenda underpinning the Arklow disturbances of 1891–92 concludes that both sides were 'clear and open as to the
political issues at stake'.[87]

The ICM alerted supporters to the potential consequences of Home
Rule. *The Banner* told how violence and boycotting against converts and
mission agents in Connemara at Moyrus in 1893 were 'a good foretaste of
what might be expected if this disastrous Bill passes into law'.[88] The *Irish
Ecclesiastical Gazette* reported that a local priest had earlier warned that he
would not be surprised if the 'jumpers' boat sank'.[89]

Revd Hallowes, the organiser of the Arklow street preachers, did not
command the support of many Irish Protestants; an editorial in the *Irish
Ecclesiastical Gazette* of 27 February 1891 considered that 'Our church is
disgraced and discredited by these Sunday orgies … the respectable portions
of the community, Protestant and Roman Catholic alike, are saddened and
disheartened'. The ICM conferred a clear vote of approval on the Arklow
preachers by inviting Revd Hallowes to address its 1893 annual meeting, the
occasion when the Society promised to increase its itinerating mission.[90]

Coinciding as it did with the threat of Home Rule, street preaching
conferred a political component on Protestant mission and ensured, in
a manner reminiscent of English anti-popery hysteria of the 1850s, that
the spiritual aim of the ICM to introduce the Gospel to Irish Catholics
could not be easily disentangled from its supporters' political agendas.
Evangelical unionists had long believed that Irish nationalism could only
be overcome through conversion but in the 1890s the possibility of Home
Rule politicised issues such as the freedom to preach the scriptures in
the open air.[91] A Protestant home-ruler from Cork, who admitted that he
knew no Protestants who approved of street preaching, acknowledged its
political consequences and added that there were many who '*seem* glad
it is serving a political end'.[92] By highlighting violence towards Protestantism, controversial open-air preaching provided unionists with a cause
that appealed to the more unstable sections of British public opinion,
strengthening unionism's appeal. Although there is no evidence that street
preaching was an official component of the campaign against Home Rule,
Catholic responses could easily be utilised in the anti-Home Rule rhetoric
of potential Catholic oppressiveness.[93]

In later life, T. C. Hammond (ICM superintendent 1919–32) recalled
his active involvement in the Cork open-air mission as a young man, telling
how detachments of police would arrive in Cork on Saturday in anticipation
of violence during the open-air preaching on the following day, and how
Mrs Ainley, the wife of the ICM's missionary, never recovered from being
struck by a stone during a riot.[94] *The Banner*'s extensive coverage of the
Cork violence shows that the ICM stood firmly behind the street-preaching

movement. It denounced Cork Corporation's 'tyrannical enactment' of a byelaw prohibiting open-air preaching, made vigorous representations, and later triumphantly reported that this byelaw had been revoked.[95] The ICM did not acknowledge the political implications of its open-air mission work, making few references to Catholic hostility. Aside from the Cork disturbances, *The Banner* rarely mentioned the political situation, confining its content to the superiority of Protestantism, the 'errors of Romanism' and its efforts to evangelise the Irish, telling how its itinerants sold 11,747 books including over 5,000 bibles in 1895.[96]

Catholic authorities were quick to protest at the spread of street preaching, recognising that the tactics of proselytising missions were changing. John Clancy, bishop of Elphin, told Sligo Catholics that this approach was being tried where 'the confiscations of Elizabeth, the butcheries of Cromwell, the penal enactments of three hundred years' had failed. He advised that the best course of action was to totally ignore 'those hireling missionaries', but where this was not possible, that every legal means should be employed to frustrate their 'fiendish efforts'.[97]

The state's role was ambiguous, compelled to protect the preachers but aware of the danger posed by their existence, as demonstrated in Arklow where stringent policing and the intervention of Catholic clergy brought an end to the episode.[98] Unionists capitalised on the state's obligation to protect street evangelists; their outrage provoked by a leaked RIC circular advising that a service likely to result in a riot should not take place, which proved impossible to implement.[99] The unresolved conflict between the right of free speech and the dangers of inflammatory preaching had been demonstrated in Britain in a celebrated case between the Skeletal Army and the Salvation Army which revealed the uncertainty of legal right when religious principles were involved.[100]

The right to preach the Gospel was depicted by unionists as an essential civil and religious liberty and came to symbolise the potential restrictions that might be placed on Protestantism by an Irish and largely Catholic parliament. In the mid 1890s, the output of the Protestant media became increasingly inflammatory, declaring that opposition to street preaching proved that 'religious liberty would cease to exist' if Home Rule came to pass.[101] Leading politicians voiced their opinions: Michael Davitt wrote that 'to deny the right to these preachers is to proclaim the principle of coercion', while the Quaker MP, Alfred Webb, considered that Catholic street preachers would not be tolerated in England.[102] Since English support for or against Home Rule was crucial, Irish nationalists considered it essential to convince public opinion that Home Rule would not threaten Protestant religious liberties. Nationalists understood that ongoing violent opposition to street preaching would damage the prospect of Home Rule by giving weekly examples of what might be perceived in England as Catholic Ireland's intolerance of Protestantism and denial of free speech.

Street preachers did not command the unanimous support of Irish Protestants. The Cork episode was strenuously condemned in an editorial in the *Irish Ecclesiastical Gazette* of 12 January 1894; one clergyman judged that almost all Wexford Protestants considered that it could only arouse 'bitter feeling and do no possible good',[103] and J. Duncan Craig of Kinsale (who could never be described as well disposed towards Catholics) considered that open-air preaching outside of Ulster would be 'a service of the utmost peril [to Protestants]'.[104] W. E. H. Lecky of Trinity College, Dublin, a strenuous opponent of Home Rule, thought that Irish and English societies differed so fundamentally that what might be acceptable in England might not be suitable for Ireland and that the placarding of Irish towns 'with questions and argument subversive to the Catholic faith ... ought not to have been permitted'.[105] Mr Balfour, cognisant that Ireland differed greatly from England, wrote that

> In Ireland, the divisions between different sections of the community, caused by difference of creed, are so deep and far-reaching, religious convictions are so closely interwoven with political passions, that a course which would be innocent, even praiseworthy, on one side of St. George's Channel, may be morally, if not legally, indefensible on the other.[106]

Liberal Irish Protestants, while not supporting street preachers, were influenced by violent hostilities against their coreligionists. As with the Papal Aggression of 1851, the threat of Home Rule galvanised diverse sections of Protestantism: those who favoured the conversion of Irish Catholics, those who opposed Home Rule, and some formerly liberal Protestants who now felt threatened by the hostility and intolerance of Catholic opposition to street preaching. Support for street preachers divided along class lines, with middle-class Protestants withholding support and the more threatened lower orders lining up behind the preachers. It appears that this increased sense of threat engendered a partial rehabilitation of the ICM in the eyes of Irish Protestantism, which was seen to provide a buttress against increasing Catholicism. There was, however, no significant increase in Irish donations at this juncture. The *Irish Ecclesiastical Gazette* wrote approvingly in 1898 that

> One could not but wish that some of those who are accustomed to give the cold shoulder to this much abused society had been present to hear of the success with which God has been pleased to accompany the humble, self-denying efforts of the colporteur, Scripture reader, and text teacher, to bring the Gospel within the reach of those who otherwise would remain in a state of ignorance of essential truth, such as only those who have worked amongst them would believe possible.[107]

The attitude of the Church of Ireland bishops to the ICM reflects the ICM's changing role from a missionary organisation to a bastion of Protestantism. During the first decade of its existence, a small number of Irish bishops were vice-presidents of the Society, but by 1860 no Irish bishop was included in its list of officers. The board of the ICM remained devoid of Irish bishops until 1884, when W. C. Plunket, archbishop of Dublin and five others were appointed vice-presidents.[108] These were joined by the bishop of Down in 1891, bishop of Meath in 1893, bishop of Derry in 1895 and bishop of Limerick in 1907. The inclusion of the archbishop of Armagh in 1910, bishop of Cork in 1915 and bishops of Cashel, Kilmore and Meath between 1916 and 1919,[109] followed by the bishop of Killaloe in 1924, provided the ICM with a full complement of Irish bishops. Table 6.3 masks the considerable variation in personal attitudes, as can be seen in Table 6.4. It would appear that most bishops either supported the ICM throughout their lives or abstained altogether from becoming a vice-president. The post of vice-president was usually taken up at a change of bishopric. For instance, the bishops of Limerick, Kilmore, Meath and Cashel resigned/died in 1907, 1915, 1919 and 1919 respectively, never having held an ICM office. Their successors, Raymond Orpen (Limerick, 1907–21), William Moore (Kilmore, 1915–30), Benjamin Plunket (Meath, 1919–26) and Robert Millar (Cashel, 1919–31) were all ICM vice-presidents.

The patronage of Irish bishops may be inferred as a vote of approval for the ICM, either as a missionary organisation or as a self-appointed guardian of Irish Protestantism. The amalgamation of the IS with the ICM in 1918 may have been a contributing factor, as the IS commanded considerable support among Irish bishops and clergy. The Plunket dynasty demonstrated exceptional family commitment to the cause, with three generations lending their support to the mission. Thomas Plunket (Tuam, 1834–67, i.e. the years of the ICM's inception) was followed by his nephew, William Conyngham Plunket (Dublin, 1884–97), founder of the West Connaught Church Endowment Society, who in turn was followed by his son, Benjamin Plunket (Tuam, 1913–19; Meath, 1919–26). In contrast, the three generations of Gregg bishops appear to have withheld support from the ICM. Although primarily an IS supporter, John Gregg wrote extensively in support of the ICM in its earlier years but distanced himself from the mission after the dissolution of the merger with the IS in 1856.[110] His son Robert, bishop of Cork during the street-preaching disturbances and later archbishop of Armagh, refrained from supporting the movement. Robert Gregg's Cork successor, William Meade (1894–1912), also refrained from involvement as did his successor as Primate, William Alexander, 1896–1911. Robert Gregg's nephew, Primate John Gregg (1939–59) would deliver a sharp rebuke to the ICM, as discussed later.

Table 6.3 Patronage of the ICM by Irish bishops, 1880–1937

Source: ICM, *Annual reports*, 1880–1937. No reports available 1916–18.

John Baptist Crozier is the only significant exception to this pattern. As bishop of Ossory (1897–1907) and Down (1907–11), Bishop Crozier was not associated with the ICM. In spite of taking over from William Packenham Walsh in Ossory and Thomas Welland in Down, both of whom were ICM vice-presidents, John Crozier did not hold an ICM office until he was transferred to the archbishopric of Armagh in 1911. In 1911, Archbishop Crozier, now Primate, announced that he felt deeply the 'action of the Irish Church Missions in carrying out its work along loyal Church lines ... [and had] much pleasure in agreeing to your desire that I should be one of the Vice-Presidents of the Society'.[111] The absence of Primates Gregg and Alexander from the ICM board and the late involvement of Primate Crozier prove that the ICM did not command unanimous support in the church at the start of the twentieth century. Their involvement may be interpreted as an endorsement of the ICM's mission to convert Roman Catholics or, alternatively, for its role in buttressing Protestantism at this time of crisis. The rapid involvement of many south of Ireland bishops between 1915 and 1923 lends support to the 'buttressing' argument and suggests a growing fear that the edifice of Irish Protestantism was about to crumble. It is striking, however, that this occurred while many of the laity were withholding support from the movement.

Table 6.5 identifies parishes in the Tuam diocese where collections were made for the ICM. This shows that most parishes consistently supported Protestant causes both missionary (Church Missionary Society) and philanthropic (Protestant Orphan Society) but did not support the ICM, which encompassed both missionary and philanthropic works. In view of this, it must be inferred that the ICM did not have the support or approval of most of the Protestants of the very diocese wherein its activities had been most concentrated. Tuam's Catholics were equally disinterested in sectarian issues. Despite the recent history of proselytism, the Catholic Protection and Rescue Society of Ireland received the second smallest contribution from the Tuam diocese (£3 10s. 0d.) while the much smaller neighbouring diocese of Killala gave almost £15.[112]

It can be seen that there was little support for the ICM in parishes outside its sphere of activity. The large towns of Castlebar, Ballinrobe and Westport (Aughaval) donated nothing to the ICM. Most parishes which apparently supported the ICM had connections with the organisation via their clergy. Revd Day, incumbent of Kilcoleman parish, where collections for the ICM were taken up in 1894, 1897, 1900 and 1906, had been missionary at Castlekerke 1877–81. Revd Colvin, on his transfer from Killanin mission to Kiltullagh in 1905, initiated collections for the ICM in his new parish. Collections in the Athenry parish of former ICM Belfast missionary, Revd John Ford, ceased on his replacement in 1903. Collections were taken in

Knappagh, which itself was a missionary parish and had briefly been under the auspices of the ICM (1853–56).

Table 6.4 Patronage of the ICM by individual Irish bishops,
1880–1938

	Diocese	*ICM vice-president*
Irish bishops as vice-presidents of the ICM (1880–1938)		
Alexander, William	Armagh 1899–1911	not a VP
Archdall, Mervyn	Killaloe 1897–1912	1897–1912
Barton, Arthur William	Kilmore 1930–38	1930–38
Bernard, Charles B.	Tuam 1867–90	1884–90
Bernard, John H.	Ossory 1911–15 Dublin 1915–19 Provost 1919–27	1911–27
Berry, Thomas S	Killaloe 1913–24	not a VP
Bunbury, Thomas	Limerick 1899–1907	not a VP
Chadwick, George Alex.	Derry 1895–1916 d. 1923	1895–1923
Chester, William Bennett	Killaloe 1884–93	1884–93
Collins, Thomas G. G.	Meath 1926–27	1926–27
Crozier, John Baptist	Ossory 1897–1907 Down 1907–11 Armagh 1911–1920	1911–24
D'Arcy, Charles F.	Clogher 1903–07 Ossory 1907–11 Down 1911–19 Dublin 1919–20 Armagh 1920–38	1904–38
Day, John G. F.	Clogher 1908–20 Ossory 1920–38	1908–38
Day, Maurice F.	Cashel 1872–99 d.1904	1884–1904
Dowse, Charles Benjamin	Killaloe 1912–12 Cork 1912–1933	1915–33
Elliott, Alfred G.	Kilmore 1897–1915	not a VP
Flewitt, William	Cork 1933–38	1933–38
Gregg, John Allen F	Ossory 1915–20 Dublin 1920–39	1915–39
Gregg, Robert Samuel	Cork 1878–93 Armagh 1893–96	not a VP
Grierson, Charles T.	Down 1919–34	1919–34
Harden, John M.	Tuam 1928–32	not a VP

	Diocese	ICM vice-president
Harvey, Thomas Arnold	Cashel 1935–58	1935–
Holmes, William Hardy	Tuam 1932–38	1932–38
Irwin, Charles King	Limerick 1934–42	1934–
Keene, James B.	Meath 1897–1919	not a VP
MacManaway, James	Clogher 1923–43	1923–
McNeice, John Frederick	Cashel 1931–35	1931–
	Down 1935–42	
Meade, William	Cork 1894–1912	not a VP
Miller, Robert	Cashel 1919–31	1919–31
Moore, William R	Kilmore 1915–31	1924–31
O'Hara, Henry	Cashel 1900–1919	not a VP
Orpen, Raymond	Limerick 1907–21	1907–29
	d.1929	
Orr, John	Tuam 1923–1927	1923–37
	Meath 1927–37	
O'Sullivan, James	Tuam 1890–1913	1890–1914
	d. 1915	
Patton, Henry E.	Killaloe 1924–43	1924–
Peacocke, Joseph F.	Meath 1894–97	1894–1944
	Dublin 1897–1915	
	Derry 1916–44	
Plunket, Benjamin John	Tuam 1913–19	1913–26
	Meath 1919–26	
Plunket, William C.	Meath 1876–85	1884–97
	Dublin 1885–97	
Ross, Arthur Edwin	Tuam 1920–23	1920–23
Shone, Samuel	Kilmore 1884–1897	1884–1900
	d. 1901	
Stack, Charles Maurice	Clogher 1886–1903	
Walsh, William Packenham	Ossory 1878–97	1884–1901
Welland, Thomas J.	Down 1892–1907	1892–1907
White, Henry Vere	Limerick 1921–24	1921–24
Wynne, Frederick R	Killaloe 1893–97	1893–97

Source: *Crockford's Clerical Directory* (London, 1941); ICM *Annual reports 1880–1938* (reports for 1916–19 missing).

This lack of support among western Protestant congregations for missionary activity targeted at Catholics raises doubts about the feasibility of the entire venture and poses the question of how welcome converts would have been in the wider Anglican community of Connaught. This was observed in 1909 by a Catholic national school-teacher who noted the church attendance of converts whose 'filthy raggedness raised disgust in

Table 6.5 Support for the ICM in the Tuam diocese, 1890–1910

	Irish Church Missions		Church Missionary Society			Protestant Orphan Society		
Non-ICM Parishes	1890	1900	1890	1900		1890	1900	
Achill								
Annaghdown								
Aran								
Athenry								
Aughaval								
Balla								
Ballinrobe								
Ballyovie								
Burrishoole								
Castlebar								
Cong								
Dunmore								
Headford								
Kilcoleman								
Kilcommon								
Kilmaine								
Kiltullagh								
Knappagh								
Louisburg								
Monivea								
Moylough								
Turlough								

Irish Church Missions · **Church Missionary Society** · **Protestant Orphan Society**

1890   1900 (per society, columns marked 1–0)

ICM Parishes:
- Aasleagh
- Ballyconree
- Ballinakill
- Castlekerke
- Errislannan
- Errismore
- Kilcummin
- Killannin
- Moyrus
- Omey
- Roundstone
- Sellerna
- Tuam
- Galway

Source: Report of the Committee for Missions contained in the *Report of the Tuam Diocesan Council*, 1891–1910.

the habitual worshippers'.[113] This was also observed in the Presbyterian missions of north Mayo, where converts experienced 'a deep spirit not only of distrust, but of actual hostility' from the original congregations.[114] George Moore MP, a Catholic landlord near Partry, with extraordinary prescience had astutely predicted this. In 1852 he had warned Partry's Catholics against mission involvement, saying, 'This fashion will pass ... and those who have lost their faith will be left like scuttle boats upon the strand – a despised and derided race – loathed by the Catholics – shunned by the Protestants.'[115]

Table 6.5 shows that, even at the height of the Home Rule crisis, street-preaching episodes and activities of the United Irish League, at the very time when the ICM was perceived by some as a stalwart of Protestantism, it commanded little support among western Protestants. This contrasts with the strong support given by Connaught Protestants to the missions in the 1850s, when the western Protestant media gave significant support in papers such as the *Ballina Chronicle*, *Connaught Watchman*, *Mayo Constitution* and *Galway Express*, which urged that 'All that is required for the continuance and furtherance of this great work appears to be pecuniary supplies'.[116] It is clear that little support was given to the mission in the Tuam diocese fifty years later. Lack of success and dislike for the mission's methodologies displaced many of the movement's former benefactors, as explained by one Donegal landlord, writing in the 1880s, who described aggressive missionary work as 'bad feeling kept up by well-intentioned but ill-judging Protestants'.[117]

Forty years later, an Anglican clergyman from the north Connaught diocese of Killala, although a former student and fond admirer of Edward Nangle of Achill, urged that Protestant churches should divert their monies to causes other than 'that of turning Catholics into Protestants' as it was 'silly to be fishing up conversions, perversions, etc.'.[118] It could be argued that the newly formed Church of Ireland, no longer a constituent part of the United Church of England and Ireland, was empowered to discourage English proselytism within its territory. Whereas the Irish Society presented its report to the annual General Synod each year, the ICM was not as closely involved with the Church of Ireland.

Although an increasing portion of the Church of Ireland withheld public support from missions to Catholics, some Protestants urged support for the ICM and the Irish Society. A letter-writer to the *Church of Ireland Gazette* claimed in 1913 that if sufficient resources had been spent on proselytism in previous decades, the Church of Ireland would not be 'face to face with the bogey of Home Rule', which was a punishment from God for 'the neglect of her most obvious duty – the duty of spreading the light of truth in the land where God has placed her'.[119] Not everyone agreed with this correspondent; a letter from 'Anglicanus' seven months later condemned the 'souper system' and urged the Church of Ireland to set its own house in order and not to treat Roman Catholics as if they were heathens.[120]

The demise of the evangelical *Christian Examiner* in 1868 deprived the mission of an Irish publication sympathetic to its objectives and motivations. From that time the ICM went almost unnoticed in the Irish media. Little mention is to be found in the *Irish Ecclesiastical Gazette*. While readers of *The Banner* were kept abreast of the mission's claimed successes, the general public was becoming less and less aware of its activities.

Perhaps the most striking case of omission is the complete lack of reference to the ICM in the obituary of Revd Hyacinth D'Arcy, founder and superintendent of the Clifden mission, and the man who had originally invited Dallas to Connemara.[121] Gradually, the ICM disappeared from notice. The *Irish Ecclesiastical Gazette* mentioned damage to the ICM boat and vandalism of property belonging to Protestants at Moyrus in 1894, but when a report of the schoolhouse at Lavally near Tuam appeared in 1894 there was no reference to the ICM, although it had provided teachers since 1869 and would continue to do so until 1904.[122] When it was reported in 1890 that there were twenty-two persons confirmed in Oughterard church and when a new church-organ was dedicated there in 1897, no mention was made of the ICM, although the Oughterard mission functioned until 1900.[123] In 1894, when Roundstone church was re-opened following renovations, a long article appeared in the *Irish Ecclesiastical Gazette* reviewing the history of the parish, but no reference whatsoever was made to the ICM, which had operated a mission there since 1851.[124] Clearly by 1894, the ICM did not feature prominently in the lives of Roundstone Protestants. After 1900, little mention was made of the ICM in the various reports of movements of clerical personnel into and out of missionary parishes, and reports detailing transfers and deaths of long-serving ICM clergymen.[125] The re-opening of the Mission Church in Dublin, which was attended by the ardent mission supporter, Archbishop W. C. Plunket, was reported.[126] The reception of converts at the Mission Church, Townsend St. is reported in 1893 and again in 1896.[127] Plunket's successor, Joseph Peacocke (1897–1915) clearly approved of the ICM's work. In 1908 he dedicated the Mission Church's new pulpit, lectern and prayer desk at a reception ceremony for four converts.[128] In 1902 an article in the *Irish Ecclesiastical Gazette* on Connemara as a tourist resort suggested that the visitor might take the 'opportunity to visit the pretty little church at Ballinahinch' but no reference was made to the origins of the building or to the ICM.[129] Mission work in Connemara had once been a magnet for interested observers, eagerly advertising its successes. Fifty years later, in the principal organ of the Church of Ireland, the mission at best went unnoticed.

The ICM's 1902–3 *Annual report* described the mission's work among lapsed Protestants or 'perverts', mostly the result of mixed marriages. The ICM consistently and strenuously protested against the Ne Temere decree (1908) which demanded that children of mixed marriages be raised as Catholics.[130] It is probable that this defensive aspect of its work, rather than its aggressive missions to Catholics, won the approval of the Irish bishops, as evidence exists that the Church of Ireland had adopted a more confrontational attitude by that time. For example, in 1915 the Dublin diocese published *An Elementary Catechism* which detailed Protestant objections to Catholicism.[131]

In 1908 an extremely anti-Catholic publication by the ICM's superintendent, Henry Fishe, clearly demonstrates the unspoken political agenda of the ICM in the early twentieth century. The fact that this work was originally printed in the *Church of Ireland Gazette* shows that these opinions commanded support among the main body of Irish Protestantism. Revd Fishe explained the Protestant duty to 'make known this fraud [Catholicism] to those upon whom the burden is imposed', adding that Catholicism was not just a 'mere religious society' but was an 'overgrown political machine ... utterly unscrupulous in her methods'. He considered that history as taught by the Irish Christian Brothers was 'steeped in untrue pictures of the past' and calculated to make children disloyal to the crown and bitter towards Protestants. The ICM was by then clearly targeting Protestants as well as Catholics, arguing that 'our duty towards our Roman Catholic brethren lies largely in the carrying out of our duty towards our own Church',[132] while Catholic opinion considered that Revd Fishe's works were designed to hold Protestants back 'from the one True Church'.[133]

The ICM's popularity was increased by its public stance, not only against the errors of Rome, but also against any erosion of Protestant interests, whether political or cultural. J. O. Alston, a former ICM agent, protested in 1913 against the history text book written by Mrs Stephen Gwynn, which was a 'decidedly anti-English and anti-Protestant book'; this sentiment was supported by Revd W. L. Giff, ICM superintendent, who objected to the tone of history books used in some Catholic schools, a matter which was 'of the deepest importance to the future of Protestantism in Ireland'.[134]

A telling episode occurred in 1919, which helps reveal the location of the ICM within Irish Protestantism. The Priests' Protection Society, which aided convert-priests, needed a room in which to hold meetings, having recently sold its own premises. On being approached, the YMCA declined to accommodate them, stating that it considered that it was 'not in the best interests of Protestantism in Dublin for the Priests' Protection Society to have the same premises as the YMCA'.[135] The ICM had no such concerns and henceforth Priests' Protection Society meetings were held in the Mission Buildings, Townsend Street. A suggestion in 1923 that the two societies amalgamate did not proceed due to legal difficulties.[136] Clearly the Priests' Protection Society, which was shunned by the evangelical YMCA, was acceptable to the ICM.

The ICM may have maintained a lower profile in the twentieth century, as a contributor to the *Church of Ireland Gazette* of 4 February 1921 made no reference to the ICM when he argued the need to expose the errors of Rome, bemoaning the fact that the Church of Ireland was content to support 'Missions to the heathen', while ignoring 'Missions to our own'. The *Gazette* regularly outlined the need for societies such as the ICM, which would clearly address the dangers to which young people were exposed.[137] This need was echoed in a letter from Revd William Colgan, formerly missionary at Inverin, who urged a thorough grounding of Protestant principles as 'every army, if not forearmed, is in danger of absorption'.[138]

When an article in the *Church of Ireland Gazette* of 26 January 1917 pessimistically outlined the demise of Irish Protestantism, Revd Goff, ICM superintendent 1910–19, informed the readership that 350 adults had publicly converted in the Mission Church over the previous years, stating that over 100 Anglican clergy in Ireland and England were converts or sons of converts.[139] In spite of this, the Society had to admit its difficulty attracting workers, writing that

> the bulk of Evangelical opinion has moved away from the original position of the Society; the Society has not kept in touch with the development of thought even of those whose general sympathy with the Evangelical tradition would naturally draw them to it; and the Society is narrower than the Church.[140]

The Banner grew increasingly political in the early years of the twentieth century, detailing victimisation of Protestants at the hands of the Catholic Association, such as the non-employment of Protestants following the passing of the Local Government Act of 1898, the boycotting of Protestant businesses, the sacking of Protestant staff and physical violence against Protestants.[141] The editor wished that the English public would realise the difficulties of Protestants living in the south and west of Ireland and advised that 'it was time for Protestants to combine in self-defence'.[142] It detailed activities of Protestant societies, explaining how power in Ireland was being transferred from the 'loyalists to the disloyalists' and advised supporters to read the monthly *Grievances from Ireland* which reported abuses suffered by Protestants.[143] In an article entitled 'Why Irish Protestants fear Home Rule', supporters were warned that Irish Protestants had 'good cause to fear if power is placed in the hands of men who are still under the domination of the Roman bishops and priests', and a Connemara missionary reported how, under priestly orders, boycottings of earlier years had recommenced and the windows of a mission church were broken, informing readers that he had to 'go armed'.[144]

Even unionists were disturbed at some intemperate pronouncements emanating from England. In the tense atmosphere of the United Irish League campaign against both Catholic and Protestant grazing farms, arrogant 'unwise Protestants' and 'over-confident Protestants of the United Kingdom' who spoke out publicly were criticised in *Grievances*, which reminded readers of Catholic promises that Ireland would never 'recover herself' until 'Protestant Missionaries and Protestant Ministers generally and Protestant landlords and Protestant places of worship are swept out of the land'.[145]

The contest for control in Ireland between Irish separatists and the British state, which dominated Irish politics between 1885 and 1920, although portrayed as a conflict of nationalities was experienced by many as a conflict of religions. From the Protestant perspective, superstitious Catholics were less suitable to govern the country than bible-reading Protestants.[146] The sense of terror of the Protestant minority may be gleaned from *Real pictures of clerical life in Ireland*, which told horror stories of violence meted out to Protestants at the instigation of priests. One story told of a priest's visit to a dying convert scripture reader, mortally injured by a Catholic mob. The author described his own efforts to prevent the priest's attempt to anoint the reader and that a Catholic crowd shrieked and hooted at the subsequent burial. Another story told of a convert being stoned to death. The veracity of these stories is doubtful as they went unmentioned in *The Banner* and although the area may have been associated with a different missionary society, it is unlikely that a sectarian murder of this nature would have gone unreported.[147] The popularity of works of this nature may be inferred by a second printing of this book in 1900, fifteen years after its original publication.

The Banner regularly reiterated its conviction that Catholic education fostered disloyalty and rebellion among the Irish. Supporters were told that the 1916 rising was 'largely the result of a closed Bible and the fruit of that education which Rome in Ireland has given to her children' and that the *Catholic Bulletin* advised its readers that taking part in the rising was 'in perfect keeping with the religiousness of some of the leaders'.[148] This observation is not without substantial foundation,[149] as teachers in Catholic schools had been urged to breed a spirit of nationalism in their pupils.[150] As the lawlessness continued into 1918, the need for increased missionary activity was outlined. *The Banner* told readers that 'never before was there more clear a call for the work of the Irish Church Missions',[151] and the Primate urged the merits of disseminating the scriptures as

There is only one thing that can make Ireland great and glorious and free. That is the very gift denied her at the time of the Reformation – God's Word in a tongue understanded [sic] by the people. God's Word proclaimed, received and obeyed. What no Act of Parliament can do, God's Word can do. It can destroy sedition, enmity, hatred, lawlessness, disobedience.[152]

Following the election of the Sinn Féin government in 1918, a three-day meeting held at the ICM's Dublin headquarters but convened by the Evangelical Alliance, heard that, although Ireland had been spared the Bolshevism of Russia, republicanism was widespread. According to *The Banner*, republicanism was supported by the priests who were largely responsible for the state of the country.[153] This meeting marked a turning point for the ICM, indicating a movement towards pan-Protestant mission in the face of increasing Romanist power. *The Banner* became a voice for beleaguered Protestants; it bemoaned the betrayal of loyal Irish Protestants and urged that 'Great Britain must reconquer Ireland' as the prospect of southern Protestants being handed over 'to be ruled by the Empire's bitterest enemies' could not be permitted.[154] By 1921 the ICM was desperately appealing for increased funds, asserting that 'the ICM exists for a time such as this', since it was surely 'not the will of God that we should weaken the outposts for God's Truth in the midst of the domains of Rome'.[155] Immediately after the Irish Free State was formed, *The Banner* asserted that 'the present distress is largely the result of unhappy divisions ... separation, suspicion, distrust and hatred between man and man'. It asked *'How is a divided people to be unified?'* and replied that this could only happen through the evangelisation of Ireland, which, it argued, had never been properly attempted by the Protestant churches.[156]

Copying Dallas' sending out of 20,000 copies of *A Voice from Heaven* in 1846, the ICM sent out 20,270 copies of 'An appeal to thoughtful Irishmen' in April 1921, which encouraged Irish Catholics, in much more moderate language, to embrace the scriptural truth, very gently explaining the errors of Rome. Supporters were assured that 'wonderful opportunities' existed if only the means were provided, that the ICM would 'lead our fellow countrymen into the way of Righteousness and Peace'.[157] Even in the face of unremitting danger and Catholic supremacy, the ICM clearly considered that it was duty-bound to bring the Gospel to Irish Catholics. Its 1921 report concluded with a rallying call to evangelise Ireland, arguing that

> when we see ... on the one hand deeds of butchery which would be a disgrace to the lowest tribes of darkest Africa, and on the other hand through a perverted form of our Christian religion, God robbed of His honour, and many of our devout fellow-countrymen deprived of that knowledge of a full, free, present salvation which is more precious than life itself, then we are verily guilty if, passing on the Message to others, we pass by those in deepest need at our very doors.[158]

The ICM in the Irish Free State, 1922–50

The work of the Irish Church Missions was largely uninterrupted by the creation of the Irish Free State in 1922, although its 'loyal Protestants were disappointed and disgusted at the weak-kneed attitude of the British authorities towards the papacy'.[159] Mission buildings and personnel came under attack during the ensuing civil war: Ballyconree Orphanage, Connemara, was burned on 22 June 1922; Limerick mission was attacked in August 1922; Moyrus church and parsonage were gutted by fire in November 1922 and Ballinaboy was attacked in February 1923. The children of Ballyconree and Glenowen were evacuated to England in July 1922.[160] When Ballyconree's boys were subsequently relocated to the Burnside Homes at Parramatta, near Syndey, *The Banner* observed that this ended 'a chapter of Christian work amongst boys in Ireland which has lasted for seventy years, and which made the greatest possible difference in the lives of hundreds of boys who are now worthy sons of the British Empire in different parts of the world'.[161] It is likely that the home's overt identification with the crown resulted in its destruction. Alannah Heather remembered Ballyconree's Boy Scouts saluting the British flag on the lawn every morning.[162] It is remembered locally that the boys marched to Clifden church on Sundays behind the Union Jack. With the orphanage's closure, Ballyconree church ceased to function. Moyrus church was not rebuilt.[163] By then mission work in Connemara had effectively ceased.

Throughout the first half of the twentieth century the ICM continued to focus much of its missionary work on children, especially in Dublin, to where it gradually relocated all its western orphanages; Galway Children's Home was turned into a 'Soldiers' Rest' in 1917. Nead na Farraige was transferred from Spiddal to Dublin in 1917 due to local boycotting; it was amalgamated with the Birds' Nest, Kingstown in 1920.[164] Aasleagh Orphanage moved from Leenane, on the Mayo–Galway border to Lurgan Street, Dublin in 1929. Work continued through the ICM's Dublin schools, augmented by house visiting and street preaching at fairs and in the capital. As the caption which accompanied a photograph of Dublin schoolchildren printed in *The Banner* demonstrates, it had raised many children above the 'flotsam and jetsam of humanity' (see figure 6.2).

Opposition to open-air preaching did not end with the passage of the Home Rule Bill and the creation of the Irish Free State. ICM agent, Edward Savage, told how an abusive crowd drove a herd of bullocks at mission workers, requiring a police escort from town.[165] The ICM claimed that there was 'no religious freedom in a large portion of the Irish Free State' although the ICM was granted permits for weekly open-air meetings at Dun Laoghaire (Kingstown).[166] Protestant clergymen directed 'enquirers'

This picture shows a group taken at the Boys' Home, Grand Canal Street, Dublin. The teachers are three members of the Dublin Mission Staff, Messrs. Winch, Strahan, and Flores. Many of these boys would be growing up as part of the flotsam and jetsam of humanity to-day were it not for the work of Miss Annie D. Smyly, in co-operation with the I.C.M. Now they are growing up in the knowledge of God as their Saviour, and are being trained for useful citizenship. We thank you for your prayers and offerings towards the continuance of this good work.

6.2 Residents at Grand Canal Street Boys' Home, 1924.
Source: *The Banner of the Truth*, October 1924

to the ICM by, as if a potential convert were seen approaching the local rector

> [he] is cursed by the priest, he is boycotted or beaten, probably both, and so compelled to leave the place; the Rector is marked out as a 'souper' … he becomes the scorn of all the priest's bodyguard, he is probably insulted by day or raided by night; his vestry, for the sake of peace, will very likely ask him to refrain from interference with Roman Catholics, and so he is compelled to desist or take the consequences. This is the plight of inquirers in the rural districts of the Free State; this is Rome's idea of tolerance.[167]

In 1928 the ICM delivered 143 indoor lectures in church halls and schools throughout the country, along with sixty-three open-air meetings.[168] By then audiences were predominantly Protestant as the mission increasingly responded to Protestant needs. A week's mission in County Cavan drew average nightly attendances of over 200 persons.[169] The ICM claimed they were 'sowing the seed of inquiry', which led some to leave the Church of Rome; the extent of these conversions cannot be ascertained.[170]

The Banner related ICM successes, naming its converts and enquirers,[171] such as J. E. McCrory from the north of Ireland, who realised that it was Rome's ambition 'to keep the Bible wholly out of the hands of their people'. He subsequently underwent training to become an ICM agent but was transferred to colporteur work due to academic weakness.[172] As was common, his conversion and that of Monica Farrell (see below) resulted in severe persecution, forcing them to leave home and family. Another convert similarly told how he dared not visit his home as his father 'would have turned me out owing to his fear of the priests, but the powers of the latter are declining since the establishment of the Free State'.[173] This former Sinn Féin supporter must have indeed undergone a cathartic change, as he aptly described the intertwining of religion and ethnicity in early-twentieth-century Ireland, when Irishmen looked on England not only as a political enemy but 'also as an enemy of their faith, in fact they look upon the name England and Protestant as synonymous terms'.[174] The veracity of this statement is borne out in the literary work, *Creideamh agus gorta* [*Faith and famine*], as discussed in Chapter 7.

With twenty-five to thirty public conversions annually, a sizeable convert community in Dublin was in regular contact with the ICM through mission services, house visits[175] and convert reunions.[176] Opposition from family and neighbours forced many to emigrate such as Michael S—, an obviously well-educated man who had converted in Townsend Street in 1928. Without doubt, his conversion was doctrinal in nature; he wrote that 'one was confronted [in Catholicism] with an infinite variety and number of codified and tabulated sins, venial and mortal, sins against the Decalogue, and sins against the commandments of the Church'. Intense opposition and lack of employment forced him to place his three older children in Smyly homes and move himself, his wife and two younger children to Middlesex. Throughout his struggles, he drew strength from the scriptures since reading the New Testament was 'like putting on a suit of armour'.[177] Few converts were as eloquent or as erudite as Michael S— and most lived in the very poorest areas of Dublin, regularly appealing to the ICM for relief.[178] One suggested that he received little aid from the ICM because he was a steadfast convert, unlike those who lived with 'one foot in Gardiner St. and the other in Townsend St.',[179] while another complained that he had not received his 'conversion grant', writing that

> I have not gone back to be a RC as I do not want to go. I do not believe in their teachin [sic] and I mean to stick to it and I would like to get confermed [sic] with you and become a proper Christian ... Well Mr Hammond, have I not to get the grant that you promised me as I did not get any money sens [sic] I was speaking to yourself as I tout [sic] that grant was to help me to be safe from any one people in case they might put me out.[180]

Correspondence from this man reveals that he felt entitled to six months' income of 30s. per week, which was eventually paid to him in instalments. He was dissatisfied with this arrangement as he had hoped to use a lump sum to purchase a lorry. Reliance on the ICM to source employment was commonplace among converts, such as Patrick C— from Ballylinan, County Leix, who wrote that he had 'turned over for the Church of Ireland last year and the Roman Catholics would not give me any work so you promised to me that if I did not get work, the Church of Ireland would not let me down'.[181] Dublin's poor proved adept at securing relief by astutely manipulating the rivalry between religious organisations. Lily O'Connor, a Dublin child of a mixed marriage, told how her mother was provided with turf and coal by the local rector, and with vouchers from the St Vincent de Paul Society when she agreed to send her children to Catholic schools.[182]

It is difficult to estimate the extent of the ICM's success in the twentieth century. *The Banner* insisted that a great interest in the doctrinal merits of Protestantism existed among the Catholic population: 'I never remember such an influx of inquiring Romanists and interested Protestants'[183] and that many received 'the vision of the Saviour through one of the Testaments sold by the I.C.M. agents in fairs and markets'.[184] The ICM claimed that 'hundreds of Roman Catholics are only so in name and would revolt at any time, if only some man strong enough to lead would appear'.[185]

Opposition and antagonism were an ongoing problem for converts and mission agents.[186] It was claimed that the last rites were forcibly administered to dying converts,[187] while elsewhere an agent told how a relative of a potential convert 'grasped the bread knife and made to disfigure my face with it'.[188] Although correspondence and a list of converts in the ICM's archives verify the presence of a considerable number of converts and enquirers, the sincerity or longevity of conversions cannot be ascertained. The validity of the convert list has to be accepted at face value, but it should be considered that agents may have been under pressure to produce evidence of success for the London Committee. The 1932 listing of converts includes sixty-nine persons denoted 'Mrs' without any mention of husbands, suggesting that mothers may have associated with the ICM to receive aid for the families (although the term 'Mrs' was regularly applied to respectable unmarried women).[189] Cross-referencing the 1932 convert list with an ICM roll book of 1935 reveals that some families on the convert list were recorded as original Protestants on the school-roll, suggesting that the 1932 record of converts may not be wholly factual.[190] In spite of this caveat, ICM correspondence and an address book of pupils at its Coombe School verify that the mission attracted converts from Dublin's most destitute and depressed districts, although it also appealed to a small number of more educated converts.[191]

The prevalence of Protestant missionary activity was a great concern to the Catholic church. One priest told how he regularly 'in every corner ... comes across the manoeuvrings of the proselytiser',[192] while another reported that 'the work of the Soupers is changed in method only, it flourishes in our land ... Still their work goes on stealthily and is well paid for'.[193] Eleven consecutive journal articles in the (Catholic) *Irish Ecclesiastical Record* during 1922–23 warned the Catholic reader that it was not

> a bygone occupation, a lost art, an out-of-date pastime. It is wholesale in some of our cities; it is met with in our towns, and quiet country places are sniped, and the victims sent to receiving stations in big centres ... priests should know that the traffic in servants' souls goes on amongst the populace of Ireland.[194]

The intolerance of Catholic Ireland to Protestantism in the early years of the Irish Free State was shown by the intemperate letter of Bishop O'Doherty of Galway which warned his people 'against the despicable endeavours of the so-called Bible Societies' and denounced the distribution of an edition of the New Testament 'without note or comment', admonishing that if 'these heretics persist in ignoring the laws of our Church further action will be necessary'. It should be noted that the Testament in question was authorised by the Catholic church.[195]

Catholic authorities showed little sympathy to those who availed of mission services, considering that there was 'ample Catholic charity, which may however be inferior or more crowded'.[196] They considered that the availability of Catholic education and relief diminished the ICM's appeal, and therefore 'proselytising inducements have correspondingly lost in power'.[197] This author patronisingly described the recipients of ICM relief as generally 'troubled with drink' whose daughters had 'gravitated to the streets'.[198]

The ICM's Dublin schools functioned into the mid twentieth century and its children's homes continued until changing social attitudes and policies resulted in the almost complete demise of institutional care in the late twentieth century. By 1922, its pupils were predominantly from Protestant or mixed families; 74 per cent of pupils came from Protestant homes in 1935 (compared with 34 per cent in 1885). Between 1885 and 1934, attendance at the ICM's Dublin schools decreased from 1,203 to 564. By then, all its western schools had closed.

Although it was repeatedly suggested that money could be saved by placing schools under the National Board, this was strongly resisted by the ICM as control of teaching would pass from the mission and also because ICM-trained teachers were not qualified national school-teachers. However, as academic standards in its schools declined, the mission was forced to employ trained national school-teachers.[199] In 1964 the last remaining mission school closed when the children of the Birds' Nest, Kingstown were transferred to Monkstown Parish National School.[200] This severed the connection which had existed for over a century between the ICM and its various children's homes.

The Irish Church Missions acknowledged that it bolstered Irish Protestantism against the incursion of Catholicism, explaining that an important part of its work was frustrating the efforts of 'the Roman Catholic Church to snip off our people, one by one, from our Faith'.[201] During the first half of the twentieth century it provided backing to Protestant parties in contentious mixed marriages.[202] It also functioned in linking vacancies in Protestant firms with those seeking employment.[203] A Dublin employer 'naturally wished to help my own people, although this is difficult for various reasons' while an English supporter offered work to someone who might need a position 'out of Ireland'.[204] As employment was highly dependent on personal recommendation, it could be utilised by Catholics and Protestants alike to entice conversions. One Protestant, who had been offered work if he converted, complained to the ICM that the Church of Ireland was unconcerned about 'the young men of their parish's [sic] and what becomes of them'.[205]

The ICM was not alone in its efforts to disseminate the scriptures. The need to evangelise the Catholics of the Irish Free State was shared across the Protestant denominations, but less aggressively. Fourteen Presbyterian colporteurs systematically covered the country in the early years of the Free State, 'not to proselytise, not to bring Roman Catholics into the Presbyterian Church but to bring them to "vital union with Christ"'. The Presbyterian church considered this essential as Catholics were beginning to read the scriptures and think independently but were in danger of becoming involved in communism.[206] Convert mission worker, Monica Farrell, also considered that it was only a matter of time until Ireland 'either declares on the side of Protestantism or joins the number of other disillusioned, but unenlightened Roman Catholics, which swell the ranks of the Communist Party'.[207] When an accusation of exaggerated colporteur sales was made in 1932, the ICM, the Methodist Church Colportage Society and the Presbyterian Church in Ireland produced a combined response.[208] In 1951, the Presbyterian church asserted that 'never more was the work of the Irish Mission more urgently needed than at present' and there were 'many devout Roman Catholics, dissatisfied with the teaching and practices of their Church'.[209]

Although Protestant missions in general became less overtly controversial during the twentieth century, accessing Catholics in domestic settings where colporteurs advocated personal access to the scriptures rather than outlining the 'errors of Romanism', the ICM continued its direct denunciation of Catholicism in 'Townsend Mission Hall' which Catholic authorities described as 'the most evil of all the Souper activities, and probably the least successful'.[210]

The experience of The Children's Fold, founded in 1920 to receive Catholic infants, shows how an ICM activity, founded to convert Catholic children, came to answer Protestant needs. By the early twentieth century, ICM homes catered increasingly for Protestant children.[211] In 1920 the ICM founded The Children's Fold, a home and adoption service for children born to unmarried Catholic mothers, who were excluded from its existing homes.[212] It differed from the other homes associated with the mission in that it was directly managed by the ICM itself. A detailed exploration of the workings of The Fold is outside the scope of this study, but the following observations may be made. The Fold was originally located in Newmarket Street, in the recently vacated Coombe Boys' Home,[213] and subsequently at Sheeana in County Wicklow until 1945 where the children's presence bolstered numbers in the local school; a small number of children remained in Sheeana until 1949.[214] It was located at 'The Boley' in Monkstown from 1945 until the mid 1960s, when its children were transferred to the Birds' Nest in Dun Laoghaire which modified its constitution to accept children born out of wedlock.

Although a minority of Catholic children were admitted to The Fold, most applications came from Protestants of all denominations from both northern and southern Ireland. Initial contact was generally made by a clergyman. Parents were required to agree to their children being brought up in the Church of Ireland. Some parents also agreed to adoption although this was not obligatory. Catholic children were not re-baptised, but those whose baptism could not be verified were baptised in the Mission Church, Townsend Street. Parents were required to contribute varying amounts from ten shillings to two pounds monthly until adoption was arranged but payment was not universally forthcoming. It was common for more than one child of the same family to be admitted and these were not necessarily kept together. Babies under two years were boarded with nurse mothers, who sometimes had two or three children at a time. Some children were transferred to residential care in The Fold at two years of age but others stayed with their nurse mothers throughout childhood. From the correspondence of nurse mothers and ICM staff, it is obvious that these children were generally well cared for.

Prior to the Adoption Act of 1952, The Fold organised adoptions on a fairly *ad hoc* basis. In common with Catholic adoption agencies, there was a surplus of children over prospective adoptive parents. Children were occasionally returned as 'unsuitable' and from today's viewpoint the selection process for adoptive parents appears inadequate. Extra details regarding the child's health and the background of the adoptive parents are contained in the files of children adopted to the United States. After 1952, many existing adoptions were retrospectively legalised; in some cases the birth-mother was untraceable, frustrating but not always totally blocking this process. Prior to 1952, school-going children were adopted into rural areas for the expressed purpose of maintaining numbers in Protestant schools. For example, the ICM declined to take a house near Ballintone, County Wicklow in 1936 to ensure the continuance of the local school, as this was 'scarcely fulfilling the object of the Irish Church Missions to Roman Catholics', but suggested that 'a number of children could be procured and placed in the homes of the local Protestants'.[215]

The Fold provided a much needed service for unmarried Protestant girls, who constituted the vast majority of its birth-mothers. The London Committee, however, felt that this did not fall within its remit, i.e. the conversion of Irish Catholics and in January 1950 ordered the closure of The Fold. The Irish Committee was aware that this was not merely a financial decision. When the Dublin superintendent was subsequently severely rebuked for admitting Protestants, he explained that these children would otherwise be placed in Catholic institutions and expressed great surprise that Protestants should have to 'make Roman Catholics of their children', while 'we assisted Rome by spending much time and money in rearing their children for them'. The London Committee could not appreciate this argument and the superintendent was ordered to henceforth admit only Catholic children.[216]

Throughout the first half of the twentieth century, ongoing tension between London and Dublin is evident. In 1937 the Dublin Committee disclaimed all responsibility for *The Banner* and when the London Committee proposed in 1939 that a memorial be brought before the General Synod of the Church of Ireland to commemorate the anniversary of the Society, the Irish Committee very strenuously opposed the suggestion as 'many Southern members will not co-operate because they are afraid'.[217] It was constantly inferred that the London Committee was unaware of the reality of the Irish situation and proposed that the English committee members should make efforts to acquire 'a personal knowledge of the work and prevailing conditions' in Ireland.[218]

The gulf between the Dublin and London committees reflected a lack of sensitivity on the part of committed English evangelicals to the reality of Protestant life in the increasingly Catholic dominated Free State. It is evident that the ICM was merely a component of global evangelicalism which focused on the errors of Rome, as shown by its 1932 correspondence which indicates an intense interest in detailing the short comings of Catholicism and in counteracting the potential danger of mixed marriages.[219] In this role, the Society maintained steady communication with like-minded persons and organisations in Britain and overseas,[220] many of whom sought blessings on the work of the ICM.[221] Deputations from biblical societies preached in the Mission Church[222] while others invited ICM agents to address audiences throughout Britain. As editor of *The Catholic*,[223] T. C. Hammond's opinion of Catholicism was widely disseminated and his regular output of sermons and publications was held in high esteem in evangelical circles, leading to frequent invitations to preach and write for scriptural societies.[224] The sources of these invitations ranged from the extreme Scottish Reformation Society[225] to the moderate Peter Gibson of Ridley Hall, Cambridge.[226] The ICM, and especially T. C. Hammond, commanded a global influence. In 1932 he was appointed principal of Moore Theological College Sydney, where he was instrumental in developing a college which has remained at the forefront of evangelicalism. It is directly due to the influence of T. C. Hammond that the bishop of Sydney does not wear a pectoral cross.

The ICM was not a uniquely Irish movement, but it was almost unique in Ireland, partnered by *The Catholic*, a periodical which focused almost entirely on the errors of Rome. Although its ethos and methodologies concurred with those of global evangelicalism, the ICM differed from other Reformation organisations in that it operated in a country where Protestants were greatly outnumbered by Catholics and where aggressive proselytism might have been considered unwise.

It is evident that the ICM was not universally supported among Irish Protestants. When an anonymous letter was circulated among supporters in 1936, the Irish Committee decided not to publish a reply in *The Banner* lest they give too much information to their critics, opting instead to produce a pamphlet for circulation among their supporters.[227] In 1938, the *Evening Mail* refused to accept ICM advertisements and four bishops threatened to resign their vice-presidencies; in 1939 the bishop of Cork did so.[228] W. E. Stanford, commenting in 1946 on how southern Protestants could be of spiritual benefit to Ireland, considered that missionary campaigns such as open-air preaching would be unacceptable since most would dismiss them as 'more proselytism'[229] and in 1949 the Fold children at Sheeana were removed to the Boley as the rector was 'no longer in favour of continuing the present connection with [the] ICM'.[230]

The celebration of the ICM's centenary in 1946 casts much light both on the location of the ICM within Irish Anglicanism and on the insensitivity of the London Committee to the realities of a minority religion in the newly formed, largely Catholic, Irish Free State. The Primate, John Allen Fitzgerald Gregg, declined an invitation from the ICM superintendent to its centenary celebrations. The Primate's disapproval of aggressive missionary work among Irish Catholics is glaringly obvious; he considered that 'a public commemoration ... would be in my opinion an ill-advised step'.[231] He understood the realities of Protestant life in the newly formed Free State, having served over forty years of his career within its territory. In spite of his strong protests against Roman Catholic doctrine, the Primate was a close personal friend of Cardinal Logue and of his successors, Cardinals O'Donnell and McRory.[232] The Primate stated that the Church of Ireland was currently 'on sufferance' in southern Ireland and that Catholicism was 'in the saddle'. He decried the use of controversial literature and reminded the ICM that Protestants in southern Ireland had to reside and earn their living among the now-dominant Catholic population. He clearly outlined that he had personally lived in the republic and had first hand justification for his refusal. Thus, a hundred years after the foundation of the Society, the Primate of the Church of Ireland was distinctly out of sympathy with the objectives and methodologies of the Irish Church Missions while the London Committee were clearly out of touch with the sensitivities of southern Irish Anglicans.

The activities of missionary societies of other Protestant denominations seem to mirror the ICM's shift in direction, functioning less as direct missions to Catholics and more as organisations to safeguard the Protestant population from any form of erosion; the Dublin missions of the Presbyterian church concentrated on visits to former Protestants, often to participants in mixed marriages. In contrast to the ICM (whose operations in Ulster were limited), the Presbyterian missions increasingly concentrated their efforts in the northern counties but maintained their existing missions in Connaught. The Presbyterian Church of Ireland maintained its Ballina orphanage until 1904 and subsidised the fourteen congregations of the Connaught presbytery, but also subsidised 'weak congregations' in the three other provinces.

Although the Presbyterian Home Mission prioritised the needs of its existing churchmen, as when it ministered at Kinsale to fishermen from Scotland and the north of Ireland, it also strove to aggressively win 'the conversion of Roman Catholics to the faith of the Lord Jesus Christ', asserting in 1891 that it had already led many 'from the darkness of Romish superstition'.[233] It maintained its mission to the Catholics of the Irish Free State, reminding its members in 1951 that 'as an Evangelical Church, our supreme task is to circulate the Scriptures as never before' but, unlike the ICM, the Presbyterian mission did not openly denounce the doctrines of Rome.[234]

As well as overtly missionary societies, the Irish poor were served by a large number of societies which could variously be described as both charitable and religious, and which served the needs of the Catholic and Protestant poor, such as the 'Island and Coast Society … for the education of children and the promotion of scriptural truth in remote parts of the coast and adjacent islands'. This Society answered the needs of fifteen Protestant families in Glencolmcille, County Donegal who had suffered from the want of 'a safe and suitable school', while at Tourmakeady in

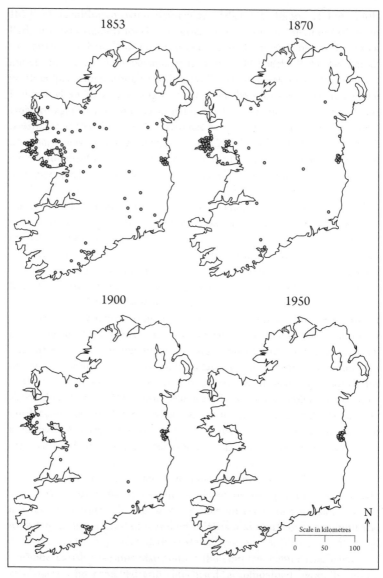

6.3 ICM mission stations in 1853, 1870, 1900 and 1950

County Mayo, a former mission district of the ICM, its superintendent triumphantly reported that 'converts who formerly attended this school are doing good work among their Roman Catholic neighbours'.[235] The large quantities of clothing that were distributed in these schools may have attracted some Catholic pupils. Although the extent of 'soft' proselytism by societies of this nature cannot be quantified, it should not be overlooked, as discussed in the following chapter.

The shifting location and focus of the ICM over the first century of its existence reflects the changes that took place in Ireland over the period. It can be stated that, in many respects, the ICM responded less to the political and social changes than did other proselytising societies, which became more circumspect in their operations. It is clear that not all Irish Anglicans appreciated this approach. It is likely that more progress was made by the other proselytising societies, whose more covert methods may have been more successful in achieving their unvoiced objectives.

Notes

1 This table includes paid missionaries, teachers, scripture readers, bible women, bookshop workers, students and bill distributors; it excludes honorary superintendents, office staff, boatmen, caretakers and local helpers. It excludes agents formerly associated with the Colporteurs Society and Scripture Readers and Irish Society which amalgamated with the ICM in 1894 and 1918 respectively.

2 Sarah Davies, *Other cities also; the story of mission work in Dublin* (Dublin, 1881), p. 1.

3 ICM Archive, ICM minutes, Training School Committee (TSC), 17 Dec. 1889.

4 SBO, *Annual report*, 1881, pp. 6–9 reported the following attendances at ICM homes and schools: Grand Canal Street Boys' Home (160–200), Grand Canal Street schools (80 girls and 132 infants), Elliott Home (admitted 200–300 annually and forwarded them to other homes), Townsend Street schools (130 boys, less girls and more infants), Townsend Street Girls' Home (60), Birds' Nest (212 'in house' and 26 'at nurse'), Coombe Boys' Home (30–40), Coombe schools (160), Lurgan Street (c.50 boys, 50 girls and 100 infants).

5 ICM, *Annual report*, 1891–92, p. 11.

6 *Report of the schools for little ragged children ... Grand Canal-Street, 1885* (n.p., n.d.).

7 E. W. Allden, *Records of gospel work in the streets and lanes of the city* (Dublin, n.d.), p. 6.

8 ICM Archive, ICM minutes, TSC, 14 Dec. 1898.

9 ICM Archive, ICM minutes, TSC, 9 Sept. 1908.

10 ICM Archive, ICM minutes, TSC, 19 Sept. 1900.

11 *Banner of the Truth*, Apr. 1902, p. 27; ICM Archive, ICM agency books.

12 *Banner of the Truth*, Oct. 1891, p. 58.

13 It is not possible to state which schools were open after 1940, as from that date individual school listings were replaced by a single listing of 'Dublin Teachers'.

14 Davies, *Other cities also*, p. 54.

15 Sarah Davies, *St. Patrick's armour: the story of the Coombe Ragged School* (Dublin, 1880), p. 13.

16 Davies, *Other cities also*, pp. 3–4.

17 Personal communication, Violet Oxley, Nov. 2004.

18 Oonagh Walsh, *Anglican women in Dublin: philanthropy, politics and education in the early twentieth century* (Dublin, 2005), p. 88.

19 ICM, *Annual report*, 1908–19, p. 16.

20 Ibid., 1914–15, p. 13.

21 Ibid., 1899–1900, pp. 16–17.

22 Ibid., 1906–07, p. 12.

23 Ibid., 1908–19, p. 13.

24 Allden, *Records of gospel work*, p. 9.

25 SBO, *Annual report*, 1880, p. 5.

26 A Catholic clergyman, *The life of the late Cardinal McCabe, archbishop of Dublin, primate of Ireland, etc. who died on Wednesday, the 11ᵗʰ February 1885, to which is added his last pastoral* (Dublin, 1885), p. 23 (Pastoral dated 9 Feb. 1885.)

27 Thomas J. Morrissey, *William J. Walsh, archbishop of Dublin, 1841–1921* (Dublin, 2000), p. 242; Patrick Walsh, *William J. Walsh, archbishop of Dublin* (Dublin, 1928), pp. 191–5.

28 Walsh, *Anglican women*, pp. 166–7; Jacinta Prunty, *Dublin slums, 1800–1925: a study in urban geography* (Dublin, 1998), p. 273; SBO, *Twenty eighth annual report*, 1885, p. 5; C. H. K. Broughton, *What I saw in Dublin, an address delivered in the Church House, Westminster on May 8ᵗʰ 1914* (Dublin, n.d.), p. 11.

29 *Irish Catholic*, 3 May 1913; 'Record of Irish Eccles. Events 1913' in *Irish Catholic Directory*, 1914, pp. 516–17.

30 *A report of the Saint Vincent de Paul Society on proselytism*, 11 Feb. 1914.

31 Quoted in ICM, *Annual report*, 1902–3, p. 13.

32 ICM, *Annual reports*, 1910–11, p. 12; 1911–12, p. 10; 1912–13, p. 12.

33 *The Leader*, 31 May 1913.

34 ICM, *Annual report*, 1910–11, p. 22.

35 Ibid., 1911–12, p. 18; 1924–25, p. 10; 1925–26, p. 9.

36 *Irish Ecclesiastical Gazette*, 17 Nov. 1893, p. 922.

37 ICM, *Annual report*, 1899–1900, pp. 14, 28–30.

38 Ibid., 1900–1, p. 21.

39 Letter from Benjamin Irwin, *Irish Ecclesiastical Gazette*, 4 June 1885.

40 Martin Maguire, 'The Dublin working-class 1870–1932: economy, society, politics' (MA dissertation, University College, Dublin, 1990), p. 155.

41 Joseph Long, *Medical missions in Ireland* (Dublin, 1925), p. 10.

42 Miriam Moffitt, *Soupers and Jumpers: the Protestant missions in Connemara, 1848–1937* (Dublin, 2008), pp. 136–51.

43 Long, *Medical missions in Ireland*, pp. 13–17.

44 *Banner of the Truth*, July 1899, p. 39.

45 Long, *Medical missions in Ireland*, pp. 19, 66.

46 Colonel Sanderson, Armagh; William Johnston, Belfast.

47 M. Joyce, P. J. O'Shaughnessy and W. Lundon.

48 *Hansard's Parliamentary Debates*, 4th series, 1901 (vol. xcvi), p. 339, hereafter *Hansard 4*.

49 'Parliamentary report', *Irish Times*, 19 June 1901.

50 *Hansard 4*, 1901 (vol. xcv), p. 722.

51 ICM, *Annual report*, 1901–2, p. 35.

52 Ibid., 1907, p. 15.

53 Dermot Keogh and Andrew McCarthy, *Limerick Boycott, 1904: anti-semitism in Ireland* (Cork, 2005), p. 34; *Banner of the Truth*, Jan., Apr., July, Oct. 1904.

54 *Banner of the Truth*, 1 Oct. 1870, p. 55; 1 Oct. 1871, p. 63.

55 ICM, *Annual report*, 1889, p. 10; *Banner of the Truth*, Oct. 1870, p. 55.

56 ICM, *Annual report*, 1892–93, p. 11.

57 Ibid., 1892–93, pp. 10–12, 13.

58 Society for Irish Church Missions, *Irish Church Missions, The itinerating work of the Irish Church Missions, brief jottings of the work in fairs, markets, and villages from itinerants' journals, for private circulation* (London, 1894), pp. 9–10.

59 *Banner of the Truth*, Jan. 1893, p. 10.

60 ICM, *Annual report*, 1884, p. 25.

61 RCBL, MS No. P. 315/4/1, Burial register of Knocktopher.

62 As Anthony McGinley entered the Male Training School in 1857, he must have been at least 85 years of age in 1925.

63 John Ennis was continuously employed by the ICM from 1856 to 1904. ICM Archive, ICM agency books.

64 RCBL, MS Nos P315/2, P315/3, P315/4.

65 ICM, *Annual report*, 1883, p. 12.

66 The ICM's correspondence for 1932 contains evidence of converts being forced to leave their native areas. As the ICM archive does not contain correspondence prior to the late 1920s, earlier evidence of movement of converts is not available, although it is probable that it was a frequent occurrence.

67 ICM, *Annual report*, 1900, pp. 10–11.

68 Ibid., 1899–1900, p. 12.

69 *Sligo Champion*, 22 Aug. 1914.

70 ICM, *Annual report*, 1866, p. 108. £1,269 was paid to five deputation secretaries in England, plus £200 and £358 for clerical and travelling expenses.

71 Among the long-serving agents who died at this time were: Revd Tim Clesham*, Aasleagh (1894); Honor Cafferkey, Moyrus (1893); Miss English, Training School (1893); Maria Nee, Errismore (1894); Revd Peter Davin, Sellerna (1898); Revd Roberts, Oughterard (1899); John Irwin, Dublin (1899); Revd John Conerney*, Sellerna (1900); Mr Harris, Ballyconree Orphanage (1900); John Dormer, Dublin (1900); P. J. Bergin, Louth (1902); William Manning*, Connemara (1902); Canon Thomas Fleming, Connemara (1904); Richard Marks, Dublin (1903); Mrs Julia Coleman, neé Fair, Galway (1904); Benjamin Bennett, Dublin (1907); Thomas O'Malley, Dublin (1907); John Brennan*, Bayleek (1907); Revd Charles MacDonald, Castlekerke (1907); John Ennis, Knocktopher (1907); John Alexander, Dublin (1908); Mrs Agnes Payne, neé Whiteside, Dublin (1908); James Lowry, Dublin (1909); Mrs

Elizabeth Carleton, Renvyle (1909); Thomas Condron, Dublin (1910); Pat Gallagher*, Connemara (1910); John Mellett*, Connemara (1911); Thomas Coleman, Galway (1913); Michael Mannion*, Connemara (1913); John Lavelle*, Connemara (1914); George Coulter, Limerick (1915); John Conry*, Connemara (1916); James Lyden*, Errismore (1918); Stephen Coursey*, Connemara (1919); Samuel O'Malley*, Dublin (1919); Miss Bloomer, Dublin (1919); Mrs Michael MacNamara*, Connemara (1919); Miss McGreal, Bunlahinch (1920); Pat McNamara*, Connemara (1920); Francis Quinn, Dundalk (1920); Miss Johnson, Dublin (1920); John B. King*, Connemara (1921); Val King*, Moyrus (1921); Mrs John Irwin, Dublin (1922); Miss Hughes, Birds' Nest (1922); Revd James Agnew, Dublin (1924); Revd Thomas Nee*, Connemara (1924). Most of these had served for fifty years; those marked with an asterisk have been verified as converts.

72 ICM, *Annual report*, 1926–27, p. 15.
73 Ibid., 1908–9, p. 20; 1910–11, p. 19. Others in the 'little band' were sisters Helen Leaper Newton d. 1902, Mrs H. A. Norman, formerly Miss L. B. Newton d. 1900, and Mrs E. S. Rogers, neé Pitter, d. 1907. *Banner of the Truth*, Apr. 1900, p. 29; Apr. 1902, p. 27; Apr. 1907, p. 96.
74 *Banner of the Truth*, Jan. 1922, pp. 3–4.
75 Ibid., Apr. 1891, p. 18; ibid., Apr. 1894, p. 6.
76 Ibid., Jan. 1891, p. 15; ibid., Oct. 1891, p. 56.
77 ICM, *Annual report*, 1887, p. 19.
78 Ibid., 1890, p. 17.
79 Ibid., 1887, p. 17.
80 Ibid., 1891–92, p. 11.
81 Ibid., 1898–99, p. 27.
82 ICM Archive, ICM minutes, TSC, 26 June 1900.
83 Matthew Kelly, 'The politics of Protestant street-preaching in the 1890s', *Historical Journal*, xxxxviii (2005), 101–25; Martin Doherty, 'Religion, community relations and constructive unionism. The Arklow street-preaching disturbances 1890–92' in James H. Murphy (ed.), *Evangelicals and Catholics in nineteenth-century Ireland* (Dublin, 2005), pp. 223–34.
84 *Cork Examiner*, 27 Dec. 1893.
85 *Cork Examiner*, 21 Apr. 1894.
86 *Irish Times*, 26 Dec. 1893.
87 Doherty, 'Religion, community relations and constructive unionism', p. 234.
88 *Banner of the Truth*, Oct. 1893, p. 2; ibid., Jan. 1894, pp. 5–6.
89 *Irish Ecclesiastical Gazette*, 8 Dec. 1893, p. 982.
90 *Banner of the Truth*, July 1893, p. 6.
91 David Hempton, *Religion and political discourse in Britain and Ireland* (Cambridge, 1996), pp. 106–13.
92 *Cork Examiner*, 13. Apr. 1894.
93 Kelly, 'The politics of Protestant street-preaching', p. 108.
94 Warren Nelson, *T. C. Hammond: his life and legacy in Ireland and Australia* (Edinburgh, 1994), p. 38.
95 *Banner of the Truth*, Apr. 1896, p. 2; Jan. 1901, p. 8; Apr. 1901, p. 21.

96 Ibid., Apr. 1896, p. 6.
97 Paul Ledoux, *The Church of Ireland and the Roman mission in Ireland, which has orders from St Patrick: a controversy which arose out of the street-preaching riots in Sligo* (Sligo, 1896), pp. 5, 7.
98 Strict orders from Catholic clergy to ignore the preachers and a systematic police curtailment of preaching contributed to the end of the affair. Doherty, 'Religion, community relations and constructive uinionism', p. 231.
99 *Cork Examiner*, 12 Apr. 1894.
100 D. G. T. Williams, 'The principle of Beatty v. Gillbanks: a reappraisal' in Anthony N. Doob and Edward L. Greenspan (eds), *Perspectives in criminal law: essays in honour of John Lt. J. Edwards* (Toronto, 1985), pp. 105–31, quoted in Kelly, 'The politics of Protestant street-preaching', p. 115. (The Skeletal Army had been founded at Weston-Super-Mare to oppose Salvation Army preaching.)
101 *Cork Constitution*, 29 Jan. 1894.
102 *Cork Examiner*, 24 Jan. 1894; Kelly, 'The politics of Protestant street-preaching', pp. 112–13.
103 Quoted in Peter Murray, 'A colporteur kicked by a priest on a Westport street: the MacAskill assault case of 1906', *Cathar na Mart*, xxi (2001), 134.
104 J. Duncan Craig, *Real pictures of clerical life in Ireland* (London, 1900), p. 217.
105 W. E. H. Lecky, *Democracy and liberty* (2 vols, London, 1896), i, pp. 440–1, quoted in Kelly, 'The politics of Protestant street-preaching', p. 111.
106 Quoted in Murray, 'A colporteur kicked by a priest on a Westport street', p. 134.
107 *Irish Ecclesiastical Gazette*, 10 June 1898.
108 Bishops of Ossory, Kilmore, Tuam, Cashel and Killaloe.
109 Precise dates are impossible as reports for 1916–19 have not been located.
110 John Gregg, *A missionary visit to Connemara and other parts of the county of Galway* (Dublin, c.1850); John Gregg, *A missionary visit to Achill and Erris, and other parts of the county of Mayo* (Dublin, c.1850).
111 ICM, *Annual report*, 1910–11, p. 18.
112 *Report of the Catholic Protection and Rescue Society of Ireland*, 1943 (Down and Connor gave £2 15s. 0d.)
113 Stephen Lucius Gwynn, *A holiday in Connemara ... with sixteen illustrations* (London, 1909), p. 282.
114 Hamilton Magee, *Fifty years in the Irish Mission* (Belfast, 1905), p. 77.
115 Quoted in P. M'Closkey, A.B., *Trial and conviction of a Franciscan monk at Mayo spring assizes, 1852, for burning and blaspheming the holy scriptures with observations of the fact and the defence made for it* (Dublin, 1852), p. 50.
116 *Ballina Chronicle*, 2 Apr. 1851.
117 D. James, *John Hamilton of Donegal 1800–1884: this recklessly generous landlord* (Dublin, 1998), p. 223.
118 James Greer, *The windings of the Moy with Skreen and Tireragh* (Ballina, 1986, first published 1927), p. 92.
119 Letter from C. E. Keane, Edgeworthstown, County Longford, *Church of Ireland Gazette*, 31 Jan. 1913.

120 *Church of Ireland Gazette*, 15 Aug. 1913.

121 *Irish Ecclesiastical Gazette*, 21 Sept. 1874.

122 Ibid., 1894, p. 589.

123 Ibid., 1890, p. 651; ibid., 1897, p. 517.

124 Ibid., 1894, p. 710.

125 *Church of Ireland Gazette*, 1906, p. 70. In the notice of Revd Arthur Manning's transfer to Killanin in 1906, no mention was made of the ICM.

126 *Irish Ecclesiastical Gazette*, 10 Apr. 1891.

127 Ibid., 1893, p. 373 and 1896, p. 703.

128 ICM, *Annual reports*, 1908–9, p. 15.

129 *Church of Ireland Gazette*, 1902, pp. 720–1.

130 ICM, *Annual report*, 1902–3, p. 28 (report of Dublin mission); *Banner of the Truth*, Apr. 1911, pp. 19–21; ibid., July 1911, p. 36; Kurt Bowen, *Protestants in a Catholic state: Ireland's privileged minority* (Dublin, 1983), p. 43; Jack White, *Minority report: the Protestant community in the Irish Republic* (Dublin, 1975), p. 131.

131 Association for Promoting Christian Knowledge, *Roman claims, or an elementary catechism on the chief points of Roman controversy, prepared by a committee appointed by the Board of Education of The United Diocese of Dublin, Glendalough and Kildare* (Dublin, 1915).

132 Henry Fishe, *The duty of the Church of Ireland towards her Roman Catholic brethren, a paper read before the C.M.S. clergy union, abbreviated and slightly revised by the Rev. Henry Fishe, M.A., Dublin Superintendent Irish Church Mission, reprinted by request, from the Church of Ireland Gazette* (Dublin, 1908), pp. 4–5, 7, 14.

133 *Catholic Bulletin*, ii (1912), 731.

134 Ibid., 12, 26 Sept. 1913.

135 ICM Archive, minutes of Priests' Protection Society, 22 Dec. 1919.

136 Ibid., minutes of Priests' Protection Society, 22 June 1923 and 9 Nov. 1923.

137 *Church of Ireland Gazette*, 28 Mar. 1918.

138 Ibid., 3 Dec. 1915.

139 Ibid., 9 Feb. 1917.

140 Ibid., 30 Nov. 1917.

141 For example see *Banner of the Truth*, July 1902, p. 35; July 1904, p. 35; Oct. 1904, p. 60; Oct. 1906, p. 63.

142 Ibid., Oct. 1904, p. 51; Jan. 1905, p. 2.

143 Ibid., Apr. 1905, p. 21; Jan. 1907, p. 68.

144 Ibid., Oct. 1908, pp. 63–4; ibid., Apr. 1911, p. 31.

145 *Grievances from Ireland*, June 1908, pp. 377–8.

146 Martin Maguire, 'The Church of Ireland and the problem of the Protestant working-class of Dublin, 1870s–1930s' in Alan Ford, James McGuire and Kenneth Milne (eds), *As by law established* (Dublin, 1985), p. 197.

147 Duncan Craig, *Real pictures of clerical life*, pp. 72–5, 191.

148 *Banner of the Truth*, Apr. 1917, p. 15.

149 *The Catholic Bulletin* advised that Irish mothers should 'impress indelibly on the memory of their children … those sad days when women and children

were brutally murdered, when homesteads were levelled and fields laid waste, when the openly expected desire of the oppressor was not to conquer but to exterminate'. Thomas H. Burbage, 'Patriotism is a Christian virtue', *Catholic Bulletin*, v (1915), 612–13.

150 The teachers' preface to the Christian Brothers, *Irish history reader* (Dublin, 1907) states that pupils 'must be taught that Irishmen, claiming the right to make their own laws, should never rest content until their native Parliament is restored; and that Ireland looks to them, when grown to man's estate, to act the part of true men in furthering the sacred cause of nationhood'.

151 *Banner of the Truth*, Apr. 1918, p. 14.

152 Quoted in ICM, *Annual report*, 1919–20, p. 17.

153 *Banner of the Truth*, July 1919, pp. 17–18.

154 Ibid., Oct. 1919, pp. 34–5; Apr. 1920, pp. 9–10.

155 Ibid., Jan. 1921, p. 1.

156 Ibid., Jan. 1921, p. 9.

157 Ibid., Apr. 1921, pp. 16–17, 18; July 1921, p. 22.

158 Ibid., July 1921, p. 23.

159 Monica Farrell, *From Rome to Christ: the story of a spiritual pilgrimage* (6th edn, Belfast, 1955), p. 28.

160 Glenowen later re-opened for boys and functioned until the 1940s.

161 *Banner of the Truth*, Jan. 1923, p. 9.

162 Alannah Heather, *Errislannan: scenes from a painter's life* (Dublin, 1993), p. 58.

163 RCBL, MS No. P. 170/8/2, Ballyconree Preacher's book. No further services were held in Ballyconree church after the evacuations from Ballyconree and Glenowen Orphanages.

164 Raymonde Standún and Bill Long, *Singing stone, whispering wind: voices of Connemara* (Dublin, 2001), p. 27.

165 Edward Savage, *Work in the fairs and markets* (n.p., n.d. [after 1922]), pp. 1–3.

166 ICM Archive, MS No.1932/c/51, Garda Siochána Permit, 1 June 1932.

167 Anonymous, *The Irish mission field* (n.p., n.d. [c.1937]), pp. 4–5.

168 ICM, *Annual report*, 1928–29, p. 10.

169 Ibid., 1928–29, p. 1.

170 J. H. Bradshaw, *Lantern missions in Ireland* (n.p., n.d. [c.1922]).

171 For example, *Banner of the Truth*, Apr. 1922 told of the conversion of the Roman Catholic, John Brophy; the return to Protestantism of Mrs McCrossan (who had lapsed on marriage to a Catholic); the repentance and death of Thomas Barnwell (who had married a Catholic), and the ICM's ongoing work with an impoverished family.

172 J. E. McCrory, *A Portadown open-air* (London, Dublin, n.d. [1930]), p. 15. Although this book is dated to 191– by the National Library of Ireland, it cannot have been written before 1925 as it refers to McCrory's period in the ICM Training School which occurred 1925–26.

173 Farrell, *From Rome to Christ*, pp. 19–22; Anonymous, *Why I left the Church of Rome* (Dublin, n.d. [after 1922]), pp. 1–7.

174 Anonymous, *An ardent Sinn-Féiner* (Dublin, n.d. [after 1922]), p. 11.

175 ICM Archive, MS No. 1932/c/50. This lists the names and addresses of 149 converts in 1932 arranged by ICM agent. Convert names and addresses are given in ICM correspondence; in view of the sensitivity and recent date of this material, they have been obscured in this publication.

176 ICM Archive, MS No. 1932/f/4. Isobel F—'s invitation to a converts' reunion in the Mission Building on 14 Jan. 1932 was returned to the ICM as she no longer lived at the address used.

177 ICM Archive, MS No. 1932/2/33, Michael S— to T. C. Hammond, 21 Nov. 1932, MS No. 1932/s/34 and Michael S— to T. C. Hammond, 20 Oct. 1932.

178 The poverty of the children in ICM schools is evident in correspondence. One letter told of the H— children of Lurgan Street School whose father was dying of consumption with some children also infected, while another letter told of extremely impoverished Grand Canal Street pupils, children of original Protestants (father from Northern Ireland, mother from England) who lived in the 'Basement Kitchen' at 25 Grattan Street. ICM Archive, MS Nos 1932/h/48, 1932/r/1.

179 ICM Archive, MS No. 1932/b/91, John B— to T. C. Hammond, 22 Feb. 1932. There is a large Jesuit church in Gardiner Street.

180 ICM Archive, MS Nos 1932/d/11/12/13/14/18, William D— to T. C. Hammond, n.d. [filed with Jan–Jun. 1932], see also MS No. 1932/d/10.

181 ICM Archive, MS No. 1932/c/27, Patrick C— to T. C. Hammond, 19 Dec. 1931. See also MS Nos 1932/d/46 and 52, T.D— to T. C. Hammond, n.d. [filed Jan–Jun. 1932]; MS No. 1932/b/1, Oliver B— to T. C. Hammond, 15 Feb. 1932.

182 Lily O'Connor, *Can Lily O'Shea come out to play?* (Dingle, 2000), pp. 16, 75.

183 Anonymous, *The Irish mission field*, p. 2.

184 Savage, *Work in the fairs*, p. 4.

185 Anonymous, *The Irish mission field*, p. 6.

186 ICM Archive, MS No. 1932/b/66, Bridget B— to T. C. Hammond, 18 May 1932. This Mountrath convert was forced to emigrate. Although her family accepted her decision, she had been contacted in England by the priest of her native parish. In this letter she states that she would like to visit her parents and 'tell them too the good news of the Gospel' but wonders would she be safe.

187 Bradshaw, *Lantern missions in Ireland*, p. 8.

188 Anonymous, *The Irish mission field*, p. 7.

189 Of the 149 converts listed in 1932, ninety-one were designated as 'Mrs', fifty as 'Mr' and eight as 'Miss'. The list included twenty-two entries of 'Mr and Mrs'. ICM Archive, MS No. 1932/c/50, Listing of converts, 1932.

190 For example Mrs T— of Allingham Buildings appears on the convert list (1932). Her son, Joseph, was identified as an 'Original Protestant' in the 1935 Coombe School return. This only available return of pupils in ICM schools (1935) specifies religions as O.P. (Original Protestant); R.C. (Roman Catholic) and M. (mixed marriage). Identities can be confirmed by cross-referencing this list of pupils, addresses of pupils in the address book of pupils in the Coombe School and the 1932 listing of names and addresses of converts.

191 ICM Archive, MS No. 1932/c/50 list of converts in 1932; Address book of pupils at the ICM's Coombe School.

192 M. Creedon, *Proselytism: its operations in Ireland, a paper read at the annual meeting of the Maynooth Union, June 1926 (archdiocese of Dublin)* (Dublin, 1926), p. 3. Fr Creedon was a curate at Francis Street, near the ICM's Coombe mission.

193 Creedon, *Proselytism*, p. 3; E. J. Quigley, 'Grace abounding, a chapter of Ireland's history, part XI', *Irish Ecclesiastical Record*, xxii (1923), 619.

194 Quigley, 'Grace abounding, part XI', *Irish Ecclesiastical Record*, xxii (1923), 610.

195 Letter from Bishop T. O'Doherty, *Galway Sentinel*, 12 Dec. 1933.

196 Creedon, *Proselytism*, p. 7. The author details numerous Protestant charities which catered for Dublin's poor.

197 Ibid., p. 11.

198 Ibid., p. 6.

199 ICM Archive, ICM minutes, TSC, 10 Dec. 1940, 3 Oct. 1947.

200 ICM Archive, Birds' Nest roll book.

201 Anonymous, *Irish Church Missions, a letter and a reply* (n.p., n.d. [c.1940]), p. 4.

202 For example, the case of the Geoghegan children in 1932. Copious correspondence indicates that the ICM played a pivotal role in this custody battle. ICM Archive, MS Nos 1932/s/20–31 (corresponding with solicitors); MS Nos 1932/a/15; 1932/g/39–42; 1932/h/37–38; 1932/s/66 (correspondence with sympathisers).

203 ICM Archive, MS No. 1932/b/21, C. Bolton to T. C. Hammond, 23 Feb. 1932, informs of three vacancies in Thom's printers.

204 ICM Archive, MS No. 1932/s/52, Arthur H. Smith, grain merchant, Corn Exchange, Burgh Quay to T. C. Hammond, 9 Sept. 1932; MS No. 1932/s/53, R. Shipman, Wayke Lodge, Chichester to T. C. Hammond, 9 Nov. 1932.

205 ICM Archive, MS No. 1932/c/5, James Cully to T. C. Hammond, 7 Feb. 1932.

206 Fred C. Gibson, *Gleanings from harvest fields, extracts from monthly reports of Colporteurs* (Belfast, c.1930), pp. 14–15.

207 Farrell, *From Rome to Christ*, p. 32.

208 ICM Archive, MS Nos 1932/d/5/6/7, Methodist Church Colportage Society to T. C. Hammond, 18, 24 Feb. and 3 Mar. 1932; MS No. 1932/d/8, Fred. Gibson, Presbyterian Church in Ireland to T. C. Hammond, 29 Feb. 1932.

209 General Assembly of the Presbyterian Church in Ireland, *Annual report, 1951* (Belfast, 1951), p. 5.

210 Creedon, *Proselytism*, pp. 7–9.

211 Based on an analysis of the surnames of children listed in the homes in the 1901 and 1911 censuses.

212 Application forms for Mrs Smyly's Homes asked the date and place of parents' marriages.

213 The residents of the Coombe Boys' Home were transferred to the Grand Canal Street home in 1922, *Banner of the Truth*, Apr. 1922, p. 11.

214 ICM Archive, ICM minutes, TSC, 16 June 1936, 29 Nov. 1949.

215 ICM Archive, ICM minutes, TSC, 10 Dec. 1936, 23 June 1937.

216 ICM Archive, ICM minutes, TSC, 5 Jan. 1950; 25 Apr. 1950.

217 ICM Archive, ICM minutes, TSC, 13 Apr. 1937; 6 Mar. 1939.

218 ICM Archive, ICM minutes, TSC, 25 Mar. 1943.

219 For example, T. C. Hammond was asked to recommend a book outlining the difference between Protestantism and Catholicism and recommended *Blakeney's Manual*. See ICM Archive, MS Nos 1932/b/33–34, Jean Bell, Cork to T. C. Hammond, 18 Jan., 1 Feb. 1932.

220 In 1932 alone, the ICM corresponded with the Bible Churchmen's Missionary Society; British Gospel Books Association; British Syrian Mission; China Inland Mission; Church of England in South Africa Aid Society; Colonial and Continental Church Society; Church Book Room; The English Churchman; Evangelical Alliance; Fellowship of Evangelical Churchmen; Hibernian Bible Society; Irish Evangelisation Society; Johannesburg Scriptural Holiness Convention; Mission to Lepers; National Church League; North Africa Mission; The Officers' Christian Union; Paris Evangelical Society; Protestant Truth Society; Religious Tract Society; Scottish Prostant League; Scottish Reformation Society; Scripture Gift Mission; Spanish Gospel Mission; Southport Evangelical Conference; Sudan Interior Mission; Women's Protestant Union (Belfast).

221 For example a *Quarterly Intercession Paper* of the Fellowship of Evangelical Churchmen asked for prayers that 'the change of government in Ireland may result in more liberty from Rome, and readiness to hear the Gospel'. ICM Archive, MS No. 1932h/71, and for prayers for the work of the ICM, MS Nos 1932h/71 and 1932/e/26.

222 A deputation of the Paris Evangelical Society preached in the Mission Church on 4 Oct. 1932 and Miss Pennefather, missionary of the British Syrian Mission, preached on an unspecified date in 1932. ICM Archive, MS Nos 1932/g/46 and 1932/g/64.

223 This periodical was started in 1892 by convert-priest, later Church of Ireland clergyman, Thomas Connellan, whose brother Joseph was also converted to Protestantism. Their publications echoed ICM sentiments: Thomas Connellan, *Landmarks* (Dublin, n.d. [after 1890]); Thomas Connellan, *Hear the other side* (Dublin, n.d. [after 1890]); Thomas Connellan, *Scenes from clerical life* (Dublin, n.d. [after 1890]); Joseph Connellan, *From bondage to liberty* (Dublin, n.d. [after 1890]). T. C. Hammond would later become editor of *The Catholic*.

224 For example T. C. Hammond was invited to speak on 'The Roman Yoke', ICM Archive, MS No. 1932/b/37, Ernest Bateman to T. C. Hammond, 22 Nov. 1932, and to produce an article on 'The Articles, A Safeguard against Romanism', ICM Archive, MS No. 1932/b/96, National Church League, London to T. C. Hammond, 25 May 1932.

225 The printed notepaper of the Scottish Reformation Society stated that it was founded to resist the aggressions of popery, to watch the designs and movements of its promoters and abettors, to diffuse sound and scriptural information on the distinctive tenets of Protestantism and popery, and to

promote the instruction of Roman Catholics in the bible truth. ICM Archive, MS No. 1932/g/65, 1932.

226 This gentleman was confident that T. C. Hammond could explain to ordinands 'how they may meet all the objections that are raised v Anglicanism in the spirit of love and fellowship' but stressed that he wanted no 'anti-Romish propaganda or violent pro-Protestant talk'. ICM Archive, MS No. 1932/g/62, Peter Gibson to T. C. Hammonds, 1932.

227 ICM Archive, ICM minutes, TSC, 23 Sept. 1936. This pamphlet has not been located.

228 ICM Archive, ICM minutes, TSC, 9, 16 June 1938, 22 June 1939.

229 W. B. Stanford, *Faith and faction in Ireland now* (Dublin, Belfast, 1946), p. 37.

230 ICM Archive, ICM minutes, TSC, 29 Nov. 1949.

231 ICM Archive, John Allen Fitzgerald Gregg to Mr Coates, 26 Oct. 1945.

232 See private correspondence between Primate Gregg and Cardinal Logue, reproduced in George Seaver, *John Allen Fitzgerald Gregg, archbishop* (Dublin, 1963), pp. 312–16.

233 General Assembly, *Annual Reports of Missions ... 1896* (Belfast, 1896), p. 4; ibid., 1891, p. 4.

234 General Assembly of the Presbyterian Church in Ireland, *Annual report, 1951*, p. 5.

235 *Annual Report of the Island and Coast Society* (Dublin, 1883), p. 17; ibid., 1885, p. 23.

Chapter 7

The legacy of
the Irish Church Missions

Underpinned by an over-riding evangelical obligation to rescue Roman Catholics bound for eternal damnation, the Irish Church Missions was established to fulfil the religious needs of committed scripturalists whose immense responsibility to those trapped in the perceived 'errors of Rome' created indistinct boundaries between religious and political objectives.[1] As Bowen acknowledged, there was no doubt about the 'terrible purity of Dallas's motives'.[2] However, by seeking to Protestantise and Anglicise Ireland, the ICM indirectly contributed to unforeseen religious and sociological changes. By engendering interdenominational mistrust and by reinforcing the existing connection between Irishness and Catholicism, the mission conferred an unplanned and long-lasting impact on the Second Reformation, an impact which Bowen considered was to be 'deeply regretted'.[3] Connections between Catholicism and Irishness had existed since the reformation era, but the overt anti-Catholic approach and methodologies of the Society provided a public platform through which the increasingly confident Catholic population could voice their resentment. Bowen's work, concluding in 1870, does not examine the influence of the ICM on contemporary Ireland. This study will attempt a more extensive study of the legacy of proselytism and of its impact on inter-confessional relations into the present day.

Paul Cullen's dislike and distrust of Protestants was nurtured by the proselytising movement. Indeed Bowen remarked that in the 1850s and early 1860s Cullen had 'an almost paranoiac obsession with the Protestant Evangelicals, particularly the agents of the ICM in Connaught and in Dublin'.[4] His inability and/or unwillingness to differentiate between proselytising and non-proselytising Protestants ensured that both were considered equally objectionable, as when he commented that Protestants 'have no religion'.[5] This was unfair on liberal Protestants who had, as early as the 1820s, objected to efforts to convert Irish Catholics,[6] and many clearly and publicly disapproved of the ICM, its aims and its methods. Although inter-faith tensions undeniably existed in the early nineteenth century, these were greatly augmented by the aggressive efforts of the ICM. It is debatable whether this deterioration in inter-confessional trust and respect can be laid directly on the shoulders of the Irish Church Missions, whose efforts admittedly aroused intense animosity and gave to the increasingly powerful Catholic church a sturdy stick with which to beat all Protestants. The cultural and religious interdenominational gulf which emerged in Ireland during the late nineteenth and early twentieth centuries was to render all Protestant interests, aims and philosophies irrelevant in the emerging Catholic ascendancy. It eventually contributed to the creation of an intolerant Catholic-dominated state where, as observed by Primate John Gregg in 1946, 'R.C.ism is in the saddle'.[7]

Just as the ICM attacked the Catholic church as a body: its practices, its doctrines and its clergy; segments of the Catholic church attacked Protestantism in general, refusing to distinguish between Protestants who supported or who opposed proselytising missions. While this may initially appear harsh, it should be remembered that considerable support was shown for the ICM in early years from 'rank and file' Protestants and it appears that in its first decade the movement had the tacit, if not overt, support of many Irish Protestants which became eroded as the mission's false claims and objectionable methodologies became apparent. However, even as Protestant opposition to the ICM became evident from the 1860s, Paul Cullen persisted in condemning all things Protestant.[8] This attitude was emulated by some Catholic writers, as when the author of *Tim O'Halloran's Choice* criticised those who embraced Protestant friends and literature.[9]

The ICM had a profound effect on Irish Catholicism. William Wilde observed at the time of its inception that Ireland was growing 'more and more Protestant every year ... even the priests are becoming more Protestant in their conversation and manners'.[10] Clerical discipline, which had improved in pre-famine decades, was even more strictly supervised with the arrival of Paul Cullen in 1850, whose discouragement of liberal or independent thought and whose efforts to bring Irish Catholics who were 'culturally Protestant' into line contributed to the confessional divide which developed, especially from the mid century.[11] Increased pastoral care consequent on proselytism imposed strict discipline and adherence to church authority at parish level through sodalities and confraternities. In spite of this, a lack of conviction among some Irish Catholics in the 1920s was attributed to the influence of proselytising societies which had caused them 'to doubt Catholicism and to remain weak, cold, formal Catholics'.[12]

This phase of the 'Second Reformation' could more correctly be viewed as the final phase of the first Reformation; it had two important, but unforeseen consequences. Firstly, it established that the majority of Ireland's population gave their allegiance to the Church of Rome, and secondly, it ensured that Tridentine practices and reforms were followed in all dioceses, regardless of geographical location, wealth of the laity or disposition of the clergy. In this manner, the proselytising crusades of the nineteenth century helped banish forever the remnants of pre-modern folk religion and galvanised the position of the Ultramontaine church. While change of this nature was underway even before the famine, the establishment of such an aggressive organisation as the ICM ensured the completion of this process.

The ICM unintentionally advanced Catholic philanthropy and education as it forced the provision of improved services to combat proselytism, mirroring the results of Protestant missions in Britain.[13] If the Society did nothing else, it obliged the Catholic church to throw new efforts into desolate regions which had been starved of pastoral care. Supporters of Protestant missions acknowledged that their chief result was the increased attention paid to the poor, which they expected would continue 'when the names of Whately, Dallas and Co. shall have been forgotten'.[14]

The ICM's presence in Connemara secured a substantial educational network and forced reform of its Catholic administration, especially after John MacHale's death in 1881. Connemara's poor educational infrastructure had originally attracted the ICM to the area, and conversely the mission can claim credit for the remarkable educational establishments subsequently located therein. The Third Order of Franciscans, MacHale's favourite educationalists, established schools at Clifden and Roundstone in the 1830s and at Tourmakeady in 1848 and, after the advent of the ICM, national schools were established throughout the mission region. In 1886, the ICM model farm at Letterfrack was surreptitiously purchased on behalf of the Catholic archbishop of Tuam as the ICM had ordered that it not be sold to a Catholic. Here, Irish Christian Brothers founded an industrial school and model farm. Education was similarly provided for Connemara's girls. Following the introduction of the Sisters of Mercy to Clifden in 1855, they established an elementary school, an orphanage and a model farm. They were at the forefront of progressive farming, being the first to introduce milking machines to Connemara and incubators for chickens. In the twentieth century they added a technical school, assumed charge of a state-run hospital and opened a boarding school to provide secondary education for girls from outlying regions. They also opened a convent and schools in Carna (near the ICM's Moyrus mission). Due to the ICM's activities, by the early twentieth century Connemara had a better network of educational establishments than was found elsewhere in the impoverished west of Ireland.

The ICM fed thousands of Connemara's starving during and after the famine. Whatever its motives, and irrespective of conditions attached, thousands would certainly have died had Dallas not turned his attention to the area. The compassion and concern of mission workers such as Fanny D'Arcy are without question: 'we are kept weekly anxious waiting upon God for the daily bread for these schools'[15] and it must be acknowledged that in 1851 over 10,000 persons were fed weekly by the ICM.[16] However, the association of charity with proselytism, especially in folk tradition, has tainted the memory of this work and obliterated the very real good carried out by the ICM. As Christine Kinealy argues, although the extent of proselytism was much less than popular belief would have it, and although it was widely condemned by many Protestant clergy, the fact that it existed at all has conferred a legacy of distrust and bitterness on all famine relief.[17] This was certainly the case in Connemara. When folklore collectors visited in 1937, they discovered that the ICM's Herculean efforts to feed the poor had been forgotten, replaced by memories of animosity with missioners cast as 'droch-dhaoine' [bad people].[18]

The nation-wide philanthropic work of Ireland's Protestant clergy during and after the famine years has been forgotten in the subsequent souperism debate and a legacy of inter-confessional animosity has overshadowed the very real but perhaps misguided charity on the part of some. Most Anglican clergymen had no connection with the ICM and attached no conditions to their relief. Many died in the course of the famine, their efforts largely unacknowledged. In his detailed and extensive study of souperism, which is located in the west of Ireland but outside the ICM region, Bowen concludes that

> The parsons of Killala and Achonry were not guilty of proselytism or Souperism during the crisis of 1847 ... but it can be argued that the Second Reformation failed when it moved into Mayo and Sligo because most of the parsons showed little enthusiasm for Bishop Plunket's proselytising program ... There is no evidence to indicate that the Killala and Achonry clergy were any different from the rest of their Established Church brethren when they showed great reluctance to support missions to the Catholics.[19]

Protestant clergy in Tuam's adjoining dioceses of Killala and Achonry worked alongside their Catholic counterparts in procuring and distributing Quaker relief and in denouncing callous landlords.[20] Catholic authorities, who did not differentiate between soupers and non-soupers, showed the same contempt for these as for the proselytising Dallas and D'Arcy, an attitude which coloured Protestant–Catholic relationships in the following decades.

Although the ICM was the best resourced and the most extensive agency which attempted the conversion of Irish Catholics, it was not alone in its efforts and its legacy is inextricably tied to the manner in which Catholics 'remembered' all organisations founded for the same purpose. Although these societies operated independently, and adopted a variety of missionary methods which ranged from the ICM's forthright denunciation of Romanism to the 'soft proselytism' of the Island and Coast Society, their activities became coalesced in the popular memory. Little, if any, distinction was made in the Catholic mind between the different societies, or even between denominations; as Protestant organisations, whether missionary, educational or philanthropic, were represented as Protestant efforts to bribe Catholics to convert.

Connemara, Achill and Ventry were the only regions of Ireland that were comprehensively 'proselytised'; despite the intensity of missionary work in Dublin, the degree to which it impacted on the slum-dwelling population was minimised by the sheer weight of their numbers which rendered effective proselytising impossible. Protestant missionary activity was conducted in a less concentrated fashion in the rest of the country. The Irish Society maintained sixty-eight missions in twelve counties from Waterford to Donegal but was most active in the province of Munster. In 1861, its income of £8,395 enabled the employment of seventy-four scripture readers, seventeen teachers and 239 'Irish teachers', who taught over 8,000 pupils, while 500 scholars attended its seventeen mission schools; ten years later its income and operations were much reduced.[21] Presbyterian and Baptist missions concentrated their efforts in north Connaught and isolated locations such as Birr (Parsonstown), and maintained ineffectual itinerating missions into the early decades of the Free State.

The fact that proselytising societies operated in every county should not suggest the practice was commonplace or commanded widespread support as segments of Irish Protestantism had opposed proselytising missions from the outset.[22] Eugene Broderick has shown that although a few localised pockets of proselytism occurred in Waterford,[23] this work was repudiated by 'intelligent and impartial Protestants'.[24] Neither should the 'remembering' of a Protestant mission confirm its existence, as the following example shows.

Proselytism is etched deep in the folk memory of the Kilrush area of County Clare, despite a lack of evidence of its existence during the famine. The ICM was not active in County Clare in 1861 (population 166,000), there is no evidence of Presbyterian or Baptist missions and the Irish Society spent a mere £141 on its four missions (including one at Kilrush). It is clear, however, that 'memories' of famine missions to Catholics, with accompanying offers of relief, are ingrained in the minds of the inhabitants of Kilrush. A memorial erected in 1967 near the site of famine graves in old Shanakyle graveyard in the Kilrush parish was almost exactly replicated twenty years later when a second memorial was erected in the same parish. The 1967 memorial reads

> Erected by the Very Rev. Peter Canon Ryan, PPVE, in memory of the numerous heroes of West Clare, who died of hunger, rather than pervert during the Great Famine of 1847–48, and were buried here coffinless in three large pits. May they rest in peace.[25]

Research into famine proselytism in this district revealed that very good relations existed between the Catholic and Protestant churches during the famine of 1845–48, described as a 'kindly feeling' by Very Revd Timothy Kelly, parish priest in famine times. This conciliatory attitude deteriorated from 1849, when strenuous allegations were made that the St Vincent de Paul Society, a Catholic charity, tried to entice Protestants to convert. Fr Michael Meehan, curate in Kilrush from 1837 to 1849, was subsequently appointed parish priest of Moyarta and Kilballyowen, fifteen miles away, where he waged a bitter war in the early 1850s against bible schools run by the proselytising landlord, Marcus Keane. Fr Patrick White, curate at Kilballyowen from 1862, wrote an account of Fr Meehan's battle against the proselytisers which was published in the *Irish Ecclesiastical Record* in 1887.[26] This article was reproduced in *Molua*, the official annual of the Catholic diocese of Killaloe, in 1954 and in the Clare magazine, *Dal gCais*, in 1977. It is reasonable to suppose that it was read by Fr Peter Ryan, who was appointed parish priest of Kilrush in 1961, and by Fr Michael Donoghue, who erected the second memorial in 1987. By superimposing Fr Meehan's 1850s battle against proselytism on the famine memory of Kilrush, a hybrid story evolved in which, contrary to contemporary evidence, the starving of Kilrush died rather than accept the lure of 'the soupers'. Fr Ryan was not the first to suggest such an occurrence; the people of Kilrush may have been influenced by the initial publication of Fr White's article in 1887. Fifty years later, the grandmother of a Kilrush schoolgirl 'remembered' famine proselytism: 'Ní raibh mórán soupers anseo. B'fhearr leo bás d'fháil ná an anraith d'ól. Tá an t'ainm seo "soupers" anseo fós. Mo sheanmháthair a thug an t'eolas seo dom, [There weren't many soupers here. They preferred to die than take the soup. They are still called soupers round here. My grandmother told this to me]'.[27] These 'memories' may be attributed in part to the emotional legacy of a war waged in the 1820s by the Catholic clergy in County Clare against the schools of the Hibernian Bible Society and the Kildare Place Society, which resulted in the establishment of Christian Brothers' Schools in Ennistymon (1824) and Ennis (1827). Inter-confessional hostility was less pronounced in Kilrush, where the Christian Brothers' School was not established until 1874.[28] The Kilrush memorials are merely one example of how myths and erroneous beliefs permeated and became consolidated in the public consciousness. It is not difficult to see the insidious influence of memorials of this nature.

The legacy of long-closed proselytising missions was perpetuated in literature, frequently recounted in a subjective or biased manner. Fictional portrayals of past events are both useful and valid in appraising attitudes of previous generations as these can reveal popular opinions in a way that official or historical sources cannot, but may reveal as much about the prejudices of the author as about the episodes in question. Both Catholic and Protestant cultures assimilated myths of persecution into their famine experience and literature, which may have eased the guilt of the survivor but further soured inter-confessional relations.

The unjust branding of all Protestant clergy as opportunistic proselytisers has been depicted in the fiction of Protestant writers, for example Revd Murray in *The Hunger* and the Brooke family in *Kingston's Revenge*.[29] Catholic proselytism in workhouses, a practice which Bowen considered may indeed have occurred, is depicted in *Poor Paddy's Cabin* (1853) and in its sequel, *The Irish Widow* (1855). In the former work, Protestant orphans were brought to the poorhouse to be reared as Catholics and in *The Irish Widow*, a priest orders a Catholic purchaser of land in the Encumbered Estates Court to evict all converts. Both novels are littered with persecution and emigration of converts. Melissa Fegan has observed how these novels 'rewrite the famine in terms of the sufferings of Protestants, not only as the derided owners of large estates bankrupted by the loss of rents, but also as the most deprived and persecuted, and the most liable to starvation'.[30]

In Catholic literature, little sympathy was given to famine converts, as when Emily Bowles, an English convert to Catholicism, callously wrote in the 1860s that 'All had not the courage to hold their starving children on their knees, and see life ebbing from them drop by drop'.[31] She contrasted 'martyred' Irish Catholics with converts and Protestants, whom she depicted as having food in the midst of famine. The pages of anti-souper novels are peppered with families who died rather than convert such as the Porters in *Irish Diamonds* (1864), the Sullivans in *Frank O'Donnell* (1861) and Paddy Hayes in *The D'Altons* (1882).[32] In *The D'Altons*, the Ultramontaine dean of Limerick pens a scene in which a Protestant gentleman denounces the 'purchasing of conversion', and in *Ailey Moore*, he describes converts as the 'off-scourings of the population' but reassures the reader near the end of the book that 'the Soupers are all gone or converted'.[33]

In a preface to the 1877 Irish edition of *Tim O'Halloran's Choice* (written by Mary Frances Cusack, the 'Nun of Kenmare') the reader learns that proselytism is 'again rampant in Ireland', having been revived in the previous two or three years.[34] The author criticises those who are indifferent to its existence, asserting that currently 'systematic, deliberate, well-organized, and vile attempts' were being made on Irish Catholicism, chiefly by means of proselytising homes and charitable institutions where 'over two thousand Catholic children are kept in these abodes of souperism'.[35] Readers learn how parents, 'debased by the demon drink', sell their 'hapless offspring to these vile dealers in souls' and how one mother was driven to suicide by remorse.[36] This novel recounts the snatching of a Catholic boy (Thade) to be reared in the Protestant 'Hawk's Nest' and tells that, although the child was eventually cunningly rescued by a Catholic neighbour (and the missionary humiliated), he was counted among the successful converts of the society.[37]

Triumphant Catholicism shines through the entire text. The pressure on mission staff to produce evidence of conversions for English audiences is emphasised, although it claims that 'they're few and far between'.[38] The publication emphasises the mission's use of bribery, readers 'hear' the scripture reader plead with the child's dying father that 'the society which I represent will undertake to feed, clothe and educate him for the moment'.[39] The work triumphantly concludes with a wealthy American Protestant converting to Catholicism, choosing 'the humble lowly laborious self-denying life of a Catholic priest', a conversion achieved through the influence of the 'rescued' Thade.[40]

An important tactic of counter-mission was the portrayal of Protestant mission as an extension of British imperialism, a concept perpetuated in twentieth-century denominational literature. There is some truth in this assertion, as the foundation of the ICM was certainly underpinned by unspoken colonising/civilising agendas. Catholics were reminded that 'What the Tudors and Stewarts and Cromwell could not do, was being done with speeches and soup.'[41] The development of an ideology that to be truly Irish one had to be Catholic contributed to the perception of Protestants as 'inferior' or 'imperfect' citizens of the Irish Free State. Recent scholarship has widely acknowledged the deep divisions caused by proselytism, as described by Liechty and Clegg: 'hoping to bequeath to future generations a legacy of social peace, they left behind instead an intensified sectarian animosity'.[42] This was further explored by Patrick O'Farrell, who asserted that 'the association of food with proselytism burnt anti-Protestantism even deeper into Catholic minds'.[43] Whether the ICM's proselytism or the subsequent portrayal of its proselytism caused this 'intensified sectarian animosity' is open to question.

Following in the vein of Fr Cahill, the writings of Catholic clergy from the 1870s linked Protestant mission with English domination, telling how in the 'period of writhing national agony ... the arch-enemy of our holy religion ... attempt[ed] the spiritual ruin of the faithful Irish people' and how what could not be effected 'by the sword, by confiscation, by corruption' was undertaken 'by money and want'.[44] Anti-souper sentiments came to pervade almost all aspects of Irish life,[45] aided by the demonising of all Protestants and Protestant interests. This was assisted by a fiercely nationalistic teaching of history which forged strong connections between Catholicism and Irishness,[46] and where those in power (Protestants or English or both) were depicted as attempting to exploit the poverty of Irish Catholics: 'the Irish poor had to choose between the Bible and beggary – but they chose beggary'.[47] Although no direct mention of souperism has been identified in textbooks used in Catholic schools, pupils were warned to 'remember that no worldly gain, no social advantage, can justify with principle of any, even the slightest, act of infidelity'.[48]

Opportunistic missionary work was demonised by an t-Athar Pádraig Ua Duinnín [Fr Padraig Dinneen] in his 1901 play, *Creideamh agus gorta* [Faith and famine], which centres on the 'nefarious system of souperism', when a young boy's refusal to accept mission relief during the 1847 famine is depicted as martyrdom: 'a mháthair, is fearr an bás' [mother, death would be better].[49] This quote was recently reused verbatim in a factual account of the famine, demonstrating the power of literature.[50] Ua Duinnín's emotive use of a simple form of standardised Irish uncompromisingly portrays the cruelty and arrogance of mission agents and the futility of their cause.[51] It is noteworthy that the author uses the term 'Sagsanach' [Englishman] in place of 'Protastúnach' [Protestant] throughout the work, reinforcing the association between Protestantism and Britishness and equally between Catholicism and Irishness. The strength and depth of Irish Catholicism are emphasised; audiences 'saw' that soup was distributed to the starving only if they denounced the Pope and studied the bible. They 'observed' that even nominal converts received large sums of money but that most Catholics maintained their distance although, according to the missionary, he was 'making Protestants/Englishmen all over the place'.[52] They also 'heard' mission agents contemptuously insult the Irish and their faith and hope that the famine would worsen as Catholics deserved far worse.[53] An air of validity was conferred on this work by its publication by the Gaelic League and its production in the Abbey Theatre in 1903. It was greatly praised by Lady Gregory although she considered that 'its picture of Protestant bigotry to not be only a caricature, but an impossibility'.[54] Souperism even made an appearance in *Ulysses* when Leopold Bloom recalled how the Birds' Nest Home gave soup to poor children 'to change to protestants in the time of the potato blight'.[55]

Over time the terminology and concept of souperism were relocated to different battlegrounds. By the 1870s it had evolved from the proffering of food to the starving in exchange for religious conversion, encompassing instead the provision of preferential treatment to those who availed of

Protestant facilities. For example, the Jesuit, Augustus Thébaud, comparing funding for Catholic colleges with that granted to the Protestant Trinity College, asked 'Why has a Protestant university so many privileges, while a similar Catholic institution is refused recognition?' and continued with the crucial question 'is souperism so completely dead that it can never revive?'[56] Suspicion hovered over all forms of Protestant philanthropy. Archbishop Walsh of Dublin, 1885–1921, opposed the scheme to send children of striking workers to England during James Larkin's 1913 lockout, as this was proselytism under another guise,[57] while nationalist Alice Millington even considered that the public health crusade of Lady Aberdeen was a form of 'modern souperism'.[58] In 1914, the Gaelic League used the term 'athletic souperism' when it criticised a Wexford member for attending a rugby club dance.[59] It may be argued that, by shifting the usage of the term 'souperism' from the localised proffering of famine relief to the provision of Protestant educational, philanthropic and social services, its impact was rolled out over the entire country.

By overt (direct priestly commands) and covert (rhetoric, literature and street-ballads) means, contempt was fostered among Irish Catholics for those who became involved with Protestant missions. Fr Peadar Ó Laoghaire remarked on the dearth of reading material in the Irish language, except for the Irish bible, which could not be used 'toisg an droch ainm a bheith fáchta aige ós na Soupers' [due to the bad name left it by the Soupers'].[60] Protestants were taunted in street-rhymes which connected the distribution of food to bible reading.[61] Abhorrence at mission involvement has continued to the present day; recently an Irish-American was admonished for belonging to the Republican political party in the United States as this was 'almost worse than your forefathers taking the soup during the famine'.[62]

Memory is subject to a number of influences and should not be accepted uncritically: 'Folklore and popular belief have taken over from historical research and have left us with a number of caricatures'.[63] Through 'mistaken' memories and 'nurtured' mis-assumptions, proselytism came to be interpreted as a ubiquitous occurrence to the extent that by 1937, what was, in effect, a fairly localised provision of mission relief was perceived as a generalised 'hurt'. This was demonstrated in folklore evidence collected in 1937, although by its nature folklore evidence can be problematic, especially when relating to traumatic events.[64]

In the study of folklore, retention of memories has been divided into global, local and popular.[65] Niall Ó Ciosáin has shown that the global had been assimilated into the popular in famine recollections gathered in 1937. Whereas memories of proselytism in Connemara may be interpreted as local, popular memories of proselytism were 'remembered' in areas like Kilrush, places where its actual existence was doubtful.[66] This perception of a 'universal' injury greatly magnified the legacy of the ICM. Ó Ciosáin considers that this exaggeration was nurtured by a 'Catholic meta-narrative, whether in a written or printed form or indirectly through sermons or speeches'.[67] However, it must be remembered that while occurrences of proselytism were indeed local, Catholic fears of landslide conversions to the Protestant faith were experienced on a global scale throughout the country, maintaining the climate of religious tension and anxiety that had existed since the reformation.

The depiction of souperism as a universal experience provided a convenient but inaccurate sub-text for the widespread (but now largely discredited) Mitchelite portrayal of the famine as an English tool of deliberate Irish extermination.[68] It is likely that the demonisation of the roles of England and of Protestants during the famine may have served a distinct purpose among a section of Irish society, which could malign both with impunity (rarely distinguishing between the two groupings).[69] As Bryan Fanning asserts, through souperism 'anti-Protestantism found expression within anti-British discourse'.[70] The verifiable but localised wrongs perpetrated on Irish Catholics by English Protestant missions enabled political rhetoric to deflect attention from the classes of Irishmen who profited by famine and prospered in its aftermath, and who held a firm grip on power in the early decades of the Free State. Such Irish beneficiaries of the famine may have wanted their countrymen to forget how their forefathers took advantage of the 'poorest of their neighbours ... [to] offer rent to the landlord and grab their farms'.[71] In the early decades of the state, the continued existence of public proselytism in the shape of the ICM with its ongoing, albeit small-scale and ineffectual, mission work among Irish Catholics created suitable conditions where the newly arrived Catholic ascendancy could exaggerate and exploit the activities of Protestant mission to their own ends. Although its impact was limited, famine souperism took its place alongside the (inconsistently applied) penal laws in the armoury of politicised Catholics, in the same way that the 1641 massacre could be used by Protestant propagandists.

In this way, Catholics were galvanised to resist Protestantism under any guise, as all Protestant education and relief were perceived as opportunistic scavenging for Catholic souls. It is probably unfair to blame the ICM for the sufferings of southern Protestants and to charge it with the creation of a Roman Catholic dominated state, which was not caused solely by its actions or by a direct response to its actions. Instead it should be recognised that this was caused by the acquisition of power by Catholics in the wake of generations of subservience and insult, with the ICM being merely one of many examples of institutions and organisations offering such offence, albeit one of the most recent and most public. In fact, the efforts of the ICM, although intensely felt in Connemara and some slum areas of Dublin, were of relevance only to a minority of Irish Catholics, contrary to 'memories' from the 1920s to 1950s. But it should also be considered that the continuation of the ICM's activities gave weight to this inaccurate depiction of Protestant mission and negatively influenced the location of Protestants within Irish society, where in Primate John Gregg's opinion, they lived 'almost on sufferance'.[72]

Although the ICM undeniably showed overwhelming arrogance in the face of increasing Catholic power with its uncompromising denunciations of Catholicism inviting unrelenting indignation, it is likely that mainstream Catholics were more affected by subtle manifestations of Protestant power, such as preferential employment and promotion of Protestants in many businesses.[73] However, the ICM, with its public profile and weekly controversial discussions, set itself up as a magnet for Catholic anger and subsequent Protestant blame. By ignoring the changing political realities of the early twentieth century, and by following the *modus operandi* of Reformation Societies in Protestant counties, irritation of both the Catholic majority and the Protestant minority was inevitable. Displaying naivety and arrogance, the ICM set itself up as a scapegoat on whom was piled centuries of wrongs perpetrated on Irish Catholics.

It was predicted from the outset that the enterprise would damage social stability. Archbishop John MacHale asserted that the peace of the country was too important for 'such peddling schemes of bigotry and perversion',[74] while Quaker MP, Alfred Webb, reported that missionary efforts had sullied the good name of Protestants and that

> Those who really became Protestants were few and far between. The movement left seeds of bitterness that have not yet died out, and Protestants, not altogether excluding Friends, sacrificed much of the influence for good they would have had if they had been satisfied to leave the belief of the people alone.[75]

To this day, evidence exists of the 'seeds of bitterness' observed by Alfred Webb. The obliteration of mission buildings from Connemara's landscape is testament to the sensitivity regarding the subject. Few mission schools survive; those that do have been converted to private houses. When services at Sellerna mission church ceased in 1926, Ballinakill Select Vestry ordered that it be demolished; Derrygimla church was knocked down in the 1950s and its stones used to build Ballyconneely Community Centre, to where its pews were relocated; one local Protestant recently remarked 'but they never had any luck with it'.[76] Ballyconree church was replaced by a Catholic national school. No trace remains of the churches at Bunlahinch, Omey Island or Renvyle, while that at Castlekerke is in ruins; Partry and Killanin have been converted to private houses. In contrast, Ballinahinch church was handed over to the Catholic diocese, who replaced the plain tracery in the East Window with a stained-glass picture of the Virgin Mary. The mission churches at Aasleagh, Ballinakill and Errislannan are still used by the Church of Ireland, along with the churches of the pre-existing parishes: Clifden, Roundstone and Oughterard.

Contempt for those who associated with Protestant missions ran deep in Catholic communities. The scars of conversion, ostracism and resentment were so indelibly ingrained and so bitterly divisive that after the closure of the missions, the subject was frequently off-limits to subsequent generations. Many have been reared in total ignorance of the movement, others have been reared to regard Protestant missions with contempt. The term 'Souper' has not yet died out, as evidenced by the controversy surrounding the production of Eoghan Harris's Play, *Souper Sullivan*, in the Abbey Theatre in 1985.

Nowadays, few persons feel free to speak of mission memory; most Protestants are sensitive regarding the subject. Evidence gathered in 2005 for an oral history study of Protestantism and Irishness identified many instances where Protestants were embarrassed at being 'branded to be part of that whole forcing people to turn their back on their religion so as to be fed', while another interviewee acknowledged a 'resentment about how people changed from one religion to the other during the famine times, that you don't want to stir things up'.[77] Recent research has also shown that some Protestants considered that

> the severity and enmity of the Catholic church of the 1920s, 1930s, 1940s and 1950s was 'understandable', given the scorn with which Catholicism had been treated in Ireland by Protestants in previous centuries, mentioning in particular the sustained attempts to convert (or coerce) Catholics to Protestantism.[78]

Jack White, a Cork Protestant, writing in the 1970s, was more direct in his appraisal of the negative legacy of proselytism: 'The wave of evangelical zeal claimed at its height many thousands of converts; yet it subsided leaving hardly a trace behind – hardly a trace, that is, but the bitter belief, indelibly etched in the Irish folk-memory, that the missionaries came to buy souls for soup.'[79]

If compelling evidence of enduring hostility towards proselytising missions were needed, it was provided by the production of Eoghan Harris' play, *Souper Sullivan*, in the Abbey Theatre in 1985. On Sunday 29 September, a Dublin priest, Fr Christy Walshe, was applauded by his Monkstown congregation for condemning the play, which he had not even seen. He asserted that its central character, Revd Fisher, an Anglican clergyman in

west Cork, had used relief money to establish a church during the famine
years, an allegation which Harris considered as dubious. Although the
actions of Revd Fisher may be variously interpreted, as Harris stated, 'the
venom of folklore went down the years', symbolised by the corruption of
the name of Revd Fisher's church from 'Teampal na mBocht' [church of the
poor] to 'Teampal na Muc' [church of the pigs].[80]

What is of interest here, is not whether Revd Fisher bribed or did not
bribe the peasantry of west Cork to convert to Protestantism, but the
spontaneous manifestation of deep-seated resentment of souperism nearly
a century and a half later. Since the practice of applauding a sermon is an
extremely rare occurrence, this episode confirms the depth of bitterness felt
by Catholics in an affluent Dublin suburb as late as the 1980s.

Little evidence exists of positive results from the ICM's crusade, except
its initial provision of famine relief, its education of poor children and
its founding of children's homes. If measured in terms of numbers of
permanent converts in Ireland, the enterprise was an abject failure, although
a sizeable number of converts and their descendants remained in the
reformed faith, but overseas. Indirectly, its presence facilitated an adequate
educational provision throughout the island; for this increased Catholic
infrastructure the ICM can take credit. In the long run, the ICM had little
direct impact on Irish Catholics while many southern Protestants regret
its operations in former years. However, Protestant mission, and memories
of Protestant mission, merely amplified the already extant resentments of
Irish Catholics towards their Protestant countrymen, consequent on the
pre-existing association of the Protestant faith with English occupation and
domination, and with the subsequent oppression of the majority population.
The modifications in ethnicity consequent on the creation of the ICM
were largely products of Catholic counter-mission and are only indirectly
attributable to the Society. These were initially fostered by the imposition
of an unwelcome Protestant mission in a predominantly Catholic country
and later by the intolerant rebound ideologies of a formerly oppressed
community. Animosity towards Protestants, engendered by the creation
of the ICM in 1849 and astutely nurtured in Irish Catholics during the
following century by clever rhetoric and astute exploitation of Protestant
mission, gave little scope for a benign treatment of Protestants in the early
decades of the Irish Free State.

The Church of Ireland suffered more from the ICM's efforts than did the
Catholic church. What damage was inflicted on Catholicism was compara-
tively small scale and short lived whereas, even in early decades, Protestant
opinion observed that aggressive evangelicalism by 'stimulating the spirit
of proselytism and deepening religious animosities ... has added greatly
to the social and political divisions of the nation'.[81] Although the harm

inflicted on Protestantism in general, and on the Church of Ireland in particular, has repercussions to this day, it must be considered that this may have been caused as much by a Catholic manipulation of proselytism as by proselytism itself.

Notes

1 David Hempton and Myrtle Hill, *Evangelical Protestantism in Ulster society, 1870–1890* (London, 1992), p. 81.

2 Desmond Bowen, *Souperism: myth or reality?* (Cork, 1970), p. 139.

3 Bowen, *Souperism*, p. 175.

4 Desmond Bowen, *The Protestant crusade in Ireland, 1800–70* (Dublin, 1978), p. 267.

5 Peadar MacSuibhne, *Paul Cullen and his contemporaries, with their letters, 1820–1902* (5 vols, Naas, 1962–74), iii, p. 118.

6 Jennifer Ridden, 'The forgotten history of the Protestant Crusade: religious liberalism in Ireland', *Journal of Religious History*, xxxi, no. 1, 78–102.

7 ICM Archive, John Allen Fitzgerald Gregg to Mr Coates, 26 Oct. 1946.

8 For instance Cullen boasted to Tobias Kirby that he had never dined with a Protestant and considered that 'Catholics who mix with Protestants are hostile to all of us'. Paul Cullen to Tobias Kirby, 28 July 1865 in 'Irish College, Rome: Kirby Papers', edited by Patrick J. Corish, *Archivium Hibernicum*, xxx (1972), 48.

9 Mary Francis Cusack, *Tim O'Halloran's choice; or from Killarney to New York* (London, Dublin, 1877), pp. x–xii.

10 W. R. Wilde, *Irish superstitions* (Dublin, 1852), p. 17.

11 Bowen, *Protestant crusade*, pp. 270–3; *Irish People*, 9 Apr. 1864; John A. Murphy, 'Priests and people in modern Irish history', *Christus Rex*, xxiii (1969), 354; S. J. Connolly, *Religion and society in nineteenth century Ireland* (Dublin, 1987, first published Dundalk, 1985), pp. 12–15.

12 E. J. Quigley, 'Grace abounding', *Irish Ecclesiastical Record*, xxii (1923), pp. 59–60.

13 Catholics and Jews formed their own charitable organisation in nineteenth-century Britain when faced with Protestant missions. Frank Prochaska, *The voluntary impulse: philanthropy in modern Britain* (London, 1988), p. 23.

14 SBO, *Twenty-eighth annual report*, 1885, p. 5; C. H. K. Broughton, *What I saw in Dublin, an address delivered in the Church House, Westminster on May 8th 1914* (Dublin, n.d.), p. 11.

15 CP, MS No. GRE/G3/2/20, Fanny D'Arcy to Elizabeth Copley, 22 Mar. [1854].

16 Fanny Bellingham, *Fourth account of the fund entrusted to Miss Fanny Bellingham ... for the Relief of the Converts and Children of Connemara* (Wonston, 1851).

17 Christine Kinealy, 'Potatoes, providence and philanthropy: the role of private charity during the Irish potato famine' in Patrick O'Sullivan (ed.), *The meaning of the famine* (London, 1997), p. 144.

18 IFC Archive, MS No. S4: 308, told by Brighid Bean Uí Thuathaith, Sellerna.

19 Bowen, *Souperism*, pp. 223–34.

20 For example in Swinford, County Mayo, Benjamin Eames, rector, and Bernard Durkin, parish priest, worked side by side to alleviate famine conditions. Ibid., pp. 200–7.

21 In 1861 the Irish Society had missions in the following counties: Clare (4), Cork (9), Donegal (7), Down (1), Galway (5), Kerry (9), Limerick (9), Mayo (6), Roscommon (1), Sligo (1), Tipperary (4) and Waterford (8). Irish Society, *Report for 1861* (Dublin, 1861); Irish Society, *Report, 1871* (Dublin, 1871).

22 Ridden, 'The forgotten history of the Protestant Crusade', 78–102.

23 At Bunmahon, Fourmilewater, Waterford, Lismore, Tramore. See Eugene Broderick, 'The famine and religious controversy in Waterford', *Decies*, li (1995), 11–24.

24 *Waterford Chronicle*, 22 Mar. 1848.

25 Joe Power, 'Proselytism and perversion in west Clare', *The Other Clare*, xxx (2006), 55–60.

26 P[atrick] White, 'Proselytism in West Clare: a retrospect', *Irish Ecclesiastical Record*, viii (May 1887), 411–21.

27 Entry of Máire Ní Iubaurd, Cill Rush [Kilrush], in the Schools Collection (1937), quoted in Power, 'Proselytism and perversion', 56.

28 Dáire Keogh, *Edmund Rice and the first Christian Brothers* (Dublin, 2008), pp. 173–9.

29 Elizabeth Hely Walsh, *Kingston's revenge: a story of bravery and single-hearted endeavour* (London, 1917), pp. 280, 298. First published as *Golden hills, a tale of the Irish famine* (London, 1865).

30 Melissa Fegan, *Literature and the Irish famine, 1845–1919* (Oxford, 2002), p. 225.

31 Emily Bowles, *Irish diamonds: or a chronicle of Peterstown* (London, 1864), p. 174.

32 Richard Baptist O'Brien, *The D'Altons of Crag: a story of '48 and '49* (Dublin, 1882), p. 129, see also Allan H. Clington [David Power Conyngham], *Frank O'Donnell: a tale of Irish life* (Dublin, 1861).

33 O'Brien, *The D'Altons*, p. 129; Richard Baptist O'Brien, *Ailey Moore, A tale of the times* (London and Baltimore, 1856), pp. 40, 308.

34 Cusack, *Tim O'Halloran's choice*, pp. x, xviii. The preface entitled 'The new departure in Ireland, souperism revived' was not included in the edition published in New York.

35 Ibid., pp. x–xii, xxvii.

36 Ibid., p. xxviii.

37 Although the story is set in Kerry, it clearly refers to the work of the ICM: the Birds' Nest Orphanage is called the Hawks' Nest and the fictional missionary organisation is called the 'Society for the Conversion of the Irish Nation'.

38 Cusack, *Tim O'Halloran's choice*, pp. 26, 70–1.

39 Ibid., p. 18.

40 Ibid., p. 257.

41 Quigley, 'Grace abounding', *Irish Ecclesiastical Record*, xxii (1923), 615.

42 Joseph Liechty and Cecelia Clegg, *Moving beyond sectarianism: religion, conflict and reconciliation in Northern Ireland* (Dublin, 2001), p. 91. See also Kinealy, 'Potatoes, providence and philanthropy', p. 144; Hempton and Hill, *Evangelical Protestantism in Ulster society*, p. 81; Bowen, *Souperism*, p. 175; Bowen, *Protestant crusade*, p. 314.

43 P. O'Farrell, *Ireland's English question: Anglo Irish relations, 1534–1970* (London, 1971), p. 113 quoted in Bryan Fanning, *Racism and social change in the republic of Ireland* (Manchester, 2001), p. 52.

44 C. Davis, 'Cape Clear: a retrospect', *The Month and Catholic Review*, 24 (1881), 476–88, see also White, 'Proselytism in West Clare'.

45 For example, a Dáil debate on the need for increased tillage during World War II heard that 'a hungry people are easily enslaved ... in another epoch, because of shortage of food, men were tempted to abandon Faith and Fatherland', *Clare Champion*, 1 Mar. 1941 (P. J. McLoghlen, TD for County Clare).

46 Although the numerous textbooks produced by the Irish Christian Brothers contain no direct account of proselytism during the famine, connections are fostered between the Irish nation and the Catholic faith, especially in English readers. For example, 'A nation's history told in its ruins' in Christian Brothers, *The second book of reading lessons by the Christian Brothers* (Dublin, 1846), p. 54, tells how ruined churches revealed a 'road of three hundred years ... that leads to martyrs' and patriots' graves, it is the road wet with the tears and with the blood of a persecuted and down-trodden people ... the emblem of the nation's undying fidelity to God'.

47 Mary Francis Cusack, *A history of the Irish nation, social, ecclesiastical, biographical and antiquarian* (London, 1876), p. 953.

48 Christian Brothers, *Irish history reader* (Dublin, 1907), p. 339.

49 Pádraig Ua Duinnín, *Creideamh agus gorta: faith and famine, a tragic drama relating to the famine period* (Dublin, 1901), p. 6.

50 Susan Campbell Berloletti, *Black potatoes: the story of the great Irish famine, 1845–50* (New York, 2001), p. 71.

51 Ua Duinnín, *Creideamh agus gorta*, p. 15, 'Beidh Cáith na Sagsanach mhaith fós' [the English/Protestant struggle will come right yet.]

52 Ibid., pp. 9, 18 'ní fheaca riamh fear ná bean ná páiste ag teacht ag iarradh unbhraithe' [not man nor woman nor child was ever seen to be looking for soup]; 'ní raibh aoinne chun é d'ól ach is dóigh leis an sean-buachaill go bhfuil sé ag déanamh Sagsanach ar fuaidh na dúthaighe' [there was nobody to drink it but the old lad supposes he is making Protestants [or Englishmen] all over the place].

53 Ibid., pp. 14–15 'daoine fiadhainne, droch-bhearacha, gan eagla roimh Dhia ná daoine acu' [wild, bad-mannered people, without fear of God nor man]; 'is mór atá sé tuillte acu' [there is more than that due to them].

54 *The Arrow*, 1 June 1907.

55 James Joyce, *Ulysses* (Picador edn, London, 1997), p. 172.

56 Augustus Thébaud, *The Irish race in the past and the present* (New York, 1878), p. 358.

57 Lucy McDiurmid, *The Irish art of controversy* (Dublin, 2005), pp. 123–66.

58 Emily Reilly, 'Women and voluntary work' in Adrian Gregory and Senia Peseta (eds), *Ireland and the great war: a war to unite us all* (Manchester, 2004), p. 51.

59 *Church of Ireland Gazette*, 20 Mar. 1914.

60 Peadar Ua Laoghaire, *Mo scéal féin* (Dublin, c.1920), p. 140.

61 'Proddy woddy on the wall / Half a loaf would feed you all / Half a candle would show you light / To read your bible in the night.' Éilis Brady, *All in, all in: a selection of Dublin children's traditional street games with rhymes and music* (Dublin, 1975), p. 172.

62 George Hook, speaking on 'The Right Hook', on Newstalk 106FM, 6 Jan. 2006, 5.50 pm.

63 Written by Peadar O'Flanagan in *Mayo News*, quoted in Patrick Riddell, *The Irish – are they real?* (London, 1972), p. 49.

64 The difficulties associated with folklore and memories of traumatic events are outlined in Cormac Ó Gráda (ed.), *Ireland's great famine: interdisciplinary essays* (Dublin, 2006), pp. 224–5; Niall Ó Ciosáin, 'Approaching a folklore archive: the Irish Folklore Commission and the memory of the great famine', *Folklore* (Aug. 2004), 222–32.

65 Global or national memory refers to events on a large or nation-wide scale and is generally derived from written sources. Local memory, at the other end of the spectrum, consists of intimate local knowledge, folklore, and oral histories, often naming individuals and places. Popular memory exists between these two extremes and assimilates a stylised repertoire of images and stories, setting them within the larger narrative of global memory. Ó Ciosáin, 'Approaching a folklore archive', 224–6.

66 Cathal Póirtéir, *Famine echoes* (Dublin, 1995), pp. 166–81. Portéir cites evidence from counties Antrim, Cavan, Clare, Cork, Donegal, Down, Galway, Kerry, Limerick, Longford, Wexford and Tipperary. In many instances proselytisers are depicted as being outwitted by converts who made brief conversions for relief or who kept rosary-beads in their pocket throughout divine service.

67 Ó Ciosáin, 'Approaching a folklore archive', 228.

68 R. Dudley Edwards and T. Desmond Williams, *The great famine* (Dublin, 1944, first published 1956), *passim*; Brendan Bradshaw, 'Nationalism and historical scholarship in modern Ireland' in Ciarán Brady, *Interpreting Irish history* (Dublin, 1994), p. 204.

69 For example an editorial in the *Catholic Bulletin* described Church of Ireland clergy as being still 'in the grip of Cromwell's army', *Catholic Bulletin*, xxiii (1933), 618.

70 Fanning, *Racism and social change*, p. 52.

71 Unidentified response to Folklore Commission Enquiry on the famine, collected in 1940, quoted in Kevin Whelan, 'Tionchar an ghorta' in Cathal Póirtéir (ed.), *Gnéithe an ghorta* (Dublin, 1995), p. 43.

72 ICM Archive, John Allen Fitzgerald Gregg to Mr Coates, 26 Oct. 1946.

73 Lily O'Shea tells how Protestant girls were promoted to office work while Catholic girls remained on the shop floor. Lily O'Connor, *Can Lily O'Shea*

come out to play? (Dingle, 2000), p. 186. Correspondence in the ICM Archive contains many examples of Protestant businesses notifying the ICM of vacancies.

74 Bernard O'Reilly, *John MacHale, his life, times and correspondence* (2 vols, New York, 1890), ii, p. 440.

75 Quoted in R. F. Foster, *Modern Ireland* (London, 1989), p. 329n.

76 Personal communication, August 2004. This person did not want to be identified.

77 Interviewees No. 16, 6 in Heather Crawford, 'Protestants and Irishness in independent Ireland: an exploration' (Ph.D. dissertation, National University of Ireland, Maynooth, 2008). This oral history study has encountered many examples of Protestant sensitivity regarding missionary activities at the time of the famine; see also interviewee No. 21: 'I wonder to myself whether the people who converted, because they couldn't feed themselves and had to take soup … Because not everybody has, not every Protestant has been Protestant through and through. Em, maybe their family was Catholic before.'

78 Stephen Mennell, 'Protestants in a Catholic state: a silent minority in Ireland', in Tom Inglis et al., *Religion and politics: east–west contrasts from contemporary Europe* (Dublin, 2000), p. 85.

79 Jack White, *Minority report: the Protestant community in the Irish Republic* (Dublin, 1975), p. 46.

80 *Irish Times*, 3 Oct. 1985, p. 3.

81 Lecky, *History of England*, ii (ed. 1878), p. 611, quoted in M. Hurley, *The Furrow*, Apr. 1965, 237, fn.

Conclusion

The Society for Irish Church Missions to the Roman Catholics, founded by committed evangelicals to rescue those 'trapped in the errors of Rome', quickly acquired social and political objectives. Anti-Catholic sentiments, which had flourished since the Act of Union, intensified in the face of campaigns for Catholic emancipation (1829) and the relief of tithes (1838). The sense of threat to the Protestant *status quo* was amplified by the active participation of Roman clergy in these political crusades. The increase in the government grant to Maynooth (1845) was perceived as an indulgence of the seditious Church of Rome so that there was a considerable support-base in Britain for efforts to suppress Catholicism, even prior to the arrival of tens of thousands of famine migrants into British cities. For those embracing millenarian beliefs, the cause held additional appeal. The restoration of the English Catholic hierarchy in 1851 and the ensuing furore would further intensify anti-Roman sentiments, increasing the attraction of the ICM. This coincided with 'the high-water mark of Protestant activity' in the 1840s and early 1850s, symbolised by the foundation of the National Club (1845) and in Reformation Societies.[1] From its inception, the ICM targeted the poor, inviting their attendance with offers of relief and education. By advertising an ability to convert idle, lawless Irish Catholic peasants to industrious Protestant citizens of the empire, it naively promised to effect ethnological change and to resolve the 'Irish problem'.

The Society for Irish Church Missions was an English organisation, all power remaining with a body of English gentlemen, many of whom were without intimate knowledge of Ireland, its history or its people. Above all, the Society's inability to perceive that Ireland differed fundamentally from Britain ensured that the movement could not aspire to permanent successes. Its naïve assumption that attendance at 'feeding' schools and services equalled devout and permanent doctrinal conversions demonstrates an immense ignorance of the character of the Irish poor. Its extravagant claims of effecting not only religious but also political and ethnological change galvanised Catholic forces to redouble their efforts to combat the movement. Its lack of understanding of the affiliation between the Irish poor and their Catholic faith led the Society to launch an attack on the religion and culture of Ireland's poorest, who of course 'converted' to survive; the poor have always remained alive by living on their wits. Taking soup was merely another tactic whereby the underprivileged acquired their most basic requirements of food, clothing and warmth. Indeed, it can be successfully argued that starving, uneducated persons were not in a position to engage with sophisticated theological concepts.

The global movement of mid-nineteenth-century evangelicalism, of which the ICM was a part, focused as much on the eradication of Catholicism as on the dissemination of the scriptures. As mainstream Protestant interests shifted to other concerns, such as the anti-slavery movement and the conversion of 'heathens' in foreign lands, support for the anti-popery cause waned and the campaign to convert Ireland's Catholics became a mere footnote in the religious history of the nineteenth and twentieth centuries.[2] That is not to say that anti-Catholicism was entirely lacking in supporters. It is clear that a near obsession with the errors of Rome held a tenacious grip on the minds of a small group of committed biblicals well into the twentieth century. Although this represented only a very small minority of public opinion, well-structured networks of conventions and meetings, reinforced by a substantial body of anti-Roman publications, ensured the continuance of anti-Catholic sentiments. Examination of the ICM's twentieth-century correspondence indicates that the Society was merely part of a world-wide scriptural movement which focused on the denunciation of Catholic doctrines and influences. However, the ICM was unique within global English-speaking evangelicalism, in that it operated in a Catholic environment where its forthright condemnation of Roman errors was counter-productive and even hazardous. This should not suggest that it was alone in its desire to convert Irish Catholics to scriptural Protestantism; many other societies were founded for this purpose, both within and without the Established Church. The ICM differed from these proselytising societies in its direct denunciation of Catholicism, an approach it maintained even in the Catholic-dominated Irish Free State.

The initial appeal of the ICM, consequent on famine conditions, ensured a substantial uptake of its relief programme, which was responsible for maintaining thousands who might otherwise have perished. It rapidly developed a sophisticated publicity machine of monthly magazines and mission tour publications which depicted Irish peasant attendances at 'feeding-services' as proof of devout conversions. Once the falseness of this portrayal was exposed in the 1860s, especially after the production of the 1861 census results, much material of a highly critical nature was produced. They cast grave doubts on the ICM's claimed successes and on its methodologies as many considered that controversialism, a part of the ICM's armoury from the outset, was counter-productive and insulting in its denunciation of Catholicism.

After a short period of success, the ICM's appeal diminished as Catholics distanced themselves from its activities, partly due to an amelioration of famine conditions and partly due to counter-missionary tactics. These included the provision of Catholic relief, alternative educational facilities, improved pastoral care and the social ostracism of converts. Association with proselytising missions was discouraged in street-ballads, by which Catholic contempt for converts and mission agents was disseminated down to and through the illiterate levels of society, the very people targeted by the ICM. The success of the Catholic counter-missionary action should not, however, blind us to the enormous successes of the ICM in its early years, nor to the likelihood that the mission might have won more converts if it had adopted a less controversial approach.

By the time of widespread Catholic dissociation in the late 1850s, a large mission infrastructure of newly constructed churches, schools and homes served to promote the work of the ICM; its supporters incorrectly interpreting the existence of buildings as proof of thriving congregations. Research has shown that in Connemara, mission agents formed a small, closely inter-related network and that those who remained in connection with the ICM benefited materially through employment as trained agents or as Irish teachers, or by living in mission cottages. Permanent conversions were most likely among the school-going cohort of the early 1850s, with occasional mission involvement in subsequent generation although reversions to Catholicism were commonplace from the 1860s and 1870s, often involving the return of entire families.

The movement, initially supported in both Ireland and England, soon lost the backing of some Irish Protestants, mostly due to allegations of bribery, dislike of controversialism and exposure of exaggerated claims of success. Its missionary income, which emanated almost entirely from England, declined markedly from its high-point of £40,039 in 1854, the effect of which was exacerbated by increased salary costs. Its philanthropic income was primarily raised in Ireland, where minimal reference was made to the missionary objectives of its schools and homes, stressing instead its charitable efforts to feed and clothe the poor. The disestablishment of the Church of Ireland and the departure of the landed classes had little impact on the viabilities of newly formed parishes of west Galway, which were supported by missionary funds from England.

Intense violent opposition to ICM agents and converts in Connemara from 1878 to 1884, assisted by the simultaneous terror of land-war activity, forced the reversion of a large number of 'luke-warm' converts, many of whom testified that they had been bribed to profess Protestantism or to send their children to mission schools. The lack of sympathy shown to mission agents by the London Committee in the aftermath of this episode demonstrates the emotional distance between the architects of ICM policies and both the providers and recipients of its efforts.

The ICM's gradual withdrawal from rural areas to urban locations reflects an acknowledgement that strong social and family influences ran counter to successful mission. By the late nineteenth century, almost all its efforts were concentrated in Dublin and larger towns, supplemented by itinerant preaching at fairs and sea-side resorts, where it increasingly attracted the interest of original Protestants as by then it encompassed an additional objective: the preservation of Protestantism. Its street preaching was unofficially assimilated into the anti Home Rule movement, with Catholic hostility to evangelising agents portrayed to English supporters as a foretaste of the treatment Protestants might expect if Home Rule came to pass. The patronage of the Irish House of Bishops at this juncture probably reflects this role of protecting Protestant interests, although it did not command the support of the entire House of Irish Bishops until the mid 1920s. The Society's missionary work received little backing from the Irish Protestant laity, many of whom felt that its methods were likely to provoke unrest. As two Irish rectors acknowledged, Irish clergy of the late nineteenth century were less antagonistic to Catholics than some of their English counterparts, finding that 'the R.C. population are very friendly, and even affectionate' and that Irish clergymen held 'much less of a party feeling and much less of extreme opinions'.[3]

The work of the ICM was largely untouched by the creation of the Irish Free State; it continued its mission of street preaching and house visiting, supplemented by its Dublin schools. In 1920 it added The Children's Fold, a home for children of unmarried mothers. Although this was established to rear children of Catholic mothers in the Protestant faith, in the absence of adequate services for Protestant mothers it drew most of its intake from within Protestantism, to the intense displeasure of the London Committee. The ICM's 1932 correspondence reveals little contact with either the laity or clergy of the Church of Ireland.[4] By then some Protestants considered that the ICM had become an embarrassing peripheral anachronism in Irish Protestantism.

The ICM's legacy to Ireland lies not in a convert community, but rather in the bitter memories of bribery and insult, as localised 'memories' were nurtured and stage-managed to create a universal experience. The Irish Free State was an uncomfortable place for many Protestants, due in part to the connection fostered in the mentality of some Irish Catholics between

Catholicism and Irishness, while many Protestants questioned the wisdom of continuing with aggressive proselytism in the Catholic-dominated Irish Free State.

With hindsight, it can be argued that the ICM answered more the fears of Protestants than the needs of Catholics. Mainstream support for the ICM waxed and waned in response to perceived Catholic aggression, an observation also made of support for the Orange Order.[5] Its foundation coincided with the influx of famine Irish to Britain and the restoration of the Catholic hierarchy; its partial rehabilitation occurred under threat of Home Rule. Although conceived and delivered for the spiritual and material benefit of Catholics, in reality the Society answered primarily to the religious, social, cultural and political needs of Protestants, both Irish and English.

So was there ever any likelihood of permanent success? For a variety of reasons, it appears there was not. The obvious cause is the lack of empathy of the English policy makers with the Irish character and Irish social structures. Potential success was also hampered by the ICM's urgency for results, a factor which led to its dissociation from the Irish Society in 1856 and to the loss of support among Irish clergy. Dallas might well have heeded Revd M'Ilwaine's advice to *festina lente*, as under less combative conditions, exposure of multiple generations to the influence of scriptural schools might have yielded more satisfactory results.[6]

The ICM was also hampered by the pre-existing association in the Irish mind of Protestantism with English occupation, a connection astutely exploited in counter-missionary literature and street-ballads which depicted mission involvement as a treacherous coupling with the English enemy. Steeped in recent memories of penal restrictions and armed with a new confidence from their ability to force through emancipation, Irish Catholics might have been expected to repel an aggressive, full-frontal attack on their faith and culture while a more kindly and subtle appeal to their educational needs might have prospered.

The pre-existence of a long-established Anglican community in Ireland also contributed to the failure of the ICM. Unlike Protestant missions to foreign lands, the ICM sought to assimilate peasant-converts into an already extant church structure, which had clearly defined social, political and cultural strata and where the peasant class was under-represented and probably unwanted. Henry Venn, who led the Church Missionary Society from 1841 to 1872, had insisted on a policy of 'triple autonomy', ordering that missions should be led towards financial, administrative and missionary control and arguing that convert communities should assume responsibility to nominate pastors and show that they were not 'the agents of a foreign society'.[7] Such an approach was not available to the ICM, whose converts could never aspire to preferment within the class-ridden structure of nineteenth-century Anglicanism.

The ICM's greatest, albeit unwitting, impact on Ireland was to strengthen and reinforce the belief in the minds of Irish Catholics that to be truly Irish one had to be Catholic. This was initially nurtured by the counter-missionary tactic of connecting efforts to protect Irish Catholicism with the struggle against British rule. Missionary activities during the famine were depicted in literature as cruel, but futile, efforts of arrogant proselytisers, which were shunned even by the starving peasantry. Over time the concept of souperism was broadened to include all forms of Protestant philanthropy. Utilising clever rhetoric of this nature, and capitalising on the over-riding fears that Protestantism might triumph in Catholic Ireland, the very real but localised effects of the ICM and other proselytising societies were interpreted by Irish Catholics as a nation-wide attack on their church and culture, and contributed to the harsh treatment of Protestants in the early decades of the Irish Free State.

And the lessons to be learned from this exploration of the Irish Church Missions? As this study explores the experiences of mission in a predominantly English-speaking environment, the attitudes and perceptions of both the providers and recipients are readily accessible.[8] It questions the merits of ardent missioners who seek to impose their beliefs even where they are unwelcome, an experience mirrored in foreign missions.[9] It demonstrates how an ostensibly religious movement can encompass cultural and political overtones. It reveals the hostility felt by an indigenous people when deeply held beliefs are attacked and long-existing traditions vilified.[10] It questions the benefits of imposing one's opinion, regardless of 'knowing' that one is right, and shows how persons can justify dubious methodologies to achieve strongly held objectives. Indeed, this entire study might question whether mission in general serves to answer to the needs of the donor or of the recipient community. It demonstrates how religion pervades all aspects of life and shows how seemingly secular events and decisions can mask unspoken and maybe unacknowledged religious agendas while ostensibly religious movements always contain political, social or ethnological aspects.

Viewed through twenty-first-century eyes, the activities of the ICM seem, at best, questionable but they should be viewed in the context of missionary methods of the nineteenth and early twentieth centuries. In its time, controversialism was not only condoned, but also inculcated in both Protestant and Catholic seminaries and was an accepted *modus operandi* of mission work. Similarly, the ethnological objectives of the ICM must be situated in the nineteenth century, when colonising agendas of both Catholic and Protestant missions showed little regard for native traditions and lifestyles. In seeking to effect cultural change, Protestant missions did not have a monopoly on obliterating native customs.[11] The strife caused by the imposition of 'colonising' religions has been acknowledged, as Michael MacDonald observes: 'Religion serves, therefore, to reproduce the original and dominant conflict between the native and settler populations.'[12]

Those who founded the Irish Church Missions did so out of an overwhelming sense of responsibility to rescue Irish Catholics from the eternal fires of hell. They viewed any ensuing confrontation as an unfortunate but inevitable by-product of their divinely inspired crusade. Despite the considerable social discord caused by the ICM, it must be recognised that its founders and agents acted out of sincere religious conviction, even compulsion, to attack the doctrines of Catholicism and to rescue those souls trapped in its clutches. However questionable their methodologies, it would be unjust to dismiss or even question the integrity of their motivations. Their zeal to save Catholic souls must temper the justifiable criticism of the methods they employed.

Notes

1 Many ICM office-holders were members of the National Club (duke of Manchester, earl of Cavan, earl of Roden, Viscount Bernard, marquis of Blandford, Charles Frewen, G. A. Hamilton, C. A. Moody, J. Napier, J. Plumptre, W. Verner, John Colquhoun, Dibgy Mackworth, Edward Bickersteth, Robert Bickersteth, Lord Ashley, later earl of Shaftesbury. Source: National Club members in 1848 in John Wolffe, *Protestant crusade in Great Britain, 1829–1860* (Oxford, 1991), pp. 212–14; ICM, *Annual reports*, 1850–60).

2 Sheridan Wayne Gilley, 'Evangelical and Roman Catholic missions to the Irish in London, 1830–1870' (Ph.D. dissertation, University of Cambridge, 1970), p. 114.

3 A. W. Edwards, 'Historic sketch of the Church of Ireland' in J. Byrne, A. W. Edwards, W. Anderson and A. T. Lee (eds), *Essays on the Irish Church by clergymen of the Established Church in Ireland* (London, 1866), p. 143; Courtney Moore, *A chapter of Irish church history, being some personal recollections of a life and service in the Church of Ireland* (Dublin, 1907), p. 27.

4 A small number of individuals including clergy corresponded regularly with the ICM, and a small number of clergy invited T. C. Hammond to preach in their churches.

5 Patrick Mitchel, *Evangelicalism and national identity in Ulster, 1921–1998* (Oxford, 2003), p. 135.

6 William MacIlwaine, *Irish Church Missions to the Roman Catholics: supplement to correspondence* (London, 1861).

7 Peter Williams, '"Not transplanting": Henry Venn's strategic vision' in Kevin Ward and Brian Stanley, *The Church Mission Society and world Christianity,*

1799–1999 (Cambridge, 2000), pp. 153–4; Jean Comby, *How to understand the history of Christian mission* (London, 1996), p. 122.

8 Although the ICM operated in the Irish-speaking region of Connemara and some material *as Gaeilge* has been located, which adds considerably to the study, most contemporary observations, both supporting and opposing the mission, were written in English, an occurrence which might not be commonplace if studying either Catholic or Protestant missions abroad.

9 An East India Company employee noted that 'I perceived that I must be watchful whenever I encountered in others an ostentatious profession of zeal for religion.' G. Crawshay, *Proselytism destructive of Christianity and incompatible with political dominion* (London, 1858), p. 3.

10 As in Renvyle, where a mission school was built on top of a ring fort.

11 The (Catholic) Foreign Missions of Milan were established in 1850, the (Catholic) African Missions of Lyon in 1856, the (Catholic) Scheut Fathers in Belgium in 1860 and the (Catholic) Mill Hill Fathers in England in 1866. Comby, *How to understand the history of Christian mission*, pp. 119–21.

12 Michael MacDonald, *Children of wrath: political violence in Northern Ireland* (Cambridge, 1986), p. 8.

Appendix: years of operation of ICM stations, 1848–1949

Location	Station	1850	1860	1870	1880	1890	1900	1910	1920	1930	1940
Connemara	Ballyconree										
Connemara	Barnatrough										
Connemara	Innisturk										
Connemara	Turbot Island										
Connemara	Bayleek										
Connemara	Cliften										
Connemara	Derrylea										
Connemara	Fakeragh										
Connemara	Coolaklei										
Connemara	Ballinaboy										
Connemara	Derryoughter										
Connemara	Errislannan										
Connemara	Aillebrack										
Connemara	Derrygimla										
Connemara	Duholla										
Connemara	Errisbeg										
Connemara	Mannin										
Connemara	Moyrus										
Connemara	Ballinahinch										
Connemara	Cashel										
Connemara	Roundstone										
Connemara	Barnahalia										
Connemara	Claddaghduff										
Connemara	Dolan										
Connemara	Omey Island										
Connemara	Patches										

Location	Station	1850	1860	1870	1880	1890	1900	1910	1920	1930	1940
Connemara	Russadilisk										
Connemara	Sellerna										
Connemara	Streamstown										
Connemara	Connemara Medical										
Connemara	Ballinakill										
Connemara	Cleggan										
Connemara	Clonluan										
Connemara	Letterfrack										
Connemara	Renvyle										
Connemara	Salruck										
Connemara	Casla										
Connemara	Garumna Island										
Connemara	Killeen										
Connemara	Lettermullin										
Connemara	Lettermore										
Connemara	Inverin										
Connemara	Spiddal										
Connemara	Aasleagh										
Connemara	Bundoraha										
Connemara	Delphi										
Connemara	Bunlahinch										
Connemara	Cappanalaura										
Connemara	Castlekerke										
Connemara	Curnamona										
Connemara	Lyons										
Connemara	Kilmilkin										
Connemara	Bunakyle										
Connemara	Glengola										
Connemara	Loughgannon										

Location	Station	1850	1860	1870	1880	1890	1900	1910	1920	1930	1940
Connemara	Ross										
Connemara	Glan										
Connemara	Kilmilken										
Connemara	Oughterard										
Connemara	Cappaghaduff										
Connemara	Drimcoggy										
Connemara	Partree										
Connemara	Tourmakeady										
Dublin	Annuitants										
Dublin	Aasleagh										
Dublin	Booterstown										
Dublin	Barrack St										
Dublin	Childrens Fold										
Dublin	City mission										
Dublin	Coombe Male										
Dublin	Coombe Female										
Dublin	Elliott Home										
Dublin	Female Training School										
Dublin	Gr Canal St Female										
Dublin	Gr Canal St Male										
Dublin	Irish Church Colportage										
Dublin	Irish Society										
Dublin	Irishtown & Donnybrook										
Dublin	Kingstown										
Dublin	Kingstown School										
Dublin	Kingstown Stanhope										
Dublin	Ladies Home										
Dublin	Luke St School										
Dublin	Lurgan St Female										

Location	Station	1850	1860	1870	1880	1890	1900	1910	1920	1930	1940
Dublin	Lurgan St Male										
Dublin	Male Training School										
Dublin	Manor House Home										
Dublin	Monkstown										
Dublin	Rath Row School										
Dublin	Readers Branch										
Dublin	Spiddal Birds Nest										
Dublin	Supplementary										
Dublin	Townsend St School										
Dublin	Training School Mixed										
Dublin	Visiting Branch										
Achill Island	Achill										
Achill Island	Ashleaem										
Achill Island	Brianasgal										
Achill Island	Cloughmore										
Achill Island	Cashel										
Achill Island	Derreen										
Achill Island	Duogh										
Achill Island	Duniver										
Achill Island	Duega										
Achill Island	Keel										
Achill Island	Meelan										
Achill Island	River										
Achill Island	Salia										
Achill Island	Shraheens										
Achill Island	Shievemore										
Achill Island	The Sound										
Achill Island	Dugort										
Achill-mainland	Curraun										

Location	Station
Achill-mainland	Pulranny East
Achill-mainland	Pulranny West
Achill-Burrishoole	Burrishoole
Achill-Burrishoole	Tiernard
Achill-Burrishoole	Mulranny
Antrim, North	Antrim, North
Aran	
Ardee	Ardee
Armagh & Lough	Newtown Hamilton
Antrim, North	Antrim, Glens of
Aughrim	Aughrim
Aughrim	Loughrea
Balla Upper	Ballaghaderreen
Balla Upper	Kiltamagh
Balla, Lower	Balla
Balla	Ballinrobe
Balla, Lower	Ballyheane
Ballycroy	Ballycroy
Bandon	Bandon
Bandon	Courtmacsherry
Bandon	Desert
Bandon	Dunmanway
Bandon	Timoleague
Belfast	Belfast
Borris	Borris
Borris	Enniscorthy
Borris	New Ross
Cashel	Cashel
Clontuskert	Clontuskert

Chart columns (years): 1850, 1860, 1870, 1880, 1890, 1900, 1910, 1920, 1930, 1940

Location	Station	1850	1860	1870	1880	1890	1900	1910	1920	1930	1940
County Clare	County Clare										
County Limerick	Askeaton										
County Limerick	Pallaskerry										
County Wicklow	County Wicklow										
Collooney	Collooney										
Coolaney	Coolaney										
Cork	Cork City										
Down & Antrim	Down & Antrim										
East Cork	Fermoy										
East Cork	Queenstown										
Erris	Bangor Erris										
Forkhill	Forkhill										
Galway	Ardrahan										
Galway	Ballagh										
Galway	Barna										
Galway	Galway										
Galway	Gort										
Galway	Moycullen										
Galway	Oranmore										
Headford	Annaghadown										
Headford	Cong										
Headford	Headford										
Headford	Shrule										
Headford	The Neale										
Innishowen	Innishowen										
Kilkenny	Ballyragget										
Kilkenny	Callan										
Kilkenny	Carlow										
Kilkenny	Graignemanagh										

Location	Station	1850	1860	1870	1880	1890	1900	1910	1920	1930	1940
Kilkenny	Kilkenny										
Kilkenny	Knocktopher										
Killala	Killala										
Kingscourt	Kingscourt										
Kinsale	Kinsale										
Knappagh	Knappagh										
Leitrim & Cavan	Leitrim & Cavan										
Lough Derg	Nenagh										
Lough Erne	Lough Erne										
Lough Foyle	Lough Foyle										
Lough Glynn	Lough Glynn										
Louth	Baronstown										
Louth	Drogheda										
Louth	Dundalk										
Louth	Louth										
Meath	Meath										
Middleton	Middleton										
Morne	Morne										
North Antrim	Ballymoney										
North Antrim	North Antrim										
North Eastern	Cushendall										
North Mayo & Sligo	Rathlackan										
North Mayo & Sligo	Stonehall										
North Sligo	North Sligo										
North West Sligo	Sligo										
Ossary	Graigue										
Ossary	Ross (Ossary)										
Portarlington	Portarlington										
Rooveagh	Moyode										

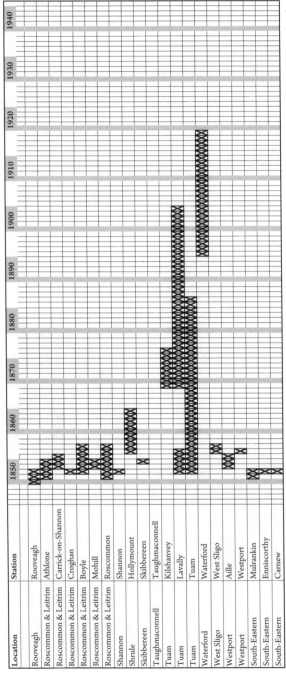

Location	Station	1850	1860	1870	1880	1890	1900	1910	1920	1930	1940
Rooveagh	Rooveagh										
Roscommon & Leitrim	Athlone										
Roscommon & Leitrim	Carrick-on-Shannon										
Roscommon & Leitrim	Croghan										
Roscommon & Leitrim	Boyle										
Roscommon & Leitrim	Mohill										
Roscommon & Leitrim	Roscommon										
Shannon	Shannon										
Shrule	Hollymount										
Skibbereen	Skibbereen										
Taughmaconnell	Taughmaconnell										
Tuam	Kilshanvey										
Tuam	Lavally										
Tuam	Tuam										
Waterford	Waterford										
West Sligo	West Sligo										
Westport	Aille										
Westport	Westport										
South-Eastern	Mulrankin										
South-Eastern	Enniscorthy										
South-Eastern	Carnew										

Lighter shading symbolises stations which were not officially closed but which had no paid employees. Source: ICM Archive, Agency books, 1856–1940.

Select Bibliography

Primary sources

Manuscript sources

Archives of the Congregation of the Mission, Sybil Hill Road, Dublin (Vincentian archives)
  Life of Fathers Dowley and Lydon
  A memoir of the Congregation of the Mission in Ireland, England and Scotland

Ballyconneely Parish Office,
  Baptismal Registers 1, 2

Birmingham City Archives http://www.birmingham.gov.uk/archives.bcc
  Records of the Ecclesiastical Parish of St James, Edgbaston (1852–1926)

Claddaghduff Parish Office,
  Baptismal Register 2

Clifden Parish Office,
  Parish Registers 1–4

Corish, Patrick J., 'Irish College, Rome: Kirby Papers', *Archivium Hibernicum*, xxx (1972) and xxxi (1973)

Department of Irish Folklore, University College Dublin www.ucd.ie/irishfolklore/
  Schools Survey (collected in Connemara in 1936–37)
  Irish Folklore Commission Collection (collected in Connemara in 1936–37)

Dublin Diocesan Archives (DDA)
  Murray Papers (1849–52)
  Cullen Papers (1852–74)
  Walsh Papers (1885–1921)

Durham University, Special Collections http://aesica.dur.ac.uk/delores/asc/
  Copley Papers (1850–70)

ICM Archive, Dublin
  Minute books (1849 – present)
  Agency books (1856–1955)
  ICM correspondence (1927–50)
  Minutes of the Priests' Protection Society (1880–1927)
  Address book of pupils in Coombe School, 1925–50
  Roll books, ICM schools, 1894–1964

London Metropolitan Archives www.cityoflondon.gov.uk/Corporation/leisure_
  heritage/libraries_archives_museums_galleries/lma/lma.htm
  Records of Saint Paul's, Dock Street: Dock Street, Tower Hamlets (1863–64)
  Christ Church, Barnet: Saint Albans Road, Barnet (1857)

National Archives of Ireland www.nationalarchives.ie/
  Manuscript returns of 1901 and 1911 census, Clifden (on microfilm)
  Department of Education files (ED) (1858–80)

National Library of Ireland http://webdev.eircom.net/nci2005_beta/site/library/
  Default.asp
  Catholic parish registers of Omey and Ballinakill parishes (on microfilm)
  (1845–80)

Pontifical Irish College Archives, Rome
  Kirby Papers, New Collection

Representative Church Body Library, Dublin (RCBL) www.citc.ie/library.htm
  Leslie, Canon, Biographical succession list of clergy for the diocese of Tuam,
  1938
  Journal of the General Synod (1870–1950)
  Extant parish records (registers of baptisms, marriages and burials, register of
  vestrymen, vestry and select vestry minute books, preachers' books of the
  following parishes): Aasleagh, Ballinakill, Renvyle, Sellerna, Clifden (Omey),
  Errislannan, Errismore, Roundstone, Moyrus, Killannin, Oughterard,
  Castlekerke and Knocktopher

Valuation Office, Dublin www.valoff.ie/
  Cancelled Books, County Galway (1855–1940)

Printed sources, official records
Reports, appeals and statements of the Irish Church Missions and associated
Children's Homes
Bellingham, Fanny, *Fourth account of the fund entrusted to Miss Fanny Bellingham …*
  for the relief of the converts and children of Connemara (Wonston, 1851)
Brief Report of the Honorary Secretary for Missions on his return from the official tour
  in Ireland in April 1853 (n.p., 1853)
Connemara Orphans' Nursery, statement and appeal (Wonston, 1850)
Eleventh account of the Fund for the Relief of Converts and Children of Connemara, 3
  April 1857–3 April 1858 (n.p., n.d.)
First annual report of the Connemara Orphans' Nursery for the year 1850 (n.p.,
  1851)
First report of the West Connaught Church Endowment Society 1861 (Dublin, 1861)
Further report and appeal of the committee of the special fund for the spiritual exigencies
  of Ireland, whose proceedings will hereafter be carried on under the title of the
  special fund for church missions to the Roman Catholics of Ireland (n.p., n.d.)
ICM, *Annual reports* (London, 1850–1937)
ICM, *Report of the proceedings at the first annual meeting, held on the 26th April 1850*
  (n.p., 1850)

ICM, *Report of the proceedings at the second annual meeting, held on the 2ⁿᵈ May 1851* (n.p., 1851)

ICM, *Report of the proceedings at the third annual meeting, held on the 30ᵗʰ April 1852* (London, 1852)

Irish Church Missions, *Yearbook for 1934* (n.p., 1934)

Report of the schools for little ragged children ... Grand Canal-Street, 1885 (n.p., n.d.)

Report of the special fund for spiritual exigencies of Ireland (London, 1849)

Report or general summary of information communicated by the Hon. Sec. for missions to the committee, upon his return from a journey in Ireland, undertaken for the purpose of meeting a number of clergy, and of arranging various matters in connection with the missions; occupying from 28ᵗʰ April to 3ʳᵈ June, 1854 (London, 1854)

Second annual report of the Connemara Orphans' Nursery (Wonston, 1852)

Second report of the West Connaught Church Endowment Society 1863 (Dublin, 1863)

Society for Irish Church Missions to the Roman Catholics, *Appeal on behalf of the Society* (London, February 1851)

Society for Irish Church Missions to the Roman Catholics, *Appeal on behalf of the Society* (London, June 1851)

Society for Irish Church Missions to Roman Catholics, *Information respecting the progress of the Society of the Irish Church Missions to the Roman Catholics* (London, 1850)

Society for Irish Church Missions to the Roman Catholics, *Occasional Paper*, numbers 1–11 (n.p., 1851–53)

Society for Irish Church Missions to the Roman Catholics, *Principles and arrangements of the Society for Irish Church Missions to the Roman Catholics: Adopted by the committee, for the guidance of the agents, January, 1851* (London, 1851)

Society for Irish Church Missions to the Roman Catholics (n.p., c.1853)

Society for Irish Church Missions to the Roman Catholics, Nov. 1850 [appeal for funds, with extracts from pastoral, &c.] (n.p., n.d. [c. 1850])

Statement of the Society for Irish Church Missions to the Roman Catholics (London, January 1852)

Thirteenth account of the Fund for the Relief of Converts and Children of Connemara from 3ʳᵈ April 1859 to 3ʳᵈ April 1860 (n.p., n.d.)

Thirteenth report of the Dublin Mission Visiting Branch of the Society for Irish Church Missions to the Roman Catholics for the year ending December 31ˢᵗ, 1861 (Dublin, 1862)

Reports, appeals and statements of other contemporary organisations

A report of the Saint Vincent de Paul Society on Proselytism, 11 Feb. 1914 (Dublin, 1914)

Annual Report of the Island and Coast Society (Dublin, 1883–1910)

Annual reports of the Ladies' Association of Charity of St Vincent de Paul (Dublin, 1851–62)

CMS, *Annual reports* (London, 1850–1950)

CPAS, *Annual reports* (London, 1850–1950)

Dublin City Mission, *Annual report* (Dublin, 1873)

English Church Missions, *Annual report* (London, 1853)

Fourth Report of the General Irish Reformation Society for the restoration in Ireland of her primitive religion, and the necessary protection of converts (Castle-Douglas, 1850)

General Assembly, *Annual Reports of Missions ... Meeting of the General Assembly, 1896* (Belfast, 1891–1920)

General Assembly of the Presbyterian Church in Ireland, *Annual report, 1951* (Belfast, 1951)

Irish Reformation Fund, *Report (Second Report) of the General Irish Reformation Fund for the restoration in Ireland of her primitive religion, and the necessary protection of converts for the years 1847 and 1848* (Dublin, 1847)

Irish Reformation Society, important and interesting information, March 1854 (n.p., n.d.)

Irish Society, *Annual reports*, 1818–52, 1857–62, 1868–72

Minutes of the General Assembly of the Presbyterian Church in Ireland, consisting of the General Synod of Ulster and the Presbyterian Synod of Ulster, distinguished by the name Seceders, held in Belfast, July 1840 (Belfast, 1840)

Primitive Wesleyan Methodist Missionary Society, *Report of the committee for the year ending June 1860* (Dublin, 1860)

Proceedings of the Irish Society (1847)

Protestant Reformation Society, *The sixty-seventh annual report* (London, 1894)

Report and statement of accounts of the Dublin Bible-Woman Mission, in connection with the Church of Ireland (Dublin, 1877)

Report of the Catholic Protection and Rescue Society of Ireland (1943)

Report of the Home Mission of the Synod of Ulster (Belfast, 1840)

Report of the Protestant Reformation Society and Church Missions to Roman Catholics in Great Britain (London, 1893, 1894, 1895)

Reports of the Tuam Diocesan Council (Dublin, 1879–1910)

Scottish Association for the relief of Irish children attending scriptural schools, *Report for 1851, with notes of a two months' residence among the Irish Church Missions in west Galway and Mayo* (Edinburgh, 1851)

Scottish Reformation Society, *Popery, its progress and position in Great Britain, and the relative duty of Protestants; being the ninth report of the Scottish Reformation Society* (Edinburgh, 1860)

Second [3rd][4th] annual report of the Home and Foreign Mission of the General Assembly of the Presbyterian Church in Ireland: July 1842 [1843] [1844] (Belfast, 1842–44)

St Brigid's Orphanage, *Annual reports* (Dublin, 1857–96)

The Irish Society Record, containing a general statement of the society's progress as shewn in extracts from the reports and correspondence of its superintendents and other friends (Dublin, 1850, 1852, 1854)

The seventh report of the Irish Missionary School, Ballinasloe for the year ending 21st December 1853 (n.p., n.d.)

Parliamentary material and official publications

1861, Census of Ireland, Pt I, Area, population and number of houses by townland and electoral divisions, provinces of Ulster and Connaught, 1863 [3204] LIV.1

1861, Census of Ireland, 1861, Pt IV, Report and tables relating to religious professions, education and occupations, 1863 [3204–111] LIX.

Census for Ireland, 1911, Area, population and number of houses, occupations, religion and education. Vol. IV Province of Connaught, 1912–13 [Cd. 6052.] cxvii.1

Census of Ireland, 1871, Pt, I, Area, population and number of houses, occupations, religion and education. Vol. IV Province of Connaught, 1874 [C.1106] LXXIV Pt.II.1

Census of Ireland, 1881, Area, population and number of houses, occupations, religion and education. Vol. IV Province of Connaught, 1882 [C.3268] LXXIX.1

Census of Ireland, 1891, Area, population and number of houses, occupations, religion and education. Vol. IV Province of Connaught, 1892 [C.6685] XCIII.1

Census returns for Ireland, 1901, Area, population and number of houses, occupations, religion and education. Vol. IV Province of Connaught, 1902. [Cd. 1059] cxxvii. 1

Educational census: Return showing the number of children actually present in each primary school 25th June 1868; with introductory observations and analytical index, H.C. 1870 [C.6v] XXVIII, Part v.1

First report of the Commission of Enquiry into Irish Education, H.C. X11 (1825)

First report of the Commissioners of Public Instruction, Ireland, with Appendix, 1835, xxxiii (45) (46)

Hansard's Parliamentary Debates, 3rd series, 1847–81 (vols lxxxix–cclix)

Hansard's Parliamentary Debates, 4th series, 1901 (vols xcv–xcvi)

Religious census of Hampshire, 1851 (Winchester, 1993), p. 123

Second report of the Commissioners of Public Instruction in Ireland, 1835, xxxiv (47)

Contemporary newspapers and periodicals

Achill Missionary Herald

The Arrow

Ballina Chronicle

The Banner of the Truth in Ireland, monthly journal concerning the Irish Church Missions to the Roman Catholics

Banner of Ulster

Belfast Newsletter

The Bulwark

Catholic Bulletin

Christian Guardian

Church Examiner and Church of Ireland Magazine

Church of Ireland Gazette

Clare Champion

Connaught Patriot and General Advertiser

Connaught Watchman

Cork Examiner

Daily Express

Dublin Evening Mail
Dublin Evening Post
Erin's Hope: the Irish Church Missions' Juvenile Magazine
Evangelical Magazine and Missionary Chronicle
Evening Mail
Free Church Magazine
Freeman's Journal
The Furrow
Galway Express and General Advertiser for the counties of Galway, Mayo, Roscommon,
    Clare and Limerick
Galway Vindicator and Connaught Advertiser
Grievances from Ireland
Irish Catholic
Irish Catholic Directory
Irish Chronicle
Irish Church Advocate
Irish Ecclesiastical Gazette
Irish Ecclesiastical Journal
Irish Ecclesiastical Record
The Irish Missionary Record and Chronicle of the Reformation
Irish People
Irish Times
John Bull
Mayo Constitution
The Month
The Nation
Northern Whig
The Primitive Church Magazine
The Record
The Rock
Saunder's Weekly Newsletter and Daily Advertiser
Sligo Champion
The Tablet
The Telegraph, later *The Catholic Telegraph*
The Times
Tuam Herald
Waterford Chronicle

Printed handbills and ballad sheets

Collection of street-ballads, in Trinity College, Dublin (3 vols, MS nos OLSX–1–
    530, 531, 532)
Irish Church Missions to the Roman Catholics, advertisements of sermons 1852–
    57, in Trinity College, Dublin (2 vols, MS nos Gall.6.m.71, 72)

Contemporary books and pamphlets

Achill Mission, *An Irish and English spelling-book: for the use of schools, and persons in the Irish parts of the country* (Achill, 1849)

Aikman, John Logan, *Cyclopaedia of Christian Missions* (London, 1860)

Alcock, Deborah, *Walking with God, a memoir of the Ven. John Alcock by his daughter* (London, 1887)

Alcock, John, *Antichrist, who is he, two sermons preached on Wednesday evenings, 22 and 29 March, 1848 in Christ Church, Cork* (Cork, 1848)

Allden, E. W., *Records of gospel work in the streets and lanes of the city* (Dublin, n.d.)

Andrews, Thomas, *The Church in Ireland, a second chapter of contemporary history* (London, 1869)

Anonymous, *Information respecting the progress of the Society of the Irish Church Missions to Roman Catholics* (London, 1850)

Anonymous, *Cardinal Wiseman and the canon law of Rome, 'The Oscott Provincial Synod' or can the cardinal be a loyal subject of Queen Victoria?* (Edinburgh, 1852)

Anonymous, 'Conversion and persecution in Ireland', *The Dublin University Magazine*, xl (August 1852), 244–8

Anonymous, *A day at Clifden* (London, 1853)

Anonymous, *Protestantism essentially a persecuting religion, by another convert from Anglicanism* (York, 1853)

Anonymous, *Results of an investigation into the cases of Protestant persecution on the continent* (London, 1854)

Anonymous, *Stories about the mission work in Ireland* (Dublin, 1854), numbers 1, 2, 4, 5, 7

Anonymous, *The Protestant in Ireland* (London, 1854)

Anonymous [Angelo Maria Rinolfi], *Missions in Ireland: especially with reference to the proseltizing [sic] movement; showing the marvellous devotedness of the Irish to the faith of their fathers, by one of the missioners* (Dublin, 1855)

Anonymous, *What are the Irish Church Missions?* (London, 1855)

Anonymous, *Two months in Clifden, Co. Galway, during the summer of 1855* (Dublin, 1856)

Anonymous, *'Them also', the story of the Dublin mission* (2nd edn, London, 1866)

Anonymous, *Pastoral address of the Catholic archbishops and bishops of Ireland to the clergy, secular and regular, and the laity of their flocks* (Dublin, 1870)

Anonymous, *The story of the Connemara Orphan's [sic] Nursery from its commencement to the year 1876* (Glasgow, 1876)

Anonymous, *An ardent Sinn-Féiner* (Dublin, n.d. [after 1922])

Anonymous, *Irish Church Missions, a letter and a reply* (n.p., n.d. [c.1940])

Anonymous, *The Irish mission field* (n.p., n.d. [c.1937])

Anonymous, *The religious state of Ireland* (London, n.d.)

Anonymous, *Why I left the Church of Rome* (Dublin, n.d. [after 1922])

Armstrong, Thomas, *My life in Connaught, with sketches of mission work in the west* (London, 1906)

Ashworth, Henry, *The Saxon in Ireland* (London, 1851)

Association for Promoting Christian Knowledge, *Roman claims, or an elementary catechism on the chief points of Roman controversy, prepared by a committee appointed by the Board of Education of The United Diocese of Dublin, Glendalough and Kildare* (Dublin, 1915)

Aurich, Edward, *Report made to the ICM Committee by the Rev. E. Aurich and the Rev. E. Bickersteth of their third visit of inspection to a portion of the missions of the Society* (London, 1868)

Barbour, A. M., *Connemara, on the eve of the twentieth century* (London, 1899)

Begg, James, *A handbook of popery; or, text-book of missions for the conversion of Romanists: being papal Rome tested by scripture, history and its recent workings ... with an appendix of documents* (Edinburgh, 1852)

Bernard, Charles *What is truth? A sermon preached on behalf of the Society for Irish Church Missions to Roman Catholics in the parish church of St. Multose, Kinsale on Sunday, November 12th, 1854* (Cork, 1854)

Bickersteth, Edward, *Special Fund for the Spiritual Exigencies of Ireland* (n.p., 1848)

Bickersteth, Robert, *The designed end of affliction; a sermon preached at St. John's Church, Clapham ... March 24, 1847* (London, 1847)

Bickersteth, Robert, *Irish Church Missions, a sermon etc.* (London, n.d.)

Bourke, Ulick, *The life and times of the Rev. John MacHale, archbishop of Tuam and metropolitan* (Baltimore, 1882)

Bowles, Emily, *Irish diamonds: or a chronicle of Peterstown* (London, 1864)

Bradshaw, J. H., *Lantern missions in Ireland* (n.p., n.d. [c.1922])

Braithwate, Robert, *The life and letters of Rev. William Pennefeather* (London, n.d.)

Brannigan, Michael, *Connaught Mission, its past and present* (n.p., n.d. [c.1848])

Broughton, C. H. K., *What I saw in Dublin, an address delivered in the Church House, Westminster on May 8th 1914* (Dublin, n.d.)

Bullock, Charles, *What Ireland needs, the gospel in the native tongue* (London, c.1880)

Burke, Oliver J., *The history of the Catholic archbishops of Tuam, from the foundation of the see to the death of the most Rev. John MacHale of Tuam* (Dublin, 1882)

Burnside, William Smyth, *The Connemara peasant; or, Barney Brannigan's reasons, in a discussion with the priest of his parish, for reading the scriptures without asking the priest's leave* (Dublin, 1854)

Cahill, D. W., *The first [2nd], [3rd], [4th], [5th], [6th] letter from D. W. Cahill to the Roman Catholics of Ireland* (Dublin, 1851–60)

Cahill, D. W., *The first and second [and third] letters of the Rev. D. W. Cahill, D.D. Upper Gloucester-Street, Dublin, to the Right Hon. Lord John Russell* (Dublin, 1851)

Cahill, D. W., *Letter 4: from D. W. Cahill to the Right Honourable Lord John Russell ... November 4, 1851* (Dublin, 1851)

Cahill, D. W., *Important letter from the Rev. D. W. Cahill to the Rt. Hon. the earl of Derby* (Dublin, 1852)

Cahill, D. W., *Letter V from the Rev. D. W. Cahill to the Right Honourable Lord John Russell* (Dublin, 1852)

Cahill, D. W., *Controversial letter from the Rev. D. W. Cahill in answer to seven Church of England ministers who have challenged him to a public discussion in Sligo* (Dublin, 1855)

Cahill, D. W., *Letter of the Rev. D. W. Cahill D.D. to the Right Hon. Lord Viscount Palmerston* (Dublin, 1855)

Cahill, D. W., *Extract of a letter from the Rev. D. W. Cahill of this day* (Dublin, 1856)

Cahill, D. W., *Letter from the Rev. D. W. Cahill, D.D., to his excellency, the earl of Carlisle* (Dublin, 1856)

Cahill, D. W., *Letter from the Rev. D. W. Cahill on the souper government to the people of Ireland* (Dublin, 1856)

Cahill, D. W., *Most important letter ... to ... the earl of Carlisle affecting the Irish Catholics at home and abroad* (Dublin, 1856)

Cahill, D. W., *Powerful address from the Rev. Dr Cahill to the tradesmen and labouring classes of Ireland* (Dublin, 1856)

Cahill, D. W., *Sixth letter from the Rev. Dr. Cahill to his Excellency, the earl of Carlisle* (Dublin, 1856)

Cahill, D. W., *Eigth letter from the Rev. Dr. Cahill to his Excellency, the earl of Carlisle* (Dublin, 1856)

Cahill, D. W., *Eloquent and impressive sermon of the Rev. Dr. Cahill in the Augustine Church, Limerick, on St. Patrick's Day* (Dublin, n.d.)

Cambrensis, Giraldus, *The history and topography of Ireland*, trans. by John J. O'Meara (rev. edn, Portlaoise, 1982)

Carlile, James, *Fruit gathered from among Roman Catholics in Ireland* (London, 1848)

Carlile, James, *Birr mission, obituary of Mary Kehoe* (n.p., 1851)

A Catholic clergyman, *The life of the late Cardinal McCabe, archbishop of Dublin, primate of Ireland, etc. who died on Wednesday, the 11th February 1885, to which is added his last pastoral* (Dublin, 1885)

Catholic Truth Society, *A roll of honour, Irish prelates and priests of the last century, with preface by Most Rev. John Healy, D.D., archbishop of Tuam* (Dublin, 1905)

Christian Brothers, *The second book of reading lessons by the Christian Brothers* (Dublin, 1846)

Christian Brothers, *Irish history reader* (Dublin, 1907)

Clay, W. L., *The prison chaplain, a memoir of the Rev. John Clay* (London, 1861)

Clington, Allan H. [David Power Conyngham], *Frank O'Donnell: a tale of Irish Life* (Dublin, 1861)

Colquhoun, J. C., *The system of national education in Ireland, its principle and practice* (Cheltenham, 1838)

Colquhoun, J. C., *On the object and uses of Protestant associations* (London, 1839)

Colquhoun, J. C., *Irish Church Missions. Reply ... to certain charges against the Society made by the Rev. George Webster, M.A., Chancellor of Cork* (n.p., c.1864)

Connellan, Joseph, *From bondage to liberty* (Dublin, n.d. [after 1890])

Connellan, Thomas, *Hear the other side* (Dublin, n.d. [after 1890])

Connellan, Thomas, *Landmarks* (Dublin, n.d. [after 1890])

Connellan, Thomas, *Scenes from clerical life* (Dublin, n.d. [after 1890])

Connelly, Pierce, M.A., *The coming struggle with Rome, not religious but political; or, words of warning to the English people* (London, 1852)

Conybeare, William, *Church parties, an essay* (London, 1854)

Costello, Francis, *Hymns for the festivals of the Blessed Virgin Mary for the whole year* (Cork, n.d.)

Creedon, M., *Proselytism: its operations in Ireland, a paper read at the annual meeting of the Maynooth Union, June 1926 (archdiocese of Dublin)* (Dublin, 1926)

Crotty, William, *The mission in Connemara* (Belfast, n.d.)

Cullen, Paul, *The pastoral letters and other writings of Cardinal Cullen, archbishop of Dublin etc., etc.*, edited by the Right Reverend Patrick Francis Moran, D.D., bishop of Ossory (3 vols, Dublin, 1882)

Cumming, John, *The Pope, the Man of Sin, a lecture ... third thousand* (London, n.d. [1851])

Cumming, John, *The church: a sermon preached in St. George's Church, Edinburgh, June 4, 1856 on behalf of the Society for Irish Church Missions to the Roman Catholics* (London, 1856)

Cunningham, Henry Stewart, *Is 'Good news from Ireland' true? Remarks on the position and prospect of the Irish Church Establishment* (London, 1865)

Cusack, Mary Francis, *A history of the Irish nation, social, ecclesiastical, biographical and antiquarian* (London, 1876)

Cusack, Mary Francis, *Tim O'Halloran's choice; or from Killarney to New York* (London, Dublin, 1877)

Dallas, Alexander R. C., *Correspondence of Lord Byron, with a friend ...* (3 vols, Paris, 1825)

Dallas, Alexander R. C., *A sermon upon the present distress in Ireland, preached at Highclere, in the county of Hants, etc.* (London, 1822)

Dallas, Alexander R. C., *My church-yard. Its tokens, and its remembrances* (2nd edn, London, 1848)

Dallas, Alexander R. C., *Pastoral superintendence: its motive, its detail and its support* (London, 1841)

Dallas, Alexander R. C., *The certainty of the restoration of Judah and Israel at the end of the 'Times of the Gentiles' – the scripture signs of those times drawing to a close, compared with present events.* (n.p., 1841)

Dallas, Alexander R. C., *The restoration of Israel to be anticipated from the unchangeable nationality of the Jews, and God's miraculous dealings towards them* (n.p., 1841)

Dallas, Alexander R. C., *Look to Jerusalem: a scriptural view of the position of the Jews in the great crisis of the world's history* (2nd edn, London, 1842)

Dallas, Alexander R. C., *The pastor's assistant. Intended to facilitate the discharge of the pastoral office in the Church of England* (3 vols, London, Wonston, 1842)

Dallas, Alexander R. C., *Harvest hints for Christian labourers* (London, 1843)

Dallas, Alexander R. C., *The pleasure-fair* (London, Wonston, 1843)

Dallas, Alexander R. C., *The prophecy upon the Mount; a practical consideration of Our Lord's statement respecting the distinction of Jerusalem, His own appearing and the end of the age* (London, 1843)

Dallas, Alexander R. C., *Real Romanism, as stated in the creed of Pope Pius the Fourth* (London, 1845)

Dallas, Alexander R. C., *What shall we do for Ireland?* (Wonston, 1846)

Dallas, Alexander R. C., *Popery in Ireland, a warning to Protestants in England, etc. being a lecture delivered before the Islington Protestant Institute on Monday, January 18th, 1847* (London, 1847)

Dallas, Alexander R. C., 'The Promised Land' in *Good things to come: being lectures during Lent, 1847, at St. George's, Bloomsbury* (London, 1847)

Dallas, Alexander R. C., *Revelation readings: an aid in searching the Apocalypse* (London, 1848)

Dallas, Alexander R. C., *Castelkerke* (London, 1849)

Dallas, Alexander R. C., *The point of hope in Ireland's present crisis* (London, 1849)

Dallas, Alexander R. C., *Introduction to prophetical researches: being a brief outline of the divine purpose concerning the world, as it may be gathered from Holy Scripture, historically and prophetically* (London, 1850)

Dallas, Alexander R. C., *A sermon preached by the Rev. Alexander R. C. Dallas ... in the church of St. Dunstan's-in-the-west, Fleet Street on Wednesday evening, May 14th, 1857, in behalf of the Society for Irish church missions* (London, 1851)

Dallas, Alexander R. C., *Lecture delivered at the Town Hall, Brighton ... on the sacramental delusions of Romanism* (Brighton, 1851);

Dallas, Alexander R. C., 'The Christ of Romanism, not the Christ of Scripture, a lecture delivered before the Church of England's Young Men's Society, 28 February 1851' in *Lectures delivered before the Church of England's Young Men's Society for aiding missions at home and abroad* (London, 1851)

Dallas, Alexander R. C., *The boasting of the Mystic Babylon, a prophetic sign of her approaching overthrow* (London, 1851)

Dallas, Alexander R. C., *Proselytism in Ireland, correspondence between Rev. Alexander R.C. Dallas and Rev. Henry William Wilberforce, the Catholic Defence Association, versus the Irish church missions, on the charge of bribery and intimidation* (London, 1852)

Dallas, Alexander R. C., 'The present position of popery and Protestantism in Ireland. A lecture, etc.' in Church of England Young Men's Society, *Six lectures on Protestantism Delivered before the north of London auxiliary to the Church of England Young Men's Society in October, November and December 1851* (London, 1852), pp. 157–96

Dallas, Alexander R. C., *A voice from heaven to Ireland* (Wonston, 1853)

Dallas, Alexander R. C., *Missionary scenes second series: a letter from an eye-witness after a missionary tour during the summer and autumn of 1853* (London, 1854)

Dallas, Alexander R. C., *Irish Church missions to the Roman-catholics* (Dublin, 1856)

Dallas, Alexander R. C., *The light thrown by prophecy on the recent development of popery* (n.p., 1856)

Dallas, Alexander R. C., *The following letters on the state of missions to the Roman Catholics in Ireland has* [sic] *recently been addressed to the editors of newspapers by the Rev. Alexander R. C. Dallas* (London, 1860)

Dallas, Alexander R. C., *The 'Birds' Nest': Missionary addresses to children. By the Rev. A. R. C. Dallas ... and the Rev. J. C. Ryle* (Bath, 1863)

Dallas, Alexander R. C., *A popish political catechism. The reprint of an old tract preserved in a volume of 'Pamphlets mostly relating to Dissenters,' in Oriel College Library. To which is added some extracts from authorized and approved Romish writings* (London, 1867)

Dallas, Alexander R. C., *The story of the Irish Church Missions, part 1* (London, 1867)

Dallas, Alexander R. C., *My life, &c* (n.p., n.d. [1869])

Dallas, Alexander R. C., *The story of the Irish Church Missions. Continued to the year 1869, etc.* (London, 1875)

Dallas, A[nne] Mrs, *Incidents in the life and ministry of the Rev. Alexander R.C. Dallas A.M.* (London, 1871)

Dalton, G. W., *Irish Church Missions ... Lecture delivered in Dundalk ... third lecture on the reformation, occasioned by the republication of Cobbett's letters, in the 'Dundalk Democrat'* (Dundalk, 1859)

Dann, Arthur G., *George Webster: a memoir* (London, 1892)

Davies, Sarah, *Holly and Ivy, the story of a winter Birds' Nest* (Dublin, 1871)

Davies, Sarah, *Wanderers brought home* (Dublin, 1871)

Davies, Sarah, *St. Patrick's armour: the story of the Coombe Ragged School* (Dublin, 1880)

Davies, Sarah, *Helping hand, the story of the Coombe Boy's Home* (Dublin, 1881)

Davies, Sarah, *Other cities also; the story of mission work in Dublin* (Dublin, 1881)

Denham Smith, Joseph, *Connemara, past and present* (Dublin, 1853)

Dill, E. M., *The mystery solved, or Ireland's miseries: the grand cause, and cure* (Edinburgh, 1852)

Dixon, James, *Letters on the duties of Protestants with regard to popery* (London, 1840)

Doudney, David Alfred, *A run through Connemara. By the editor of the 'Gospel Magazine,' and 'Protestant Beacon'* (London, Dublin, 1856)

Duncan Craig, J., *Real pictures of clerical life in Ireland* (London, 1900)

Eade, Henry Cory, *Irish Church Missions, are the converts bribed? a correspondence between the Rev. Henry Cory Eade ... and the Rev. George Webster* (Dublin, 1864)

Edinburgh Irish Mission, *The true way of dealing successfully with popery, being the report of the Edinburgh Irish Mission for the year 1850, with the list of subscriptions* (Edinburgh, 1851)

Edinburgh Irish Mission, *Conversion of the Rev. James Forbes, Roman Catholic priest in Glasgow* (Edinburgh, 1852)

Edinburgh Irish Mission, *History of the mission* (Edinburgh, 1852)

Edinburgh Irish Mission, *Missions for the conversion of Irish Romanists in the large towns of England and Scotland explained and recommended, being the Report of the Edinburgh Irish Mission for the year 1851, with the list of subscriptions* (Edinburgh, 1852)

Edinburgh Irish Mission, *Appeal in reference to the extension of the Edinburgh Irish Mission and Protestant Institute, addressed to the friends of Protestantism* (Edinburgh, n.d.)

Edwards, A. W., 'Historic sketch of the Church of Ireland' in Byrne, J., Edwards, A. W., Anderson, W. and Lee, A. T. (eds), *Essays on the Irish Church by clergymen of the Established Church in Ireland* (London, 1866)

Ensor, G., *Letters showing the inutility and showing the absurdity of what is rather fantastically termed 'The New Reformation'* (Dublin, 1828)

Farrell, Monica, *From Rome to Christ: the story of a spiritual pilgrimage* (6ᵗʰ edn, Belfast, 1955)

A Fellow Worker, *Patient continuance: a sketch of the life and labours of the late Rev. Doctor MacCarthy of Dublin* (Dublin, 1878)

Fishe, Henry, *The duty of the Church of Ireland towards her Roman Catholic brethren, a paper read before the C.M.S. clergy union, abbreviated and slightly revised by the Rev. Henry Fishe, M.A., Dublin Superintendent Irish Church Mission, reprinted by request, from the Church of Ireland Gazette* (Dublin, 1908)

Fitzpatrick, William John, *Memoirs of Richard Whately ... with a glance at his contemporaries & times* (London, 1864)

Forbes, John, *Memorandums made in Ireland in the autumn of 1852* (2 vols, London, 1853)

Four Rectors (eds), *The only complete copy of the correspondence between G. W ... and H. C. Eade and A. R. C. Dallas, relating to the charge of bribery against the Society ... together with a paper on conscience by A. R. C. Dallas and Mr. Colquhoun's letter to the Daily Telegraph. Edited by four Rectors* (Dublin, 1864)

A Free Churchman, *Reply to Review of Charges brought by a Free Churchman against the Scottish Ladies' Association, in aid of the Irish Presbyterian Mission to Roman Catholics* (n.p., 1864)

Freyer, Marian, *Connemara, its social and religious aspects* (Galway, 1861)

Garrett, John, *Good news from Ireland. An address to the archbishops and bishops of the Church of England* (London, 1863)

Garrett, J. P., *A brief memoir of Miss Moore, late of Warren Cottage, Lisburn ... with a preface by the Rev. Alexander R. C. Dallas, Rector of Wonston, Hants* (3ʳᵈ edn, Belfast, 1867)

Garwood, John, *The million peopled city: or one half of the people of London made known to the other half* (London, 1853)

Gibson, Fred. C., *Gleanings from harvest fields, extracts from monthly reports of colporteurs* (Belfast, c.1930)

Godkin, James, *Ireland and her churches* (London, 1867)

Godkin, James, *Religious history of Ireland* (London, 1873)

Gordon, J. E., *A letter to the Rev. Edward Bickersteth* (n.p., 1847)

Greer, James, *The windings of the Moy with Skreen and Tireragh* (Ballina, 1986, first published 1927)

Gregg, John, *A missionary visit to Achill and Erris, and other parts of the county of Mayo* (Dublin, c.1850)

Gregg, John, *A missionary visit to Connemara and other parts of the county of Galway* (Dublin, c.1850)

Gwynn, Stephen Lucius, *A holiday in Connemara ... with sixteen illustrations* (London, 1909)

Hall, Mr and Mrs, *The west and Connemara* (London, 1853)

Hall, Mr and Mrs, *Ireland north and west, its character and scenery … in one volume* (Boston, n.d.)

Hatherell, James, *A City wholly given to idolatry. A sermon [on Acts xvii. 16] preached in aid of the Irish Church Missions to the Roman Catholics* (London, 1860)

Hely Walsh, Elizabeth, *Kingston's revenge: a story of bravery and single-hearted endeavour* (London, 1917), first published as *Golden hills, a tale of the Irish famine* (London, 1865)

Hermes, *Souperism and Romanism; being a reply to the editor of the Irish Quarterly Review, in his address to His Excellency the earl of Carlisle, entitled 'Soup and sanctification', 'The Irish Church Mission' 'Scripture Readers' etc. which he designates as a public nuisance, 'Lest the people'* (Dublin, 1857)

Hobson, Richard, *What hath God wrought, an autobiography. With an introduction by the Right Rev. F. J. Chavasse* (London, 1913)

Houstoun [Matilda Charlotte], *Twenty years in the wild west; or, life in Connaught* (London, 1879)

How, F. D., *William Conyngham Plunket, fourth Baron Plunket and sixty-first archbishop of Dublin* (London, 1900)

Howard, John Elliott, *The island of saints, or Ireland in 1855* (London, 1855)

Inglis, Catherine Hartland, *Notes of a tour through the south and west of Ireland; with some account of the operations of the General Irish Reformation Society* (Castle Douglas, 1850)

An Irish Peer, *A letter to His Grace, the archbishop of Dublin on proselytism, by an Irish Peer* (Dublin, 1865)

Jones, Llewelyn Wynne, *The new reformation in Ireland: or striking facts and anecdotes illustrating the extent and reality of the movement* (London, 1852)

Kerns, Thomas, *Connemara past and present, occasional paper of the Irish Church Missions to the Roman Catholics* (n.p., 1859)

Killen, W. D., *The ecclesiastical history of Ireland from the earliest period to the present times, by W.D. Killen, D.D., President of Assembly's College, Belfast and Professor of Ecclesiastical History* (2 vols, London, 1875)

Ledoux, Paul, *The Church of Ireland and the Roman mission in Ireland, which has orders from St Patrick: a controversy which arose out of the street-preaching riots in Sligo* (Sligo, 1896)

Lighton, Christopher, *Does Rome teach salvation by faith alone? If not is her teaching Christian?* (n.p., n.d.)

M., *Connemara. Journal of a tour, undertaken to inquire into the progress of the reformation in the west of Ireland. By M.* (Dublin, 1852)

MacBeth, John, *The story of Ireland and her church, from the earliest times to the present day* (Dublin, 1899)

M'Closkey, P., *Trial and conviction of a Franciscan monk at Mayo spring assizes, 1852, for burning and blaspheming the holy scriptures with observations of the fact and the defence made for it* (Dublin, 1852)

McCrory, J. E., *A Portadown open-air* (London, Dublin, n.d. [1930])

Magee, Hamilton, *Fifty years in the Irish Mission* (Belfast, 1905)

MacHale, John, *The new testament of our Lord and Saviour Jesus Christ; translated*

*from the Latin vulgate; diligently compared with the original Greek; and first
published by the English College at Rheims, A.D. 1582 with annotations, a
chronological index, table of references, etc. With the approbation of his Grace the
Most Rev. Dr. Mac Hale, Archbishop of Tuam* (Tuam, 1846 and 1863)

MacHale, John, *Powerful letter of the Rev. Dr. M'Hale on its not yet being too late
for the people of Ireland to exert themselves in behalf of their insulted religion,
and teach a lesson of political ethics to a persecuting ministry and their selfish
retainers* (Dublin, 1851)

MacHale, John, *An Irish translation of the book of Genesis, from the Latin vulgate
with a corresponding English version, chiefly from the Douay …* (Tuam, 1859
and 1868)

MacHale, John, *An Irish translation of the holy bible: from the Latin vulgate; with a
corresponding English version, chiefly from the Douay; accompanied with notes
from the most distinguished commentators* (Tuam, 1861 and 1868)

MacHale, John, *Craobh urnaighe cráibhthighe, tioinssuighthe ar an Sgriobhain
Dhiadha, agus rannta toghtha na h-Eaglaise.* Second edition. Irish and English
(Dublin, 1866)

MacHale, John, *Sermons and discourses of the late most Rev. John MacHale, D.D.,
archbishop of Tuam,* edited by Thomas MacHale, D.D., Ph.D. (Dublin,
1883)

McIlwaine, William, *Irish Church Missions to the Roman Catholics: supplement to
correspondence* (London, 1861)

MacManus, Henry, *Sketches of the Irish highlands: descriptive, social and religious.
With special reference to Irish Missions in west Connaught since 1840* (London,
Dublin, 1863)

M'Neile, Hugh, *The famine, a rod of God, its provoking cause – its merciful design: a
sermon preached in St. Jude's Church, Liverpool on Sunday, February 2, 1847*
(London, 1847)

MacWalter, J. G., *The Irish reformation movement in its religious, social and political
aspects* (Dublin, 1852)

Maguire, Edward, *Fifty eight years of clerical life in the Church of Ireland* (Dublin,
1904)

Maher, James, *The Letters of Rev. James Maher, D.D. late P.P. of Carlow Graigue on
religious subjects, with a memoir,* ed. by the Right Rev. Patrick Francis Moran
(Dublin, 1877)

Marrable, William, *Sketch of the origin and operations of the Society for Irish Church
Missions to the Roman Catholics* (London, 1853)

Meagher, William, *Notices of the life and character of his grace, Most Rev. Daniel
Murray, later archbishop of Dublin* (Dublin, 1853)

Mecredy, James, *A brief narrative of the reformation in Iar Connaught* (Dublin,
1854)

Minton, Samuel, *Romish tactics and Romish morals* (London, 1851)

Moody, Stuart A., *Ireland open to the Gospel* (Edinburgh, 1847)

Moore, Courtney, *A chapter of Irish church history, being some personal recollections
of a life and service in the Church of Ireland* (Dublin, 1907)

Murray, Patrick, *The mendacity of souperism in Ireland, a letter to Edward G.K.*

Browne, Esq., from the Very Rev. P. Murray, D.D., concerning the unblushing mendacity of Mr. Rogers, one of the missionaries of the Irish Church Mission Society (London, 1861)

Nangle, Edward, *Protestantism in Ireland, the essence of a sermon, preached in the octagon chapel, Bath, on Sunday, July 5ᵗʰ, 1835, on behalf of the Protestant missionary settlement, in the island of Achill* (Bath, 1835)

Napier, John, *England or Rome, who shall govern Ireland? a reply to the letter of Lord Mounteagle* (Dublin, 1851)

National Club, *Report of speeches at the National Club meeting* (London, 1852)

National Club, *Address to the Protestants of the United Kingdom by the committee of the National Club. The progress of foreign popery as affecting English safety. Fourth Series, No. VIII* (London, 1852)

Neave, Digby, *Four days in Connemara* (London, 1852)

Nicholson, Asenath, *The bible in Ireland ('Ireland's welcome to the stranger; or, excursions through Ireland in 1844 and 1845 for the purpose of personally investigating the condition of the poor')*, edited with an introduction by Alfred Tresidder Sheppard (London, 1927)

Nicholson, Asenath, *Annals of the famine in Ireland*, edited by Maureen Murphy (Dublin, 1998, first published 1851)

Nolan, L. J., *A third pamphlet* (Dublin, 1838)

O'Brien, Richard Baptist, *Ailey Moore, A tale of the times* (London and Baltimore, 1856)

O'Brien, Richard Baptist, *The D'Altons of Crag: a story of '48 and '49* (Dublin, 1882)

O'Callaghan, John, *Society for Irish Church Missions and the Rev. J. O'Callaghan: Lough Corrib mission* (Dublin, 1855)

O'Donnell, Hugh Joseph, *David and Goliath, or the complete victory of a Mayo hedge-school pupil: over Sir Thomas Dross, a souper knight, and three Bible and tract-distributing ladies ...* (Dublin, 1853)

Olden, Thomas, *The national churches: the Church of Ireland* (London, 1892)

O'Reilly, Bernard, *John MacHale, his life, times and correspondence* (2 vols, New York, 1890)

O'Rourke, John, *The battle of the faith in Ireland* (Dublin, 1887)

Osborne, Sidney Godolphin, *Gleanings in the west of Ireland* (London, 1850)

Peacock, Robert Backhouse, *The reformation in Ireland. Notes of a tour amongst the missions in Dublin and west Galway in ... September 1852* (2ⁿᵈ edn, London, 1853)

Philip, John, *Researches in South Africa* (2 vols, London, 1828)

Plunket, Thomas, *Convert confirmations; a discourse delivered to converts from Romanism in the west of Ireland in September 1851, together with a report of the tour for missionary confirmations upon the same occasion* (London, 1851)

Plunket, Thomas, *The West Galway Church Building Fund, statement and account by the bishop of Tuam* (Dublin, Wonston, 1852)

Plunket, Thomas, *The West Galway Church Building Fund, an appeal from the bishop of Tuam* (Dublin, c.1860)

Plunket, W. C., *The Church and the census in Ireland* (Dublin, 1865)

Plunket, W. C., *A book for tourists in Ireland. Sights to be seen in Dublin and Connemara ... with an introd. by the Lord Bishop of Rochester* (n.p., 1863)

Plunket, W. C., *A short visit to the Connemara missions. A letter to the Rev. John Garrett ... from the Rev. W.C. Plunket, with a preface by the Lord Bishop of Rochester* (London, Dublin, 1863)

Presbyterian Church in Ireland, *Mission to the Roman Catholics* (n.p., 1867)

Roden, earl of, *Progress of the reformation in Ireland: extracts from a series of letters written from the west of Ireland to a friend in England in September 1851* (2nd edn, London, 1852)

Ross, Andrew, *Ballinglen, Killala, County Mayo, Ireland* (n.p., 1851)

Ross, John, *The Irish evangelistic mission of August, 1853, in three letters relating to its operation, fruits and lessons* (London, 1853)

Ryder, Roderick, *Transubstantiation – the confessional. A letter ... to ... Dr. French, Roman Catholic bishop at Gort, etc.* (Dublin, 1846)

Savage, Edward, *Work in the fairs and markets* (n.p., n.d. [after 1922])

Sedall, Henry, *The Church of Ireland, a historical sketch* (London, 1886)

Seymour, C. H., *Late synod in Tuam: questions for the bishops, priests and people of the church of Rome* (Dublin, 1854)

Sirr, J. D., *A memoir of Power Le Poer Trench, last archbishop of Tuam* (Dublin, 1845)

Sirr, J. D., *The children of the light and their obligations, a sermon by the Rev. J. D'Arcy Sirr, D.D., one of the secretaries of the Irish Society of London, preached on the district parish church of St. John, Notting Hill on Sunday morning, April 13, 1851 in behalf of the Irish Society of London* (London, 1851)

Society for Irish Church Missions, *Early fruits of Irish missions* (6th edn, London, 1852)

Society for Irish Church Missions, *A mission tour book in Ireland, showing how to visit the missions in Dublin, Connemara, etc.* (London, 1860)

Society for Irish Church Missions, *Irish Church Missions, The itinerating work of the Irish Church Missions, brief jottings of the work in fairs, markets, and villages from itinerants' journals, for private circulation* (London, 1894)

Stanford, Charles Stuart, *A handbook to the Romish controversy: being a refutation in detail of the creed of Pope Pius the Fourth on the grounds of scripture and reason: and an appendix and notes* (Dublin, 1868)

Stanford, W. B., *Faith and faction in Ireland now* (Dublin, Belfast, 1946)

Steele, R., *Footprints in the hands of time* (London, 1882)

Stopford, Edward, *A reply to Sergeant Shee on the Irish Church* (Dublin, 1853)

Taylor, James William, *A month's visit to Connaught and its mission stations* (Edinburgh, London, 1849)

Thackeray, William M., *The Irish sketchbook* (Dublin, 1990, first published 1843)

Thébaud, Augustus, *The Irish race in the past and the present* (New York, 1878)

Trevelyan, Charles, *The Irish crisis* (London, 1848)

Ua Duinnín Pádraig, *Creideamh agus gorta: faith and famine, a tragic drama relating to the famine period* (Dublin, 1901)

Ua Laoghaire, Peadar, *Mo scéal féin* (Dublin, c.1920)

Venables, George, *The good news is true; or, what an English clergyman saw in Connemara ... with a preface by the Rev. W. C. Plunket* (London, 1865)

Walsh, Luke, *The Home Mission unmasked; or, a full and complete exposure of the frauds, deceptions, and falsehoods practised by the agents of the Home Mission of the General Assembly of the Presbyterian Church in Ireland. In a series of letters* (Belfast, 1844)

West Galway Church Building Fund, *Statement and account by the Bishop of Tuam, with a report of his tour through parts of the united diocese of Tuam, Killala and Achonry in the months of July and August 1852* (Wonston, 1852)

[West Connaught Church Endowment Fund], *The Church in Ireland: the speeches delivered at the Hanover Square Rooms, on Thursday, June 11, 1863 ... in aid of the West Connaught Church Endowment Fund* (London, 1863)

Whately, E. J., *Life and correspondence of Richard Whately* (2 vols, London, 1866)

Wilde, W. R., *Irish superstitions* (Dublin, 1852)

Wilson, Daniel, *The Church of England in Danger. A letter to the vicar of Islington upon his recent pamphlet 'Our Protestant faith in danger'. By one of his parishioners* (London, 1850)

Reference texts

Crockford's clerical directory (London, 1865–1941)

Dictionary of national biography (London, 1886)

Leslie, James, *Biographical succession lists of the clergy of the diocese of Down* (Enniskillen, 1936)

Leslie, J. B., *Clergy of Tuam, Killala and Achonry, biographical succession lists, compiled by Canon J. B. Leslie and revised, edited and updated by Canon D. W. T. Crooks* (n.p., 2008)

Lewis, Donald (ed.), *The Blackwell dictionary of evangelical biography* (2 vols, Oxford, 1995)

Office of Public Works, *Archaeological inventory of county Galway, west Galway including Connemara and the Aran Islands* (Dublin, 1993)

Oxford dictionary of national biography (Oxford, 2004)

Religious census of Hampshire, 1851 (Winchester, 1993)

Stenton, M. (ed.), *The who's who of British members of parliament* (Hassocks, 1976)

Stenton, M. and Lees, S. (eds), *The who's who of British members of parliament* (Hassocks, 1978)

Secondary sources

Books and journal articles

Acheson, Alan, *A true and lively faith* (n.p., 1992)

Acheson, Alan, *A history of the Church of Ireland 1691–1996* (Dublin, 1997)

Akenson, D. H., *The Church of Ireland, ecclesiastical reform and revolution, 1880–1885* (London, 1971)

Akenson, D. H., *A Protestant in purgatory* (Connecticut, 1981)

Andrews, Hilary, *The lion of the west: a biography of John MacHale* (Dublin, 2001)

Bane, Liam, *The bishop in politics: life and career of John MacEvilly* (Westport, 1993)

Barnard, Toby, 'Improving clergymen' in Ford, Alan, McGuire, James and Milne, Kenneth (eds), *As by law established* (Dublin, 1995)

Bateman, Fiona, 'Defining the heathen in Ireland and Africa: two similar discourses a century apart', *Social Sciences and Missions*, xxi (2008), 73–96

Bebbington, D. W., *Evangelicalism in modern Britain: a history from the 1730s to the 1980s* (London, 2002)

Bowen, Desmond, *The idea of the Victorian church: a study of the Church of England, 1833–1889* (Montreal, 1968)

Bowen, Desmond, *Souperism: myth or reality?* (Cork, 1970)

Bowen, Desmond, 'Alexander R.C. Dallas, warrior-saint of Wonston, Hampshire' in Phillips, Paul T. (ed.), *View from the pulpit: Victorian ministers and society* (Toronto, Cambridge, 1977)

Bowen, Desmond, *The Protestant crusade in Ireland, 1800–70* (Dublin, 1978)

Bowen, Desmond, *Paul Cardinal Cullen and the shaping of modern Irish Catholicism* (Dublin, 1983)

Bowen, Desmond, *History and shaping of Irish Protestantism* (New York, 1995)

Bradshaw, Brendan, 'Nationalism and historical scholarship in modern Ireland' in Brady, Ciarán (ed.), *Interpreting Irish history* (Dublin, 1994)

Brady, Éilis, *All in, all in: a selection of Dublin children's traditional street games with rhymes and music* (Dublin, 1975)

Broderick, Eugene, 'The famine and religious controversy in Waterford', *Decies*, li (1995), 11–24.

Brown, Stewart, 'The new reformation movement in the Church of Ireland, 1801–29' in Brown, Steward J. and Miller, David W. (eds), *Piety and power in Ireland, 1760–1960* (Belfast, 2000)

Campbell Berloletti, Susan, *Black potatoes: the story of the great Irish famine, 1845–50* (New York, 2001)

Claddaghduff Development Association, *To school through the years: a history of the people and schools of the Claddaghduff area, 1853–2003* (Claddaghduff, 2004)

Clarke, Aidan, 'Bishop William Beddell, 1571–1642' in Brady, Ciarán, *Worsted in the game: losers in Irish history* (Dublin, 1989)

Clarke, Peter, *Dever and Down: a history of the parish of Wonston* (Winchester, 2002)

Comby, Jean, *How to understand the history of Christian mission* (London, 1996)

Comerford, Patrick, 'Edward Nangle (1799–1883): the Achill missionary in a new light', part i in *Cathair na Mart*, xviii (1998) 21–9; part ii in *Cathair na Mart*, xix (1999), 8–22

Comerford, R. V., *Ireland* (London, 2003)

Connolly, S. J., *Priests and people in pre-famine Ireland* (Dublin, 1982)

Connolly, S. J., *Religion and society in nineteenth century Ireland* (Dundalk, 1985)

Cooney, Dudley Levistone, *Sharing the word: a history of the Bible Society in Ireland* (Dublin, 2006)

Corish, Patrick, *The Irish Catholic experience: a historical survey* (Dublin, 1985)

Crawford, John, *The Church of Ireland in Victorian Dublin* (Dublin, 2005)

D'Alton, E. A., *History of the archdiocese of Tuam* (2 vols, Dublin, 1928)

Davidoff, L. and Hall, C., *Family fortunes: men and women of the English middle class, 1780–1850* (London, 1987)

Davis, C., 'Cape Clear: a retrospect', *The Month and Catholic Review*, xxiv (1881), pp. 476–88

Doherty, Martin, 'Religion, community relations and constructive unionism. The Arklow street-preaching disturbances 1890–92' in Murphy, James H. (ed.), *Evangelicals and Catholics in nineteenth-century Ireland* (Dublin, 2005)

Dunlop, Robert (ed.), *Evangelicals in Ireland: an introduction* (Dublin, 2004)

Edwards, R. D. and Williams, T. D., *The great famine* (Dublin, 1994, first published 1956)

Egan, Patrick, *The parish of Ballinasloe: its history from the earliest times to the present day* (Dublin, 1960)

Emerson, N. D., 'Church life in the nineteenth century' in Philips, W. A. (ed.), *History of the Church of Ireland from the earliest times to the present day* (3 vols, London, 1933)

Fanning, Bryan, *Racism and social change in the republic of Ireland* (Manchester, 2001)

Fegan, Melissa, *Literature and the Irish famine, 1845–1919* (Oxford, 2002)

Foley, Tadhg and Ryder, Seán (eds), *Ideology and Ireland in the nineteenth century* (Dublin, 1998)

Ford, Alan, McGuire, James and Milne, Kenneth (eds), *As by law established* (Dublin, 1995)

Foster, R. F., *Modern Ireland* (London, 1989)

Gray, Peter, 'Ideology and the famine' in Póirtéir, Cathal (ed.), *The great Irish famine* (Dublin, 1995)

Gribben, Crawford, 'The forgotten origins of the Irish evangelicals' in Dunlop, Robert (ed.), *Evangelicals in Ireland: an introduction* (Dublin, 2004)

Handley, James Edmund, *The Irish in modern Scotland* (Cork, 1947)

Hayton, David, 'Did Protestantism fail in early eighteenth-century Ireland? Charity schools and the enterprise of religious and social reformation' in Ford, Alan, et al. (eds), *As by law established* (Dublin, 1995)

Heather, Alannah, *Errislannan: scenes from a painter's life* (Dublin, 1993)

Hempton, David, *Religion and political discourse in Britain and Ireland* (Cambridge, 1996)

Hempton, David and Hill, Myrtle, *Evangelical Protestantism in Ulster society, 1870–1890* (London, 1992)

Hibbert, Christopher, *Queen Victoria: a personal history* (London, 2000)

Hill, Myrtle, *The time of the end: millenarian beliefs in Ulster* (Belfast, 2001)

Hill, Myrtle, '"Women's work for women": the Irish Presbyterian Zenana Mission, 1874–1914', in Raughter, Rosemary (ed.), *Religious women and their history: breaking the silence* (Dublin, 2005)

Hilton, Boyd, *The age of atonement: the influence of atonement on the social and economic thought, 1795–1865* (Oxford, 1988)

Hoppen, Theodore, *The mid-Victorian generation, 1846–1886* (Oxford, 1998)

Hume, A[braham], *Results of the Irish census if 1861, with a special reference to the condition of the Church of Ireland* (London, 1864)

Hurley, Michael, *Irish Anglicanism 1860–1969* (Dublin, 1970)

Hyde, Douglas, *Abhráin diada chúige Connacht or the religious songs of Connaught: a collection of poems, stories, prayers, satires, ranns, charms, etc* (Dublin, 1906)

Hylson-Smith, Kenneth, *Evangelicals in the Church of England, 1734–1984* (Edinburgh, 1989)

James, D., *John Hamilton of Donegal 1800–1884: this recklessly generous landlord* (Dublin, 1998)

Johnson, Máirín, 'Priests and proselytism in the nineteenth century' in Uibh Eachach, Vivian (ed.), *Féile Zozimus* (Dublin, 1992), 61–6

Johnston, Thomas, Robinson, John and Wyse Jackson, Robert, *A history of the Church of Ireland* (Dublin, 1953)

Joyce, James, *Ulysses* (Picador edn, London, 1997)

Keenan, Desmond, *The Catholic Church in nineteenth-century Ireland: a sociological study* (Totawa, New Jersey, 1983)

Kelly, Matthew, 'The politics of Protestant street-preaching in the 1890s' in *Historical Journal*, xxxxviii (2005), 101–25

Keogh, Daire, 'The Christian Brothers and the Second Reformation in Ireland', *Éire-Ireland*, xl (spring/summer 2005), 42–59.

Keogh, Dáire, *Edmund Rice and the first Christian Brothers* (Dublin, 2008)

Keogh, Dermot and McCarthy, Andrew, *Limerick Boycott, 1904: anti-semitism in Ireland* (Cork, 2005)

Kerr, Donal, *'A nation of beggars'? Priests, people and politics in famine Ireland, 1845–52* (Oxford, 1994)

Killen John (ed.), *The famine decade: contemporary accounts, 1841–1851*, edited by John Killen (Belfast, 1995)

Kinealy, Christine, *This great calamity: the Irish famine 1845–1852* (Dublin, 1994)

Kinealy, Christine, 'Potatoes, providence and philanthropy: the role of private charity during the Irish potato famine' in O'Sullivan, Patrick (ed.), *The meaning of the famine* (London, 1997)

Klaus, Robert James, *The Pope, the Protestants and the Irish: papal aggression and anti-Catholicism in nineteenth-century England* (New York, London, 1987)

Lampson, G. Locker, *A consideration of the state of Ireland in the nineteenth century* (London, 1907)

Larkin, Emmet, 'Before the devotional revolution' in Murphy, James H. (ed.), *Evangelicals and Catholics in nineteenth-century Ireland* (Dublin, 2005)

Liechty, Joseph and Clegg, Cecelia, *Moving beyond sectarianism: religion, conflict and reconciliation in Northern Ireland* (Dublin, 2001)

Liechty, Joseph and Clegg, Cecelia, *Moving beyond Sectarianism: a resource for young adults, youths and schools* (Belfast, 2001)

Long, Joseph, *Medical missions in Ireland* (Dublin, 1925)

Lyons, John, *Louisburg: a history* (Louisburg, 1995)

MacArthur, William P., 'Medical history of the famine' in Edwards, R. D. and Williams, T. D. (eds), *The great famine* (Dublin, 1994, first published 1956), pp. 263–318

MacDonald, Michael, *Children of wrath: political violence in Northern Ireland* (Cambridge, 1986)

MacSuibhne, Peadar, *Paul Cullen and his contemporaries, with their letters, 1820–1902* (5 vols, Naas, 1962–74)

McDiurmid, Lucy, *The Irish art of controversy* (Dublin, 2005)

McDowell, R. B., *The Church of Ireland, 1869–1969* (London, 1975)

McDowell, R. B., *Historical essays, 1938–2000* (Dublin, 2003)

McLeod, Hugh, *Religion and society in England, 1850–1914* (London, 1996)

Maguire, Martin, 'The Church of Ireland and the problem of the Protestant working-class of Dublin, 1870s–1930s' in Ford, Alan, McGuire, James and Milne, Kenneth (eds), *As by law established* (Dublin, 1995)

Matthews, Shirley, '"Second string" and "precious prejudice": Catholicism and anti-Catholicism in Hampshire in the era of emancipation' in Murphy, James H. (ed.), *Evangelicals and Catholics in nineteenth-century Ireland* (Dublin, 2005)

Mennell, Stephen, 'Protestants in a Catholic state: a silent minority in Ireland' in Inglis, Tom et al, *Religion and politics: east-west contrasts from contemporary Europe* (Dublin, 2000)

Miller, David, *Church, state and nation in Ireland, 1898–1921* (Pittsbugh, 1973)

Mitchel, Patrick, *Evangelicalism and national identity in Ulster, 1921–1998* (Oxford, 2003)

Moffitt, Miriam, *Soupers and Jumpers: the Protestant missions in Connemara, 1848–1937* (Dublin, 2008)

Moran, Gerard P., *The Mayo evictions of 1860* (Westport, 1986)

Moran, Gerard P., *A radical priest in Mayo: Fr. Patrick Lavelle, the rise and fall of an Irish nationalist 1825–86* (Dublin, 1994)

Morrissey, Thomas J., *William J. Walsh, archbishop of Dublin, 1841–1921* (Dublin, 2000)

Mulryan Moloney, Maeve, *Nineteenth-century elementary education in the archdiocese of Tuam* (Dublin, 2001)

Murphy, James H., 'The role of Vincentian parish missions in the "Irish counter-reformation" of the mid nineteenth-century', *Irish Historical Studies*, xxii (1984), 152–71

Murphy, James H. (ed.), *Evangelicals and Catholics in nineteenth-century Ireland* (Dublin, 2005)

Murphy, John A., 'Priests and people in modern Irish history', *Christus Rex*, xxiii (1969), 235–59

Murray, Peter, 'A colporteur kicked by a priest on a Westport street: the MacAskill assault case of 1906', *Cathar na Mart*, xxi (2001), 127–43

Neil, Stephen, *Colonialism and Christian missions* (London, 1966)

Nelson, Warren, *T. C. Hammond, his life and legacy in Ireland and Australia* (Edinburgh, 1994)

Ní Ghiobúin, Meala, *Dugort, Achill Island, 1831–1861: the rise and fall of a missionary community* (Dublin, 2001)

Ní Shúilleabháin, Máire, *An t-Athair Caomhánach agus an cogadh creidimh i gConamara* (Dublin, 1984)

Noll, M. A., Bebbington, D. W. and Rawlyk, G. A., *Evangelicalism: comparative studies of popular Protestantism in North America, the British Isles and beyond, 1700–1990* (New York, 1994)

Ó Corrán, Daithí, *Rendering to God and Caesar: the Irish churches and the two states in Ireland, 1949–73* (Manchester, 2004)

Ó Ciosáin, Niall, 'Dia, bia agus Sasana: an Mistéalach agus íomha an ghorta' in Póirtéir, Cathal (ed.), *Gnéithe an ghorta* (Dublin, 1995)

Ó Ciosáin, Niall, 'Famine memory and the popular representation of scarcity' in MacBride, Ian (ed.), *History and memory in modern Ireland* (Cambridge, 2001)

Ó Ciosáin, Niall, 'Approaching a folklore archive: the Irish Folklore Commission and the memory of the great famine', *Folklore* (August 2004), 222–32

O'Connor, Lily, *Can Lily O'Shea come out to play?* (Dingle, 2000)

Ó Duigneáin, Proinnsíos, *The priest and the Protestant woman: the trial of Rev. Thomas Maguire, P.P.* (Dublin, 1979)

O'Farrell, P., *Ireland's English question: Anglo Irish relations, 1534–1970* (London, 1971)

Ó Gráda, Cormac, *An drochshaol, béaloideas agus amhráin* (Dublin, 1994)

Ó Gráda, Cormac (ed.), *Ireland's great famine: interdisciplinary essays* (Dublin, 2006)

Ó Murchada, Brighid, *Oideachas in Íar Chonnacht sa naoú céad déag* (Dublin, 1954)

O'Neill, Thomas, 'Sidelights on souperism', *Irish Ecclesiastical Record*, lxxi (1949), 50–64

O'Rourke, John, *The history of the great Irish famine of 1847, with notices of earlier famines* (Dublin, 1902)

Parsons, Gerald, *Religion in Victorian Britain*, i, *Traditions* (Manchester, 1988)

Paz, D. G., *Popular anti-Catholicism in mid Victorian England* (Stanford, 1992)

Póirtéir, Cathal, *Famine echoes* (Dublin, 1995)

Póirtéir, Cathal (ed.), *Gnéithe an ghorta* (Dublin, 1995)

Póirtéir, Cathal (ed.), *The great Irish famine* (Dublin, 1995)

Power, Joe, 'Proselytism and perversion in west Clare', *The Other Clare*, xxx (2006), 55–60

Preston, Margaret, *Charitable words: women, philanthropy and the language of charity in nineteenth-century Dublin* (London, 2004)

Prochaska, Frank, *Women and philanthropy in nineteenth century England* (Oxford, 1980)

Prochaska, Frank, *The voluntary impulse: philanthropy in modern Britain* (London, 1988)

Prunty, Jacinta, 'Margaret Louisa Aylward' in Cullen, Mary and Luddy, Maria (eds), *Women, power and consciousness in nineteenth-century Ireland* (Dublin, 1995)

Prunty, Jacinta, *Dublin slums, 1800–1925: a study in urban geography* (Dublin, 1998)

Prunty, Jacinta, *Margaret Aylward, lady of charity, sister of faith: Margaret Aylward, 1810–1889* (Dublin, 1999)

Purcell, Mary, *The story of the Vincentians* (Dublin, 1973)

Quigley, E. J., 'Grace abounding', *Irish Ecclesiastical Record*, part I in vol. xx (1922), 561–72; part II in vol. xxi (1923), 27–38; part III in vol. xxi (1923), 126–38; part IV in vol. xxi (1923), 275–80; part V in vol. xxi (1923), 402–10; part VI in vol. xxi (1923), 513–23; part VII in vol. xxii (1923), 58–69; part VIII in vol. xxii (1923), 271–83; part IX in vol. xxii (1923), 382–97; part X in vol. xxii (1923), 500–11; part XI in vol. xxii (1923), 605–19.

Quinn, J. F., *History of Mayo* (5 vols, Ballina, 1993–2002)

Reilly, Emily, 'Women and voluntary work' in Gregory, Adrian and Peseta, Senia (eds), *Ireland and the great war: a war to unite us all* (Manchester, 2004)

Richards, Shaun, 'Plays of (ever) changing Ireland' in Richards, Shaun (ed.), *The Cambridge companion to twentieth century Irish drama* (Cambridge, 2004)

Riddell, Patrick, *The Irish – are they real?* (London, 1972)

Ridden, Jennifer, 'The forgotten history of the Protestant Crusade: religious liberalism in Ireland', *Journal of Religious History*, xxxi, no. 1, 78–102

Rowan, Myles V., *An apostle of Catholic Dublin: Father Henry Young* (Dublin, 1944)

Seaver, George, *John Allen Fitzgerald Gregg, archbishop* (Dublin, 1963)

Smyly, Vivienne, *The early history of Mrs Smyly's homes and schools*, speech by Miss Vivienne Smyly (grand-daughter) given 29 May 1976 (n.p., n.d.)

Standún, Raymonde and Long, Bill, *Singing stone, whispering wind: voices of Connemara* (Dublin, 2001)

Stock, Eugene, *History of the Church Missionary Society* (4 vols, London, 1899–1916)

Swords, Liam, *A hidden church: the diocese of Achonry, 1689–1818* (Dublin, 1997)

Swords, Liam, *In their own words: the famine in north Connaught* (Dublin, 1999)

Swords, Liam, *A dominant church: the diocese of Achonry 1818–1960* (Dublin, 2004)

Villiers-Tuthill, Kathleen, *Beyond the twelve bens: a history of Clifden and district 1860–1923* (2nd edn, Dublin, 1990)

Villiers-Tuthill, Kathleen, *History of Clifden, 1810–1860* (Dublin, 1992)

Villiers-Tuthill, Kathleen, *Patient endurance: the great famine in Connemara* (Dublin, 1997)

Villiers-Tuthill, Kathleen, *History of Kylemore Castle and Abbey* (Connemara, 2002)

Wallis, Frank, *Popular anti-Catholicism in mid-Victorian Britain* (Lampeter, 1993)

Walsh, Oonagh, *Anglican women in Dublin: philanthropy, politics and education in the early twentieth century* (Dublin, 2005)

Walsh, Patrick, *William J. Walsh, archbishop of Dublin* (Dublin, 1928)

Whelan, Irene, 'Edward Nangle and the Achill Mission, 1834–1852' in Gillespie, Raymond and Moran, Gerard (eds), *Mayo, a various county: essays in Mayo history* (Westport, 1987)

Whelan, Irene, 'The stigma of souperism' in Póirtéir, Cathal (ed.), *The great Irish famine* (Dublin, 1995)

Whelan, Irene, *The bible war in Ireland: the 'second reformation' and the polarisation of Protestant Catholic relations, 1800–1840* (Dublin, 2005)

Whelan, Kevin, 'Tionchar an ghorta' in Póirtéir, Cathal (ed.), *Gnéithe an ghorta* (Dublin, 1995)

White, Jack, *Minority report: the Protestant community in the Irish Republic* (Dublin, 1975)

White, P[atrick], 'Proselytism in County Clare: a retrospect', *Irish Ecclesiastical Record*, viii (May 1887), 411–21

Williams, Peter, '"Not transplanting": Henry Venn's strategic vision' in Ward, Kevin and Stanley, Brian, *The Church Mission Society and world Christianity, 1799–1999* (Cambridge, 2000)

Wilson, A. N., *The Victorians* (London, 2002)

Wolffe, John, 'Evangelicalism in mid-nineteenth-century England' in Samuel, R. (ed.), *Patriotism, the making and unmaking of British national identity* (London, 1989)

Wolffe, John, *The Protestant crusade in Great Britain, 1829–1860* (Oxford, 1991)

Wolffe, John (ed.), *Evangelical faith and public zeal: evangelicals and society in Britain, 1780–1980* (London, 1995)

Wolffe, John, *Evangelicals, women and community: study guide* (Milton Keynes, 2000)

Unpublished dissertations and papers

Crawford, Heather, 'Protestants and Irishness in independent Ireland: an exploration' (Ph.D. dissertation in history, National University of Ireland, Maynooth, 2008)

Gilley, Sheridan Wayne, 'Evangelical and Roman Catholic missions to the Irish in London, 1830–1870' (Ph.D. dissertation in history, University of Cambridge, 1970)

Kelley, Thomas J., 'Trapped between two worlds: Edward Nangle, Achill Island and sectarian competition in Ireland, 1800–1862' (Ph.D. dissertation in history, Trinity College Dublin, 2004)

Mac Uaid, Bearnárd, 'Stair oideachas Bráthar Triomhadh Úird Riaghalta Sain Proinsias san naomhadh céad déag' (MA dissertation in history, University College Galway, 1956)

Maguire, Martin, 'The Dublin working-class 1870–1932, economy, society, politics' (MA dissertation in history, University College, Dublin, 1990)

Majerus, Paschal, 'The second reformation in west Galway: Alexander R. Dallas and the Society for Irish Church Missions to the Roman Catholics, 1849–1859' (MA dissertation in history, University College Dublin, 1991)

Moffitt, Miriam, 'The Society for Irish Church Missions to the Roman Catholics, 1850–1950' (Ph.D. dissertation in history, National University of Ireland, Maynouth, 2006)

Nemer, Lawrence, 'Anglican and Roman Catholic attitudes on missions: a comparison of the Church Missionary Society with the Society of St. Joseph of the Sacred Heart for Foreign Missions in their home structures and life between 1865 and 1885' (Ph.D. dissertation in divinity, University of Cambridge, 1978)

Preston, Margaret, 'The unobtrusive classes of the meritorious poor': gentlewomen,

social control and the language of charity in nineteenth century Dublin' (Ph.
D. dissertation in history, Boston College, 1999)

Prunty, Jacinta, 'The geography of poverty: Dublin 1850–1900: the social Mission
of the church with particular reference to Margaret Aylward and Co-Workers
(Ph.D. dissertation in geography, National University of Ireland, 1992)

Index